Habermas: Critical Debates

Habermas

Critical Debates

Edited by

John B. Thompson and David Held

THE MIT Press
Cambridge, Massachusetts

First published 1982 in the USA by
THE MIT PRESS
Massachusetts Institute of Technology, Cambridge, Massachusetts 02142

Printed in Hong Kong

Library of Congress Cataloging in Publication Data

Main entry under title:

Habermas, critical debates.

   Bibliography: p.
   1. Habermas, Jürgen.   I. Thompson, John B.
II. Held, David.
B3258. H324H32   1982   193   81-20881
ISBN 0–262–20043–0 (hard cover)   AACR2
      0–262–70023–9 (paperback)

Contents

Preface

We began work on this volume in the summer of 1978. Since then our task, which we have shared equally, has been made all the more pleasurable by the enthusiastic co-operation of our contributors. Special thanks are due to Anthony Giddens and Thomas McCarthy who, in addition to writing essays for the volume, provided us with invaluable advice. We should like, finally, to express our gratitude to Jürgen Habermas for his willing participation in the project.

July 1980   The editors

Editors' Introduction

During the last two decades many of the established perspectives in Anglo-American philosophy and social science have been subjected to probing criticism. The philosophical approach developed by the later Wittgenstein, Austin and others has been questioned from many sides; and the erstwhile predominance of functionalism in the social sciences has given way to a plurality of methodological positions. Undoubtedly these developments have been unsettling, but their effects were not merely destructive: they prepared the way for a broadening of intellectual horizons, a relaxation of rigid boundaries between different disciplines and different traditions of thought. It is within this historical context that Jürgen Habermas has assumed an extraordinary stature. As the leading social thinker in Germany today, Habermas has elaborated a theoretical orientation which is relevant to a wide range of disciplines, from politics and sociology to philosophy, psychology and linguistics. His work reveals an astonishing grasp of intellectual traditions and a wealth of original ideas. Amid the turbulence which prevails in the humanities, Habermas stands out as a thinker of tremendous scope and vision.

In view of the relevance and importance of Habermas's work, there is an urgent need for a sustained critical discussion of his ideas. The essays contained in this volume represent an attempt to fulfil this need. All of the essays are published here for the first time; their authors include well-known philosophers and social theorists from Europe and the United States. Each essay focuses on a particular theme or themes in Habermas's work, and each presents both an exposition and a critique. In a long concluding essay Habermas replies to these and other criticisms, taking this as an opportunity to clarify and develop his views. The volume thus amounts to a critical and constructive exchange with Habermas, an exchange which will, it is hoped, serve to facilitate the sympathetic reception of his ideas.

In this introduction we shall sketch a backcloth for the critical debates which follow. We cannot, in so small a space, provide a comprehensive survey of Habermas's works; nor is there any need to, since excellent

surveys already exist.[1] Our aim is much more limited. In the first and
second parts of the introduction, we shall situate Habermas within the
tradition of critical theory and outline some of the central themes of his
work. In the third and fourth parts, we shall summarise the main
arguments of the essays in this volume and draw out some of the most
interesting aspects of Habermas's reply.

I

'Critical theory' refers to a series of ideas which emerged in Germany in
the 1920s and 1930s. The critical theorists were concerned, among other
things, to interpret the course of twentieth-century history, and especially
the effects of the First World War, the defeat of left-wing working-class
movements, the rise of fascism and Nazism, and the degeneration of the
Russian revolution into Stalinism. While rejecting Marxism-Leninism, the
critical theorists nevertheless found in Marx's thought a powerful tool for
the analysis of historical events. Among the questions which became
central for them were the following: Why did the European radical
movements fail to develop into a unified struggle? Why were tendencies
towards authoritarianism and the expansion of bureaucracies dominant?
How, in spite of these tendencies, could theory preserve hope for the
future? In changing historical circumstances, how could the revolutionary
ideal be sustained and justified?

An institutional basis for the pursuit of such questions was established in
1923, with the foundation in Frankfurt of the Institute for Social Research.
Under the guidance of Max Horkheimer, who became director in 1931, the
Institute was committed to a programme of interdisciplinary study in which
'philosophers, sociologists, economists, historians and psychologists must
unite in a lasting working partnership'. [2] Horkheimer wished to overcome
the division of labour in the humanities and social sciences, as well as to
avoid dogmatic holistic approaches such as orthodox Marxism. The
membership of the Institute during the 1930s reflects this interdisciplinary
orientation. Apart from Horkheimer (philosopher, sociologist), the Institute included an extraordinary variety of individuals who were to become
distinguished in many fields: Theodor Adorno (philosopher, sociologist,
musicologist), Friedrich Pollock (economist), Erich Fromm (psychoanalyst,
social psychologist), Franz Neumann (political scientist) and Herbert
Marcuse (philosopher, social theorist).

Horkheimer, Adorno and Marcuse were pre-eminent among the first
generation of critical theorists. Although there were important differences
between them, a number of common strands can be discerned in their
work. Trained primarily as philosophers, all three wrote major appraisals
of the German philosophical heritage. These works were conceived as both
analyses and interventions, for their goal was to break the grip of all closed
systems of thought and to counter an unreflected affirmation of society.

Adorno was foremost in thinking that only a sustained critique of philosophy could adequately dispense with old problems and set limits for new projects. All three thinkers retained many of the themes of German idealism, especially those concerned with the nature of reason, truth and beauty; but they rejected and recast the way these had been articulated by Kant and Hegel. The historical character of the social world and the mediation of nature and society through *Praxis* were key ideas in their approach. Following Marx, the critical theorists were not just concerned with interpretation: they strove to unite analysis and critique. Yet they also sought to preserve an autonomous moment of criticism; that is, they maintained that theoretical and practical claims could be adjudicated independently of particular social interests. They were committed to elucidating future possibilities which, if realised, would overcome existing contradictions and enhance the rationality of society. They stood in the tradition of those who believe in the unity of socialism and liberty.

Horkheimer, Adorno and Marcuse were agreed on the significance of Marx's political economy for social and political theory. They also agreed that the ideas elaborated in Marx's mature work were an insufficient basis for the comprehension of contemporary society. The expansion of the state into more and more areas of life, the growth of what they called the 'culture industry', the spread of bureaucracy and instrumental reason (that is, reason defined by the adequacy of means for the attainment of predetermined ends) – all implied that the terms of reference of critique had to be extended. If phenomena such as fascism and Stalinism were to be understood, it would not be sufficient to focus on the changing infrastructures of capitalist and socialist societies; one must also grasp the ways in which the attitudes and impulses of the individual are controlled by the social order. Accordingly, political economy, cultural criticism and psychoanalysis were integrated into the framework of critical theory.

Some of the key ideas of critical theory are crystallised in the *Dialectic of Enlightenment*, a work written by Horkheimer and Adorno in the 1940s. This work retraces the history of instrumental reason, from its first appearance in *Genesis* to its institutionalisation in capitalist economic growth. The Enlightenment occupies a privileged place in this history; for while on the one hand it espoused an ideal of rational self-determination, on the other hand it prescribed a method which eventually usurped this ideal. Reason ceases to be a critical tribunal, reducing itself instead to a means of describing what is already given. With the development of science and technology, nature is increasingly subjected to the reign of instrumental reason; even human beings are subsumed to objectives which appear as 'fatefully structured, pre-given'. This state of affairs is reinforced by the culture industry. Whereas the products of artists once preserved a certain autonomy from the world of economic interests, today they are enmeshed in a process of standardised production for a market. Without regard to the integrity of artistic form, the culture industry is concerned with the effect entertainment, diversion, distraction. It promotes acquiescence, affirmation and a fatalistic attitude to the *status quo*. The rise of the culture industry signals the eclipse of critical reflection.

II

The work of critical theorists had a considerable impact on German intellectual life in the post-war period. This impact is clearly discernable in the early writings of Habermas – their most influential student. Habermas's first major study, *Strukturwandel der Öffentlichkeit* (1962) [Structural Transformation of the Public Sphere],[3] reflects some of the central themes of *Dialectic of Enlightenment. Strukturwandel der Öffentlichkeit* is a historical inquiry into the formation and disintegration of the 'public sphere': a realm of social life where matters of general interest can be discussed, where differences of opinion can be settled by rational argumentation and not by recourse to established dogma or customs. Habermas traces the emergence of the public sphere from the eighteenth-century forums of public discussion – clubs, cafes, newspapers and journals of all kinds – which were at the forefront of the European literary and political Enlightenment. Such forums nurtured debate about the role of tradition and established a base of opposition to feudal authority. With the growing division between the state and civil society, a division which followed the expansion of market economies, the public sphere flourished. Merchants, traders and others with property and education became actively concerned about the government of society, recognising that the reproduction of social life was now dependent upon institutions which exceeded the bounds of private domestic authority.

The public sphere was thought by many of its leading participants to anticipate and articulate the interests of the community, the 'general interest'. The pursuit of this interest involved, in their view, both the freeing of civil society from political interference and the limiting of the state's authority to a range of activities supervised by the 'public'. The 'public' was, of course, predominantly the bourgeoisie; the earliest modern constitutions reflected their political aspirations and victories. Yet the goal of free speech and discursive will-formation was, Habermas maintains, never fully realised in the politics of capitalist societies. With the development of large-scale economic and commercial organisations, and with the increase in state activity to stabilise the economy, the realm of the public sphere was gradually restricted and compressed. Powerful organisations strove for a political compromise with one another and with the state, excluding the general public from their negotiations wherever possible. A symptom of these developments was a change in the nature of journalism: from an occupation stimulated by conviction to one motivated essentially by commerce. The extension of the principles of commodity exchange to more and more areas of life undercut the autonomy of forums potentially critical of the *status quo*. The classical idea of 'public opinion' was undermined. 'Public-relations work' and 'public-opinion research' replaced discursive will-formation.

The dissolution of the public sphere has important implications for the legitimation of contemporary capitalist society. The latter requires a form of legitimation which ensures sufficient latitude for state intervention to secure both private utilisation of capital and mass loyalty to the system. In 'Technology and Science as "Ideology" ' (1968) [see *Toward a Rational Society*] Habermas argues that this requirement is met to a considerable extent by science and technology. Since the late nineteenth century there has been a growing interdependence of science, technology and production: science and technology have become a leading productive force. Economic success appears to depend on the progress of technical innovation. Thus the problems facing capitalist economies (resource allocation, unemployment, economic stagnation) are defined as technical problems soluble only by experts, and politics assumes a singularly 'negative character'. It becomes orientated towards the avoidance of risks and dangers to the system – 'not, in other words, toward the *realization of practical goals* but toward the *solution of technical problems*'.[4] The idea of political decision-making based on general and public discussion is replaced by a 'technocratic consciousness'. Occasional plebiscitary decisions about alternative sets of leaders appear to be the only mode of government appropriate for advanced industrial societies.

Habermas develops his critique of technocratic consciousness through a study of the work of Marcuse. In an important essay,[5] Marcuse contested the account of 'rationalisation' offered by Max Weber, who used this notion to refer to the growth of societal sectors subject to the criterion of means-ends efficiency. In Marcuse's opinion this account presupposes an excessively narrow concept of rationality; and hence the process which Weber calls 'rationalisation' does not realise rationality as such, but merely an unacknowledged form of political domination. This form of domination is sustained by science and technology, in virtue of their intrinsic link to technical control. Marcuse therefore suggests that emancipation from the contemporary form of domination is conditional upon a transformation in the very structure of science and technology. It is this suggestion that Habermas does not accept. For the development of science and technology, according to Habermas, necessarily unfolds in the dimension of 'purposive-rational action' or 'labour'. Thus the critique of technocratic consciousness requires us to recognise, not the possibility of an alternative type of science and technology, but rather the existence of another type of action: 'communicative action' or 'interaction'. Whereas the rationalisation of systems of purposive-rational action may well accord with the Weberian account, this is not the case with the institutional framework of society. The rationalisation of the institutional framework demands the removal of obstacles to communication, leading not to the better functioning of the social system but to the creation of conditions for an unrestricted discussion and democratic resolution of practical issues.

The irreducibility of practical issues to technical problems was acknowledged by what Habermas calls 'the classical doctrine of politics'. According to this doctrine, first expounded by Aristotle, politics is continuous with the teaching of the good and just life. Politics is directed towards the cultivation of character and proceeds 'pedagogically' rather than technically; it is a guide to *Praxis*, to moral-political action, which is distinguished as a whole from *Theoria*. However, as Habermas shows in *Theory and Practice* (1963), the classical doctrine of politics was undermined by the rise of modern science and positivist philosophy. In the writings of Hobbes in particular, politics was conceived as a technical science which excluded practical questions, so that it had 'little more than the name in common with the old politics'.[6] The way was thus prepared for the establishment of a political science which would facilitate the administrative manipulation of the social order. Yet the Hobbesian programme has not stood unchallenged. For the Enlightenment gave rise to an alternative concept of reason, a concept that preserved the practical character of classical politics and yet did not sever this aspect from history and from theory. This concept of 'committed reason' must, Habermas argues, be regained; it must be turned against the epistemological prop of technocratic consciousness, that is, against the objectivistic self-understanding of the sciences.

Habermas undertakes a systematic study of philosophies of science and social science, with the twofold aim of unveiling the illusion of 'pure knowledge' and of elaborating a constructive framework for critical theory. The early results of this study are found in *Zur Logik der Sozialwissenschaften* (1967) [Logic of the Social Sciences], *Knowledge and Human Interests* (1968), and in the debates with Hans Albert, Hans-Georg Gadamer and Niklas Luhmann. Throughout these works Habermas maintains that critical theory cannot be conceived on the model of a natural science, nor can it be identified with those disciplines concerned to interpret and renew our cultural heritage. For critical theory is characterised above all by 'self-reflection', a concept which has been eclipsed by the rise of positivism as a philosophy. Thus Habermas opens *Knowledge and Human Interests* with the avowed hope of recovering 'the forgotten experience of reflection'.[7] Through an epistemological reflection of a Kantian type, that is, a reflection on the conditions of possibility of knowledge, Habermas conducts a critique of the conceptions of science which may be found in the writings of philosophers and practitioners of science. He seeks thereby to show that there is no single model of science, but rather several forms of scientific inquiry, each of which is governed by a particular kind of 'interest'. These interests are fundamental characteristics of the human species, characteristics which are connected to specific dimensions of the social world. Thus scientific knowledge, far from being the pure and untainted product of an objective method of inquiry, is linked via interests to the reproductive processes of social life.

By eliminating the activity of reflection, positivist philosophies of science transformed epistemology into the elucidation of scientific method. The methods of the natural sciences in general, and of physics in particular, were regarded as paradigmatic for any discipline which aspires to the production of knowledge: such is the essence of 'scientism'. Habermas maintains, however, that this transformation of epistemology has prevented positivist philosophers from grasping the conditions of possibility of natural science, as well as of its emulators in the social sphere. Habermas uses the term 'empirical-analytic' to describe those sciences which seek to formulate general laws about a domain of objects or events and to derive predictions therefrom. He then attempts to show, through a critique of the writings of Mach, Comte and Peirce, that the conduct of such sciences presupposes a framework of purposive-rational action or labour in which the environment is objectified from the standpoint of possible technical control. In other words, the knowledge produced by the empirical-analytic sciences is 'constituted' by an interest in the technical control of a world of manipulable objects. This type of science is perfectly legitimate in itself; it becomes illegitimate only when its claim exceeds the limits established by the conditions of possibility. Thus Parsons's functionalism or Luhmann's systems theory, regarded as forms of empirical-analytic inquiry, cannot provide an exhaustive approach to the social world, for neither can do justice (to mention just one limitation) to the character of meaning as a constituent feature of the social world. Similarly, on the level of the philosophy of science, Popper's contention that falsifiability is the criterion of demarcation between science and non-science must be rejected, since it precludes the possibility that there may be types of science which do not concur with the empirical-analytic model and which are constituted by fundamentally different interests.

One type of science which cannot be assimilated to the empirical-analytic model is the 'historical-hermeneutic sciences'. These are the disciplines concerned, above all, with renewing cultural heritage through the interpretation of texts and works received from the past. Habermas seeks to elucidate the conditions of possibility of these disciplines through an analysis of the writings of Dilthey. The latter author shows how, through a circular process of anticipation and corroboration, hermeneutics is able to render perplexing expressions intelligible and to remove confusions from the process of communication. This indicates, according to Habermas, that the conduct of the historical-hermeneutic sciences presupposes a framework of communicative action or interaction, and that these sciences are governed by a 'practical interest' in intersubjective under-standing. Once again, however, Habermas is critical of those hermeneutic philosophers who raise universalistic claims which, in his view, exceed the limits of validity established by the practical interest. Thus, while Haber-mas praises Gadamer's insight into the historical character of language, he criticises Gadamer's tendency to transform this insight into an absolutisa-tion of cultural tradition. For this tendency overlooks the fact that 'language is *also* a medium of domination and social force',[8] the medium of ideology *par excellence*. The distortion effected by the exercise of power implies that hermeneutic interpretation must be supplemented by a reductive critique.

The analysis of power and ideology is the concern of a third type of science which Habermas calls 'the critical social sciences'. Marx was one of the first writers to pursue this science in a systematic fashion; but Marx's emphasis on the concept of social labour prevented him, Habermas argues, from giving an adequate account of the role of reflection. Habermas therefore turns to the writings of Freud in order to uncover the conditions of possibility of critical social science. Freud shows us how the explanatory reconstruction of developmental processes can be combined with the interpretation of behavioural symptoms, so that 'in the end insight can coincide with emancipation from unrecognized dependencies'.[9] Psychoanalysis thus presupposes a framework in which action and com-munication are systematically distorted by the exercise of power and repression; and this discipline is paradigmatic for those sciences which are governed by an 'interest in emancipation'. Habermas acknowledges, however, that the interest in emancipation cannot be assumed as self-evident. For it could be alleged that this interest is itself an illusion, no less imaginary than the ideologies criticised in its name. It is in response to such allegations that Habermas has, in recent years, turned his attention increasingly to the theory of language.

Habermas's concern with language stems both from its centrality in the formation of consciousness and from its capacity to provide a foundation for critique. Language is the medium of ideology *qua* systematically distorted communication; and yet to make sense of the notion of systemati-cally distorted communication, one must have some idea of what rational or non-distorted communication would be. That we have some such idea is precisely what the programme of 'universal pragmatics' seeks to show. By reconstructing the conditions of possible communication, Habermas hopes to identify the elements which are necessarily presupposed in the successful exchange of speech-acts, and thereby to uncover 'the universal validity basis of speech'.[10] He argues, for example, that in uttering a speech-act, the speaker unavoidably raises certain 'validity claims' which can only be 'redeemed' in a discourse having the structure of an 'ideal speech situa-tion'. However distorted the actual conditions of communication may be, every competent speaker possesses the means for the construction of a speech situation which would be free from domination, and in which disputes concerning the truth of statements or the correctness of norms could be rationally resolved. Since, moreover, this situation is necessarily anticipated in every act of speech, it attests to the reality and universality of the interest in emancipation.

Throughout his writings Habermas has been concerned to elaborate a framework for the analysis of societies and social change. The basic elements of this framework are derived from Marx, whose account of liberal capitalism is accepted by Habermas as largely correct. Habermas maintains, however, that since the nineteenth century two developmental tendencies have occurred which render Marx's account inapplicable to contemporary forms of advanced capitalism. In the first place, the transformation of science and technology into a leading productive force has eroded the conditions for the application of the labour theory of value. The mechanisation of the labour process effects a qualitative change in the mode of creating surplus value, which stems no longer from labour power alone but also from the scientific development of the technical forces of production. Hence the 'tendency of the rate of profit to fall' may be checked, for the increase in productivity which accompanies the introduction of labour-saving devices may enable a steady rate of profit to be secured. The second developmental tendency affecting the adequacy of Marx's account concerns the growing role of the state. The process of the private accumulation and utilisation of capital led to increasingly severe crises which could be averted or controlled only through political intervention. This repoliticisation of the economy implies a fundamental change in the relation between the political and the economic system: they no longer stand as superstructure to base. Hence 'a critical theory of society can no longer be constructed in the exclusive form of a critique of political economy',[11] for the ideology of advanced capitalism can no longer be derived directly from the exchange of equivalents in the market.

The structural transformations of capitalism imply that the basic assumptions of historical materialism are in need of reformulation. It is this task which Habermas undertakes in his most recent work, *Zur Rekonstruktion des Historischen Materialismus* (1976) [see *Communication and the Evolution of Society*]. He conceives of historical materialism as a theory of social evolution, and he seeks to develop this theory through an analysis of some of the key concepts introduced by Marx. Thus the forces of production, according to Habermas, determine the level of control over the objectified processes of nature and society; they are bounded by the rules of purposive-rational action which govern the activity of labouring individuals. The relations of production regulate access to the means of production and thereby to the distribution of social wealth. These relations are sustained at the level of language and governed by the rules of communicative action; they crystallise around an institutional core which secures a specific form of social integration. The stability of a mode of production is endangered when the development of the forces of production generates system problems which cannot be solved within the existing relations of production. The prevailing form of social integration must then be revolutionised in order to create the capacity for alternative solutions. To account for these evolutionary steps we must assume, Habermas argues, that there is an intrinsic and autonomous learning mechanism in the institutional sphere. 'The rules of communicative action do develop in reaction to changes in the domain of instrumental and strategic action; but in doing so they follow *their own logic*'.[12] Drawing upon the developmental psychology of Piaget and Kohlberg, Habermas characterises this logic as a series of stages in the growth of consciousness in the individual as well as the species. Since the progression to a higher level of consciousness is a prerequisite for the solution of system problems which threaten stability, it follows that the development of normative structures is, in the last analysis, the 'pacemaker' of social evolution.

The theory of social evolution forms the backcloth for Habermas's current analysis of the crisis tendencies of advanced capitalism. As he explains in *Legitimation Crisis* (1973), a 'crisis' arises when the members of a society feel that their social identity is threatened by the occurrence of structural changes. In liberal capitalist societies, crises were directly linked to the vicissitudes of capital accumulation, since social integration was secured through the bourgeois ideology of fair exchange. However, as the state becomes actively engaged in ameliorating the fluctuations of the business cycle, the crises which originate in the economy are displaced into the political sphere. Caught between the contradictory imperatives of planning the economy and protecting private accumulation, the state is in a position of vulnerability to 'rationality crises'. If the government fails to manage such crises, then it may fail to secure the increasing quantity of legitimation which the growing role of the state requires. The conditions are thus created for a 'legitimation crisis' which would threaten social integration. A legitimation crisis is based upon a discrepancy between the motives necessary for the continued existence of the political-economic system, and the motivation actually supplied by the socio-cultural system. Habermas suggests that there are empirical indicators to support the view that this discrepancy is growing. The syndromes of privatism and individualism which form the core of bourgeois ideology are being irreversibly destroyed by changes in the social structure; and the emerging components of cultural tradition, which are crystallised around scientism, modern art and universalistic morality, are not suited to the reproduction of these privatistic syndromes. Thus there are, Habermas maintains, good grounds to suppose that advanced capitalist societies are facing imminent crises of legitimation.

The contention that the motive-forming components of the socio-cultural world are increasingly incapable of reproducing traditional motivational patterns is closely linked to an assumption which is central to Habermas's work, namely the assumption that norms are susceptible of rational justification. In contrast to Weber, Luhmann and others, Habermas argues that norms do not merely secure a belief in legitimacy; they also raise a claim to correctness which can be independently and rationally assessed. Habermas's analysis of the developmental tendencies of advanced capitalism here rejoins his reflections on language. For the conditions under which the validity claim of norms can be rationally assessed are those of the ideal speech situation. Universal pragmatics thus underpins Habermas's current proposals for critical theory, in so far as the latter attempts to expose relations of power by comparing 'normative structures existing at a given time with the hypothetical state of a system of norms formed, *ceteris paribus,* discursively'.[13] If such a 'counterfactually projected reconstruction' could identify generalisable interests which are suppressed by existing institutions, then the ideologies which legitimate these institutions could be criticised in a rational manner. The practical directives which emerge from such a critique would nevertheless retain a hypothetical status. For in the final analysis, Habermas insists, the tactical decisions of political struggle can be justified only by the unconstrained consensus of the subjects concerned.

III

The foregoing sketch of Habermas's work provides a backcloth for the essays contained in this volume. The essays do not purport to offer a comprehensive critique of Habermas's writings; for a thinker as prolific and provocative as Habermas, it would be presumptuous to make such a claim. The essays do, nevertheless, pursue in depth some of the most pressing problems in Habermas's work. His theories of language, action and evolution – to mention only a few examples – are examined and re-examined throughout the volume. Different essays focus on different aspects; they speak from different standpoints and bring different resources to bear upon Habermas's work. Together they form a broad and substantial basis for the development of a critical discussion.

In Chapter 1 Agnes Heller offers an analysis of Habermas's relation to the tradition of Marxism. She points out that in the writings of Marx the formulation of a theory with practical intent is characterised by the identity of the basic assumption and the addressee of the theory; for the basic assumption concerns the world-historical role of the proletariat. Heller suggests that Habermas follows the same pattern, though now the addressee is universalised to embrace human reason as such, which is exemplified by idealised speech. This universalisation of the addressee has definite advantages, but it gives rise to difficulties when we look more closely at the process of enlightenment. Thus Heller argues, for example, that the commitment to rational argument is not sufficient to secure the target-group's readiness for enlightenment: such readiness depends on the involvement of the human being as a whole, 'as a needing, wanting, feeling being'.[14] This in turn implies a greater awareness than Habermas displays of the sensuous character of human life, as well as a greater recognition of the plurality of ways of living and possible theories. The shift of addressee is closely linked to the second theme which Heller pursues. In his reconstruction of historical materialism, Habermas rejects the Marxian paradigm of production, emphasising instead the right of argumentation as the 'legacy' of capitalism and the endogenous growth of knowledge as the 'independent variable' of social evolution. Heller maintains, however, that Habermas thereby overlooks the anthropological significance of labour, and tends to disregard the *tragic* aspects of history. Habermas reconstructs historical materialism around one value, domination-free communication; but there are, Heller reminds us, other values and other needs, and hence other ways of interpreting the past.

The status of critical theory in Habermas's work is examined in the contribution by Rüdiger Bubner (Chapter 2). He begins by sketching the origins of the concept of *Kritik* in classical German philosophy, origins which have left the concept tainted with an essential ambiguity. On the one hand, following Kant, *Kritik* refers to the justification of a form of knowledge by way of disclosing its conditions of possibility; on the other hand, following the young Hegelians, *Kritik* implies the negation of an existing social order through the translation of theory into *Praxis*. In the writings of Marx these two concepts of *Kritik* are united, but in such a way that the problem of the status of his critical theory remains unresolved. Bubner traces the development of this problem through the writings of Lukács, Horkheimer and Adorno, arguing that the problem is confronted directly and systematically only in the work of Habermas. By searching for a foundation in language, Habermas offers the possibility of a critical theory which is free from ideology and which is not exhausted by an endless sequence of critical acts. Bubner argues, however, that this possibility is more apparent than real. For the danger of ideology lurks in the very idea of a dialogue wherein perfect mutual recognition would be achieved. Moreover, the gulf which exists between ideal discourse and actual speech cannot, Bubner maintains, be closed by recourse to transcendental reflection. Here the ambiguity in the concept of *Kritik* is fatal: rationality may be a constitutive feature of knowledge, as Kant sought to show, but it is not a defining characteristic of social *Praxis*. Thus, in attempting to ground practical critique through a quasi-Kantian reflection on language, Habermas succumbs, according to Bubner, to the 'most intricate self-deception'.[15]

In 'Rationality and Relativism: Habermas's "Overcoming" of Hermeneutics' (Chapter 3) Thomas McCarthy traces through some of the general

argumentative strategies in Habermas's work. Following the debate between critical theory and hermeneutics, Habermas has become increasingly concerned with the development of an approach to the social world
which places more emphasis on theoretical-empirical analysis than on
considerations of a historical-practical character. McCarthy shows how this
emphasis is connected with Habermas's attempt to sustain some of the
universalistic claims of transcendental philosophy, such as the Kantian
theses concerning the universal presuppositions of theoretical and practical
reason. However, Habermas seeks to establish these claims on the basis of
reconstructive-empirical research; and given the cultural variations in
structures of action and discourse, this strategy runs into serious difficulties. It is at this point, McCarthy suggests, that Habermas's argument takes
a Hegelian turn. Reason has a history as well as a universality; hence the
need to establish the development of competencies in the individual as well
as the species. McCarthy maintains, however, that substantial objections
can be levelled at the research programme initiated by Piaget and
Kohlberg, so that 'Habermas would . . . be well-advised to adopt a much
more tentative and critical posture towards cognitive-developmental
theories than he has to date'.[16] McCarthy concludes by suggesting that
Habermas's concept of reason reflects too much emphasis on differentiation, and that this concept should be modified by the idea of a unity in
difference attained through dialogue.

Henning Ottmann's essay on 'Cognitive Interests and Self-Reflection'
(Chapter 4) is a critical study of the central themes of *Knowledge and
Human Interests*. Ottmann emphasises the way in which human interests
serve to bridge the gap between pre-scientific forms of life, science and the
application of scientific knowledge. The mediating character of interests
implies that they cannot be based exclusively in life or in knowledge: they
are, as Habermas says, 'quasi-transcendental'. Ottmann argues, however,
that this status is unstable, threatening constantly to collapse into one
sphere or the other and failing to do justice to either. Thus the technical
interest, for example, pertains to nature only in so far as the latter is
susceptible of control and exploitation; but this does not sufficiently
acknowledge the possibility of a nature which lies beyond the will-to-
control, as well as making it difficult to comprehend nature as *natura
naturans*, that is, as origin of the subject. Similarly, when we examine the
emancipatory interest and its relation to the practical interest, we find,
Ottmann maintains, an abstract opposition between historical 'positivity'
and critical reason, as well as 'a singular overestimation of the power of
reflection'.[17] In an attempt to overcome this opposition, Ottmann suggests
that the idea of emancipation can be given content only through interpretation of the reason inherent in historical positivity, thus raising the
possibility of a hermeneutic integration of critique into the framework of
tradition.

In 'Science and Objectivity' (Chapter 5) Mary Hesse examines some of the recent revisions and reformulations of Habermas's views on epistemology. Focusing primarily on 'A Postscript to *Knowledge and Human Interests*', she relates Habermas's work to current debates in analytical philosophy of science. She shows, for instance, how Habermas's combination of a pragmatic theory of meaning with a consensus theory of truth enables him to reject all three positions commonly held by Anglo-Saxon philosophers of science: realism, reductionism and relativism. Hesse argues, however, that Habermas's theories of meaning and truth are unsatisfactory. For something like a correspondence notion of truth is necessary, she contends, to account both for the meaning of descriptive terms and for the empirical constraint on scientific theories. Moreover, Habermas's consensus theory overemphasises the discursive character of science and raises complex problems concerning the relativity of theoretical frameworks to cultural backgrounds. In the final part of her essay, Hesse explores the notion of a reconstructive science and the grounds for distinguishing it from critical and empirical sciences. She maintains that the differences between reconstructive and empirical sciences are overstated, since the data of reconstructive sciences are not, as Habermas suggests, immutable. This in turn has important implications for Habermas's proposed analysis of the framework of human action.

Habermas's attempt to reconstruct the validity basis of speech is examined by John B. Thompson in his essay on 'Universal Pragmatics' (Chapter 6). In the first part of his essay Thompson situates Habermas's writings on language within the context of his social theory as a whole, underlining some of the continuities and discontinuities with his earlier work. The central themes of Habermas's programme of universal pragmatics are then presented. Thompson focuses on four of the principal themes of the programme, reconstructing and criticising the arguments on which they rest. He contends, for example, that Habermas's restriction of the analysis to speech-acts in the 'standard form' is not sufficiently justified; and hence 'the extent to which Habermas's programme qualifies as a *universal* pragmatics must be held in doubt'.[18] Thompson argues that Habermas's proposals concerning pragmatic universals are of a questionable character, and he tries to show that Habermas's argument for the presupposition of an ideal speech situation is problematic. Pointing to difficulties in Habermas's analysis of truth, Thompson suggests that these difficulties reflect the unsoundness of the basic distinction between action and discourse. In the final part of the essay Thompson discusses in more general terms the project of grounding the critique of ideology in a theory of language. He concludes with a few constructive remarks, suggesting that a more adequate theory of language and action might provide a way of integrating the spirit of Habermas's project with some of the provocative themes of his earlier work.

Habermas's contention that judgements about moral and political questions can be rationally grounded is examined by Steven Lukes in 'Of Gods and Demons: Habermas and Practical Reason' (Chapter 7). Lukes concentrates on the 'model of the suppression of generalisable interests' sketched by Habermas in *Legitimation Crisis*. The central insight of this model, according to Lukes, is the idea that in order to determine the legitimacy of social norms one must engage in a complex thought-experiment and reason counterfactually about how actors would interpret their needs, etc., if they were to do so autonomously, that is, under conditions of undistorted communication. Lukes maintains, however, that there are two serious problems with this proposal. The first concerns the identity of the actors involved in the thought-experiment, the second concerns the nature of the norms about which they are supposed to agree. In both cases it is difficult to elicit a clear and consistent view from Habermas's writings. Lukes draws upon the work of Anglo-Saxon philosophers, such as Mackie and Rawls, in an attempt to clarify and criticise Habermas's position. He also casts doubt on the philosophical soundness of Habermas's appeal to the work of Piaget and Kohlberg. These investigations lead Lukes to the conclusion that Habermas has not succeeded in establishing a vantage-point for the critical analysis of the social world, and hence 'we have not yet escaped the Weberian gods and demons'.[19]

In 'Labour and Interaction' (Chapter 8) Anthony Giddens focuses on a distinction which is fundamental to Habermas's social theory. Giddens returns to the original formulation of this distinction in Habermas's discussion of Hegel's Jena lectures, and then traces its elaboration and ramifications throughout Habermas's writings. The distinction enables Habermas to illuminate a number of important issues, such as the positivistic features of Marx's thought and the limits of technical reason. Giddens argues, nevertheless, that the distinction is unsound and that it creates serious inadequacies in Habermas's work. In the first place, 'labour' and 'interaction' oscillate between being 'analytical' and 'substantive' types, attesting to their mixed derivation from the writings of Weber and Marx. Moreover, each of these categories presents specific difficulties. Thus, according to Giddens, Habermas tends to confuse 'interaction' with 'action', and 'action' with 'communicative action'; and he tends to assume that communicative action can be analysed at the level of norms. One implication of these confusions is that Habermas has little to say about the mechanisms which sustain patterns of social interaction; as Giddens says, 'there is an "absent core" in Habermas's writings: an adequate conceptual scheme for grasping the production and reproduction of society'.[20] The emphasis on norms reveals, in Giddens's view, the proximity of Habermas's work to that of Parsons. With Habermas as well as with Parsons, there is a tendency to underplay the importance of power and contradiction, of struggles for scarce resources and clashes of material interest, in the process of social change.

The main elements of Habermas's attempt to develop a theory of social evolution are analysed in the essay by Michael Schmid (Chapter 9). He focuses his critical analysis on two central concepts: 'organisational principle' and 'developmental logic'. The former concept refers to a set of 'abstract rules', determined by the level of learning of a society, which fixes the range of variation for structural change. The latter concept denotes a sequence of stages of development through which all societies must pass. Schmid argues that neither of these central concepts is satisfactory. Organisational principles are too abstract for differentiating types of social formation; and the attempt to relate these principles to particular social structures threatens to become a mere question of definition rather than a matter of empirical interpretation. The notion of developmental logic rests, according to Schmid, on questionable assumptions concerning the relation between the ontogenesis of the individual and the development of world-views. Moreover, this notion burdens the theory of evolution with normative/descriptive ambiguities. Schmid therefore maintains that the notion of developmental logic should be jettisoned; it has no explanatory power and a theory of evolution can be elaborated without it. A theory thus freed of developmental-logical elements would, Schmid concludes, provide no basis for commitment or critique.

David Held's 'Crisis Tendencies, Legitimation and the State' (Chapter 10) examines Habermas's analysis of advanced capitalist societies. After locating this analysis in the context of Habermas's early work and his theory of social evolution, Held elaborates Habermas's conception of the changing relation between state and society. The themes of *Legitimation Crisis* are then expounded. In the second part of his paper, Held shows how a number of Habermas's formulations lead to difficulties. For example, he argues that Habermas's emphasis on the centrality of legitimation crisis derives from an inadequate conception of the way societies cohere; and that this detracts from an appraisal of the fragmentation of culture and the atomisation of people's experiences of the social world. He also challenges Habermas's attempt to develop a crisis theory centred on problems that occur within the boundaries of the nation-state. According to Held, no analytic account of crisis is satisfactory if it does not take sufficient account of international conditions and pressures. In the final section of the essay, questions concerning political transformation and the role of critical theory are explored. Held contends that the practical implications of Habermas's theory are left undeveloped and that this, at a time when there is greater need than ever to establish the credibility of socialism, leaves Habermas's work in an unsatisfying state of abstractness.

In 'Critical Sociology and Authoritarian State Socialism' (Chapter 11) Andrew Arato discusses the relevance of Habermas's work for the analysis of East European societies. While Habermas himself has not written systematically about these societies, Arato reconstructs his general views from remarks scattered in several key texts. A variety of positions emerge from these writings and while they contain provocative insights, they do not amount to an adequate and coherent conception. Arato argues none the less that Habermas's ideas, especially those developed in *Legitimation Crisis*, constitute an important resource for understanding state-socialist societies; and in the main body of his essay he attempts to formulate the organisational principle and the crisis tendencies of those societies. Focusing on developments in the Soviet Union, he examines whether or not its central administrative apparatus – the party-state – is threatened by crisis. Although there are clear dangers facing the party-state, Arato cannot find a direct parallel to the accumulation of problems that, according to Habermas, face Western capitalist states. Pointing to the considerable legitimation reserves in the Soviet Union, he questions Habermas's postulation of a single logic of legal and moral development in history. He finds no reason to share Habermas's views concerning the erosion of traditional world-views and the moral development of humanity.

IV

Habermas's reply to the criticisms developed in these essays (Chapter 12) represents a major restatement and clarification of his views. While firmly defending his over-all project, he acknowledges that many of the objections point to serious and unresolved difficulties. Habermas does not undertake to deal with all of these difficulties here; he confronts only a selection of those which, at the current stage of his work, he regards as most crucial. The relevant issues are regrouped and divided into six sections. In our brief synopsis we shall follow this format, seeking to draw out some of the most interesting and innovatory aspects of Habermas's reply.

Habermas begins with a reconsideration of his relation to the tradition of Marxism. Affirming that his approach, like that of Marx, is guided by the aim of uncovering an emancipatory potential in social life, he nevertheless argues that today we are separated from Marx by inescapable historical truths, for example the contemporary absence of a definite social class which could be regarded as the representative of the general interest. Such truths have fundamental implications for the problem of the relation between theory and practice; and in this regard Habermas finds himself in agreement with much of what Heller says. Habermas does not accept, however, the suggestion that he has filled the place once reserved for the proletariat with a 'universal subject', with human reason as such. 'Both *revolutionary self-confidence* and *theoretical self-certainty* are gone',[21] so that practice must be stripped of false certitude and handed over to the deliberations of responsible subjects. Habermas grants that his concept of labour is quite distinct from the Romantic notion of *Praxis* which is found in the writings of the early Marx, and which is forcefully defended by

Heller. He maintains, however, that this does not leave his theoretical framework incapable of accounting for the distortions effected by the process of production in modern societies. Moreover, a theory developed at the appropriate level of abstraction would not preclude differing conceptions of 'the good life'.

In the second section of his reply Habermas considers the arguments of Bubner concerning the status of critical theory. Returning to the writings of Marx and the early generation of critical theorists, Habermas seeks to show that these authors were not guilty of the confusion which Bubner detects in the concept of *Kritik*. This is not to say that Habermas wishes to follow these authors in every respect, and he clearly restates his view that critical theory can be sustained today only on the basis of a theory of rationality. The latter theory cannot, as Bubner suggests, be detached from speech and action and hence from the social world. 'Rational' is not a term applicable to knowledge but rather to the implementation of knowledge in utterances and actions; and in the natural sciences no less than in ethics and critical theory, 'the unsettled ground of rationally motivated agreement among participants in argumentation is our only foundation'.[22] Those who suppose that the attempt to link reason, language and society must necessarily fall prey to sophism and self-deception have, in Habermas's view, by no means established their case.

In a section entitled 'Reason and Nature' Habermas explores a series of issues which arise from his analysis of the concept of reason. As Ottmann, McCarthy and others argue, this analysis seems to preclude the possibility of establishing a non-objectivistic relation to nature, that is, of encountering a nature-in-itself which would set limits to the human interest in technical control. Habermas distinguishes two threads in this argument, one epistemological and the other ethical. On the epistemological level, Habermas does not deny that human beings can assume different attitudes with regard to nature; but he argues that 'there is for *this* domain of reality only one *theoretically fruitful* attitude, namely the objectivating attitude of the natural-scientific, experimenting observer'.[23] Of the various possible attitudes that may be adopted towards the natural world, only a few have been selected historically, precisely because they alone have proved appropriate for the accumulation of knowledge. 'Nature-in-itself', while not accessible to the objectivating attitude, serves as a *limit concept* of the transcendental-pragmatic theory of knowledge. Similarly, on an ethical level, Habermas does not deny that human beings can have certain feelings, such as compassion or solidarity, with regard to nature. Once again, however, these feelings do not enter into a discursive ethics but function rather as limit concepts of the latter. For while living creatures are certainly *affected* by the moral behaviour of human beings, such creatures could never become equal and effective *participants* in a practical discourse.

Habermas pursues the ethical implications of his position through an examination of the relation between reason and history. In the modern era the structures of reason have become detached from the contents of traditional world-views, thereby creating the conditions for the formulation of a universalistic ethics. However, as Heller, McCarthy and Lukes point out in differing ways, this account gives rise to the following problem: how can such an ethics be related back to historically concrete situations and forms of life? In reply to this question, Habermas emphasises that from the formal structures of reason one cannot derive criteria for the evaluation of particular forms of life: 'Ethical universalism does indeed have a utopian content, but it does not *sketch out* a utopia.'[24] This important clarification enables Habermas to counter specific criticisms of his work. Focusing on the role and significance of developmental psychology, he argues that the latter involves a peculiar division of labour between philosophy and psychology, whereby the truth of empirical theory functions as a 'coherence test' for the rightness of reconstructions of moral intuitions. One should not expect, however, that developmental psychology could resolve the debate between rival ethical positions, such as those of Kant, Rawls or Apel. For these positions are already situated at the level of postconventional morality, and therefore cannot be further ordered by a theory which, hitherto, has been unable to demarcate clearly between different postconventional stages.

Habermas turns, in the subsequent section, to the criticisms of his theories of action, language and science. His reply to Giddens takes the form of a detailed and much-needed clarification of his basic concepts of action. Habermas argues that these concepts provide a means of approaching problems of social reproduction which is more adequate than the alternative account proposed by Giddens. Habermas accepts the latter's claim that his concept of power is bound to the domain of communication; but by introducing the related notion of force, Habermas tries to show how he could deal with the phenomenon of domination in modern societies. The theory of communicative action is based on the analysis of the use of language orientated towards reaching an understanding and is therefore closely linked to the programme of universal pragmatics. Habermas defends his methodological decision to initiate this programme by analysing speech-acts in the 'standard form', while acknowledging that this decision, especially in so far as it neutralises contextual features, is in need of additional support. The criticisms which Thompson and Hesse make of the 'consensus' or 'discourse' theory of truth elicit from Habermas a substantial development of his views. Emphasising that the 'truth-*claim* advanced for *"p"* is . . . not identical with the truth or validity of *"p"*',[25] Habermas seeks to show how his account could be freed from certain difficulties. He nevertheless admits that the relation between the truth of propositions and the objectivity of experience presents a problem which remains to be resolved.

In the final section of his reply, Habermas discusses the contributions by Held and Arato concerning the analysis of modern societies. He grants that there are obscure points in his formulation of the theory of legitimation crisis and that these are linked to difficulties in his attempt to integrate 'life-world' and 'system'. Within a revised framework for such an integration, Habermas introduces a distinction between 'the deficits that inflexible structures of the life-world can give rise to in maintaining the economic and political systems, on the one hand, and manifestations of deficiencies in the reproduction of the life-world itself, on the other'.[26] Legitimation and motivation crises then present themselves as parallel possibilities on the side of maintaining the economic and political systems, and these possibilities are both to be distinguished from the manifestation of deficiencies in the reproduction of the life-world. Such a view could, Habermas believes, account for the complexities of social integration and the division of labour in capitalist societies. Turning to the analysis of state-socialist societies, Habermas suggests that differentiating between the initial conditions of modernisation and the subsequent paths of development may help to clarify some of the issues which Arato raises. State-socialist and capitalist societies can be conceived as two variants of an evolutionary stage characterised by an extensively rationalised life-world. Both types of society display peculiar patterns of crisis tendencies which, Habermas concludes, are urgently in need of analysis.

The critical essays in this volume and Habermas's extensive reply raise issues which, in our opinion, are of fundamental significance for philosophy and social science. To say that these issues are raised is not to suggest that they are resolved. Indeed, Habermas frequently emphasises that his ideas are in an unfinished state, that they sketch out a programme of collaborative research which remains to be developed. It is our hope that the material contained in this volume will help to demonstrate the importance of pursuing this task.

1

Habermas and Marxism

AGNES HELLER

In a study written in 1957 Habermas drew up a sketchy typology of the main trends in Marxism at that time.[1] In the postwar period Marxism was either one scholarly subject among many, or the official ideology of various communist parties. A change, however, could be discerned and Habermas described it with sympathy at a distance: out of the womb of party Marxism, 'humanist' and 'critical' tendencies were born, as a sign of the pluralisation and individualisation of the doctrine which may help to reintroduce it into the realm of public discourse.

Habermas is part of the same humanist/critical trend, in spite of the fact that he is the only important philosopher who has had a great impact on the self-reflection of socialism and Marxism without at the same time ever actually being committed to any particular movement, party or organisation. The fact that he never belonged to any particular movement or party has turned out to be advantageous to his theory in many respects. His horizons have never been limited by the ups and downs of actual historical developments. Proving his theory in scientific discourses *before* the 'process of enlightenment' has been his privilege. The fact that he never had in mind a particular addressee has spared him the effort of formulating a theory which would be appropriate to its possible reception. But the lack of the sensuous experiences of hope and despair, of venture and humiliation, is discernable in the structure of his theory: the creature-like aspects of human beings are missing.

Habermas has always rejected the philosophy of hope and of despair. He never wanted to be the Prince of Wales of negative dialectics; the solid core of his thinking prevents him from accepting this role. Recently, writing of Adorno and Schelsky, he passes this judgement: the philosophy of despair is 'not binding'.[2] One has to add: non-binding philosophies are irresponsible. As a matter of fact, in his polemics against Adorno, Lukács found the appropriate expression for it: 'Grand Hotel Abgrund'. Total despair is an aesthetic feeling in philosophy; even common-sense optimism involves more practical commitment.

In turning away from the philosophy of despair, Habermas gives up two basic categories of his theoretical heritage: that of totality and that of fetishism. If he does apply these – which happens more often in his early writings than in his mature work – he does so with a great deal of caution. They never provide him with *the* theoretical framework for understanding the world constellation. That explains, at least partially, his vehement rejection of Lukács's *History and Class Consciousness*.

Habermas successfully combines critical and positive philosophy. This combination means that critical theory has ceased to be negative dialectics and positive philosophy has ceased to be positivism. He does not tell the world that all its efforts are doomed to failure, but he confronts the world with the values inherent in it, which although distorted still imply the possibility of progress. This is, indeed, a philosophy of responsibility. The theorist takes the risk of becoming a modest fighter in 'making progress', if there is any. Although Habermas never participated in any kind of movement, one should not misunderstand him: he is a fighter. Critical positive philosophy is in itself a daring project in our times.

Habermas turns to Marx with a sovereign gesture. He never undertakes to dissect the delicate fibres of the tissues called the *oeuvre* of Marx, nor does he attempt to understand a *cogito* called Karl Marx. His Marx is the institutionalised one: Marxism, historical materialism. Marx's *oeuvre* is a kind of raw material for him, in a twofold sense. He reinterprets the Marx who was already interpreted by Marxism, on the one hand; and he uses the raw material from the standpoint of his theory as a contrast or background, on the other. That is why it is irrelevant to point out that his explanations of Marx's texts vary, even contradict each other, in different works (sometimes even in the same one), or that he criticises Marx from a standpoint which was precisely Marx's own standpoint, or that he often excludes basic texts from his interpretations. The raw material is incorporated in the product and it is the product that really matters. If we appreciate the product, we have to accept the creator's sovereignty.

There is, however, one characteristic aspect of Habermas's interpretation of Marx which has to be mentioned. He completely neglects the 'romantic' features of Marx, the same ones which have been heavily exploited by Adorno and still more by Marcuse. Although the Feuerbachian element had faded in the work of the later Marx, its bittersweet taste could be felt right to the end. The sensuous, the needing, the feeling human being never ceased to be one of his main concerns. Habermasian man has, however, no body, no feelings; the 'structure of personality' is identified with cognition, language and interaction. Although Habermas accepts the Aristotelian differentiation between 'life' and 'the good life', one gets the impression that the good life consists solely of rational communication and that needs can be argued for without being felt. A striking example of this neglect is his analysis of the chapter on estranged labour in *The Economic–Philosophical Manuscripts*. This odyssey of human suffering – one of the greatest ever written – exemplifies for Habermas the structure of instrumental rationality. I will return later to Habermas's criticism of Marx's concept of work. However, I should mention in advance that Marx's theory had one advantage, as well as a certain grandeur which disappears in Habermas's interpretation: Marx grasped human progress as suffering. He conceives of the fate of the individual human being together with the development of production and of institutions. In rejecting the 'romantic' elements in Marx, Habermas has to give up the theory of alienation – although this theory, as opposed to those of fetishism and totality, *could* have a place in it. Habermas's profession of the 'old European' value of human dignity tacitly includes the value of individuality as a 'whole'. I think that no theoretical consideration should exclude the unification of the 'humanist' and 'critical' heritage of Marx.

Habermas understands Marx's *oeuvre* as science *and* philosophy. Only in this way can criticism of Marx be combined legitimately with the acceptance of some of his basic assumptions. Moreover, this is the only way to avoid ideological and religious attitudes in accepting Marx as a theoretical heritage. By interpreting Marx exclusively as a scientist, the present-day thinker has only two alternatives. First, given that at least some of the basic statements of Marx have been falsified, the theorist may take the position that Marx has no relevance whatsoever in and for our times. The motivation for this position is highly ideological, especially in the case of those who were once dogmatic Marxists themselves and now want to discard their own tradition. The second alternative is the use of the concept of science as a means of ideological legitimation. According to this view, the *corpus* of Marx's work is scientific and that is why it has validity. Those who accept this view disregard all scientific counter-arguments as irrelevant. Thus the *corpus* of Marx is introduced into practice as a system of dogmas. On the other hand, to understand Marx exclusively as a philosopher can be an enterprise that runs the same risk. Lukács's paradigmatic formulation of the 1920s, that even if all of Marx's actual assertions were falsified his method would remain true, implies the conclusion that assertions do not matter at all. Indeed, a philosophy cannot be falsified.[3] Marx, however, has not been understood by Marxist movements mainly as a philosopher; hence the falsification of some of his statements must have a bearing on our relation to him, not only in theory but in practice as well. In understanding the *oeuvre* of Marx as both science and philosophy, Habermas avoids the dangers of both extremes. His reconstruction of historical materialism is perhaps the best example of the soundness and viability of this attitude – irrespective of one's agreement or disagreement with all its theoretical proposals.

There are two basic problems – or rather two clusters of problems – in Marx and Marxism which are continuously interpreted, elaborated, applied and criticised by Habermas. One is the problem of the relation between theory and practice, the other is the problem of historical materialism. The main issues discussed under the latter headings are the concept of productive forces and the conception of the relation between base and superstructure. I shall take up each of these two clusters of problems in turn. Of course, both themes have ramifications which run throughout Habermas's theoretical framework, touching upon a range of problems which I am unable to cover in this study.

I

Habermas is very sceptical about Marx's eleventh thesis on Feuerbach, according to which philosophers hitherto have only interpreted the world, whereas their task is to change it. His scepticism is highly justified. The theoretical attitude is different from the practical one, even when practice is intended. Yet whatever the shortcomings of the eleventh thesis, a theory with practical intent has a particular construction that can be found in Marx. The particularity of the construction is the *identity* of the basic assumption and the *addressee* of the theory. The basic assumption of Marxian theory was the world-historical role of the proletariat: that was the focal point of the system, from which 'the riddle of history' could be solved. All specific theoretical problems were reflected upon in the light of this premiss. The theory with practical intent is a theory constructed *for* the addressee. Of course, the addressee becomes an addressee because of prior theoretical considerations and values.

In the construction of his own theory Habermas follows the same patterns he explores in Marx. First he finds an addressee, human reason, and then works out his basic theorem as the focal point of his theory. The theorem and the addressee are, once again, identical. Human speech *is* practical reason and there is, of course, no human existence without speech. All speech-acts are related to the ideal speech-act; all speech-acts contain – even if only in a hidden way – the four aspects of rational communication.

Habermas differentiates, in the same way as Marx did, between 'in-itself' and 'for-itself'. According to Marx, the proletariat develops from a class in-itself to a class for-itself and thus realises its historical mission. For Habermas, distorted communication is reason in-itself, domination-free argumentation is reason for-itself; the second stage *means* the realisation of the historical mission of practical reason. That is why Habermas's theory is really a theory formulated with practical intent: the realisation of the theory depends on the addressee. We do not need to invent 'the good state' or 'the good society' where reason can flourish and where motivations serve the goal of the Good. Precisely the opposite: the less distorted communication is, the more rational our institutions can become.

If an addressee is universal and not a particular social class, the theory has to cope with special difficulties. I have mentioned one difficulty already: Habermas is compelled to disregard the whole motivational system of human beings.[4] Marx was not compelled to do so: he attributed many kinds of motivations to the proletariat, though often not in a very conclusive manner (they suffer, they feel unhappy in their alienation, etc.). The question of whether, and, if so, how, distortion of communication is motivated cannot be answered by Habermas; nor can he answer the question of what would motivate us to get rid of the distortion. The assumption that consensus can be achieved in a process of enlightenment is in fact no answer: the *will* to achieve consensus is the problem in question. The universalisation of the addressee is also exposed to other theoretical difficulties which I shall discuss later on. At this point I want to consider the advantages.

Habermas refers back to Marx's famous formulation according to which the head of the revolution is philosophy and its heart is the proletariat. The revolution has lost its heart, Habermas argues. The proletariat cannot be the addressee of a theory with practical intent, because it has not developed the emancipatory interest attributed to it by Marx. The latter's conception of political revolution has to be given up, because it has no bearer at all. Moreover, even if it had, political revolution would not lead to human emancipation. Domination can be only gradually transcended. This concept of gradualness, however, has nothing to do with Popperian 'piecemeal engineering'. Habermas insists on the transcendence of domination and on a highly Marxian conception: emancipation is a collective affair depending on the emancipatory interest of the dominated, in the optimal case on the emancipatory interest of every human being. Moreover, the birth-place of the emancipatory interest can be detected in the crisis of capitalism – again an orthodox Marxian idea. Consequently, Habermas's concept of gradualness cannot be described as a liberal idea. Liberalism and democracy have always been divided over one important issue, namely whether change has to be realised from above (by reforms) or from below (by the action of the people). The idea of domination-free communication related to the emancipatory interest of everyone can be properly described as 'radical democracy'.

In the following I shall refer primarily to the new introduction to *Theory and Practice,* in which the political implications of Habermas's theory are made explicit by the author himself. Habermas describes here the 'normal' relationship between theory, the target-group (*Zielgruppe*) and political action. The introduction is meant as an answer – at least partially – to critical remarks which accused him of lacking a theory of organisation. However, it does not offer any theory of this kind; moreover, it tacitly refuses the arrogance of a theory which would suggest 'proper' organisations for political action. If it comes to action, Habermas argues, the theorist cannot have any privileged position: he is one among the many who make decisions and take responsibility. Habermas replaces the theory of the organisation-for-action by that of the organisation of enlightenment, in which – according to Habermas – theory *does* have a privileged position. The theory of the organisation of enlightenment is definitely not identical with the theory of organisation, which has always been understood as a theory of the organisation-for-action. I do not see any shortcomings in this tacit refusal; moreover, it seems to me that organisational theory was a misconceived innovation of Marxism. Marx never suggested any organisational theory; according to Georges Haupt, he refused again and again suggestions along these lines made by some parties in the International.[5] The liberation of the proletariat is the task of the proletariat, the workers have to decide upon their own organisation.[6] Habermas thus follows Marx in declining to elaborate an organisational theory proper.

Nevertheless, the organisation of enlightenment cannot be conceived without contradictions within the framework of Habermas's theory. The relation of theory and target-group is simple when the addressee of the theory and the target-group are identical. In terms of orthodox Marxism it would mean the enlightenment of the proletariat as the particular target-group of the theory. I have argued, however, that Habermas's addressee is practical reason, this being identical with the basic assumption of his system; and human reason is not a 'group'.[7] Humankind has no interests which can be formulated into an argument against the interests of others, humankind as such cannot take any actions. The target-group as the addressee of the theory cannot be conceived together with Habermas's overall account in a clear and conclusive way. Still, this contradiction is understandable, and is even to Habermas's credit. The partiality for reason does not exclude the partiality for the oppressed. Both the dominated and the dominators are equally endowed with reason; the partiality for reason cannot make any distinctions in this respect. The value of domination-free communication ascribes distortion of communication to the system of domination. According to this value, it has to be assumed – though only tacitly – that those who are dominated, from different aspects and in different relations, might have a greater impulse to follow emancipatory interests than those who dominate. Without this tacit presupposition, the notion of the 'target-group' would not make sense at all.

In spite of the introduction of the notion of the target-group and the partiality for the oppressed, Habermas maintains the priority of the partiality for reason. Rational argumentation has to be carried on in two stages: first, inside the target-group; and second, between the target-group and other groups. The theory turns to the target-group, triggering a process of self-reflection on the interests of its members. The process of enlightenment ends (ideally) when the target-group recognises itself in the theory, or at least in a version of the theory which took shape in this process. This self-recognition has to be (again ideally) consensual, and serves as a basis for action. All consensual actions can be replaced by rational argumentation. Substitution can mean two different procedures: either only such actions should be undertaken as can be argued for rationally at any time, or the substitution has to be factual. The difference between the two explanations has no bearing at all on the enlightenment process inside the target-group, but turns out to be important in the ingroup–outgroup relationship. To put it briefly, the gist of the matter is whether class struggle[8] as action can be replaced by rational argumentation. According to Habermas's theory and his supreme value (partiality for reason), it has to be replaced; but Habermas knows that it cannot be. Thus he draws the conclusion that the reflexive theory cannot be applied to strategic activities, that force and discourse cannot be conceived together. I would argue, however, that class struggle cannot be described – at least not in all of its forms – as merely strategic activity and that the models of force and of discourse could be interconnected without giving up Habermas's basic theorem.

When Rousseau said that 'burning is not an argument', he did so from the standpoint of a possible future. Burning was never a 'substitute' for argumentation, because no one who ever burned a book wanted to persuade anyone, least of all those whose books were burnt. Only civil society, based on the formal equality of citizens and the system of contract, universalised (at least virtually) the *right* of argument. The acknowledgement of formal equality in pluralistic democracies ensures the *possibility* of discourse for everyone. However, the right cannot be put into practice forthwith. The social system is one of domination, and the dominating party cannot be brought to listen to an argument or accept any kind of reciprocity unless it is forced to pay attention.

In formal democracy, as opposed to despotic political systems, political revolutions can be replaced by rational discourse. If this holds true, then class struggle has one aim: to create situations in which the other party is forced to listen to argument and has to accept the reciprocity of the situation. This can happen, however, only in situations of momentary equality of power, which can only be achieved by force. Although force cannot be replaced by argumentation, it can be applied 'on behalf of argumentation'. Moreover, if we take democracy seriously, we have to accept that the only legitimation of force is the realisation of the virtually existing right of argumentation. If it holds true that argument cannot replace action, it holds true as well that action cannot replace argument. If, however, the goal of action is argument (forcing the other party to 'pay attention'), then class struggle cannot be conceived exclusively in terms of strategic action: the partiality for reason is included in the concept of success.

This is by no means mere speculation invented on behalf of the partiality for reason. The process described above happens everyday. Both particularistic interests and universalistic needs are often formulated in the process of forcing argumentation. To mention the particularistic ones: arbitration commissions are institutions for argumentation where rational compromises can be achieved; but strikes have to precede arbitration, because without them the employers would not be forced to listen. This is why unions refuse to replace strikes by arbitration. The expression of universalistic needs can (and often does) take the same form, though no arbitration institutions are established for this kind of argumentation (but they are not excluded in principle). Nor can mass demonstrations against nuclear sites, uranium mining, wars, unemployment or women's oppression be replaced by argumentation. Force has to be shown, the dispute has to be made explicit, the dissenting delegation has to be backed by force to make the other party pay attention. Movements such as pressure groups do the same. In the case of mass demonstrations, class struggle can even less be identified with 'strategic action' than in the case of a strike. Action *is* communication, class struggle *and* enlightenment occur at the same time, not only because the slogans of the posters can trigger enlightenment processes, but because the conscious aim of action is (at least partially) an enlightenment process which will counterbalance the distorted communication of the media. The more mass demonstrations there are, the more counter-institutions and counter-movements express universalistic (mostly radical) needs, the greater the chances for progress through rational discourse – though only if discourse is set as an aim. The enlightenment process of reflexive theory might have no other task but one: namely, to establish the target-group's readiness for rational argumentation. If reflexive theory would be satisfied with this substantial task, it could address *any* group, movement, or party and the partiality for reason would be achieved.

It seems to me, however, that Habermas has something 'more' in mind. I put 'more' in quotation marks, because – if I understood him correctly – the enlightenment of the 'target-group' described by Habermas is 'less' than what has been described above, so far as human emancipation is concerned.

The organisation of enlightenment presupposes the emancipatory interest inside the target-group, which means two things: the tutelage is self-imposed and the outcome from it is intended. Habermas does not convince us that this *is* the case, only that this *might* be the case. Readiness for emancipation is explained by the transcendental theorem: we are rational beings, consequently we do not *choose* rationality as a value. In his efforts to eliminate decisionism, he identifies a conditional assertion with a statement. The conditional assertion is this: if we choose at all, we cannot choose anything but rationality. The statement is this: we do not choose rationality, because we *are* rational beings. Habermas only establishes the first (conditional) assertion, not the second one, but in fact he substitutes the second for the first. I think, however, that these two are theoretically and practically different statements and that the first does not prove the second. We can choose the priority of instrumental or strategic rationality over communicative rationality, and we may not choose at all but simply follow drives, emotions or habits. Acceptance of this possibility would not mean relapsing into the trap of decisionism, because it does not assert that there is a choice between rationality and irrationality. What it does state is that communicative rationality is a choice, a *value-choice*. Our rationality, as Habermas shows, is a rationality in-itself; but to transform it into a rationality for-itself we have to choose communicative rationality as a value. The decisive question is not, as Habermas presumes, whether the target-group accepts (or transforms) reflexive theory in and through arguments; rather, the decisive question is whether it is ready for argumentation. Reflexive theory turns either to groups in which rational argument is already accepted as a consensual value, or to groups where it is not accepted. In the latter case its task is twofold: to argue for the value of rational discourse *and* to introduce the premises of the theory into the target-group – the second can be achieved only when the first has been completed.

Habermas does not describe how consensus regarding the abovementioned value should be achieved (indeed, he refuses to acknowledge it as a value at all); he describes only how consensus concerning a theory can be attained. A theory has to be proven as true in scientific discourse before it can enter into the process of enlightenment. At the same time, Habermas does suggest that a theory accepted in the enlightenment process can be corrected, and that a consensus achieved at the end of the process does not mean acceptance of the theory as a *whole* (which would presuppose that everyone becomes a scientist). This is not only a sound idea, but again a conception based on awareness of responsibility. Whoever turns to a target-group has to be aware of his or her responsibilities. In our times, when modern myths and dogmatic systems have attracted groups and led them into catastrophes, it is especially important that all theories prove whether they hold true in rational discussions before offering any kind of solution for a particular group. Proving the theory first does not mean, of course, that a consensus of scientists should or could be achieved. In the social sciences this is never the case. But it means that the theory has to be open for discussion; the theorist has to consider all counter-arguments and must be ready to amend the theory or defend it rationally. Moreover, the explanation of why other theorists do not accept a theory does not exempt the theorist from taking their arguments seriously: ascribing arguments to different interests is no argument in itself.

A theory can *offer* itself only after being proven. Up to this point I can follow Habermas and I agree with him. My problems are connected with the second step, with the enlightenment process itself and with the relation of the theory to the target-group in general. Habermas writes:

The theory serves primarily to enlighten those to whom it is addressed about the position they occupy in an antagonistic social system and about the interests of which they could become conscious in this situation as being objectively theirs. Only to the degree that organized enlightenment and consultation lead to the target groups' recognizing themselves in the interpretations offered do the analytically proposed interpretations actually become consciousness, and does the objectively attributed situation of interests actually become the real interest of a group capable of action.[9]

The end of the process of enlightenment is, as I have already mentioned, consensus. However, this is not a consensus about values (or about one value), but a consensus about *theory* ('the acceptance by those concerned, free of any compulsion, of the theoretically derivable interpretations').[10] Hence this is a model of one theory/one target-group. If all reflective theories offer an interpretation of the latent interests of one group, then either the theories have to be particularised (different interests, different theories), or else we must accept that all groups share the same interest. In the first case a theory could not claim universality; in the second case it could not claim to be interpreting interests at all. There is only one way out of this deadlock: the presupposition that the interests of one particular social group are *identical* with the emancipatory interest as such, that universality is inherent in its particularity. But this was precisely the proposal Lukács made in his *History and Class Consciousness*, a proposal vehemently rejected by Habermas. The consensual acceptance of a theory by a group which recognises its interest in the theoretically 'imputed' or 'possible' consciousness is nothing but the 'imputed consciousness' *(zugerechtnentes Bewusstsein)* of Lukács. Consensus *is* the collective consciousness which enters into emancipatory action. There are political differences between Lukács's and Habermas's theories, but no important theoretical ones. The political differences are obvious: Habermas speaks of 'groups' and not of one particular historical class, a highly obscure point in his argument. Further, the enlightenment process is not led by a political party but immediately by theory. This modification breaks with only one tradition (with the identification of true knowledge and a social organisation), but not with the other tradition: elitism. The theorist's pretension to know the interests of *others* better than they do themselves, and the claim that others can recognise their *real* interests only through the interpretation of *the* theory (indeed, through *one* single theory) – these claims must be renounced. The imputation of needs and interests cannot and should not be the task of theory.

Later I shall return to the question of what can be offered by theory, but before doing so one question has to be raised: is consensus regarding theory a precondition of consensual action? Moreover, is consensus in the interpretation of needs and interests a precondition? The answer does not refer to real actions but to the ideal one, which is domination-free.

By 'action' we may understand two different things: a particular action undertaken in an actual situation; or the norm of practical procedure. The first can be disregarded because it is obvious that consensus regarding one single practical action does not presuppose consensus in theory or regarding all needs and interests. (Let us consider the example of organising a demonstration. Anybody is free to join a demonstration if he or she agrees on just one point: the cause being demonstrated for.) It is indeed the second meaning that matters.

Human beings do not accept social theories (philosophies) from the standpoint of their group-interests, but from the standpoint of their lives as a whole, from their system of needs. 'Readiness' for rational argumentation about values and theories presupposes the involvement of the human being as a whole, as a needing, wanting, feeling being. The system of needs is identical with the form of living. If we accept the plurality of ways of life, we have to accept the plurality of theories as well. Consensus regarding *one* theory would mean consensus in one single way of life. To exchange pluralism for consensus would be a bad bargain (not only for me, but for Habermas as well).

Is this exchange a necessity? I do not think so. A plurality of ways of life and consequently of theories can be conceived of together with consensus for and in action. One thing is, however, obvious: preliminary consensus about the value of rational argumentation *alone* is not enough to ensure consensus for action in the case of diverse ways of life and theories. A preliminary consensus about *one other* value is presupposed to enable us to think of this possibility without self-contradiction.

Robert Owen formulated the practical rule of action in a future society as follows: 'One man has no more power over the thoughts of another, than that which *fair argument,* expressed in the spirit of *charity* . . . shall give him'; and he concluded: 'Without charity, pure practical charity, for all mankind, there can be no real virtue of rationality in the mind and conduct of men.'[11] To replace the word 'charity' with a more modern (but not a better) one: the acknowledgement and satisfaction of the *needs of others* has to be accepted as a universal value in a preliminary consensus, for otherwise domination-free argumentation cannot be conceived of at all. One accepted theory, one way of life, excludes rational argumentation too: only different theories and forms of living can lead to discourse. Different ways of life, different theories, make practical discourse possible only together with the value Owen called 'charity'. If someone gives his or her consent to an action because it satisfies the needs of others, it is not a wrong consent: accepting the 'good' without being forced to do so does not differ from accepting the 'true' in the same way. The ethics formulated by Habermas (in *Legitimation Crisis*) cannot fill the gap caused by the lack of any kind of positive moral value.

Returning to the first question: what would be the task of the theory of society if not the organisation of the enlightenment process about the needs and interests of others? The theorist is in a privileged position: he or she has access to the products of the human mind in which social life as a whole is reflected, and acquires the ability to reflect upon social life following the rules of his or her own objectivation. Theories of the past are already more or less proven in one respect: we know whether or not they met basic needs or interests on the basis of their reception and the consequences of their reception (if there were any). The theorist's construction of a 'world' has always been related to his or her own needs and interests; the more the theorist shared interests and needs with others, the more generally the theory was received. In our present time this is the case to a no less extent. In historical epochs when there was actual consensus regarding basic values, the theorist could proceed less cautiously. Since this is no longer the case, the theorist must now proceed with caution. The theorist has to be aware that in constructing a world he or she expresses his or her own needs and interests; the desire to universalise them does not allow them to be imputed to others. Social theory is a kind of service and has to be understood as such. We offer it and you take it or leave it according to *your* needs, even if we hope that you will take it. The theorist cannot organise any kind of enlightenment for others; this can only be done by the others themselves. The 'asymmetry' of theory and possible target-group is exclusively the 'asymmetry' of scientific/philosophical explanation, but *not asymmetry in the awareness of needs and interests*. Nevertheless, reflexive theory – especially that of Habermas – has one advantage over all other theories: it can offer a universally valid *form* of procedure. It is not more authorised to inform others about their real needs and interests than other competing theories, but it can tell you that, whatever your interests or values, you must argue for them, you must relate your needs to values with rational arguments.

II

The second main cluster of problems with respect to which Habermas always refers to Marx – pro or con – is the complex of forces and relations of production, basis and superstructure. From the outset Habermas rejects the Marxian paradigm of production. This rejection can be explained not only by his philosophical education but also by historical experience. The development of the forces of production has changed society without leading to emancipation. This conclusion is valid for both constituents of the forces of production. The proletariat does not represent emancipatory interests on the one hand, nor has technology had emancipatory effects on the other. Moreover, the growth of technology has led to the instrumentalisation of human activities and has become – together with science – an ideology legitimating the system of domination. Thus one has to look for possible liberating influences in another realm of human activity, the system of communication. The 'liberating force' in and for human society is attributed by Habermas to communication. It can be easily seen that Habermas conceives of all traditional universal values within the framework of a theory of communication. Rational discourse stands for practical rationality and is the supreme value: domination-free communication stands for freedom, the ideal speech situation for equality, consensus for truth.

Following Max Weber, Habermas distinguishes two basic forms of rationality: goal-rationality and value-rationality (rational communication). He further subdivides goal-rationality into instrumental-rationality (work) and strategic-rationality (goal-rational decisions in human interaction). Genuine rationalisation as humanisation of society would mean the primacy of communicative rationality over goal-rationality – the actual primacy of practical reason over pragmatic-instrumental reason.

The shift of the paradigm turns our theoretical and practical attention in a different direction. It highlights some basic problems neglected by Marx while failing to take into consideration others which were solved in Marx's theoretical framework. The main question is that of historical legacy. First I am going to discuss the heritage of capitalist society for a future (socialist) one, and then discuss the over-generalisation of this issue in a philosophy of history.

I have analysed already how the 'shift' from the paradigm of production to the paradigm of communication implies the replacement of the theory's addressee. This implication is interwoven with several others. Marx considered the productive forces to be the main legacy of capitalism, not only because they destroy the traditional relations of production but because they can be taken over just as they are, though they may develop further in the future. Later on Marx even included in this legacy those aspects of the relations of production that are described by Habermas as relations of strategic rationality. Civil society, with its contractual procedure, its right of debate, and so on, could not serve as a heritage for Marx; he conceived of a society without a state, without any kind of market and with a complete division between the management of persons and things. Not only have the latter attributes turned out to be utopian, but they cannot serve as regulative practical ideas either. At the same time – and for this very reason – the progressive preservation of strategic rationality became highly problematic as well. Herein lies the importance of Habermas's 'shift'. In reconsidering the question of heritage he turns to a different sphere: to that of civil society, to the right of argumentation, to formal democracy, to the growing impact of reflexivity in the ethical world. The possibility of progress can be grasped precisely in terms of the 'ethical' subsystem:[12] the latter has to subjugate pragmatic activities, which cannot be simply taken over but must become the matter of reflexion. In this case there is no clash but rather gradual progression. This new understanding of the problem of heritage is a convincing one, particularly in the light of a new and (at least for orthodox Marxists) surprising historical fact, namely that socialism is not the only alternative to capitalism. In the Soviet Union and Eastern Europe a mode of production has emerged which cannot be described as either capitalist or socialist; it is simply different. One characteristic of this difference is the absence of civil society and its heritage, an absence which restricts rational communication and cancels out progressive institutions already achieved in the course of history. Habermas's theory is a good one. It fulfils a double task: that of promise and that of warning.

Habermas, however, pays a price for these new insights. By rejecting the paradigm of production he almost completely neglects the anthropological meaning of work, which was conceptualised by Marx in depth.

The notion of 'work' cannot be defined; it is entirely a question of what we *call* 'work'. If, for example, we depart from the division of labour, then rational communication – even discourse – can be defined as work (done by social scientists, lawyers, politicians, teachers). There is only *one viewpoint* in which work is identical with material production: that in which we define it as the metabolism of society with nature. Marx did define it in this way, but not exclusively; with Habermas the definition becomes exclusive. This exclusivity is completely legitimate in all cases where Habermas refutes Marx's philosophy of history based on the inherent dynamics of material forces of production. It turns out to be illegitimate only from the standpoint of anthropology.

If we define work as goal-rational activity, we must consider the possibility that the division of rules into 'social' and 'technical' is a fairly recent development in the history of the human species. On the other hand, up to the present time the development of skills has taken place not only in production but also in interaction. In our everyday activities the appropriation of norms and skills is completely interwoven; the same is true in artistic creation. If, however, we analysed work since the time when technical and social rules were differentiated, we are obliged to raise the question of whether this division is always a characteristic of goal-rationality (*techne*).

If we define goal-rational work exclusively through 'following technical rules', then we must accept Habermas's proposal to describe it as 'instrumental-rationality'. Habermas refers back to the Aristotelian definition of *techne*, which was accepted by Marx in the fourth chapter of *Capital*. Following technical rules is, however, only one element in the latter author's analyses, and not even the basic one. Goal-rationality is comprehended primarily as teleological activity, where the unity of *noiesis* and *poiesis* is achieved in the work process by the same individual. Following sheer technical rules is, according to Aristotle, not *techne*, not the work of free men, but *banausis*, the work of slaves. One may wonder why Marx turned back to this older concept in a book in which production is identified with modern industrial production, and why he reformulated the 'one-man/one-work' model (a very abstract one) which had no bearing whatsoever on the actual processes of production in his own time. This becomes understandable if we take into account a new distinction which he drew concerning a new phenomenon in modern capitalist industrial labour. He emphasised that the division of mental and manual labour took a new form: the mental and manual aspect of the *same* productive process became divided, the unity of *noiesis* and *poiesis* is gone, production follows technical rules without any longer being goal-rational from the standpoint of the individual. [13] Hence what is rational socially is no longer necessarily rational individually. This differentiation between goal-rationality and instrumental-rationality has many theoretical and practical advantages over Habermas's view. First, it provides us with a double yardstick to evaluate societies: production and the producers. Second, it enables us to pose a historical question: if, as Habermas maintains, production does not socialise our inner nature, then is this an inherent characteristic of work or is it merely a consequence of a historical development in which productive activity has ceased to be goal-rational from the standpoint of the producers? Finally, it allows us to raise a question concerning the possible rehumanisation of work in a future society: how could goal-rationality be regained, presupposing the continuation of modern industrial production?

In contrast to Habermas, I would argue that goal-rationality is not concerned solely with the appropriation of outer nature, but that goal-rationality and value-rationality together accomplish the socialisation of our *inner nature* as well. I would go so far as to say that the same feelings – fear, anger, pleasure, disgust – are channelled, repressed and withheld in work as in interaction. Work cannot be done properly without concentrating on it, enjoyment must be postponed. If one is afraid, shaky hands will not accomplish the task; if one is angry, the raw material will be broken rather than shaped. We may approach goal-rationality in its 'pure' form and grasp it as a model of socialisation of our inner nature without any kind of repression. We must recognise, however, that work is always done in definite social settings. Undistorted goal-rationality has been no less and no more present in human history than undistorted communication. I agree with Habermas: every instance of human speech is a claim to rational communication; but I would add that every instance of human work is a claim to goal-rational creativity. Accomplished human freedom means socialisation of our inner nature without repression, both in communication and creation.

The need to 'make sense' of our lives always includes the need for creativity. If this need is not met, then we are deprived of one of the greatest joys attained by effort; and being deprived is discomfort, or, worse still, misery. Even institutionalised discourse could not replace this need, which is basic in us. Envisaging the most ideal possible future, we may assume that work will take up more time in our very limited life than public debate. We can argue about our lives and those of others, but living our lives is prior to this. Even in a world of organised discourse, our main needs will be those we once attributed to God: creation and love. Hence I oppose Habermas's identification of work with instrumental-rationality and with the transformation of outer nature.

From the beginning Habermas has been concerned to show that Marx was in some way wrong to assign priority to the forces of production. Precisely why he was wrong is a question that Habermas has answered in different ways. The counter-argument began to take shape in *Technik und Wissenschaft als 'Ideologie'*, and it was worked out in detail in *Zur Rekonstruktion des Historischen Materialismus*. In the following analysis I shall concentrate on the latter work.

Habermas, no less than Marx, offers a theory of historical evolution. He understands history, not as histories in the plural, but as history in the singular, as *the* history. He accepts Marx's idea that the anatomy of humans is the key to the anatomy of apes, that the higher stage of development is the key to understanding a lower stage. The present stage of history is the highest, which means that history as a whole can be understood as a sequence of social forms which led to the present one. Like Marx, he envisages the future as the outcome of our history, which is at the same time the outcome of History. It is a teleological reconstruction of history, where teleology is not identical with the concept of tending towards a hidden goal, but with the logic of evolution. It does not presuppose the necessity of every step undertaken in history, but an 'if – then' necessity. We can conceive a social formation as a progressive one only if it follows the logic of evolution;[14] and decisive social formations have followed the logic of evolution (otherwise our own historical stage could not be conceived as the highest one).[15] In spite of many cautious restrictions, what Habermas offers us is not a theory of history but a new philosophy of history, with all the beauties and problems of such an enterprise.

Habermas differentiates between the logic of evolution and its dynamics. That is, he wants to distinguish between the problem of the independent variable of progress and the problem of the indicators of progress. Without presupposing an independent variable, a philosophy of history is never 'complete'. The temptation to make a complete conception is very great: Habermas cannot resist it. As we shall see later on, he reintroduces the independent variable, though very cautiously.

Marx located the dynamics of historical development in the development of the forces of production. In this conception the forces of production fulfil a triple function: they engender progress, they indicate progress, and they provide continuity of progress. This triple function secures the totalisation of the historical mission of the proletariat. The substance (work) becomes subject; the decisive element of the forces of production is identical with the class which wages the struggle. The continuity of progress (development of the means of production) is ensured by a *conscious dynamics*: logic and dynamics are conceived together. Habermas cannot accept this independent variable, for he, rightly, does not believe in the emancipatory role of the development of the forces of production.

In reconstructing history Habermas's main focus is the learning processes which make possible the emergence of higher social structures. 'The introduction of new forms of social integration . . . requires knowledge of a moral-practical sort and not technically useful knowledge that can be implemented in rules of instrumental and strategic action.'[16] Hence he rejects the Marxian independent variable, together with the *model* of transformation. The question is no longer whether forces of production are prior to relations of production, but whether new relations of production can be introduced at all without previous learning processes in the realm of the 'superstructure'. Marx's assumption of the development of forces of production is reduced by Habermas to its simple but relevant meaning: it is 'the endogenous growth of knowledge'.[17] This reduction unveils the secret of Marx's 'independent variable': it is nothing other than the increase of human knowledge, with priority given to one type of knowledge (knowing how). Progress in knowledge equals progress in freedom. However, in unveiling Marx's 'secret', in discarding his independent variable, and in replacing it with parallel learning processes, Habermas dispenses not only with a highly problematic explanation of history but also with all of the *tragic aspects* inherent in it.

Of course, Marx never denied the existence of new learning processes in all fields of human interaction: the progressive modes of production were characterised as totalities of new learning processes. The theory of the development of forces of production as the independent variable in history allowed him to apply the same independent variable as a double indicator of progress: the level of production and the fate of the producers. The producers carry progress on their shoulders, they suffer from the progress which they themselves create. Progress is a contradiction between the wealth created and the impoverishment of the creators of wealth. Marx's idea of progress is a conditional one: only the perspective of the abolition of alienation (or at least a process of de-alienation) makes us conceive of history as progress at all. We cannot weigh gains against losses, for losses are incommensurable. Only the perspective of gains without any kind of losses allows us to speak about 'progress' in history. In Habermas's work the concept of progress is not a tragic one; it is not conditional, it is absolute. For him, progress is a fact – at least he wants to persuade us that it is. We are developing splendidly. The question is on our lips: Towards

Auschwitz? Towards the Gulag? Towards Hiroshima? Towards our self-destruction? Later on I shall return to these questions.

In order to understand history in terms of consecutive sequences of progressive forms of interaction, Habermas works out a parallel between the ontogenetic development of ego structures and the phylogenetic development of systems of social integration. The stages of development of the ego structures are: the symbiotic, the egocentric, the sociocentric-objectivistic and finally the universalistic (based on Piaget's description). Habermas is aware that the parallel cannot be complete; for example, 'egocentric' social integrations are, by definition, impossible. Nevertheless, in spite of the cautious formulation, the use of the theory of ego development for understanding progress in history would make no sense at all if Habermas did not want us to believe that there *is* a parallel which enables us to grasp the evolutionary logic as such. Moreover, the parallel would provide us with this grasp only on the assumption that ontogenesis has priority over phylogenesis. If we could demonstrate the priority of ontogenesis, we could kill two birds with one stone: we could establish the logic of progress in history for the past and for the future. Habermas's cautious and conditional formulations in no way change the ontological overdetermination inherent in the parallel itself. Either we discard the parallel completely or we overdetermine the understanding of history. There is *no* third possibility. If ontogenesis is prior to phylogenesis (and without this assumption the parallelism is pointless), then progress is teleologically conceived; and however often we repeated that development is not unilinear, that regression is not excluded, etc., it would not make any difference. Moreover, the priority of ontogenesis reintroduces the independent variable into history: ontogenesis becomes the independent variable.

How can we argue for the priority of ontogenesis? We might accept the following thesis: the only societies which developed were those in which new ontogenetic structures appeared. This thesis is, however, theoretically and empirically unsound. Put a newborn Polynesian child into a German family and it will go through the same ontogenetic development as everyone else in German society. The hidden racism of this explanation would be, of course, repulsive to Habermas. We might try another thesis: the inheritance of acquired faculties; but this would be disproved from a biological point of view. Last but not least, we could use the 'inbreeding' of high cultures in our argument and conceive of progressing ontogenetic structures as outcomes of this inbreeding. However, the history of the twentieth century refutes this presupposition as well. If ontogenesis is prior to phylogenesis, how could it happen that children who had been through the stages of development as described by Piaget later dropped all universal values, reflexivity and individuality in sanguinary acts of killing and destroying, as well as worshipping new myths and self-imposed leaders? Regression, perhaps. But where is the logic of ontogenesis if it is *fragile* enough to break into pieces when challenged by a social integration which does not grant reflexivity, universal values and individuality? The theory of the priority of ontogenesis suggests that regression is an interlude which does not endanger the march of progress. Let us hope so. We cannot, however, base our hope on the ontogenesis of the ego structure.

The theory is, none the less, a great and all-embracing one. There are no loose threads, everything is ordered around the basic message and at the same time explained by it. This is a philosophy of the old style, totalised as a philosophy of history, as a theoretical expression of the traditional European value of human dignity.

The theorist, however, steps outside of his or her own theory. Habermas writes:

> Evolutionary-theoretical statements about contemporary social forma-
> tions have an immediate practical relevance, insofar as they facilitate
> the diagnosis of developmental problems. The restriction to the re-
> trospective explanation of historical material is thereby renounced in
> favour of a *retrospection which is projected from an action perspective*:
> the diagnostician of the present assumes the fictitious standpoint of an
> evolutionary-theoretical explanation of a past belonging to the
> future . . . Marxist analyses share in principle this asymmetrical posi-
> tion of theoreticians, who analyse the developmental problems of
> contemporary social systems with respect to the structural possibilities
> which are not yet institutionalised – *and* perhaps *never will find an institu-
> tional embodiment.*[18]

This asymmetrical position of the theorist emphasised by Habermas is what I call the theorist's 'stepping outside his or her own theory'. The theory is that of the theorist, but the same theorist reflects upon his or her own theory as a conditional one. The theory itself is not self-reflective, but the relation of the theorist to the theory is a self-reflective one. The theory can validate itself only in the future: if there is a progressive future at all, this will be the theory of the future; if there is progress at all, our history has to be comprehended (and will be comprehended) in this way.

Hence the totalisation (and overdetermination) no longer serves to grant knowledge about the future of society. It is, rather, an *offer* to create progress, an *invitation* to it. The theorist participates in this creation by formulating a philosophy of progress; this is his or her contribution to the collective enterprise. The theorist does not *know* whether there will be any progress, but he or she *ought* to act for it and *may* hope there will be.

In this respect it is therefore misplaced to use Auschwitz, Gulag and Hiroshima to argue against Habermas's viewpoint. The theory of progress is conceived *for* progress and hence it will be valid only in the case of realised progress. Habermas follows the logic of his own objectivation in constructing the logic of evolution. If we accept the genre, we have to accept this 'one-sidedness' as well. For my part, I do.

Nevertheless, as far as the *retrospective* rather than the prospective is concerned, it is not out of place to argue against Habermas using Auschwitz, Hiroshima and the Gulag – and all of their predecessors. Here one has to return to the comparison between the Marxian and the Habermasian reconstruction of history. Marx understood the progress of 'pre-history' as an alienated one: progress *itself* is conditional; losses and gains cannot be balanced against one another, for losses are incommensurable. Marx promised us that future progress is inevitable; Habermas does not promise it – he speaks in conditional terms with regard to the future. However, he does not speak in conditional terms retrospectively, because he drops the concept of alienation and thus the fate of individuals as one indicator of progress or regression. If there is to be future progress, the whole of history should be understood as progress without contradictions, he suggests. It is to this point of his 'reconstruction of historical materialism' that one reacts with uneasy feelings. No future will give back the lives destroyed in their youth, no future can make us forget the horrors, the miseries, the bloodshed and the tears of the past and the present. If people of the future committed the insult against our fathers, sisters and brothers of conceiving the epochs in which they were killed, tortured and oppressed as part of a smooth process of evolution, they would be very inhumane indeed. In constructing a pre-history for the possible future, we cannot avoid making it to remember. We may reconstruct the past more tragically than Habermas does without endangering the prospect of progress theorised with practical intent.

As I have said, Habermas constructs a complete (totalising) theory, but steps outside his own theory, making the promise a conditional one, whose condition is our readiness to create a progressive future. If, however, his theoretical overdetermination does not serve the same aim as it did for Marx, namely to ensure the realisation of the promise, then what kind of aim does it serve? The underlying idea may be to provide a positive answer to Mannheim's challenge: to present a self-reflexive theory which is at the same time not relativistic. But it is possible to answer this challenge without overdetermination, even if it is not easy.

Let us look again at Habermas's conditional formulation: if there is progress, it will be like this. All overdeterminations serve one purpose: to define what progress might be. Progress can be nothing but the realisation of rationality, with priority given to communicative rationality. Hence there is only one true theory of progress, the one which conceives it as the realisation of rationality; and progress (if it happens) can only validate *this* theory. However, domination-free argumentation can be conceived only as a precondition of the good life – it is not the good life itself. Moreover, why the 'good life' and not 'good lives', each of which can reconstruct its *own* history in *different* ways? Habermas reconstructs historical materialism around *one* universal value: his own. But there are other universal values too. He overdetermines his theory in order to make us accept his own value as the exclusive or at least the highest one. He cannot be blamed for this, because here, too, he is only following the logic of his own objectivation, that of philosophy. But those who are ready to create progress are confronted with different philosophies. They can express their needs for the future in the conceptual framework and value system of the one among many which formulates this need-expression in the most perfect way – but they ought to do it in the *form* of a rational argument. This is the real message of Habermas's historical materialism, a message which has to be accepted even if one refuses the theory as a whole. No one who is ready to create progress can neglect it – and thus it creates progress *unconditionally*.[19]

2

Habermas's Concept of Critical Theory

RÜDIGER BUBNER

Preliminary

The concept of critical theory is ambiguous. It combines in a productive way *two meanings* of the word *Kritik* which were developed in classical German philosophy. The one meaning stems from the Kantian programme for a transcendental philosophy and signifies the testing of legitimacy. The other meaning goes back to the Young Hegelians' attitude to the opposition of theory and practice and signifies negation. Ever since Marx developed his concept of a realist science, which sought to draw the consequences from the faltering beginnings and eventual failure of German idealism, the two meanings of the concept of *Kritik* have been fused together. Thus the ambiguity of the concept has been passed on from generation to generation and can be traced even to present-day neo-Marxism. This is what I wish to demonstrate in what follows.

For *Kant, Kritik* was to be the primordial act of an unprejudiced testing of the validity claims of knowledge, a testing carried out by the force of reason alone. He considered his own enlightened age to be particularly suitable for such a task of critical testing, which would finally put an end to the errors and squabbles of dogmatic metaphysics. Reason must reflect upon itself and draw a definitive line between valid knowledge of reality and empty excesses of speculation. As if recalling the classical origin of the concept, Kant speaks of *Kritik* as the 'high court'[1] of reason where judgement is passed on legitimate and illegitimate claims to science.

An entirely different sense of *Kritik* emerges in the *post-Hegelian* era. As is well known, Kant's attempt to ground empirically objective knowledge had given rise to contrary developments. The principle of this grounding – namely, the synthetic achievement of self consciousness – was turned by idealist philosophy in the wake of Kant into the basis for a renewal of metaphysics; Hegel's doctrine of absolute spirit, as the mediation of all substance of reality in an encyclopedic system, marked the end of this development. Post-Hegelian philosophy bore everywhere the stamp of this successful integration of all reality into unbounded knowledge. Only one more step remained to be taken, and the final barrier, this side of which Hegel's speculation had admittedly halted, would be surmounted once and for all – *the perfect theory had to be translated into the historical Praxis of the human world.*

This demand, which is made in unison by the Young Hegelians, Bauer, Ruge and the early Marx,[2] in fact carries Hegel's argument beyond Hegel. If philosophical concepts can take possession of all reality, and if historical progress is to be seen as the ever more complete unification of prevailing reality and thought, then it is inexplicable that Hegel restricted his mediation to pure theory from which the reality of social life was excluded as alien. The extension of fully developed theory into real *Praxis* is a transformation of bad *Praxis* into reasonable *Praxis*. The intervention of reason in the given circumstances of socio-historical reality is termed *Kritik*. In this context *Kritik,* strictly speaking, signifies a negating reflection.

Marx immediately noted that although this passage of thought into reality is meant to bridge the abstract discrepancy between theory and *Praxis*, it in fact succumbs to an essentially idealist illusion. He took leave of his former fighting companions by mercilessly branding Young Hegelianism as the 'German Ideology'. Alongside his critique of the ideology of these critics, who believed that their abstract reflections could arrive at reality, there emerges the concept of a *new science*, which is to provide the true theory of socio-historical reality. According to this concept, the truth about reality emerges only when one removes the ideological illusions beneath which the relevant structures and factors are concealed. The prevailing circumstances are in fact dependent for their continued existence on those theories which stabilise the circumstances by suppressing the possibility of real change. The ahistorical laws of bourgeois economics are, as far as this function is concerned, on a par with the illusory hopes of the Young Hegelians' abstract *Kritik*.

The new science is called the 'critique of political economy'. The critical demonstration of the illusions in economic theories, which had been presumed to be universally valid, forms the methodological presupposition for genuine knowledge of social reality. In one sense Marx's science contains a clearly Kantian component, in so far as the 'natural laws of capitalist production' are unveiled in a critical manner, as promised by the preface to the first edition of *Capital*. Simultaneously, however, this concept of *Kritik* contains also the intention of transforming reality by thought, in so far as laying bare the real factors of the social nexus puts an end to the false blockade of the historical process by ideological theories. In Marx's project the two meanings of the concept of *Kritik* are inseparably united.

This is the origin of the much-debated difficulties in Marx's methodology,[3] a methodology which pursues the scientific explanation of given reality with a view to the future transformation of that reality. It is only thanks to the anticipation of a better, unalienated society that we can critically penetrate the illusion which freezes the prevailing social relations. Nevertheless, we should not conjure up any image of a utopia which might itself contribute to ideological self-deception. The difficulties of this methodology come to a head in the question: what kind of theory is it that can accuse all philosophical and economic theories of ideologically masking reality, and which can itself still lay claim to theoretical status? If it is itself an ideology, then it is not a science; but if it is a science, then it is not a *Kritik*.

The role of reflection
This is a difficulty under which Marxism has been labouring up to the present day, so far as it has placed its interest in theoretical explanation above blind partisanship. In his important book *History and Class Consciousness*[4] Lukács showed the way forward. For the Lukács of the 1920s, who had developed from a bourgeois intellectual into a Marxist theorist, the orthodox doctrine of Marx must be combined with the active formation of class consciousness in that social group which has to bear the contradictions of capitalist production. Unless the *proletariat* is enlightened as to its own role in the overall social nexus, the ideological spell of an all pervasive reification cannot be broken. Thus Marxist science is supplemented by an activity of critical reflection. For the mere laying bare of the laws of motion of capitalist production in Marx's 'critique of political economy' had not, in the historical experience acquired in the interim, brought about the expected revolutionary transformation. The necessary progress of history, which is in itself predetermined, must still be furthered by critical reflection.

Essentially, the *Frankfurt School* takes up these thoughts of Lukács. The belief in the world-shaking power of a formation of consciousness in the proletariat has, however, definitely diminished. The historical phenomenon of fascism and, just as much, the Stalinist perversion to which Marx's theory had succumbed, for all its emancipatory intentions, have undermined the concept of class. 'In this society, the situation of the proletariat is no guarantee of correct knowledge.'[5] There remain only the few clear-sighted subjects who are able to escape the universal deception of ideology by their critical reflection. The 'subjects of critical activity' no longer have on their side any objective grounds for their conviction other than the act of critical reflection. Thus, with a historical crisis of credibility in Marxian science, we witness once again a retreat into the 'holy family' of pure critics, which Marx had sought to overcome through his quasi-scientistic programme.

In this context Horkheimer introduced in 1937 the distinction between 'traditional and critical theory', a distinction which founded a school of thought. Traditional theory designates the model, which has been dominant ever since Descartes, of a closed system of statements constructed according to logical rules, while critical theory is governed by an 'interest in rational conditions' and takes as its paradigm Marx's 'critique of political economy'. The traditional type of value-neutral theory conceals the covert dominance of practical interests and hence is in permanent danger of ideology. The critical turn of the theory explicitly reflects on such interests, and there remain only those interests which are posited by the theory's own measuring-stick of rationality. Knowledge and interest no longer diverge but coincide.

Now it can scarcely be denied that in establishing the new philosophical paradigm, Horkheimer is guilty of overstepping the mark. First, Marx's 'critique of political economy' is, for all its declared interest in the emancipation of humanity, basically a science of economic laws and hence at least as 'traditional' as it is 'critical theory'. Economics, modelled as it was on the *natural sciences*, consequently gave rise to objections against the continuing acceptance of Marx's conception.[6] Second, in Horkheimer and in the entire Frankfurt School, critical theory was reduced to an *unending sequence of acts of critical reflection* on the new forms of ideology which were forever emerging, and never attained the closed unity of a theory. Further work along the lines of the old programme had therefore to lead beyond these remnants of a Young Hegelian position.

Adorno chose a path which is not in fact a real way out of this problem. He believes that it is only in the form of *aesthetics* that one can confront the dilemma of a critical theory which would not be prone to ideology in the traditional sense and which could nevertheless claim to be a fully fledged and coherent theory. Art is the only appearance which does not lie. A philosophy which concerns itself with art, therefore, is never under an illusion as to the discrepancy which separates beautiful appearance (*schönen Schein*) from reality. At the same time, however, art portrays a reconciliation which is not – or not yet – attained in the historical world where men and women labour and suffer. Art anticipates a condition which has yet to be established: a condition of freedom and harmony, in which people in society live in untrammelled and unalienated communion both with each other and with nature.

In the aesthetic sphere Adorno's essayistic work continually contrasts this utopia with reality as it is. This contrast and its brilliant exploitation have given rise to compelling individual studies on numerous literary and musical topics, studies whose prismatic refractions offer clear and startling insights into the relationship between art and society. But a wealth of essays does not constitute a theory. It is only in his *Ästhetischen Theorie*, published posthumously in 1970,[7] that Adorno offers a grand *résumé* of how *Kritik* can evade its dilemma by turning to the analysis of art.[8] I consider this work to be a significant contribution to philosophical aesthetics and to be Adorno's real intellectual bequest. Nevertheless, he has not succeeded in elevating critical theory on to a systematic plane. Nor could he succeed in this, since aesthetic theory represents an evasion of the dilemma.

A fundamental shift in the situation of critical philosophy comes only with Habermas. He resolutely exchanged the role of the fault-finding cultural critic and political columnist – which, incidentally, he could perform brilliantly when required – for the project of a *systematic philosophy*. Even if, hitherto, his philosophy has deliberately remained at the stage of prolegomena and sketches, one can nevertheless pass judgement on this beginning and on its general principles. It will, however, become apparent that even Habermas's attempt suffers from the legacy of an ambiguous concept of *Kritik*.

The systematic framework
In contrast to his predecessors, Habermas chooses to ground his work not in the idealist tradition of the analysis of consciousness but in the more recent philosophy of *language*. With the help of this springboard he can set about the task of developing a theory which on the one hand is not endangered by ideology, in the sense of the traditional model of science, while on the other hand its critical thrust is not exhausted by the endless repetition of acts of reflection which have no theoretical consistency. He first formulated a doctrine of 'dialogue free from domination', which then appears in modified form as a 'universal pragmatics'. In his inaugural lecture at Frankfurt, which explicitly refers to Horkheimer's distinction between traditional and critical theory, Habermas presents this thesis as follows.[9]

Sciences cannot be understood without reference to the *knowledge-constitutive interests* which govern them. What accounts for the various forms of science is not – as has been assumed ever since the neo-Kantian methodological struggle between natural sciences and sciences of culture – an alternative method, but rather the difference between their constitutive interests. We should distinguish between three forms. The *empirical-analytic* sciences obey a technical knowledge-constitutive interest in the instrumental regulation of objectivity. The *historical-hermeneutic* sciences, on the other hand, correspond to a practical interest in intersubjective understanding. The *emancipatory* sciences, finally, are in the service of critical self-reflection. The first two forms reflect the traditional division between the natural sciences (*Naturwissenschaften*) and the humanities (*Geisteswissenschaften*). The third category, however, is new.

On close analysis the third category can be seen to contain the legacy of idealist philosophy, which is not unreservedly affirmed but which returns in the guise of two modern quasi-sciences – ideology critique and psychoanalysis. It is plain that their scientific character is highly questionable. At first sight the critique of ideology would seem to be an activity which presupposes some given body of knowledge, whereas psychoanalysis seems to be a therapeutic *Praxis* dealing with psychic illness. Habermas would therefore have to demonstrate what is here simply presumed, namely that these two methods of the elucidation of false consciousness are forms of science and not forms of the transcending of science.

It is hardly fruitful to argue about the scientific character of ideology critique and psychoanalysis. It is more illuminating to ask how their special status is legitimated and why the shortcomings, which the philosopher has to detect in the empirical and hermeneutic sciences by reflecting upon their constitutive interests, do not hinder us here. Habermas says:

> It is no accident that the standards of self-reflection are exempted from the singular state of suspension in which those of all other cognitive processes require critical evaluation. They possess theoretical certainty. The human interest in autonomy and responsibility is not mere fancy, for it can be apprehended *a priori*. What raises us out of nature is the only thing whose nature we can know: *language*. Through its structure, autonomy and responsibility are posited for us. Our first sentence expresses unequivocally the intention of universal and unconstrained consensus. Taken together, autonomy and responsibility constitute the only Idea that we possess *a priori* in the sense of the philosophical tradition.
>
> However, only in an emancipated society, whose members' autonomy and responsibility had been realized, would communication have developed into the non-authoritarian and universally practiced dialogue from which both our model of reciprocally constituted ego identity and our idea of true consensus are always implicitly derived. To this extent the truth of statements is based on anticipating the realization of the good life. The ontological illusion of pure theory behind which knowledge-constitutive interests become invisible promotes the fiction that Socratic dialogue is possible everywhere and at any time. From the beginning philosophy has presumed that the autonomy and responsibility posited with the structure of language are not only anticipated but real. It is pure theory, wanting to derive everything from itself, that succumbs to unacknowledged external conditions and becomes ideological.[10]

Reason in language

We learn that the particular knowledge-constitutive interest of critical science is plain for all to see: there is no need for ideology critique to prise it out of the appearance of pure theory in the traditional sense. This interest cannot be disregarded by reason, for it is reason's own interest. There is a direct connection between rationality and liberation from appearance, between autonomous responsibility (*Mündigkeit*) and knowledge. Where is the proof for this? In *language*! Language is not only a logically structured system of sentences, not merely a self-sufficient nomenclature. Language is primordially concerned to communicate, and dialogue is its primordial form. Since every linguistic utterance receives its actual meaning in the to and fro of dialogue, every sentence reaffirms the idea of autonomous responsibility for all participants, speakers and listeners.

Thus the grounding of the critical knowledge-constitutive interest refers one to a fact. Language reveals itself to be an interest of reason. Admittedly this fact takes on an *a priori* status and is hence in no way a purely empirical datum of experience. The particular designation given to language is given on the basis of an idea. Dialogue, as the true realisation of the linguistic ability of human beings, represents the concretion of the partners' mutual recognition of each other as subjects with equal rights. What the philosophical tradition of idealism had dreamed of becomes reality in the material form of linguistic communication. The idea is more than an empty (lofty) postulate: it can be grasped.

Not every dialogue, however, is the expression of an unforced consensus, so that we need only to take refuge in speech in order to find that freedom which we lack amid the violence of historical *Praxis*. Further, the naive belief in free discourse, to which philosophical theory traditionally seems to fall prey, is itself ideological and itself a contributory factor to the prevention of true freedom. This idea of freedom or the interest in emancipation must always be considered, therefore, as an *anticipation* of a condition which by definition does not yet exist. Only the future can promise one the 'fulfilled life' which echoes the ancient ideal of political *eudemonia*, whereas the history known to us must be reconstructed as a process of the suppression of dialogue. After language as dialogue has offered philosophy the prospect of grasping a rationality of life in a manner more direct than the old dichotomy between ideal and reality, between life as it is and life as it ought to be, the *a priori* evidence shifts away once again into a utopian assumption of a condition which does not yet exist and which hitherto never has existed.

For all its refinements, the complex argument of Habermas contains several problems. First, it is an odd argument to say that language represents *per se* a rational principle, but that to name this principle one must call upon an *a priori* ideal, which is not identical with language as such. For one has to fall back upon language in order to show what the principle means. Where else could an elucidation be found? Thus, either that elucidation is superfluous, since it only shows an obvious fact, namely rationality incorporated in language, or the elucidation does not work, since it has to draw upon a higher principle of rationality which is not given, but postulated.

It may be presumed that Habermas is implicitly taking his bearings from Kant's doctrine of the 'fact of reason'.[11] Now, this doctrine of Kant[12] is based on precisely that strict separation between a theoretical and a practical use of reason which Habermas wishes to annul. One can speak of the moral law as a fact of reason only if moral obligation, which is irrefutably present in the sense of duty, cannot be deduced from any theoretical principles: for each and every theoretical elucidation or recourse to higher principles would place restrictions on the absoluteness of the obligation in which, according to Kant, our *Praxis* as rational subjects is directly affected by pure, unconditional reason. Kant emphasises that this fact is not an empirical given but a special mode of reason which, as he puts it, 'imposes itself' directly and unrestrictedly on the subject's self understanding.

There is no possible way in which language, which is Habermas's starting-point, can be likewise interpreted as a fact of reason. Admittedly, language is a given which is not theoretically derived and in which we continually live in our practical dealings with each other and with the world. But the interpretation of language as a medium of free dialogue goes back to an idea of rationality in the sense of intersubjective recognition which is neither identical with language as such nor to be found unreservedly in every act of speech. So the customary dialogues which we conduct every day, and which Habermas recognises in all previous human history, must be clearly distinguished from that ideal dialogue which mirrors the anticipation of a completely different *Praxis*. We must first make the presupposition of a free society before we are in the position to look for undistorted and unrestricted rationality in the linguistic medium of social communication.

To put the same problem differently: if dialogue is to be acclaimed as the proper form of communication, then there must somewhere be an underlying conception of the rational *Praxis* of society. The linguistic nature of the dialogue is of secondary importance when compared with the principle of the *mutual recognition* of subjects as subjects. In dialogue, the equality of the social partners, or the distribution of the principle of rational subjectivity to all lay actors, takes on a concrete linguistic form. Yet the notion of equality itself does not, as Habermas believes, originate in the model of Socratic discourse which, he claims, has haunted the philosophical tradition like an alluring though deceptive illusion.

Behind this notion, on the contrary, is the dialectic of the relationship between *master and slave*, which Hegel develops at a decisive point in his *Phenomenology of Spirit*.[13] Hegel there tries to resolve the unequal distribution of roles evident in social interaction, through a process of debate between partners which ends in universal equality. The mutual recognition of subjects, whose initial relationship was one of superiority and inferiority, concludes the debate between master and slave. In this condition of mutual recognition the two relinquish their existence as separate subjects altogether and are elevated into the unity of *Geist*, which joins all people together. Ever since the dictum of Marx[14] that the *Phenomenology* is the 'source and the secret' of the Hegelian dialectic, inasmuch as it grasps the real movement of history while at the same time reflecting it idealistically in thought, Marxism has extracted the relation of subjectivity from the Hegelian phenomenology and employed it in the reconstruction of historical class conficts. The unity of *Geist* is transformed into the communist society of the future, while the socio-philosophical realisation of the idealist conception is achieved only in a utopian perspective.

Habermas continues this reinterpretation of the Hegelian motif by introducing ideal dialogue as an *anticipation* of improved social *Praxis*. At the same time, he hopes to avoid the problem of Marx's methodology, which vacillates between *Kritik* and scientism, by disconnecting the real economic basis of society in the dimension of labour from its forms of political organisation in the sense of the mutual recognition of subjects. [15] For Hegel and for Marx the liberation of the slave is brought about by *labour*, in which the subject acts productively on the objective world and, in changing that world, experiences his or her own superiority. Habermas, on the other hand, projects, independently of the productive labour process, an ideal of free *interaction*, which is not the result of a change in social relationships brought about by labour.

Habermas wants to provide the critical study of society with a standard which is not dependent on a science of economic laws prescribing the development of capitalism towards revolution or on a speculative philosophy of history promising a final reconciliation to come. The element of *Kritik*, which, as in Horkheimer, is contrasted with traditional theory, is no longer reduced to the unending sequence of acts of reflection carried out by self-appointed critics. In ideal dialogue the 'holy family' expands to include all subjects. Thus critical theory is put in command of a model which makes possible the critique of ideology, while at the same time satisfying the claims of theory. Nor is this achieved by borrowing from traditional scientism and paying the price of latent ideology. Meanwhile, however, the danger of ideology is lurking in another area where Habermas does not suspect it.

The problem of sophistry

Is dialogue the realm where intersubjective recognition takes on concrete form without any of the traditional assumptions of an ontology of the mind or of history? The Socratic model hardly supports this. Every reader of Plato knows that the dialogues in which Plato rehearses philosophy are anything but ideal media for the exchange of pure rationality. On the contrary, they sketch in everyday situations in which, as a rule, the interlocutors are not philosophers but representatives of common sense or of the would-be wisdom of scientific specialists. Naive prejudices and the arrogance of authorities, false conclusions, misunderstandings and insoluble stalemates – all the inadequacies of the dialogues with which we are acquainted and which are not acted out in a future 'kingdom of ends' – are essential constituents of the Socratic dialogues. For in the Platonic conception of dialectic, dialogues are considered to be means of gaining knowledge or of freeing oneself from a prevailing lack of knowledge; they are not considered to be the parade-ground of perfect rationality or the playing-field for an ideal model of society.

The sharp distinction between the model of dialogue and the concrete conditions of speech – a distinction which is not made evident as such but is rather smoothed over because in all speech we ought to follow the ideal rules – contains the seeds of a further misunderstanding. Following Plato here, I should like to call it the *sophistic* danger. The Platonic dialogues' sharp-sighted diagnosis of the false wisdom of the sophists does not rest on an *a priori* distinction between truth and deception or between the ideal conditions of rationality and ideological appearance. Making the distinction seems to be incumbent upon one precisely because dialogues in their linguistic form can promote both knowledge and sophistry. *Logos* alone is *not* a sufficient condition of the discovery of truth, for *logos* can be deceptive.

The problem of sophistry arises when language, which is merely a means towards knowledge, becomes the one and only end. The perfection of the means, which is the aim of the speaker's technique, surreptitiously produces a perversion of the alleged rationality. Belief in the reliability of language or in perfect forms of communication ends in rhetorical delusion. Perhaps that form of speech which appears so entirely rational is only a new, enhanced form of deception, all the more difficult to see through since it seems so dissimilar to manifest power relations. This deception conceals a coercion of the most dangerous kind, one which embraces everyone without exception, even the most radical critics.

What criteria, however, are at one's disposal to separate out true reason in interhuman *Praxis* from that superficial appearance of rationality which is present in refined forms of social intercourse and which charms everyone but really satisfies no one? Horkheimer and Adorno inquired into this phenomenon once the auspicious prospects for emancipatory enlightenment had been disappointed and the critical intentions of the theory had given birth to the dominance of dogma. They encapsulated these experiences of unexpected reversal in the term 'dialectic of enlightenment',[16] which infuses all of human history up to the present. Rationality, which promises liberation from the dominance of dullardness and obscurantism, always wins the most ambivalent victories. In expressing this scepticism Horkheimer and Adorno are legitimate heirs of Nietzsche.

With the systematic conception he has in mind, Habermas wishes to go beyond this position. He is not prepared to acquiesce in the scepticism implicit in the notion of a dialectic of enlightenment: he has undiminished hopes that his dialogical model of critical reflection will be a dynamically emancipatory force. The passage quoted from his inaugural lecture (p.47) explicitly elevates *Kritik* to the status of a compelling and unshakeable scientific theory. Only later, in the context of an interpretation of Walter Benjamin, does Habermas chip away at the linking of ideology critique with historical progress, which had been customary since the Young Hegelians. He is now prepared to reckon with the possibility of an enlightenment which in fact changes nothing and fosters only false hopes.[17]

Over and above the ideology of an ideology-free discourse, it does not help us much to find that Habermas is aware of the difference between ideal dialogue and actual history. Even if one concedes that an ideal does not always correspond to reality, the ideal must nevertheless be meaningful as an ideal. That is, it must be an appropriate criterion for testing whether a reality is inadequate, in so far as the reality must correspond to the ideal, at least in principle. It seems to me, however, that ideal dialogue and historical human society do not – without proviso – have any such a relationship of correspondence.

Precise and explicit criticism would have to examine the particular structure of each communication network, instead of universalising *one* single model. The particular *pragmatic* context would also give criticism a more suitable measuring-stick. One must not forget the important insight of Wittgenstein that the plurality of possible language-games can be grouped together only in loose family likenesses. Wittgenstein deliberately formulated this view when taking issue with the thesis of the one logically correct ideal language which he himself had once considered to be the measuring-stick for all forms of speech. The rich spectrum of human communication should not be reduced to a single model of a scientific system of exact statements.

There is just as little justification, however, for considering every actual use of language to be based on one model of intersubjective recognition to which the various forms of language-games, such as commanding, teaching, advising, conversing, etc., can all be uniformly related. Not with every sentence that we speak do we imply the 'general and unforced consensus'. Not all intersubjective relations in the medium of language lose their meaning if they do not conform to the pattern of equality. Habermas continually invokes the pragmatics of language as a fruitful starting-point; but in compressing the entire spectrum of practical communication in society into the model of the seminar discussion in Humboldt's sketch for university reform,[18] he is essentially abandoning this starting-point.

Transcendentalism?

The recollection of *transcendental reflection* promises to solve the paradox. The gulf between ideal conditions and actual circumstances seems to be necessary and legitimate if one notes that it is only from a transcendental viewpoint that the gulf exists at all. Just as Kant's transcendental reflection distinguished the *quid facti* from the *quid iuris*, and nevertheless related the one as condition of possibility to the other as reality, so too, according to Habermas, we assume the ideal conditions to be present in all real speech.

> The conditions of empirical speech are clearly not identical with those of the ideal speech situation (and of pure communicative action), at least they are often or mostly not identical. Nevertheless, it is inherent in the structure of possible speech that while carrying out speech-acts (and actions) we contrafactually so proceed as if the ideal speech situation (or the model of pure communicative action) were not merely fictitious but real – precisely what we call a presupposition.[19]

It is clear that no actual speech is even possible without this reaching out towards those ideal conditions which are not realised in any actual speech.

This terminology deliberately approaches that of Kant. Above, the theme of the transition from theory into practice referred to the 'fact of reason' in Kant's ethics; now, the point of reference is the Kantian *critique of knowledge*. The transcendental conditions for the possibility of knowledge are, of course, projected on to linguistic findings. Kant's concern was to ground objective knowledge on the basis of subjective representations. He did this by identifying in all knowledge a synthetic achievement without which human consciousness was a chamber of mirrors reflecting a welter of images devoid of rhyme or reason. The synthetic achievement implies a form which every subject as such provides spontaneously. In this respect all subjects are alike – regardless of their particular individuality – thanks solely to the organising principle of self-consciousness. Structurally, therefore, this 'general subject' may be presumed present in every individual subject under the rubric of transcendental apperception.

Over and above this assumption, Kant sought a proof of the *legitimacy* of all knowledge of experience with a view to the constitution of science. Since time immemorial, critics have argued about the strategy and validity of this deduction.[20] Whatever their decision on this matter may be, the transcendental reflection of Kant finds its *raison d'être* in the struggle to legitimate a claim to objectivity. Once metaphysical dogmas have been renounced, the desired legitimation emerges solely from the proof of an irreducible constitutive relation between *a priori* and *a posteriori* elements in the transcendental argument. Now, there are at least two points where the concept of an ideal dialogue does not correspond to the Kantian project.

Kant's transcendental reflection is valid without any restriction whatsoever for all representations of all subjects, since all representations are potential knowledge. Not all forms of linguistic communication, however, are in themselves potential realisations of the social model of mutual recognition. The assumed analogy does not exist and the reference to transcendental reflection tends to lead astray. If the assumption is to be cogent, one must first introduce the premiss that people speak as in free communication, or that the emancipated society is already achieved. Later on in the argument quoted, therefore, Habermas says:

> The fundamental norms of possible speech built into universal pragmatics contain a practical hypothesis. The critical theory of society takes its departure from this hypothesis, which must be developed and grounded in a theory of communicative competence.

My second reservation concerns the unclear position of the *a priori* and *a posteriori* elements. I earlier drew attention to the fact that language is conceived as an empirical object of linguistics and not as a perfect construction of the philosophical mind from *a priori* principles. Nevertheless, in the *a posteriori* givenness of language, one is supposed to be able 'to see *a priori* the human interest in autonomous responsibility'. For Habermas, this ambiguity was sufficient ground to call to mind the Kantian concept of 'transcendental appearance' (*transcendentaler Schein*) which signifies an illusion to which human reason by its very nature becomes victim again and again, though it has developed the power to see through it critically:

> The ideal speech situation would be best compared with a transcendental appearance so long as this appearance was not the result of an inadmissible transference (as in the non-experiential use of the categories of understanding), but was at the same time a constitutive condition of possible speech. For every possible communication, the anticipation of the ideal speech situation signifies a constitutive appearance, which is at the same time the anticipatory apparition of a form of life.[21]

In subsequent comments on the programme for a universal pragmatics, Habermas quite correctly distances himself from any reference to the model of transcendental philosophy.[22]

The practical dimension

The present-day notion of a critical theory has inherited that underlying ambiguity which has its roots in the origins of the concept of *Kritik*. The Kantian attempt to find a reasoned legitimation of knowledge[23] and the Young Hegelian impetus to negate unreasonable circumstances of society cannot easily be reduced to one common denominator of critical reflection.[24] Transcendental grounding establishes the validity of knowledge according to premises which must always have been posited by reason. Reflection is the act of withdrawal from questionable knowledge to premisses without which all knowledge would be meaningless. In this process the linguistic form in which given knowledge is expressed is of secondary importance, because in comparison with the content of knowledge it neither needs nor is capable of reasoned legitimation. At the most, its suitability or unsuitability can be debated – a process in which, once again, the content of knowledge, as distinct from the linguistic form, would be of primary importance.

In contrast, the negation of bad *Praxis* in the sense of reflective ideology critique seeks to judge social reality as it is, by reaching forward to a normative ideal which practical reason makes desirable. The ideal names a desideratum with which we concur because of our insight into the structure of *Praxis* and society. The general ability of any given *Praxis* to concur with the ideal is, however, in no way an assumption comparable with those premisses without which knowledge would be meaningless.

Knowledge and *society* are distinguished by the fact that knowledge is just not conceivable as knowledge without certain elements of rationality which must be guaranteed in the structure of all knowledge; while a society which does not correspond to a normative ideal of practical reason can certainly be conceived as a society, and indeed coincides, by and large, with historical experience. The society of our everyday experience is still far from the anticipated ideal of fulfilled life in a free community, but it does not follow that it is not a society: it is simply not the ideally projected society. That knowledge, however, which lacks the structural conditions of order and the synthetic constitution of meaning is not factual knowledge which falls short of ideal knowledge: it is not knowledge at all. So once again we come back to the old distinction between theoretical and practical knowledge, a distinction which has exerted influence from Aristotle through Kant to the methodological dispute between the sciences and the humanities. The standards of pure theoretical reason are not identical with reason in *Praxis*.

Habermas's concern is to free himself from this tradition of a divided concept of reason. He is seeking to construct a *dialectical unity*, by presenting every theory that is distinct from practical reason as a false appearance which must be overcome. I believe, however, that this strategy itself ends up in deception. The deception is based precisely on the central category of *appearance (Schein)*. The appearance of knowledge which only seems to be knowledge but does not correspond to the appropriate conditions of rationality is different from the appearance of a society which on the surface seems to be reasonable while its real structure conceals irrationality and contradiction. The first appearance is destroyed by a critique of knowledge *à la* Kant; the second is merely disclosed by a critique of ideology. The first appearance can be countered by the argument of meaninglessness; the second can be countered only by a demand for practical action.

Rationality is one of the inalienable defining characteristics of knowledge. Rationality is not, however, an equally inalienable defining characteristic of social *Praxis*. For this to be true, a special proviso must be added equating actual society with rational society and assuming a process of development in which true society accordingly creates itself by overcoming those contradictions which are incompatible with it. *The coincidence of the concepts of Praxis and reason* must therefore be characterised methodically as a practical directive or a historical prognosis or a utopian hope. At any event it cannot simply be enlisted for all theoretical analyses as if it were in every case a fulfilled presupposition.

Habermas systematically avoids considering the issue in so differentiated a way. The result is that he is unwittingly affected by that very confusion of science and revolution which he sharp-sightedly criticises in Marx. The *mediation* between theory and practice is, however, only a semblance if they are brought together at the cost of neglecting their difference. Dialectic as a method presupposes precisely the pronounced definition of the differences which are to be overcome; otherwise the work of the dialectic would be already done before it began. It is in the interest of dialectic as correctly understood to develop a concept of *Praxis* which is resistant to theoretical projections. In order to achieve this one must break out of the spell of Hegelian speculation which ultimately relates all content to the unity of mind. In reality the concept of *Praxis* favoured by Habermas – a concept which shows isolated theory to be false illusion – is only the unacknowledged reflection of a theory which, in its eagerness to mediate, no longer perceives the actual, individual factors of *Praxis* at all.

It is my conviction that there is no way out of this most intricate self-deception unless one is first of all prepared to concede the difference between theoretical and practical reason or between knowledge and human interest. In order more precisely to define this difference, once it has been conceded, one would require a theory of *action* which is not from the very outset conceived with a view to dialectical mediation. Only on this basis does it seem possible to combine a theory of action with practical reason without artificially smoothing over the actual differences. Such a combination will be the object of a philosophy of *Praxis*,[25] for which at present we have merely the first fragments.

Translated by Richard Humphrey

3

Rationality and Relativism: Habermas's 'Overcoming' of Hermeneutics

THOMAS McCARTHY

Introduction

The debate between Habermas and Gadamer which took place in the late 1960s and early 1970s came to a provisional close on Habermas's side with a series of promissory notes.[1] While he agreed with Gadamer on the necessity for a *sinnverstehenden* access to social reality, he insisted nevertheless that the interpretation of meaningful phenomena need not, indeed could not, be restricted to the type of dialogic understanding characteristic of the hermeneutic approach. He held out instead the possibility of a theoretically grounded analysis of symbolically structured objects and events which, by drawing on systematically generalised empirical knowledge, would reduce the context-dependency of understanding and leave room for both quasi-causal explanation and critique. The types of theoretical-empirical knowledge in question, he suggested, included (i) a general theory of communication which would reconstruct the 'universal-pragmatic infrastructure' of speech and action; (ii) a general theory of socialisation in the form of a theory of the acquisition of communicative competence; (iii) a theory of social systems which would make it possible to grasp objective meaning connections going beyond what is subjectively intended or expressly articulated in cultural traditions; and (iv) a theory of social evolution which would make possible a theoretical reconstruction of the historical situations of the interpreter (or critic) and his or her object.

In some ways this appeared to signal a break with Habermas's earlier programme which had stressed the historico-practical dimensions of critical theory, the historically rooted and politically engaged character of a social thought aimed at unmasking ideological distortions and promoting the realisation of a just society.[2] And there is no doubt that the need to free critical theory from the embrace of hermeneutics once they had jointly dealt with their common positivist opponents did push Habermas in a more emphatically theoretical direction. For philosophical hermeneutics stresses that the interpreter of social phenomena is a member of a life-world, that the interpreter too occupies a specific historical, social, cultural position from which he or she tries to come to terms with the beliefs and practices of others. The understanding achieved is, as a result, inexorably situation-bound, an understanding from a point of view that is on the same level as what is understood. There are, the argument goes, no privileged positions outside of or above history from which to view human life; there can be no interpreter without a language – in Wittgenstein's full-bodied sense of the term. And there is no such thing as *the* correct interpretation.'Each time will have to understand . . . in its own way . . . One understands otherwise if one understands at all.'[3] The interest behind hermeneutics is not an interest in bringing a certain object domain under theoretical control or submitting it to a critique of ideology; it is an interest in coming to an understanding through dialogue – with others in my own culture, with alien cultures, with the past – about the common concerns of human life. The social inquirer is not, as may be mistakenly supposed, a neutral observer, explainer, predicter; nor is the inquirer a sovereign critic who may safely assume his or her own cognitive or moral superiority; the inquirer is, however virtually, a partner in dialogue, a participant rather than an observer or critic.

It was in part to oppose what he saw as the relativistic implications of this and related views that Habermas stressed the need for a theoretically grounded analysis of social phenomena. The fronts of the *Methodenstreit* in the theory of the human sciences had shifted. The positivist and empiricist views that had dominated the scene for so long were gradually yielding pride of place to the interpretative approaches they once scorned. Wittgenstein's *Tractatus* gave way to his *Investigations* and thence to the trenchant attacks by post-Wittgensteinians on the unity of scientific method. Husserl's transcendental phenomenology generated its detranscendentalised progeny as well: the phenomenological and ethnomethodological approaches to social inquiry flowing from Alfred Schutz, and the *verstehenden*, hermeneutic approaches inspired by Heidegger and Gadamer. In consequence of this shift, the universalism associated with the positivist emphasis on logic and mathematics, on universal laws and general theories, came increasingly under attack. A new front was forming along relativist versus universalist lines. Fundamental challenges to the idea of a critical theory of society no longer came solely from the direction of positivism; more and more they issued from the side of post-Heideggerian and post-Wittgensteinian versions of historicism and culturalism.

The strongly theoretical, universalist approach to social inquiry that Habermas wishes to defend does not rest on a rejection of the detranscendentalisation of philosophy since Kant. On the contrary, a central theme of *Knowledge and Human Interests* was precisely the progressive radicalisation of epistemology that led to the 'idea of a theory of knowledge as social theory'. Here and elsewhere Habermas traced the decline of the conception of the subject that had dominated modern philosophy from Descartes through to Kant. He argued that the transformation in the course of the nineteenth century to a view of the subject of knowledge and action as inherently social, historical, embodied and labouring relegated irretrievably to the past the idea of a presuppositionless 'first philosophy' – whether in its ontological or epistemological guises. Philosophy had to surrender its claim to grasp the totality of being from an extramundane position and on the basis of principles discovered in the very structure of reason. The (re-)detranscendentalisation of twentieth-century philosophy has brought this point home to us once again.[4] And again, as previously in the nineteenth century, it has left in its wake a variety of forms of relativism, images of irreducible pluralities of incommensurable language games, forms of life, conceptual frameworks, life-worlds, cultures, and so on.

But while Habermas fully endorses the decline and fall of the Cartesian ego, he does not regard relativism as its inevitable consequence. He holds that the conception of the subject that has replaced it is not *per se* incompatible with certain of the universalistic claims of transcendental philosophy – though these would clearly have to be reformulated in co-operation with the human sciences that have since taken that subject as their theme. He wants, in particular, to salvage by way of reconstruction Kant's claim that there are universal and unavoidable presuppositions of theoretical and practical reason, as well as his conception of *Mündigkeit,* autonomy and responsibility, as the essence of rational personality. But he also wants, thinking now more with Hegel, to present a reconstructed conception of the *Bildungsprozesse,* the self-formative processes of the individual and the species that have rational autonomy as their telos – a kind of systematic history of reason. Nor does he eschew the normative dimensions of this enterprise; quite the contrary, the universal scheme he espouses is both theoretical and moral-practical.

In this essay I should like to examine the types of argument that Habermas employs to make his case, to clarify somewhat their status and to offer a tentative and preliminary evaluation of their philosophical cogency and empirical plausibility. Considerations of space will make it impossible to lay out the individual arguments themselves; this has been done elsewhere and I shall have to assume the reader's familiarity with them.[5] Instead I shall focus on the general strategy of argumentation that Habermas is pursuing and the kinds of considerations to which he appeals for support, so as to make clearer both what the force of his argument would be if it were successful and the sorts of evidence that might count against it.

Variations on Kantian themes

The Kantian aspect of Habermas's programme might be represented as an analogue to the question: how is experience possible in general? The corresponding question for Habermas would then read: *Wie ist Verstän-*

digung überhaupt möglich? How is understanding (among speaking and acting subjects) possible in general? [6] And just as Kant's analysis of the conditions of possibility of experience was at the same time an analysis of the possibility of the object of experience, Habermas's investigations of the 'general and unavoidable presuppositions of achieving understanding in language' [7] is meant to elucidate the general structures of communicative social action itself. Having said this, it is important to head off possible misunderstandings by immediately adding that Habermas explicitly distances himself from the claims and procedures of transcendental philosophy in the traditional sense. His project is empirical – not in the sense of the nomological sciences of nature but rather in the sense of the 'reconstructive' approaches that have been developed above all in linguistics and cognitive developmental psychology.[8] As Habermas sees it, the basic idea behind this type of approach is that speaking and acting subjects know how to achieve, accomplish, perform, produce a variety of things without explicitly adverting to, or being able to give an explicit account of, the structures, rules, criteria, schemata on which their performances are based. The aim of rational reconstruction is precisely to render explicit the structures and rules underlying such 'practically mastered, pre-theoretical' know-how, the tacit knowledge that represents the subject's competence in a given domain. Thus it differs from hermeneutic understanding, which is primarily concerned with tracing semantic relations within the surface structure of a language or between those of different languages; its goal is not a paraphrase or a translation of an originally unclear meaning but an explicit knowledge of the 'deep' structures and rules, the mastery of which underlies the competence of a subject to generate meaningful symbolic configurations.

If the tacit, pre-theoretical knowledge that is to be reconstructed represents a universal know-how – and not merely that of a particular individual, group or culture – our task is the reconstruction of a 'species competence'. Such reconstructions can be compared in their scope and status with general theories (for example, of language or cognition). From another point of view, they can also be compared with Kant's transcendental logic. But the differences are critical here. Rational reconstructions of universal or species competences cannot make the strong *a prioristic* claims of the Kantian project. They are advanced in a hypothetical attitude and must be checked and revised in the light of the data, which are gathered *a posteriori* from the actual performances and considered appraisals of competent subjects. Any proposal must meet the empirical condition of conforming in a mass of crucial and clear cases to the intuitions of competent subjects, which function ultimately as the standard of accuracy.

Adopting this approach, Habermas advances a proposal for a universal or formal pragmatics, which is based on the idea that not only language *(langue)* but speech *(parole)* admits of rational reconstruction in universal terms, that 'communicative competence' has as universal a core as linguistic competence. The competence of the ideal speaker must be regarded as including not merely the ability to produce and understand grammatical sentences but also the ability to establish and understand those modes of communication and connections with the world through which speech becomes possible. Pragmatic rules for situating sentences in speech acts concern the relations to reality that accrue to a grammatically well-formed sentence in being properly uttered; they are general rules for arranging the elements of speech situations in relation to the external world of objects and events (about which one can make true or false statements), the inner world of my own experiences (which can be expressed sincerely or insincerely, authentically or inauthentically), and the social life-world of shared norms (with which an act can conform or fail to conform, and which are themselves either right, i.e. legitimate or justifiable, or wrong). From this pragmatic point of view it becomes clear that communication necessarily (even if often only implicitly) involves the raising, recognising and redeeming of 'validity-claims', claims to the truth of statements, to the sincerity or authenticity of self-presentations, and to the rightness of actions and norms of action.

I shall not reproduce here the details of Habermas's proposal; nor shall I trace the series of arguments with which he attempts to show that truth and rightness claims require discursive justification and thus have to be analysed in terms of the possibility of rational consensus; that a consensus is rationally motivated only if it is the result of the force of the arguments advanced and not of accidental or systematic constraints on communication; that this absence of constraint requires that the pragmatic structure of communication provide an effective equality of opportunity for participants to assume dialogue roles; and finally that the requirements of this 'ideal speech situation', the 'fundamental norms of rational speech', supply us with a non-arbitrary, because universally (if only implicitly) presupposed, 'minimal ethics'.[9] Assuming some familiarity with all this, I shall address myself instead to certain difficulties that arise from Habermas's general approach itself.

1.   Although Habermas has explicitly dropped the earlier characterisation of his project as a 'transformed transcendental philosophy' in favour of the more empirical terminology of 'rational reconstruction', the considerations he has until now adduced in support of his proposals are decidedly more 'philosophical' than 'empirical'. Thus the arguments and analyses through which his account of communication is introduced make little mention of the type of data on which rational reconstructions are said to be based. Linguistic reconstruction, for example, calls for empirical inquiries undertaken with actual speakers. In Habermas's own words:

The linguist procures for himself a knowledge *a posteriori*. The implicit knowledge of competent speakers is so different from the explicit form of linguistic description that the linguist cannot rely on reflection on his own speech intuitions. The procedures employed in constructing and testing hypotheses, in appraising competing reconstructive proposals, in gathering and selecting data, are in some ways like the procedures used in the nomological sciences.[10]

As even a cursory reading of Habermas's writings on universal pragmatics makes evident, the construction of the hypotheses he advances therein does not make essential use of such procedures. In fact, they seem to rely very heavily on just the 'reflection on his own speech intuitions', analysis of fundamental concepts (e.g. 'understanding', 'truth', 'discourse', 'rationality'), and critical appropriation of relevant literature that is so characteristic of 'philosophical' in contrast to 'empirical' modes of thought. Habermas has responded to a related objection by granting: 'Naturally one proceeds with one's own intuitions', but with the important condition that 'it must be possible to reconstruct them as such'; and this latter task depends on testing such intuitions against those of other competent subjects with the help of the empirical procedures mentioned above.[11] However, the implied separation of theory construction (based here on reflection, conceptual analysis, and the like) from data-gathering and theory-testing (based on careful, controlled procedures for ascertaining the tacit knowledge of competent objects) is certainly not typical of the empirical sciences as we know them. The identification, description, classification, etc., of data are part and parcel of the process of theory construction itself, not something subsequent to it. Now, this need not be an objection 'in principle' to Habermas's approach. He would perhaps argue that the peculiar combination of logical and empirical analysis characteristic of reconstructive (in contrast to nomological) sciences lends a much greater weight to such procedures as reflection on one's own intuitions and analyses of central concepts, such that they play a much more prominent role here in the construction and appraisal of hypotheses – it is after all a competence, a tacit know-how, a practically mastered knowledge, that we are attempting to reconstruct. And he would probably add that formal pragmatics is in its infancy, that as this line of research develops the present imbalance between the conceptual and the empirical will be righted, that working hypotheses will be refined in the light of new data, and so on.

2. The force of this response depends in part on the plausibility of supposing that Habermas's starting-point in reflection on his own intuitions – and, one should add, on intuitions central to the Western philosophical tradition[12] – has not fundamentally skewed his approach. In this connection, I shall raise only the following points. Habermas's analysis of communication has focused on *verständigungsorientierte Sprechhandlungen,* i.e. on the 'pure' case of communication orientated to reaching understanding in the following strong sense:

The goal of coming to an understanding (*Verständigung*) is to bring about an agreement (*Einverständnis*) that terminates in the intersubjective mutuality of reciprocal understanding, shared knowledge, mutual trust, and accord with one another. Agreement is based on recognition of the corresponding validity claims of comprehensibility, truth, truthfulness [or sincerity], and rightness.[13]

It is obvious – and Habermas readily acknowledges the fact – that a great deal of everyday social interaction does not fit this idealised model. In addition to cases of overtly strategic and covertly manipulative interaction, of conscious deception and unconscious self-deception, of insincerity and inauthenticity, there is the whole range of interaction in which these and other elements are combined in a variety of ways to constitute the 'organised artful practices of everyday life', 'relations in public', 'games people play', and the like, which have been so extensively studied in recent years. The point here is simply that if, as appears to be the case, instances of 'pure' communicative action in Habermas's sense are, at least in many spheres of life, the exception and not the rule, there is some question as to whether a reconstruction of the 'universal and unavoidable' structures of communication should start with this idealised case. For a reconstruction claims to represent the rules and structures that are actually operative in the object domain, those on which the production of symbolic formations is actually based. To concede that pure communicative action is unusual in many departments of life seems to entail that its analysis cannot yield 'universal and unavoidable' structures of communication.

In defence of his starting-point Habermas has maintained that action orientated to reaching understanding is not just one type of social action among others but is 'fundamental' in the sense that other forms of social action – e.g. conflict, competition, deception, manipulation – are 'derivative' from it and have to be reconstructed as such.[14]

The sphere of possible action does not coincide with the sphere of possible speech with a communicative intent. But I would like to reconstruct the universal conditions of employing language from the original mode thereof . . . speech for the purpose of coming to an understanding. Wittgenstein was right to find fault with this way of putting it; it is not possible to define 'speech' in terms of the purpose of achieving understanding, because one cannot explain what it is 'to reach an understanding' if one does not know what it is 'to speak'. The telos of reaching understanding is inherent in the concept of speech. The class of actions with which I begin my analysis is not chosen arbitrarily; it is the class of those speech actions that are carried out in an attitude oriented to achieving understanding. We can reconstruct the normative content of possible understanding by stating which universal presuppositions have to be met for understanding to be achieved in an actual case.[15]

In addition to this 'conceptual' argument, Habermas has offered several brief considerations on the centrality of this type of social action for social life. They centre on the claim that unconstrained agreement in language is a fundamental medium of social interaction which can be replaced with other, more or less coercive, options only to a certain degree and within certain spheres of life: 'In my view, it belongs to the form of life of a species that reproduces itself through labor and through understanding in language that motives are shaped primarily in communicative relationships. We can't really conceive of the family as a context of strategic action regulated by civil law.'[16] And the shift from unconstrained consensus to coercion or manipulation exacts its price:

> Acknowledged universal validity claims have a motivating force that does not derive from power or institutions. If one decides to behave strategically, one does not have all the advantages that come with behaving consensually. As the saying goes, 'lying won't get you very far'. Because it is possible to give a structural description of the built-in burdens that one takes on in detaching oneself from validity claims so that one does not follow a command of reason, it is possible on the empirical level to speak in a trivial sense of the motivating force of validity claims.[17]

Perhaps these arguments, conceptual and empirical, could be developed so as to make Habermas's starting-point plausible before the fact, that is, before research based on the programme is sufficiently far along to permit an appraisal after the fact. We might also ask: what kind of empirical results would actually count against the claim that an orientation to reaching understanding is the 'original' mode of employing speech, whereas strategic uses are derivative? There are other questions as well that arise from Habermas's rather *a priori* arguments in support of what are intended to be judgements *a posteriori*. For he has not only introduced the programme of formal pragmatics as a fruitful line of investigation; he has also advanced a number of specific proposals in regard to the basic universal-pragmatic structures of communication. These are represented concisely in his model of communicative action (action orientated to achieving understanding) and the distinctions it embodies between the different types of validity claims (truth, rightness, sincerity/authenticity); between the different attitudes in which one can use language (objectivating, conformative, expressive); and between the different 'worlds' or domains of reality to which speech relates (the external world, our social world, each individual's own inner world). Now, it is rather evident – and Habermas himself frequently remarks on the point – that this way of setting out the fundamental structures of communication reflects the influence of epistemological and ontological problematics basic to the Western philosophical tradition. And this of course raises the question of whether the model succeeds in capturing *universal* conditions of understanding, *general* and *unavoidable* presuppositions of communicative action, or whether it represents instead a thinly disguised Eurocentrism.

3.   To be sure, this is not a problem of which Habermas is unaware:

> When one no longer pursues transcendental philosophy . . . but research into universals, one must be aware of the dangers that lie in seizing upon historically limited and rather variable capabilities for cognition, communication, and action, and stylizing them as universal competences; or in reconstructing what is actually a universal pretheoretical knowledge from a culturally and historically distorted perspective, so that the reconstructive proposals are caught up in provincialism. It goes without saying that one must allow for such possibilities of error.[18]

The claimed universality of the structures Habermas singles out cannot be established inductively; for it is quite clear that they are not characteristic of communication in all cultures and in all historical epochs, nor even of all communication in advanced industrial societies. The abilities to differentiate the 'worlds' of external nature, internal nature and society, to distinguish the 'validity claims' of propositional truth, moral-practical rightness and sincerity/authenticity, to deploy these distinctions reflectively in communicative action and, at another level, in argumentative discourse, are not – as a matter of empirical fact – to be met with universally. Even if we keep separate, as Habermas suggests, the question of 'empirical generalities' from that of 'universals discovered by way of rational reconstruction',[19] the problem remains. If formal pragmatics is an empirical-reconstructive science which seeks a knowledge *a posteriori*; if reconstructions are to capture just those structures and rules that are actually operative in the domain under investigation; and if, finally, the structures of communicative action and discourse that Habermas singles out are to be found with significant frequency only in certain spheres of certain (Western) cultures at certain (modern) times, how then is it possible to defend the view that these structures are universal-pragmatic features of communication as such?

It is here that Habermas's thought takes a 'Hegelian' turn: reason does not appear at one blow; it has a history, both in the individual and in the species. The passage quoted above on the dangers of provincialism continues:

> On the other hand, I do not see how this admission amounts to an objection in principle to a research strategy directed at universals. We are normally quite prepared to regard the forms of objectivating thought as universal even though they gained institutional relevance, so to speak, only with the establishment of modern science. I assume that the forms of moral-practical insight are just as universal. This does not

mean that such cognitive structures could appear all at once, whether in ontogenesis or in social evolution.[20]

Viewed in a developmental perspective, Habermas's universalist claims appear less immediately implausible than the line of argument sketched above would suggest. Problems remain, but they are of a different kind. To put it succinctly, Habermas has to show that the ability to act communicatively (in his strong sense) and to reason argumentatively and reflectively about disputed validity claims is a developmental-logically advanced stage of species-wide competences, the realisation and completion of potentialities that are universal to humankind. To anyone familiar with the 'rationality debates' that have accompanied the development of cultural anthropology from the start, and more particularly with the neo-Wittgensteinian turn they have taken in recent years, it will be clear that the burden of this proof is considerable.

Variations on Hegelian themes
The contrasts between 'mythico-magical' and 'modern' modes of thought and action have been characterised in a number of different ways. Very often 'modern' is read as equivalent to 'scientific-technological' and the contrast takes the form of exhibiting the 'pre-' or 'proto-' or 'un-' scientific character of the 'savage mind'. Habermas rejects this starting-point as based on too narrow a conception of rationality and thus assuming in a certain way what has to be shown. He starts instead from the model of communicative action developed in his universal pragmatics and, taking Lévi-Strauss and Godelier as his guides, characterises the mythico-magical understanding of the world in a series of contrasts suggested by that model.[21] Thus he singles out for attention the 'peculiar levelling of the different domains of reality: nature and culture are projected on to the same plane', resulting in an anthropomorphised nature and a naturalised culture; the techniques of magically influencing the world connected with this 'confusion' and with the attendant failure to recognise the distinction between instrumental control of things and intersubjective relations among persons, between moral and physical success/failure, between good/evil and harmful/advantageous; the inadequate distinctions between language and the world, between names and the named, between external relations of objects and internal relations of ideas, between the validity of symbolic expressions and physical efficacy; the lack of differentiation among diverse validity claims such as propositional truth, normative rightness, and expressive sincerity; the absence of self-awareness *as* a world-view, as an interpretation of the world that is subject to error and open to criticism and revision; the lack of a clear demarcation of a domain of subjectivity, of intentions and motives from actions and their consequences, of feelings from normatively fixed stereotyped expressions; connected with this, the binding of identity-formation to the details of myth and the prescriptions of

ritual; and thus the absence of ego identity in the strict sense. In short, mythico-magical world-views are marked, in Habermas's view, by insufficient differentiation of the objective, social and subjective domains of reality, of the fundamental attitudes towards them, and of the validity claims proper to them, as well as by a lack of reflexivity that prevents them from recognising themselves as interpretative systems constituted by internal relations of meaning, symbolically related to reality, connected with validity claims, and thus open to criticism and revision. In this formal-pragmatic sense, they are by comparison 'closed' systems.

It is obvious that this characterisation is drawn from 'our' (or Habermas's) perspective. It presupposes rather than proving *quod est demonstrandum* the universal significance of the categories and assumptions on which it is based. Only when the latter has been demonstrated is the description itself warranted as more than a particularistic culturally biased account of an alien form of life. This is a particular case of a problem facing social inquiry generally, as Habermas is well aware:

If some concept of rationality is invariably built into the action-theoretical foundations of sociology, then theory-formation will be limited from the start to a culturally or historically bound perspective unless the fundamental concepts are constructed in such a way that the concept of rationality they implicitly posit is encompassing and general, that is, satisfies universalist claims. The demand for such a concept of rationality also emerges from methodological considerations . . . The experiential basis of an interpretive sociology is compatible with its claim to objectivity only if hermeneutic procedures can be based at least intuitively on general and encompassing structures of rationality. From both points of view, the metatheoretical and the methodological, we cannot expect objectivity of social-theoretical knowledge if the corresponding concepts of communicative action and interpretation express a merely particular perspective on rationality, one interwoven with a particular cultural tradition . . . The rational internal structure of processes of reaching understanding . . . would have to be shown to be universally valid in a specific sense. This is a very strong requirement for someone operating without metaphysical support and no longer confident that a transcendental-philosophical program can be carried out.[22]

Habermas's account of the contrasts between modern and mythico-magical thought makes it clear that he does not regard this 'rational internal structure' as everywhere and always characteristic of social interaction. How, then, can it be shown to be 'universally valid', if not empirically (i.e. inductively) and not through metaphysical or transcendental argument? Habermas's position, as we have seen, is that in a detranscendentalised universe of discourse the principal avenue left open for grounding such universalist claims is 'rational reconstruction'. What has to be shown is the empirical-theoretical adequacy of the reconstructive model of communicative action. Several lines of research suggest themselves: formal-pragmatic analysis of general structures of communication; investigation of pathological or distorted patterns of communication in the light of standards and conditions for normal communication established in formal pragmatics; application of formal-pragmatic perspectives to studies in the ontogenesis of communicative competence; and their application to the theory of anthropogenesis, the process of hominisation from which the sociocultural form of life emerged; as well as to the theory of social evolution itself.[23] The structures of communicative rationality singled out by Habermas would have to prove themselves adequate to the empirical materials available in all these areas. Since, as was suggested above, their universal significance cannot be established solely by the 'horizontal' reconstructions of formal pragmatics, it would have to be established principally in the 'vertical' reconstructions of developmental theories; that is, the mastery of these structures would have to be shown to represent the developmental-logically most advanced stage of species-wide competencies.

Turning the argument in this way to considerations of empirical-theoretical adequacy and fruitfulness, and thereby to the present state and future course of research in the areas mentioned, clearly takes it beyond the scope of individual reflective virtuosity. But Habermas has tried to make his (hypothetical) claims plausible with reference to existing materials in the study of ontogenesis and social evolution. [24] I am not in a position to offer a detailed evaluation of the ways in which he appropriates these materials; but I should like to make a few, very general observations concerning the use he makes of cognitive developmental psychology.

1. Habermas's appropriation of the concepts, assumptions and results of developmental studies has been noticeably less critical than one might have expected from his treatment of other research traditions. Positivist, behaviourist, phenomenological, hermeneutic, functionalist, systems-theoretic, etc., programmes were, so to speak, 'determinately negated', that is, their claims to adequacy refuted and their positive contributions critically appropriated in a more comprehensive framework. One central strategy of this approach was to exhibit the historically rooted, situation-bound character of allegedly universal concepts. Thus Habermas argued that:

Status and contract, *Gemeinschaft* and *Gesellschaft*, mechanical and organic solidarity, informal and formal groups, culture and civilization, traditional and bureaucratic authority, sacral and secular associations, military and industrial society, status group and class, etc . . . [are] 'historically rooted concepts' which, not by accident, arose in connection with the analysis of the unique historical transformation of European society from feudalism to modern capitalism . . . None of these concepts lose their situation-bound, specific content through formalization. This can be seen precisely when a theoretical framework constituted of historically substantive concepts is supposed to be employed in the analysis of culturally foreign and removed contexts. In such transpositions the instrument becomes particularly blunt. This experience leads to the suspicion that there exists in sociology a tacit connection between the categorial framework of general theories and a guiding pre-understanding of the contemporary situation as a whole. The further such theories are removed from their domain of application, the less they contribute to interpretation, the less they 'signify' or 'make understandable'.[25]

In the same vein, he criticised Parsons's simplifying assumption of a universal scheme of values, a set of basic value orientations (pattern variables) fundamental to all social action, regardless of the particular historical context:

But if one examines the list, one can scarcely overlook the historical situation of the inquiry on which it is based. The four pairs of alternative value orientations . . . which are supposed to take into account *all* possible fundamental decisions, are tailored to an analysis of *one* historical process. In fact they define the relative dimensions of the modification of dominant attitudes in the transition from traditional to modern society.[26]

The obvious question is whether something similar might not be said of Piaget's 'formal-operational thought', of Kohlberg's 'post-conventional stages of moral consciousness', or indeed of Habermas's 'communicative rationality'. Charges of ethnocentrism, of scientist and rationalistic bias have of course been levelled against cognitive developmental paradigms in general and against Piagetian/Kohlbergian cross-cultural research more particularly. In his published work to date Habermas has not given adequate consideration to these charges, nor indeed to the host of other criticisms – metatheoretical and methodological, empirical and theoretical – that have been directed against the Piagetian and, especially, the Kohlbergian programmes. And yet it is clear that his empirical-reconstructive approach to universals must prove itself precisely in the face of such objections.

2.   The Piagetian model was developed on the basis of studies carried out with urban, middle-class schoolchildren in Switzerland and, subsequently, in several other advanced Western societies. It is only recently that cross-cultural research has been carried out to any great extent,[27] and this

has consisted largely of cross-sectional studies of concrete-operational thought, focusing on different aspects of conservation (of quantity, weight, volume, etc.). There has been significantly less cross-cultural investigation of the other stages and virtually no longitudinal studies tracing particular individuals throughout the course of their development. Thus the results to date are very incomplete and open to different interpretations. Nevertheless, a number of general problems and questions have emerged which bear directly on our present inquiry.

(a) The end-state towards which the developmental process is construed as heading is decidedly Western in conception, indeed it has been characterised as 'the development of a Western scientist'. And this construal of the telos in terms of abstract, formal cognition affects in turn the conception of the earlier stages leading to it: 'The most important thing is not so much what the child can do in the concrete world as how quickly he can do without it'; the tests of concrete-operational thought 'do not track the skills of "concrete science" . . . but progress toward formal abstraction'.[28] The problems this raises for cross-cultural research are obvious:

> The typical research demonstrates either the presence of a certain structure or its absence (but negative results are clearly non-interpretable), and there is little room to find an alternative structure . . . The demonstration that all individuals are able to reason according to a certain structure does not prove that this is their usual or preferred mode of reasoning. In fact we may not be adequately sampling the culturally relevant skills. What we may be asking is the question, 'How well can *they* do *our* tricks?', whereas what we should be asking is, 'How well can *they* do *their* tricks?'[29]

The point is that without an adequate understanding of the 'end-states' of development in other cultures, and thus the modes of thought and types of knowledge valued by them, we are determined before the fact to construe their performances as exhibiting a more or less deficient mastery of our competences rather than as expressing a mastery of a different set of skills altogether. In other words, the question of whether there are alternative cognitive structures more adaptive in a given environment and more culturally valued, and thus alternative lines of development, cannot be adequately explored within the limits of the standard design for cross-cultural Piagetian research. And yet it seems quite possible that different domains of activity might call for different types of thinking (e.g. more perceptually orientated) or different types of knowledge (e.g. about altered states of consciousness), and that in such domains Western thought is rather 'primitive' by comparison – *we* can't do *their* tricks very well either.

(b) Until such questions as these are convincingly resolved, the results of cross-cultural research seem to be open to divergent assessments. In the usual interpretation the development of the Western midde-class child is taken as the norm and the 'time lag' discovered for development in other cultures is seen as a 'deficit' or 'retardation'. That is, human reason is viewed as following the same course of development in different societies, but at a faster or slower pace and with a more or less early arrest depending on the social environment. Thus the proportion of different populations ever attaining to formal operations – and even to many aspects of concrete operations – is subject to wide variation. This variation is linked to a variety of social, cultural and economic factors: urban *vs* rural setting, extent of contact with Western culture and technology, existence and nature of formal schooling, degree of industrialisation, structure of workaday activities, and so on.[30] There are, for example, studies indicating that children from pottery-making families in Mexico perform better on conservation of substance than do their peers from non-pottery-making families; that nomadic, hunting populations develop spatial concepts more rapidly than do sedentary, agricultural groups, whereas the latter attain concepts of conservation of quantity, weight and volume more rapidly; that among Australian Aborigines performance on concrete-operational tasks is directly proportional to the extent of contact with the dominant culture; in general, that the *structure d'ensemble* or inter-task consistency posited by Piaget for the concrete-operational thought of the Genevan child apparently does not hold in different cultures: 'two concepts that develop congruently in the average Genevan child may develop at very different rates in another culture if one of those concepts is highly valued in that culture . . . and the other is not';[31] further, that the development of formal-operational thought is heavily dependent on schooling, that children with formal schooling which emphasises symbolic thinking generally develop formal thought processes faster and further than those without it; and that there is a high degree of variability in performance across different materials and situations. 'This limitation creates a paradox: the formal operations which were supposed to be independent of context are in fact situation-bound . . . What is lacking . . . are studies of operational thinking in culturally relevant, real-life situations.'[32]

Results such as these inevitably raise the all-important questions of the extent to which patterns of cognitive development are determined by environmental factors; whether such factors affect only the 'quantitative' aspects (ages) of development or the 'qualitative' (structural) aspects as well; how to distinguish 'competence' – conceived as universal – from 'performance', clearly dependent on such factors; or indeed whether this distinction is at all possible. Until such problems are satisfactorily resolved, the question of 'cultural retardation' versus 'cultural difference' remains an open one: do the observed differences in task performance reflect the

non-universality of Piagetian theory, or merely quantitative differences in
the rate of acquisition of universal competences, or simply the inadequacies of cross-cultural research design?

(c) Specifically Kohlbergian cross-cultural research is in an unhappier
state: the number of cultures in which such studies have been carried out is
still relatively small; the conceptions of the higher stages of moral
consciousness (as reflected in the various editions of the 'Scoring Manual')
appear to be continually shifting; and the results obtained seem to indicate
a high degree of cultural variability – which might be expected, since the
structures in question arise from interacting with features of the social
environment. More particularly, 'principled morality' appears to occur in
significant proportions only in Western or Westernised populations – and
even here the occurrence of stage 6 morality is exceedingly rare: 'criteria
for identifying orientation 6 are now so stringent that the orientation is not
even scored in [the 1976 edition of] the Standard Form Scoring Manual'. [33]
This of course is what one would expect to find for the 'social contract
reasoning' of stage 5 – justifying moral prescriptions or evaluations by
appeal to social-contract rights, values and principles – and for the 'ideal
role-taking' of stage 6 – justifying moral prescriptions or evaluations by
decisions of conscience in accord with self-chosen ethical principles appeal-
ing to logical comprehensiveness, universality and consistency.

The questions we raised above in relation to Piagetian cross-cultural
research – of different 'developmental endpoints' and alternative cognitive
structures, of disentangling 'competence' from 'performance' and the
influence of environmental factors – are even more pressing here. And
there is the added problem of meta-ethical disagreement among the
'principled moralists' of the Western philosophical tradition as to which is
really the most adequate style of moral reasoning. The assessment of the
transition from contractarianism and utilitarianism to 'justice as fairness' as
an 'advance' to a 'higher stage' would scarcely meet with general agreement (not to mention the view that the former are developmental-logical
presuppositions of the latter).

In the face of these problems and open questions, Habermas would, it
seems, be well advised to adopt a much more tentative and critical posture
towards cognitive developmental theories than he has to date. They
certainly cannot be appealed to as providing confirmation of his universality claims. In the present state of affairs, perhaps the most they can be said
to offer is 'a heuristic guide and an encouragement'. [34]

3. The penultimate point, or series of related points, I should like to raise
is of a yet more general and programmatic nature. It strikes me as
questionable that the highest stages of cognitive development could be
investigated and established with the same methods as lower stages. As
long as we are dealing with modes of thought that are, in Habermas's

formal-pragmatic sense, not yet 'open', there is some plausibility to the model of reconstructing the intuitive, pre-theoretical knowledge underlying the performances of competent subjects. In such cases there is an asymmetry presupposed between the insufficiently decentred thought of the child, traditional culture, or whatever, and the differentiated, reflective thought of the investigator. And this asymmetry provides a foothold for the conception of explicating an intuitive know-how, of knowing 'better' in this sense the structures and rules underlying a subject's performance. Further, if the competence in question concerns basic features of human life as we know it, or even as we can possibly conceive it, there is some plausibility to the claim of universality as well. This seems to be the case, for example, with the progressive formation of a conception of the permanence of objects and of their invariance under certain operations; it seems also to hold for the child's developing ability to co-ordinate social perspectives in interpersonal relations to the extent required for role-taking in the family and society. In these cases, it seems, we are dealing with the acquisition of unreflectively mastered know-hows – in relation to the external and social worlds – which are constitutive of the human form of life. To the degree that they can be characterised formally, we might claim to have identified universal structures of human reason.

The attainment of the 'higher' cognitive stages – of formal operations and principled morality – is, by contrast, said to require a certain break with the 'here and now', that is, with the unreflective character of the 'theories in action' that underlie performance at the lower stages. As Habermas puts it:

> Only with adolescence can the youth succeed in progressively freeing himself from the dogmatism of the preceding phase of development. With the ability to think hypothetically and to conduct discourses, the system of ego-demarcations becomes reflective . . . When the youth no longer naively accepts the validity claims contained in assertions and norms, he can transcend the objectivism of a given nature and, in the light of hypotheses, explain the given from contingent boundary conditions; and he can burst the sociocentrism of a traditional order and, in the light of principles, understand (and if necessary criticize) existing norms as mere conventions. To the extent that the dogmatism of the *given* and the *existing* is broken, the prescientifically constituted object domains can be relativized in relation to the system of ego-demarcations so that theories can be traced back to the cognitive accomplishments of investigating subjects and norm systems to the will-formation of subjects living together.[35]

Thus in Kohlberg's view the attainment of his stages 5 and 6 involves a questioning of a conventional morality absorbed during childhood, a period of 'moratorium' marked by meta-ethical reflection on the origin, function and validity of received ethical sentiments. This view raises certain difficulties for the claim that we are dealing with 'natural' stages of development. It is not merely that the requisite experience of disembedding oneself from an implicit world-view and adopting a detached and questioning posture, *in an environment that favours the move to principled morality,* is hardly typical of coming of age in all societies. More to the present point, even when this does occur, 'Kohlberg's description of these orientations as natural stages seems improbable in the light of the essential role played by reflective meta-ethical thought in their construction, since natural stages are theories-in-action presumably constructed through implicit interactive processes'.[36] The suggestion I should like to advance is that Kohlberg's account places the higher-stage moral subject, at least in point of competence, at the same reflective or discursive level as the moral psychologist. The subject's thought is now marked by the decentration, differentiation and reflexivity which are the conditions of entrance into the moral theorist's sphere of argumentation. Thus the asymmetry between the pre-reflective and the reflective, between theories-in-action and explications, which underlies the model of reconstruction begins to break down.[37] The subject is now in a position to argue with the theorist about questions of morality. This discursive symmetry might help to explain why Kohlberg's attempt to get from 'is' to 'ought' (in part) by establishing the 'naturalness' of the higher stages has struck moral philosophers as questionable. He has to adopt and defend a specific position on the very meta-ethical issues they spend their lives debating; the appeal to empirical-psychological considerations brings no dispensation from participation in this debate. This is not to deny the significance of such considerations for moral theory; it is only to say that they will have to make themselves felt *within* moral-theoretical argumentation.[38]

One might advance a similar, if somewhat more controversial suggestion in relation to Piaget's studies of cognitive development. He views the underlying functioning of intelligence as unknown to the individual at lower stages of cognition. At superior levels, however, the subject may reflect on previously tacit thought operations and the implicit cognitive achievements of earlier stages, that is, may engage in epistemological reflection. And this places the subject, at least in point of competence, at the same discursive level as the cognitive psychologist. Here, too, the asymmetry between the subject's pre-reflective know-how and the investigator's reflective know-that begins to break down. The subject is now in a position to argue with the theorist about the structure and conditions of knowledge. One reason this does not emerge as clearly as it might from Piaget's own work is his focus on natural-scientific thought, on the development of those concepts (space, time, causality, number, etc.) and those operations requisite for hypothetical-deductive reasoning about objectified states and events. And, as the logic and methodology of science attest, we are inclined to assume for scientific thought a version of the pre-reflective/reflective asymmetry attributed to earlier stages in relation to reconstructive theory, that is, to assume that the methodologist can in a sense know 'better' than the scientist the structures underlying the latter's accomplishments. But if we shift our focus from 'the development of a Western scientist' to the mastery of the structures underlying the type of reflective thought in which the cognitive psychologist is engaged, the presumed asymmetry becomes less plausible. As the subject's thought itself becomes more reflective, particularly in an epistemological vein, the subject is increasingly in a position to argue with the psychologist about the latter's own presuppositions, standards, procedures, appraisals, etc. And, again, this discursive symmetry suggests the implausibility of any empirical approach which assumes that epistemological issues are settled. The appeal to empirical-psychological considerations does not exempt the developmental psychologist from engaging in epistemological debate; rather, such considerations are contributions to it.[39]

4.   Given Habermas's reliance on the model of rational reconstruction, with its assumed pre-reflective/reflective asymmetry, these considerations raise questions about his own (reconstructive) scientific self-understanding. But I shall not pursue them here. Instead I should like to close with a somewhat diferent point, which is, however, not unrelated to Habermas's 'transformation of philosophy'. Very briefly, it seems to me that in certain contexts he advances a conception of the end-point of the history of reason which borrows too heavily from developmental psychology and fails as a result to account for some of his own insights. Thus in contrasting mythical and modern modes of thought he characterises the latter primarily in terms of a differentiation of the objective, social and subjective worlds, of the fundamental attitudes towards them, and of the validity claims proper to them. The differentiation theme is reflected as well in his characterisation of the telos of ontogenesis in terms of ego autonomy:

> By that I mean the independence that the ego acquires through successful problem-solving, and through growing capabilities for problem-solving, in dealing with (a) the reality of external nature and of a society that can be controlled from strategic points of view; (b) the nonobjectified symbolic structure of a partly internalized culture and society; and (c) the internal nature of culturally interpreted needs, of drives that are not amenable to communication , and of the body.[40]

This stress on differentiation and the autonomy of the self in relation to external nature, internal nature and society represents a conception of reason strongly reminiscent of Kant – a conception of *Verstand*, as Hegel would say, rather than of *Vernunft.* Yet in other contexts Habermas has in effect sided with Hegel against Kant and his conception of the autonomous self. In regard to the relation of self and society, he explicitly rejects all monadological views in favour of a notion of co-constitution. Individuation, he has constantly argued, can be comprehended only as a process of sociation; in the formative process, the subject is inextricably involved in a network of interactions, such that personal identity can be achieved only on the basis of mutual recognition:

> No one can construct an identity independently of the identifications that others make of him . . . [the ego] presents itself to itself as a practical ego in the performance of communicative actions; and in communicative action the participants must reciprocally suppose that the distinguishing-oneself-from-others is recognized by those others. Thus the basis for the assertion of one's own identity is not really self-identification, but intersubjectively recognized self-identification.[41]

And Habermas also rejects conceptions of ego autonomy which are based on the suppression of inner nature:

> The dual status of ego identity reflects . . . an interdependence of society and nature that extends into the formation of identity. The model of an unconstrained ego identity is richer and more ambitious than a model of autonomy developed exclusively from perspectives of morality . . . need interpretations are no longer assumed as given, but are drawn into the discursive formation of will . . . Inner nature is rendered communicatively fluid and transparent to the extent that needs can, through aesthetic forms of expression, be kept articulable *(sprachfähig)* or be released from their paleosymbolic prelinguisticality. But that means that internal nature is not subjected, in the cultural preformation met with at any given time, to the demands of ego autonomy; rather, through a dependent ego it obtains free access to the interpretive possibilities of the cultural tradition . . . Naturally this flow of communication requires sensitivity, breaking down barriers, dependency – in short, a cognitive style marked as field-dependent, which the ego, on the way to autonomy, first overcame and replaced with a field-independent style of perception and thought. Autonomy that robs the ego of a communicative access to its own inner nature also signals unfreedom.[42]

Oddly enough, Habermas does not adopt the same dialectical stance in the third dimension, that is, the relation of self to nature. Here we are left with a subject/object relationship characterised exclusively in terms of technical control. Thus in *Knowledge and Human Interests* he maintains that the conditions of instrumental action 'bind our knowledge of nature with transcendental necessity to the interest in possible technical control over natural processes'.[43] I have argued elsewhere that this position is incompatible with his Marxian thesis that nature is the ground of spirit, with his notion of a 'nature preceding human history' in the sense of a 'natural process that, from within itself, gives rise likewise to the natural being man and the nature that surrounds him'.[44] In this perspective nature is 'at the root of laboring subjects as natural beings';[45] social labour, and the technical objectivation of nature that it entails, are 'founded in a history of nature that brings about the toolmaking animal as its result'.[46] Nature is in short also a *natura naturans* and thus not merely an object of technical domination. Habermas, who dealt extensively with Schelling's *Naturphilosophie* in his earlier writings, is certainly aware of what is at stake here. And he several times alludes to the possibility of a science of nature that would not be categorically rooted in an interest in technical controllability:

A theory of evolution which is expected to explain emergent properties characteristic of the sociocultural life-form – in other words, to explain the constituents of social systems as part of natural history – cannot, for its part, be developed within the transcendental framework of objectifying sciences. If the theory of evolution is to assume these tasks, it cannot wholly divest itself of the form of a reflection on the prehistory of culture that is dependent on a prior understanding of the sociocultural life-form. For the time being these are speculations, which can only be confirmed by a scientific clarification of the status enjoyed by the contemporary theory of evolution and research in ethology.[47]

This suggestion of a non-objectivistic, reflectively cast theory of evolution certainly relativises the autonomous-ego/technically-controllable-nature picture that Habermas builds into his conception of autonomy. Here, too, it seems, he would have to regard strict subject/object differentiation as less adequate than a schema of dialectical interdependence.[48]

Taken together, the above considerations suggest that on Habermas's own view the telos of rational development cannot be adequately grasped in a schema of differentiations. The strict separations of *Verstand* are only a stage, albeit a necessary one, on the way to a more complex unity in difference. The undifferentiated unity of the earlier stages of thought has to be reconstituted at the highest stages.

I shall conclude this discussion with a few very tentative remarks concerning what, in my view, the preceding considerations do and do not entail.

(1) They do not of themselves entail a rejection of the idea of qualitatively different, hierarchically ordered stages of thought. But they do suggest that once the level of discursive thought has been attained and reflective argumentation plays an increasingly important role in the development of reason, the empirical-reconstructive methods of Piaget and Kohlberg become increasingly blunt. At this level the model of pre-reflective subject/reflective investigator gradually loses its foothold; in the end we are all participants in the debate as to what is higher. To be sure, explicit reconstructions of implicit know-hows retain their point – but only as contributions to this debate. They cannot by themselves settle it.

(2) My remarks do not imply a rejection of differentiation as a mark of cognitive development. The dissolution of the undifferentiated unity of pre-operational thought does appear to be a necessary step in the progress of rationality. But the separation of domains of reality and types of validity claims, of an ego that stands over against nature, society and its own *Bedürfnisnatur,* must give way to a unity in difference, to a non-regressive reconciliation with self, others and nature, if the 'dialectic of enlightenment' is to lose its sway over our lives.

(3) They do not entail a wholesale renunciation of theoretical and critical distanciation in favour of hermeneutic participation. The interpretation of meaningful phenomena need not be restricted to dialogic understanding; it can be theoretically grounded in a systematic conception of reason and its history, and thus be joined to explanation and critique. But if differentiation is not the last chapter in this history, the relation of 'lower' to 'higher' takes on a different appearance: the undifferentiated unity at the start is broken up along the way only to be reconstituted as a unity in difference at the end. And this suggests that we have things to learn from traditional cultures as well as they from us, not only what we have forgotten and repressed, but something about how we might put our fragmented world back together again. This is not a matter of regression, but of dialogue – dialogue that is critical, to be sure, but not only on one side. From this point of view as well, 'in a process of enlightenment there can only be participants'.[49]

4

Cognitive Interests and Self-Reflection

The status and systematic connection of the cognitive interests in Habermas's *Knowledge and Human Interests*

HENNING OTTMANN

I

In his inaugural lecture[1] Habermas presented a programme of a philosophy of emancipation, according to which our knowledge is guided by our interest in emancipation, our interest in intersubjective communication, as well as our interest in technical mastery over nature. Already, at that time, Habermas indicated that a proof of the thesis that our knowledge depends on our interests was not to be given in the form of a systematic argument but rather by way of a historical appraisal of the positivistic and historicist philosophy of science. Accordingly, *Knowledge and Human Interests* turned out to be a history of philosophy, albeit of a special kind. His excursion through the idealistic (Kant, Hegel) and the materialistic (Marx) theory of knowledge, through the prehistory of positivism (Comte, Mach), pragmatism (Peirce), historicism (Dilthey), psychoanalysis (Freud) and perspectivism (Nietzsche) served as the philosophical and historical framework within which the thesis of the cognitive interests was to be *systematically* established. This was in effect the systematisation of a theory the aims of which converge in the concept of 'self-reflection'. *Knowledge and Human Interests* was an exercise in 'self-reflection' in the sense of a theory of knowledge which, while raising the question of human interests, at the same time resurrected the Kantian question concerning the conditions of the *possibility of knowledge in general*; it was also a 'self-reflection' in the sense of a critical theory which, while reflecting upon cognitive interests, was at the same time a reflection on the conditions of the *possibility of emancipation from ideologies and power structures*.

Anglo-Saxon readers might find such a history of the philosophy of science for the purpose of establishing a theory of knowledge (together with a critical theory) an unnecessarily complicated way of laying a foundation. In addition, the suspicion arises that in Habermas's previous works there were already plenty of historically well-established theoretical conceptions which could have been organised into a systematic theory of knowledge.[2] Nevertheless, we do not have to try to justify the combination of history of philosophy, epistemology and critical theory, given the extraordinarily fruitful controversies *Knowledge and Human Interests* has raised. Considering the development of the Frankfurt School toward the end of the 1960s, we see that the danger of a loss of impact on *Praxis* and a certain isolation with regard to contemporary philosophy of science called for an attempt to combine the theory of knowledge with a history of philosophy.[3] Critical theory no longer had the 'wind in its sails'. Through the loss of its hope in the proletariat as the bearer of emancipation, it had also lost its historical executor.[4] It had distanced itself from the established systems of socialism in the East and yet was not at home in the West.[5] It was no longer sure of the validity of certain fundamental theses of Marx and, in addition, was challenged by the positivistic theory of knowledge which seemed to disqualify *any* practical foundation for scientific theory. In such a situation a clarification of the foundations of one's own theory was as important as an answer to the challenge from the positivistic philosophies of science. A critical theory intending to combine knowledge and human interests was forced to meet the challenge of stronger defenders of the classical theory which maintains that science is independent of human interests.

The classical theory abstracted from human interests but was not without implications for *Praxis*. For example, we find an immediate connection of theory and *Praxis* in Plato's theory of the philosopher as a mimetic exemplification of the cosmic order, an indirect connection in Aristotle's notion of the contemplative life or in Hegel's self-illumination of reason in the present. In contrast to this, contemporary views in the philosophy of science went so far as to eliminate radically each and every interdependence between theory and *Praxis*. *Knowledge and Human Interests* attempts to meet this challenge in the enemy's own camp. Like Hegel's *Phenomenology of Spirit*, *Knowledge and Human Interests* tries to reach an all-embracing standpoint by progressing through a series of limited, and therefore only relatively valid, forms of consciousness.

A 'systematic' philosophy of history is a legitimate enterprise. Whether such an enterprise succeeds is, to be sure, another question. In such an undertaking we are always faced with the problem that the result might be prejudiced by the selection of the authors chosen for interpretation.[6] Hermeneutically questionable interpretations might result from our systematic intention. No matter how plausible, founding a theory of knowledge in the interpretation of the theory of science of a certain epoch seems to be a hazardous venture, one that possibly endangers the universality of its conclusions by its historical contingency. The interest shown by a critical theory in doing away with concrete power structures could itself be a child of the times and thereby merely reflect the interest of a particular period and not of a theory of knowledge in general.

On the other hand, objections to the choice and interpretation of particular authors is not the way to examine successfully the truth of Habermas's position. In spite of the fact that Habermas's preoccupation with contemporary philosophy and his immediate critical concern raises the suspicion that the results are only relative to the times, nevertheless the interpretations themselves could very well contain enough argumentative force to establish the status of human interests and their systematic foundation. Accordingly, in what follows, we shall try to question the general basis and coherence of Habermas's interpretations, without going into each one in depth.

II

First of all, readers of *Knowledge and Human Interests* must be impressed by the way Habermas combines his criticism of positivistic and historicist theories of science with his position on human interests. While positivism, in the name of a concept of nature existing independently of human subjectivity, and historicism, in the name of a reduction of history to a 'museum' of traditional forms of consciousness, insist on a separation of subject and object, life and knowledge, science and its application, Habermas demonstrates the participation of the subject in the constitution of the objective world, the participation of human interests in knowledge and the connection between the genesis of science and its practical application. In Habermas's critical continuation of Peirce's pragmatism as a 'self-reflection' of the natural sciences, as well as in his critical interpretation of Dilthey's historicism as a 'self-reflection' of the humanities, human interests are shown to bridge the gap between the pre-scientific form of life, science and the application of scientific knowledge. 'Human interests' are, in the literal sense of the word, the 'inter-esse', i.e. the 'being-in-between'.

In Peirce's pragmatism, the cognitive interest of natural science is seen to be the interest in technical mastery over nature. It arises in human beings' pre-scientific relation to nature through their labour; at a certain period of human development, this interest extends itself into the natural sciences where it constitutes the domain of objectivity as the domain of things and happenings (which can be manipulated). Thus this interest determines the meaning of nomological statements and finally dominates even the context of applicability within which the results of natural science are technologically applied by means of causal explanation and prognosis.

In Dilthey's historicism, the cognitive interest of the humanities is shown to be an interest in intersubjective communication. This interest has its pre-scientific genesis in interaction and communication effected through the use of symbols; it penetrates the humanities in that it constitutes the domain of 'objectivity' as the domain of persons seeking to communicate with one another. Thus this interest determines the meaning of the symbolic utterances and ultimately extends into the context of application within which the interpretation of present and past meaningful utterances serves the purpose of intersubjective communication.

In Habermas's discussion of Freud's psychoanalysis and Marx's critique of ideology, there appears – in addition to the technical and practical interests – an interest in emancipation as the concern of critical psychology and critical social science. Just as the 'self-reflection' of the patient in psychotherapy entails an insight into hidden sources of repression and at the same time a freeing from this repression, so too 'self-reflection' in the name of the interest in emancipation entails an insight into power structures and a practical freeing therefrom. As long as institutional oppression and instinctual repression distort intersubjective communication, this interest assumes the form of criticism and the anticipation of a freer society. It criticises oppression and delivers us from it in the name of a universal non-repressive communication already manifest in the structure of language: 'Our first sentence expresses unequivocally the intention of universal and unconstrained consensus'.[7]

Human interests are 'beings-in-between' or mediators between life and knowledge. Their status as mediators leads us to suspect that a systematic foundation cannot be based exclusively either in life or in knowledge. Habermas tries to do justice to this difficulty by his concept of the 'quasi-transcendental'.[8] Human interests are not 'transcendental' in a simple (i.e. Kantian) sense of the word, because they do not fit into the framework of a sharp division between transcendental constitution on the one hand and the 'empirical' as constituted on the other.

The interests are indeed conditions of the possibility of experience. They constitute the objective domain of possible experience. Similar to the forms of sensibility and the categories of Kant, they are necessary conditions of knowledge. The technical and the practical interests are even 'invariant' and 'objective', i.e. unalterable by reflection and binding on all subjects.[9] On the other hand, they are not fixed to a transcendental subject in a Kantian sense but to the human species which, as a product of nature, reproduces itself in its labour, language and forms of political authority, and at the same time forms itself as a subject over and above nature. As '*quasi*'-transcendental conditions, human interests are based in the natural history of the human species, in the history of a nature which as a whole is described by Habermas with the adjective 'contingent'.[10] In so far as interests proceed from the history of nature, their status cannot be grasped any longer in the rigid opposition of transcendental constitution and constituted empirical world. Rather, the rigid opposition is made fluid by a dialectical concept of interests, themselves the product of the very empirical world they transcendentally constitute.

This relation between the 'transcendental' and the 'empirical' is conceived as being compatible neither with a reduction of interests to the natural interests of the species nor with a relativisation to particular historical conditions. The 'quasi-transcendentality' of human interests assigns them the role of mediators. 'Knowledge-constitutive interests mediate the natural history of the human species with the logic of its self-formative process.'[11] Technical interest already implies more than the adaptation of an organism to its environment. Practical interest already entails more than an adaptation to temporarily dominant traditions and institutions. The process of self-preservation is itself embedded in the socio-cultural forms of the *Lebenswelt*, i.e. in work and intersubjective communication. 'Self-preservation' cannot be defined without a culturally formed understanding of the 'self'. In this perspective, the cumulative learning resulting from the progressive mastery over nature, as well as from the interpretations of past and present traditions, belongs to the process of self-formation. And only the latter, as the self-formation of a free being over and above nature, offers the framework within which the meaning of 'self-preservation' can be understood.[12]

In the final analysis, only the emancipatory interest of the species seems to prove that neither a naturalistic reduction nor an historical relativisation can do justice to the knowledge-constitutive role of interests. Human interests can count as 'cognitive' interests because the emancipatory interest entails an idea of reason and freedom which transcends both biological self-preservation as well as dependency on specific historical constellations. If we reflect on the process of self-formation, then instrumental reason, which leads to mastery over nature, and the practical reason of intersubjective communication (together with the respective sciences and methodologies) reveal themselves as integral parts of our interest in freeing ourselves from the arbitrary force of nature and the power structures that inhibit our capacity to understand ourselves. It is this interest in freedom which also constitutes the interest of knowledge and reason as such: 'In self-reflection, knowledge for the sake of knowledge comes to coincide with the interest in autonomy and responsibility (*Mündigkeit*). For the pursuit of reflection knows itself as a movement of emancipation. Reason is at the same time subject to the interest in reason.'[13]

For Habermas, the emancipatory interest, as the immediate unity of freedom and universal reason, testifies to the possibility of a knowledge of history and nature which is undistorted by interests too closely tied to history or nature. The nihilistic conclusion drawn by Nietzsche, that natural interests can only be knowledge-distorting interests, seems invalidated along with the historicist objection, which maintains that historical interests cannot constitute the interest of a universal reason. Via human interests, nature and freedom will be 'simultaneously *disclosed* and constituted'.[14] And yet, how is the appeal of the emancipatory interest to the court of universal reason to be judged? Can the emancipatory interest lay a systematic foundation strong enough to establish the status of the technical and the practical interests?

III

In a critical theory the emancipatory interest cannot be conceived as the ultimate starting-point which, similar to the 'origin' of classical theory, is founded in itself. Notwithstanding Habermas's claim to an *'a priori'* insight into the idea of emancipation,[15] the 'highest' interest of a phenomenology of spirit materialistically inverted is itself dependent upon successful mastery over nature and interpersonal communication. While the technical and practical interests represent 'invariant' conditions of life and knowledge, which self-reflection can only catch up with but not modify,[16] the emancipatory interest is changeable in a certain way, depending upon the state of the mastery over nature and the historically different degrees of repression. Its 'derivative status' foreshadows the difficulties which Habermas encounters in establishing the existence of an interest which unites universal reason and freedom.

The emancipatory interest marks the convergence of the problems of a 'critique' which is supposed to be both a theory of knowledge in general and a critical liberation within a historical situation. The immediate identity of knowledge and interest creates a 'theory problem' and a *'Praxis* problem'. The *theory problem* is manifested in the fact that the practical freeing from particular ideologies and power structures undermines reason's claim to universality. The *Praxis problem* arises at the opposite side of the theory problem, because the historically relativised theory cannot legitimate a universally binding *Praxis*. 'Self-reflection', as a critique interested in liberation, is so closely associated with the self-formation of a certain subject that its claim to universality cannot be anchored in the freeing of this particular subject. As a claim to reason, it must stand up to the general requirements of theories and their generalisability – independently of its attachment to a particular self-formative process. Also psychoanalysis, selected as the methodological example of a critical theory, achieves the level of a generalisable theory only when its knowledge is freed from any reference to a particular case history.[17] If, on the other hand, the theory's claim to general or universal knowledge is destroyed by too close a connection with a specific process of liberation, then such a theory cannot justify a practice binding on all subjects. A risky, theoretically unfounded *Praxis* rears its head behind the identity of knowledge and interest.

These objections to the immediate identity of knowledge and interest, which have been presented by Apel and Böhler in other terms,[18] caused Habermas to modify the position laid out in *Knowledge and Human Interests*. First of all, Habermas introduced a distinction between 'critical self-reflection' and 'reconstruction', which dissolves the immediate unity within the emancipatory interest.[19] 'Critical self-reflection' designates the practical freeing of a particular subject; 'reconstruction' undertakes the function of a theory which has been uncoupled from practical consequences and which is equally valid for all subjects. In subsequent works we see Habermas engaged in assimilating linguistic (Chomsky), genetic (Piaget, Kohlberg) and evolutionary (Marx) approaches and developing theories which, independently of the specific practice of a particular subject, 'reconstruct' communicative competence, the genesis of cognitive and moral competence and the developmental sequences of social evolution.[20] The detachment of critical self-reflection goes hand in hand with a separation of 'genesis' from 'validity'. Just as the new claim to a general reconstructable theory is detached from the emancipatory interest, so similarly the problem of the 'validity' and 'truth' of statements (now transposed to the realm of an *'a priori* of argumentation') is more clearly separated from the interests and their constitution of experience (the so-called *'a priori* of experience').[21] Validity and truth of statements – whether they refer to the domain of the technical or the practical interests – are to be examined in 'discourse'. The latter designates a dialogue in which the constraints on action are 'virtualised' and the truth of statements about facts, as well as the correctness and appropriateness of recommendations and warnings, are decided and justified argumentatively. Whereas in systems of experience and action the validity of facts and norms is assumed 'naively', it is in discourse that 'problematic' claims to validity are to be clarified and resolved by consensus. A true consensus is distinguished from a false one with the aid of a 'counterfactual' presupposition of an 'ideal situation' of discourse, in which the chances of selecting and employing speech acts are symmetrically allocated.[22]

Second, further distinctions are set up to preserve a claim to rationality on the part of emancipatory *Praxis*. Emancipation is now evidenced on three levels: (a) in freedom anticipated through the 'ideal situation' of verbal communication, without which a theoretical discourse could not be conducted; (b) as 'enlightenment' which organises the liberation from ideologies and distortions of communication, following the maxim that only the acceptance of an interpretation by those who are to be freed from repression can be the final assurance of its legitimacy; and (c) as 'strategic action' which, on account of conflicts which cannot be solved by discourse, takes refuge in political strife.[23] With the category of 'strategic action' Habermas takes the risk and potential one-sidedness of political engagements into account. Owing to the fact that enlightenment can only be confirmed retrospectively by those who have been enlightened, discourse cannot justify potential risks in advance. Nevertheless, the legitimacy of strategic action also remains dependent on discursive confirmation. The struggle has to be considered as a struggle similar to Hegel's 'struggle for recognition'. Only the future agreement of all involved is the final assurance of its legitimacy.[24]

Certainly, these distinctions relieve the emancipatory interest from some of the difficulties inherent in the immediate identity of knowledge and interest. Whether they solve the 'theory problem' and the *'Praxis* problem' is a question which, within the limitations of our topic, we cannot examine any further.[25] As it is, the new distinctions have by no means eliminated all of the fundamental problems connected with the emancipatory interest. Alongside the 'theory problem' and the *'Praxis* problem', the conception of this interest conceals a far-reaching *reflection problem:* a singular overestimation of the power of reflection.

The 'reflection problem' is documented above all in an exceedingly intellectualised interpretation of Freud. Even when, following Habermas, one does not underestimate the co-operative role of the patient during therapy, and even when one does retain the moment of insight (contrary to objectivistic interpretations), nevertheless it seems exaggerated to elevate the patient's 'self-reflection' to a means of liberation. In psychotherapy, liberation is more the result of the 'emotional acting-out of the conflict', of repetition, resistance and emotional upset.[26] Rather than being the primary cause of liberation, reflection confirms in retrospect the successful freeing from repression. In Habermas's intellectualised interpretation, reflection is attributed to what is actually accomplished by the working-out of the conflict. This may be explained by the fact that Habermas orientated his interpretation with reference to Lorenzer's linguistic approach to psychoanalysis.[27] It is also possible, however, that the intellectualised interpretation of Freud is influenced by an idealism of the Fichtean sort.

Habermas's concept of the 'emancipatory interest' has certainly been affected by Fichte's 'interest of reason in freedom'.[28] But what Fichte established upon idealistic premisses as the union of reason and freedom cannot be transposed into a synthesis for a materialistic theory of interests. Fichte was able to unite nature and freedom within the 'I' because the 'Non-I' was on the whole the product of the 'I'. From the standpoint of practical reason, freedom had to destroy the factual resistance of the 'Non-I' and dissolve it into freedom. In this philosophy, nature is only of importance as that which has always been encompassed by the 'I' or as the *Material der Pflicht.* According to the idealistic-metaphysical interpretation, nature is only freedom's 'otherness', the lost yet, through freedom, retrievable product of itself.[29]

According to the materialistic premisses of the history of the species, Habermas cannot allow nature to be only freedom's otherness. Yet the role of nature in the process of emancipation is ambivalent, a naturalistic-idealistic chameleon. It appears difficult to decide whether, within the emancipatory interest, a contingent yet self-caused nature comes into its own, or whether this nature only reveals itself as freedom's own 'otherness'. The subject (this seems to be one possible version) dissolves the alienations and objectivations which are self-inflicted upon his or her inner nature; nature, released through reflection, reveals itself undistortedly. The freeing of inner nature could, however (and this is the other version), be equivalent to its dissolution into reason. In this case, nature as such would not be able to offer any resistance to reason; emancipatory reason would encounter a barrier only in so far as its own objectivations and alienations are concerned. Considering these two possible versions, is it not plausible to suppose that the undesired naturalism of a nature coming into its own (first version) joins hands with the equally undesired idealism of a reason returning to itself (second version)?

IV

The belief in the power of self-reflection is based upon an argument according to which progress in the mastery over external nature (and the subsequent riches), as well as progress in abolishing the repression inherent in the 'second' nature of institutions, lend wings to the progress of emancipation. Progressing technical control (and the subsequent riches) is the first prerequisite for a possible relaxation of the censorship of the instincts and the institutional framework.[30] The gradual transformation of institutions into the 'anti-institution'[31] of discourse would be the second step for an emancipation which reduces 'socially necessary repression below the level of institutionally demanded repression'.[32] An optimistic technical utopia apparently combines with a political utopia inimical to what traditionally has been called our 'second' nature.

Now the successful mastery over external nature is, in a certain sense, an unproblematic precondition for freedom. We are only free if we can free ourselves from external nature (to the extent that it is natural force). However, the connection between mastery over nature and emancipation becomes problematic, when external nature as the 'material' of a boundless will-to-control is made the prerequisite for freedom. In present-day experience with an increasingly disrupted environment, it becomes apparent that external nature sets a limit to the boundless will-to-control which could result in the destruction of external nature as the foundation of survival. The conservative philosophy of technology *à la* Freyer and Gehlen,[33] Heidegger's critique of the modern metaphysics of subjectivity, or the much-discussed *Dialectic of Enlightenment*, have all taught us that the retaliation of an exploited nature is not to be understood solely in a biological sense, as the destruction of the foundation of survival. Instrumental reason may also encroach upon the inner nature of human beings as well as upon all forms of the *Lebenswelt*. In view of the possibility of 'liberation' dialectically changing into an enslavement of inner nature, into an instrumentalisation of the *Lebenswelt* or into the destruction of the biological basis for survival, the modern degree of control over nature, as well as the qualitative character of this control, can no longer be taken for granted.

To be sure, there exist conceptions in Habermas's critical theory which do not seem to agree with the optimistic utopia of an emancipation expedited by the progress of technology. Primarily, one has to take into account one of the most attractive features of Habermas's theory, the separation of work and interaction – a distinction which renews the classical difference between *poiesis* and *Praxis*. Its restoration can be interpreted as being specifically directed against instrumental action encroaching upon the social life-world. According to Habermas's own teaching, it has become imperative to keep the social world free from the manipulations of technocratic practice. The early model of a consultative communication between scientists and politicians,[34] the attempts at revitalising the 'depoliticised' public sphere and the conception of 'discourse' can, in this perspective, be considered as proposals about how the previously 'passive' adaptation of institutions to technical progress can be converted into a technical development planned according to the standards of intersubjective communication. Technical and economic progress, as Habermas points out again and again, only seems to be a particular precondition for freedom, not its realisation.[36]

In addition to his usual distrust of the emancipatory blessings of technology, Habermas is obviously aware of the problem that human beings have a need for an encounter with nature which technical exploitation cannot fulfil and growing riches cannot compensate for. In his interpretation of Benjamin's aesthetics, he even hints at the possibility of a non-instrumental and non-exploitative but 'mimetic', playful and communicative association with external nature. An aesthetic experience of 'correspondences' between living and lifeless nature which, for instance, surrealistic art brings to light is said to be capable of experiencing even '*things* in the context of a vulnerable inter-personal encounter'.[37]

Nevertheless, the idea of having to set a limit to the boundless will-to-control, as well as the desire for a different association with nature, have no impact upon the technical interest itself and its relation to nature. Some of the reasons which underlie Habermas's position come to light in his critique of Bloch's and Marcuse's philosophies. In the latter there recurs the topos of the 'resurrection of fallen nature' – a myth inspiring the hope in an 'awakening' nature which, given a more 'humane' science and technology, could in some future time reveal itself as humankind's complementary 'partner'. In Habermas's view the hope in an 'awakening' nature has very little chance of realisation, because the modern type of mastery over nature is a 'product of the human species as a whole, and not of an individual epoch, a specific class or a surpassable situation'.[38] If, in addition, we recall the 'invariance' and rigidness of the technical interest stemming from its foundation in the natural history of the species, then two conclusions seem unavoidable. First, the technical interest itself is not related to a nature which lies beyond control and exploitation. Second, a non-exploitative relation to nature has to be relegated to the role of an 'attitude' compensating for aesthetically unsatisfied needs.

However, in the history of humankind's association with nature there have existed two typical 'attitudes' towards nature which differ immensely from the modern world-view of the *'maître et possesseur de la nature'*. During the times of the 'hunter and scavenger', humankind conceived itself to be a part of the order of nature; and even during 'agricultural' periods it wanted to 'cherish and protect' nature. In those times nature was interpreted as being a realm of living 'organisms'. It is only in modern times that this paradigm of interpretation has changed and has been replaced by the model of a nature which is regarded solely as inorganic lifeless matter. Once the new paradigm was established, humankind no longer felt any obligation to refrain from the manipulation and exploitation of nature.[39]

Considering that the paradigm of a lifeless and therefore *ad libitum* exploitable nature is only part of the world-view of the last few centuries, the status of the technical interest as an interest in mastery over nature becomes questionable. The question must be raised as to whether it is possible to recognise, on the level of the technical interest itself, the dimension of a nature beyond control and exploitation. This move need not be equivalent to the exaggeration of the myth which transfigures nature into a subject, over which any form of control would be forbidden. But, even if we could discover in Bloch's and Marcuse's technical utopia traces of the *'Tischlein-Deck-Dich'* fairy tale (according to which the verbalisation of a wish immediately leads to its realisation),[40] and even if, in the name of the survival of the masses of contemporary humanity, we did not want to dispute the legitimacy of the modern type of mastery over nature entirely, nevertheless this does not mean that we should accept *carte blanche* the will-to-control and its modern form. A will-to-control, whose legitimacy is based upon our need to survive and which is itself a threat to our survival, becomes dialectical. The technical interest in mastery over nature encounters a nature taking revenge upon the boundlessness of the will-to-control. If we attempt to draw a distinction, we may say that nature has to be regarded as a *purpose-for-us*, to the extent that we have to master it in the name of survival. But even within the perspective opened up by the technical interest, nature proves to be an 'objectivity' which refuses boundless control. It reveals itself to be a *purpose-for-itself*, in the face of which the will-to-control has to impose limitations on itself.[41]

In the light of this consideration, the epistemological status of Habermas's technical interest has to be re-examined. Technical interest must, on its own level, be associated with the recognition of a nature transcending control and exploitation. And, *prima facie*, Habermas himself seems to pave the way for an interpretation of the technical interest which leaves open the possibility of distinguishing between nature as it appears relative to the interest in control and nature beyond control and exploitation. Habermas has, for instance, termed the experience guided by the technical interest a 'restricted' one.[42] It seems to be a 'restricted' experience precisely on the grounds that it is an experience relative to and dependent upon the conditions of systematic observation, experiment and control, formulated in a 'monological' language abstracted from our ordinary language and experience; and the term 'restricted experience' apparently calls for an interpretation of the technical interest which distinguishes between the technical interest's 'restricted' power of disclosing nature and an 'unrestricted' experience of what nature truly is.

It is in his interpretations of Marx and Peirce that Habermas himself is led to the idea of a 'nature-in-itself'. Indeed, in Habermas's view, 'nature-in-itself' has to be regarded as a necessary postulate. But it must be postulated neither for the purpose of relativising the technical interest instrumentalistically, nor for the purpose of leaving open the distinction between nature appearing relative to the interest in control and 'nature-in-itself'. On the contrary, the postulate seems to be designed to exclude any relativisation of the technical interest and to identify the nature appearing relative to this interest with 'nature-in itself'. Technical interest confronts a 'factual', 'external' nature which places constraints on our inquiry and 'resists' false interpretations. Referring, for instance, to Peirce's example of the 'hardness of diamonds', Habermas states that a diamond has to be regarded as 'hard' not only as it is constituted as an object of technical control but also as it is in itself 'capable of entering the behavioural system of instrumental action'.[43] By 'disclosing' natural objects within the interest in control, the technical interest brings to light at the same time what the objects are 'in themselves'. 'Nature-in-itself' is revealed within the technical interest.

We reach the same conclusion if we examine another meaning of the postulated 'nature-in-itself'. Viewed from the perspective of history, 'nature-in-itself' stands for a 'nature preceding human history'. At the level of the history of humankind, it 'separates out into the *subjective nature* of man and the *objective nature* of his environment'.[44] After this separation, nature can only be conceived of as mediated through subjective nature, through the human interest in mastery over nature and through the historical processes of labour. But although Habermas at one time states that we 'learn to master natural processes only to the extent that we subject ourselves to them',[45] this submission seems to be more reminiscent of the Hegelian *List* with which we deceive nature into letting it work for us[46] than of an attempt to recognise a nature beyond the interest in control. 'Nature-in-itself' only calls into question particular interpretations within the framework of the technical interest, and does not question the technical interest itself. Again, 'nature-in-itself' seems to be completely within the scope of the technical interest, and one wonders what knowledge of external nature, if any, is left for a recognition of the nature beyond control and exploitation. The latter, it seems, has no access to what nature truly is.

In a materialistic theory of knowledge there may exist good reasons to avoid the danger of an instrumentalistic relativisation of the technical interest. But Habermas's interpretation of the technical interest leaves, as far as our knowledge of external nature is concerned, no room for the distinction between nature only appearing relative to our interest in control and nature beyond control, no room for the distinction between external nature as 'means' for us and as 'end-in-itself'. In the final analysis, the postulate of a recognisable 'nature-in-itself' leads us back to difficulties similar to those raised by the wavering of the emancipatory interest between naturalism and idealism. On the one hand, there is the subject which, via its interest, constitutes nature with transcendental necessity; on the other hand, there is a 'contingent' nature which is also characterised as being a *natura naturans*, i.e. the origin of the subject. As a product of nature, the subject would have to be 'contingent' but nevertheless it is equipped with an interest capable of constituting its own origin with transcendental necessity. 'Nature-in-itself' is only an epistemological postulate of the subject, but at the same time it is the origin of the subject, a knowable 'thing-in-itself' – knowable, however, only within the bounds of the technical interest.

Habermas's materialistic transcendental philosophy finally dissolves the transcendental concept of 'constitution'.[47] *Prima facie*, only the *natura naturans* seems to be capable of a supreme constitution, which constitutes that (i.e. the subject) by which it itself is constituted. A materialistic *natura naturans* encompasses the subject and its 'natural' interest in control over nature. On the other side, this very nature is subjected to the interest of the subject to such a degree that the subject's interest 'discloses' nature for what it is. Nature has to obey the commands of instrumental reason; even its 'resistance' is a compliance with the demands of an interest in more successful control. Although materialism and naturalism seem to prevail at first sight, even here one finds traces of a corresponding subjective idealism. The subject, although the product of the *natura naturans,* nevertheless does not encounter a nature which creates a barrier against the subject's interest in control. The supreme constitution of the *natura naturans* is rivalled by the supreme constitution of the subject, which seems (equally?) capable of constituting that (i.e. nature) by which it itself is constituted. Nature and freedom seem to belong together like moments of a Hegelian 'relation of reflection', not unlike the relation which Hegel has exemplified in his dialectic of 'master and slave'.[48] 'Relations of reflection' are defined by Hegel as relations of moments which are constituted through each other and which, nevertheless, individually claim to be the totality. However, one of the moments can be the totality only by subjugating the other moment, by claiming to include it and by denying any dependence on it. But if one of the moments is to be the other's 'master', then the dialectic of relations will show that the master is dependent upon the 'slave'. Habermas describes the subject's interest as if we could regard it as the 'master' which subjugates nature; consequently he has to identify appearing nature and nature-in-itself. But the subject as nature's master is itself dependent on nature. The subject's 'colonial war' against nature may well turn against the aggressor. If it is true that progressive mastery over nature possibly results in the destruction of nature as the foundation for survival, one can very well claim that nature itself is the subject's master whose 'imperatives' the subject had better 'obey'. In this case nature could be conceived of as being independent of the subject's freedom to such a degree that it 'resists' not only false interpretations within the technical interest but the interest in control as such.

It may be the case that practical philosophy has to find a compromise between our interest in control (and survival) and the recognition of a nature transcending control. Nevertheless, it must include a concept of external nature which, already in the perspective of mastery and survival, means more to us than a realm of lifeless matter that can be manipulated without limit. If control and mastery results from our interest in survival, the recognition of a nature transcending control must be part of our interest in 'the good life'. Habermas, notwithstanding the merely 'restricted' experience of the technical interest, tried to establish this interest as the one and only power of disclosing nature. By doing so, he has introduced too sharp a distinction between the level of the technical interest on the one hand, and that of the practical interest on the other. It seems difficult to see how our association with external nature is to be integrated into life-forms guided by the practical interest, not to mention the danger that this technical interest may open the door for an encroachment of the will-to-control upon inner nature or the social life-world. A technical interest in itself not related to practical standards, and a practical interest which has left to the technical interest all there is to know about external nature, both seem unable to avert such a danger.

V

Habermas's conception of the technical interest finally sways between naturalism and idealism. In any case external nature does not seem capable of resisting the subject's freedom and interest in control. Similarly, Habermas depicts the traditions and institutions, or to put it differently, our 'second' nature, as a nature which has to be dissolved into the subject's freedom. If we take a closer look at the relation between the practical interest and emancipatory self-reflection, there once again recurs the overestimation of the power of reflection we first encountered in Habermas's intellectualisation of psychoanalysis. This can be explained by the fact that Habermas puts institutions on a level with neurotic behaviour and the repetition compulsion of an individual. Institutions are a collective form of defence and censorship: 'Like the repetition compulsion from within, institutional compulsion from without brings about a relatively rigid reproduction of uniform behavior that is removed from criticism.'[49] The primary task of institutions can be summarised as the external regulation of oppression corresponding to instinctual repression, the necessary degree of which is dependent upon the relative shortage or abundance of economic goods. In modern times, institutions are the object of a political pathology, no longer justifiable as the foundation of political ethics in the classical sense. The modern morality is universal; it can no longer be restricted by the claims of particular institutions like the family, the state or the nation.[50] Modern morality as the morality of humankind as such only depends on 'discourse', in which humankind rationally decides what norms it wants to 'obey'.

Similar to the technical interest in mastery over nature, the practical interest in intersubjective communication apparently enjoys an unproblematic relation to freedom. We are only free if we can free ourselves from the power of traditions and institutions which constrain our communication by violence and repression. But the reader of *Knowledge and Human Interests* may be puzzled by the extent of Habermas's anti-institutionalism. The emancipation seems to be guided by an interest in freeing ourselves not only from illegitimate power structures, but from power and authority as such. Certainly, Habermas's intention is not to be confounded with an 'activism' which believes that the existing traditions and institutions 'can and should be ignored and surpassed'.[51] For the purpose of political practice, Habermas obviously recommends moderate policies. Liberation, as he puts it, only transposes the 'logic of trial and error' to the level of world history; it is committed to the 'determinate negation of unequivocally identifiable suffering – and committed equally to the practical-hypothetical consciousness of carrying out an experiment that can *fail*'.[52] Nevertheless, the theory of institutions as purely pathological forms of behaviour and the aim of freedom from power and authority as such introduce a very questionable antithesis between our practical interest in communication and our critical interest in liberation and freedom.

First of all, the separation between the practical and the emancipatory interests presupposes a 'meta-hermeneutic' which many adherents to a hermeneutic interpretation of 'tradition' and 'authority' might find unconvincing. Hermeneutic philosophy, as developed, for instance, by Gadamer, shares with critical theory an interest in criticising the positivistic consciousness of methodology and inadequate forms of self-understanding. Hermeneutic philosophy itself seems to be a critical philosophy. Nevertheless, for Habermas it espouses a dependence of our interpretations on 'tradition' and 'authority' which seriously underestimates the necessary range of critique and the power of 'self-reflection'. Hermeneutics, as Habermas points out, relies on a 'prejudice for the right of prejudices certified by traditions'.[53] Our 'stepping into the framework of tradition'[54] is the presupposition for hermeneutic understanding. In traditions, 'authority' and 'reason' are said to converge. Language is regarded as being the 'universal' medium of understanding and communication. But for Habermas language must be equally considered as a medium in which violence and power structures systematically distort our capacity to communicate. It is therefore not the hermeneutic favouring of traditions but only the power of 'self-reflection' which enables us to distinguish between an unconstrained consensus and pseudo-communication brought about by violence.[55] Only 'self-reflection' liberates us from ideologies which the hermeneutic acceptance of traditions cannot free us from.

Habermas's attempt to separate critical 'self-reflection' from the universality-claim of hermeneutics reintroduces an abstract opposition between historical 'positivity' on the one hand and critical reason on the other. This opposition is itself a 'prejudice', which Hegel has already unmasked as the very prejudice of the 'Enlightenment'.[56] It was the Enlightenment which interpreted traditions only within the perspective of reason, challenging the 'irrationality' of historical facticity and traditions. But a price had to be paid for the abstract opposition between history and enlightened reason. In the 'traditions' of past centuries, Enlightenment only recognised itself and an 'irrationality' completely opposed to its idea of reason. It did not encounter different ways of life or different ways of understanding capable of shaking up the prejudice of Enlightenment or its idea of reason. The same 'prejudice' applies to the emancipatory interest, if its reflection on traditions is based solely on the opposition between critical 'self-reflection' and historical positivity. The idea of emancipation cannot be exempted from the 'unlimited' process of understanding. The 'dialogue that we are' is unlimited because no generation is able to exhaust the meaning of traditions; it is unlimited because we, at a certain time, can only question some of our prejudices, never all of them. The very notion of critique presupposes the acceptance of traditions and prejudices, the reasonableness of which we rely upon. If emancipation is to have more than an abstract meaning of 'freeing (us) from', it has to be embedded in a hermeneutic interpretation of the 'reason' already inherent in the historical positivity of traditions.

Corresponding to the danger of robbing the emancipatory interest of historical sense, there is the danger of depriving the repression-free communication of 'cultural' content. Freud's psychoanalysis can only partially warrant the hope in an emancipation expedited by the progress of technology and economy or a fairer distribution of economic goods. According to Habermas, Freud's theory of instincts at least does not discourage the techno-political utopia of emancipation. Yet this interpretation somehow seems to neutralise the pessimistic overtones of the theory of instincts, stemming from the inseparability of culture and instinctual repression.[57] Repression seems to be linked not only to the relative shortage or abundance of economic goods, but also to the cultural function of sacrificing the instincts as such. A discouragement with respect to the utopia of emancipation would follow if, contrary to Habermas, the loosening of instinctual repression and institutional oppression could be expected to result in an increasing aggressiveness and a reprimitivisation of instinctual demands. However much Gehlen, in the name of the archaic origin of institutions, exaggerated their 'transcendence', he has nevertheless given a vivid description of modern 'subjectivism' which can be interpreted as the opposite side of decaying institutions. Traditional institutions offered a *'bienfaisante certitude'*, a relief from the pressure of needs and the possibility of a progression to culture, because the subject restrained his or her natural and individual interests in the name of the intrinsic value of institutions acknowledged as ends in themselves. In modern times institutions are no longer regarded as ends in themselves; they are reduced to instruments of survival and utilised for the satisfaction of immediate needs. But these modern institutions no longer allow for the tranquility of mind and the dignity which dedicated service to institutions had previously offered. 'Subjectivism' can be experienced as intellectual and moral overstress, as growing irascibility, as an 'exteriorised asphyxia-tion' *(nach aussen verlegte Atemnot)*, as increasing aggressiveness, as a reprimitivisation of instincts and a 'revenge' on cultural ideals.[58] Habermas once discussed the possibility of a cultural revenge, i.e. of a culture taking revenge on an age-long 'exploitation' for the purpose of legitimising power and authority. This culture 'at the moment of overcoming age-old repres-sion could suddenly be found lacking repression, but also content as well'.[59] But if a certain higher level of culture is intrinsically linked to the repression of instincts, could one not equally foresee the danger of a liberated instinctual nature taking revenge on a successful emancipation by depriving it of its cultural contents?

The emancipatory interest in an unconstrained and universal com-munication is not the fundamental interest of stabilised behaviour as such. As an interest in argumentative discussion of problematic validity-claims, it does not cover 'the case of love, of strife, of the disinterested perception of another person, of evasion, of practical imitation or primary social-ization'.[60] The critical interest is not *eo ipso* a motivation for the stabilisa-tion of a certain behaviour. Considering the difficulties of institutionally establishing a continuous reflection,[61] it may be suspected that the critical interest promotes further insecurity, which is then 'stabilised' in discourse. The latter seems to be a special case of highly unburdened, artificially self-conscious behaviour, itself dependent upon a multitude of empirical conditions ranging from the (institutionally secured) absence of fun-damental conflicts to the rules of orderly discussion. Even when these conditions are fulfilled, one still has to take into account the pressure of time, the necessity of having to decide, the limited capacity to take up or to alter topics of communication, and the fatigue of those participating in the dialogue.[62] In summary, there seems to be a larger gap between the anticipation of an 'ideal situation' of discourse and the actual practice of communication than is suggested by Habermas's conception of an anticipated, yet already realisable form of life.

The repression-free communication, some readers might be tempted to conclude, is only an ideal of communication for intellectuals: the disguised ideal of the 'republic of scholars' transposed to the realm of society in general. Adherents of classical practical philosophy, who reckon with the inevitability of power and authority, might even suspect the idealised discourse of being an ideology of power for intellectuals who, in the name of freedom from power and authority as such, establish the new power of discussion and the written word. But if we recall Habermas's intention to secure the utopia of emancipation against objectivistic applications, another critical approach might prove more adequate. Considering the gap between the empirical conditions of discourse and its idealisation, between discourse and institution, between hermeneutically interpreted traditions and the overestimated power of critique and self-reflection, the possibility arises of reintegrating the ideal of an unconstrained communication into the framework of traditions. Within the practical interest, 'critique' could play the role of a 'regulative idea'[63] which is not in itself a form of life but a necessary and unrenounceable idea with the help of which we examine distortions in our communication. Similar to the contract theories of modern natural law, the 'regulative idea' of a repression-free communication could serve as a thought-experiment through which we can question the legitimacy of certain institutions. It is true that Habermas lately seems to have shifted his position in such a way that the 'ideal situation' of verbal communication and his model of social critique resemble more a Kantian 'regulative idea' than a form of life.[64] Nevertheless, this model of critique also starts from an antithesis between traditions, authority and power on the one hand and emancipation and critique on the other, an antithesis which a hermeneutic integration of critique into the framework of traditions has to overcome. There still remains an 'abstract' opposition, now between 'decisions' without reason and 'decisions' which are the result of a rational consensus. There still remains the contention that communication and discourse can become a 'motive forming power'. The critical interest is still an interest confined to the purpose of criticising power and authority as such, presupposing that in our society 'generalisable interests' can only be suppressed interests. In contrast to this idea of critique, the very purpose of the critical models employed in the history of natural law must not be seen in terms of a liberation from power and authority as such, but in terms of an attempt to legitimate 'just' forms of power and authority.[65] Instead of opposing the repression inherent in existing institutions and the idea of critique, a hermeneutic mediation has to reconcile traditions, power and authority with our idea of the principles we would choose in a situation free from repression. Possibly, what Rawls has termed the 'reflective equilibrium' is one way of describing such a hermeneutical process of mediating traditions and critical ideals.[66] According to this theory, we have to go back and forth between the principles we would choose in an 'ideal situation' and our 'considered judgements', modifying either the conditions of the ideal situation or revising our 'considered judgements' until we eventually find a harmony satisfying the demands of both.

Habermas's theory of interests threatens to do injustice to the external or the second nature. Therefore it also threatens to do injustice to freedom. Swaying between naturalism and idealism, it overburdens both nature and freedom. The proposal to associate the technical interest with an interest in recognising an external nature, in the face of which the boundless will-to-control has to limit itself, can possibly relieve the technical interest of some of its difficulties. The proposal to re-embed critical 'self-reflection' and the emancipatory interest in the practical recognition of institutions and traditions can possibly reconcile the idea of a repression-free communication with our 'second nature'. The latter seems to be a part of 'the good life', the realisation of which is sought by both critical theory and traditional practical philosophy.

5

Science and Objectivity

MARY HESSE

Action and discourse

Habermas has not yet explicitly addressed himself to the detailed problems of philosophy of science as these are currently being discussed in the analytic tradition. That is to say, he has not participated directly in the post-Kuhn and post-Feyerabend debates on truth and meaning, instrumentalism, realism and relativism, that are primarily associated with Davidson, Kripke, Putnam and others who more or less indirectly owe their problem-situation to the work of Quine. On the other hand, in Habermas's writings since *Knowledge and Human Interests* there is to be found a sufficiently systematic discussion of natural science to enable us to derive an account of his distinctive approach to these problems. My aim in this essay is to give a critical account of this approach.

In *Knowledge and Human Interests* (hereafter *KHI*) Habermas drew on Charles Peirce for his model of the empirical sciences.[1] He defined empirical science as being constituted by *technical interest,* that is, by the goal of successful prediction and control of nature, ensured by the method of generalisation, testing and corrective feedback. Peirce attempted to define 'truth' as the ideal permanent consensus of scientists at the limit of this self-corrective method, but logical difficulties in specifying such a 'limiting' process led Peirce to supplement his consensus theory with a form of correspondence theory in which truth is after all guaranteed by the success of science in the natural environment. The two aspects of truth sit uneasily together in Peirce's theory; consequently Habermas drops the 'contemplative' notion of correspondence with an external reality, and embraces wholeheartedly the consensus concept, the objections to which he attempts to deal with in the appendix to *KHI* and elsewhere in terms of his theory of the ideal speech situation. In his later 'A Postscript to *Knowledge and Human Interests*', however, the interpretation of Peirce is somewhat different.[2] There Habermas notes that his critics have drawn instrumentalist implications from his treatment of natural science in *KHI*, and argues that rejection of Peirce's later contemplative concept of truth does not imply an instrumentalist theory of truth either for Peirce or for himself. Peirce did indeed give an instrumentalist or pragmatic theory of the *meaning* of empirical expressions, that is, as those that 'grasp' objects with the aim of control of external nature, but his theory of truth was not determined by this pragmatic grasp of nature but by intersubjective argumentation and consensus. Habermas interprets this as an anticipation of his own (post-*KHI*) distinction between 'action' and 'discourse', that is, between habitual 'following of the rules' of pragmatic action on the one hand, and reflective and discursive argumentation about the validity of the statements and social norms thereby presupposed on the other.

This distinction between action and discourse has now become of central importance for the understanding of Habermas's theory of meaning and truth in general, and for his philosophy of natural science in particular.[3] Expressed briefly, it implies a pragmatic theory of meaning and a consensus theory of truth. First it is necessary to understand what he means by saying that technical interest in prediction and control 'constitutes the object domain' of empirical science, and what he means by use of the term 'objectivating' in relation to science. His theory must be distinguished carefully from a realism which presupposes that the aim of science is to derive true statements corresponding to an antecedently given 'real' domain of objects, and which issues in the possibility of technical control only as an incidental spin-off. On the contrary, Habermas believes (along with the Kantian tradition) that there is no antecedently given domain of objects which are the direct referents of true statements. Empirical objects and 'empirical reality', in general, are constituents of human commerce with the natural world, constituted *in the course of* human pursuit of those technical interests which are continuous with the needs of all animal species to survive in their natural environment. This does not of course mean that there is no natural environment independent of the technical interest; it means merely that there are no true empirical statements independent of this interest. What Habermas calls 'communicative action' in relation to nature is the unreflective pursuit of the feedback method of empirical science. In the course of such pursuit, scientific and indeed all empirically descriptive statements acquire pragmatic meaning. To quote F. Ramsey (to whom Habermas refers for the pragmatic theory of meaning): 'The essence of pragmatism I take to be this, that the meaning of a sentence is to be defined by reference to the actions to which asserting it would lead, or, more vaguely still, by its possible causes and effects.'[4] In other words, the empirical meaning of a sentence is not determined, as in verifiability theories of meaning, by the conditions under which the sentence would be said to be true, but rather by the conditions under which utterances are acceptably produced in the language community, including the conditions of learning to use the language to refer to that in the surrounding reality which is categorised as particular kinds of objects and events for technical purposes.

McCarthy puts Habermas's thesis thus: 'the constitution of a world of objects of possible experience has to be viewed as the result of a "systematic interplay of sense reception, action and linguistic represen-tation"'.[5] To 'objectivate' experience, then (at least as this term is used by Habermas's translator in the 'Postscript'),[6] is to take experience as the arena of communicative action, and in particular to constitute the inter-subjective object domain of the natural and social sciences in so far as these are subjected to the empirical method. The 'objectivating sciences' are thus, in the 'Postscript', contrasted to the 'self-reflective' sciences, which I shall describe later (pp. 109-14).

Truth, however, according to Habermas, is removed from direct con-frontation with experience by being asserted or denied only of statements, and only as a result of attempting to justify the speech acts produced in unreflective action. Thus truth is conceived as essentially intersubjective, that is, as concerned with conditions of utterance in the speech community, and in particular with reasoning and argument within communicative discourse. True statements do not correspond to empirical facts as things in the world. Rather, following Ramsey and Strawson, facts are what true statements state: they are interpretations or representations of the object domain in the categories of a given language. More than one true statement, and more than one 'fact', may in this way 'correspond' to the world. Thus 'Caesar's death' and 'Caesar's murder' are different facts, but the corresponding expressions refer to the same event. Or, in a scientific context, Habermas implies that different theory-languages may be used to state different facts, but nevertheless to refer to the same objects or events, for example 'particle-as-classical-object' and 'particle-as-quantum-object'.[7]

The attempted distinction between pragmatic or instrumental meaning and consensus truth, and the related distinction of action and discourse, need deeper examination than Habermas gives them. In his theory the meaning of an empirical language seems to be in an uneasy intermediate position between merely animal trial-and-error learning on the one hand, and fully discursive argumentation about an empirical subject-matter (which includes scientific theorising) on the other. Habermas wants 'truth' to enter only at the latter stage. This becomes explicit in his assertion that the interests which direct knowledge (in this case empirical knowledge) do not remove or resolve 'the difference between *opinions about objects* based on experience related to action, on the one hand, and *statements about facts,* founded on discourse that is free of experience and unencumbered by action, on the other'.[8] 'Opinions about objects' depend on understanding the meanings of categories of descriptive natural language, but they have no truth value; only statements have truth value, and this is truth-as-consensus.

The attempt to explain 'meaning' in relation to the objects of experience without explaining 'truth' follows from Habermas's desire to discard correspondence in favour of consensus. But it is difficult to see how the meanings of descriptive terms and the syntactical and semantical structure of descriptive language can be learned without an appeal to something like correspondence truth. Habermas almost admits this when he refers to such elementary empirical propositions as 'this ball is red'.[9] It is almost as if the paradigm cases for a Tarskian correspondence theory of truth become peripheral limiting cases for Habermas – limiting in the sense that he still maintains that their truth is determined by *discursive* verification (for it presupposes the intersubjective categorial system of objects, colours, etc.), but admits that this verification is 'grounded' in the experience of handling the red ball. Such 'grounding', however, cannot be absent in *any* understanding of the meaning of empirically descriptive language, and it cannot be totally separated from the truth claims of the products of scientific theorising, however complex and distant from the observable these become. There is no language or learning of language without truth claims that are *both* grounded in experience and linguistic habit, *and* are the result of discursive argumentation. Habermas seems to agree that scientific experimentation and measurement are part of truth-justifying *discourse*, but experimentation cannot be sharply cut off from ordinary experience, observation and natural feedback learning, with which it is continuous.[10]

Habermas's theory of pragmatic meaning is comparable with the taken-for-granted character of Tarski's theory of truth. Where Tarskians simply presuppose the givenness of truth for such expressions as 'this ball is red' in some antecedently understood metalanguage, Habermas simply assumes the givenness of their meaning in habitual linguistic interaction with the world. He rejects the correspondence theory of truth as such, but he is prepared explicitly to notice that an account of descriptive meaning can and should be given in terms of the concrete history of the language and of speakers' socialisation into the language – something which Tarskians tend to dismiss as being of no concern to philosophy. Habermas's theory of truth, moreover, is strong where the Tarskian theory is weak, namely in attempting to explicate truth as intersubjective consensus where the correspondence 'grounding' is weak or highly indirect. His theory of *theoretical* truth in science does help, as we shall now see, to illuminate the cluster of problems regarding 'theory-ladenness' and 'meaning variance' that have been much discussed in analytic philosophy of science.

Truth in scientific theories
The theory of theoretical truth is developed principally in the 'Postscript'. There Habermas starts by attacking the positivistic, or 'scientistic', account of science as a global philosophy, on the grounds that it does not admit of critical reflection on its own epistemological foundations.[11] It pretends that a total philosophy of nature can be 'monological', as he puts it elsewhere,

that is, that it need concern only objective descriptions of nature, and not the 'dialogue' which is involved as soon as the conditions of scientific work and language in a scientific and social community are taken into account. But, Habermas goes on, philosophy of science does now attempt to be critical, and scientism has defended itself against this kind of objection in two ways.

First it has argued for a reductionism in which the knowing self and even the scientific community are also conceived as part of external nature, and are ideally describable in objective terms as 'objects' constituted by empirical science. But this attempted reduction becomes problematic in face of the dependence of science on changing theories and paradigms, which creates difficulties for realism, and also in the light of the insistence of ordinary language philosophy that human action has to be interpreted within its own 'non-objective' framework of reason, meaning, intention, etc.

The second modern defence of scientism arises from the discussion of theory-languages by Feyerabend, Sellars, Rorty, Smart and others. Here it is admitted that changing scientific theories radically reinterpret all ordinary descriptive language, including that of empirical science and of human action. Thus ideally the scientific community itself is subject to objective reinterpretation of its own self-image with every change of global theory. Habermas has two objections to this 'displacement hypothesis'. The first is that it presupposes that the best theory in the sequence of theories (or the best to date at any given time) must be an objective theory, whereas it might be a reconstructive theory (like linguistics), or a critical theory (like psychoanalysis), both of which depend on ordinary language rather than on theoretical reinterpretations. (I shall return to this threefold distinction of kinds of science below.) The second objection is that the displacement hypothesis falls into relativism if there are *no* conditions regulating the sequence of theories except Feyerabend's 'principle of proliferation'. 'At this point belief in witches would be able to challenge seriously the place of Newtonian mechanics.'[12]

This discussion makes it clear that Habermas rejects the presuppositions of all three of the positions commonly held by philosophers of natural science: namely, realism, reductionism and relativism. All three, he maintains, rest on the common assumption that the objective method of natural science is the only source of knowledge, and that it is self-contained in the sense that there can ultimately be no critique of science that arises from outside its own framework. These presuppositions are untouched by all the local philosophical disputes between realists, reductionists and relativists.[13]

It is in the light of this analysis that one must understand Habermas's alternative account of theoretical science. This borrows some insights from the discussion of 'theory-ladenness' and 'meaning variance', but without their realist/relativist presuppositions. First, the pragmatic theory of meaning ensures that denotative terms refer to identical objects in the world. The idea that meaning is wholly dependent on theoretical context is quite unreal, because ordinary descriptive language is learned in pragmatic conditions under which identity of reference in normal cases is practically ensured. We understand the natural-language reference of 'ball' under most circumstances without having to ask whether a speaker is a Newtonian or an Einsteinian or indeed a flat-earther. It is because scientific theory is continuous with these natural-language meanings that theoretical explanation can be translated into technical knowledge. Meaning at the pragmatic observation level is therefore relatively independent of theory, and the problem of meaning variance is a pseudo-problem.[14]

Truth, however, is intimately bound to theory and is not pragmatic or instrumental. In a refutation of those who have interpreted his theory as an instrumentalism, Habermas says:

> the *objectivity* of experience could only be a sufficient condition of *truth* – and this is true of even the most elementary empirical statements – if we did *not* have to understand theoretical progress as a critical development of theory languages which interpret the prescientific object domain more and more 'adequately'. The 'adequacy' of a theory language is a function of the truth of those theorems (theoretical statements) that can be formulated in that language. If we did not redeem these truth claims through argumentative reasoning, relying instead on verification through experience alone, then theoretical progress would have to be conceived as the product of *new* experience, and could not be conceived as reinterpretation of the *same* experience. It is therefore more plausible to assume that the objectivity of experience guarantees not the *truth* of a corresponding statement, but the *identity* of experience in the various statements interpreting that experience.[15]

This somewhat opaque paragraph needs to be carefully unpacked in terms which show its relevance to the problem of the relation of theory and observation. It can, I think, be paraphrased in five points:

(1) Since even the most elementary observation statements are expressed in terms of some theory-language or other, and since these theory-languages change with time, truth cannot inhere in observation statements simply as correspondence between statement and the empirical world.

(2) We therefore have to understand theory-languages not as directly describing the world, but as *interpreting* it more and more 'adequately' as science develops.

(3) 'Adequacy' is measured by experimental verification, but also necessarily by argumentative reasoning from the truth of theoretical postulates

formulated in the language, by means of which we 'redeem' the implicit truth-claims of empirical statements.

(4) If adequacy were measured by empirical verification alone, we should fall into the meaning-variance problem, because there would be no linguistic means of identifying the experiences expressed in the language of one theory with those expressed in the language of another.

(5) Therefore, in order to guarantee the identity of reference of observation statements made in different theoretical languages which are 'about' the same subject-matter, we cannot rely on their correspondence truth, but rather we need communication and argumentation between and within different theory-languages. The possibility of such communication is ensured by the pragmatic theory of meaning which shows how the subject-matter is constituted in a theory-independent way by technical interest.

This explains why, in Habermas's view, scientific truth is not instrumental, and consequently provides his resolution of the problems of theory-ladenness and meaning variance. It still does not, however, answer the question 'Why can we not regard science as the pragmatic non-discursive continuation of animal-like learning behaviour?' Habermas presupposes throughout that scientific progress *does* consist of the attempt to justify the truth of hypotheses, and that it is therefore essentially discursive and detached from action. But suppose this is just a contemplative illusion? In view of Habermas's rejection of contemplative realism, we cannot suppose that the truth-redeeming features of theoretical discourse are due to any correspondence truth of their premises. How, then, does the concept of consensus truth, bound as it must be to one theory or another, overcome the tendency to relativism that Habermas has objected to in Feyerabend's account?

There are several possible answers to the question 'Why do we need discourse as well as action in science?'

(a) Habermas clearly rejects the contemplative reply that science just aims to describe the world truly, and that technical knowledge is a mere spin-off from this aim.

(b) Habermas asserts that 'the practice of a form of life [in this case pursuit of the technical interest] . . . can only reproduce itself with the aid of potentially true statements'. And again, 'it is evidently a fact of nature that the human species, confined to its socio-cultural form of life, can only reproduce itself through the medium of that most unnatural idea, truth'.[16] But this is only an assertion of what has in fact happened in the history of science – it has indeed spawned sequences of highly discursive theoretical systems. The traditional understanding of these systems, namely contemplative realism, has been rejected, and we have not been told *why* the human species can only reproduce itself through the medium of 'truth'. If Habermas replies in terms of the truth-claims presupposed in all human language, this still does not show that *theoretical* science necessarily raises truth-claims, for there are many societies which pursue technical interests and reproduce themselves but do not develop complex theoretical systems. The argument that I have paraphrased in points (1) to (5) above does not demonstrate their necessity. Moreover, even where they occur, the argument does not altogether exclude an instrumental interpretation of their 'higher-level' postulates. It shows only that instrumentalism is inadequate as an interpretation of theory-laden empirical statements, but it is well known that the acceptability of theories does not only depend on verification of such statements, but also upon judgements of simplicity and intelligibility which are not obviously truth-bearing.

(c) Perhaps, somehow, this 'most unnatural idea, truth' makes pursuit of technical interest more efficient. Habermas does not anywhere say this in so many words. It does seem to be a reasonable inference from the history of science, but it is not clear that, if true, the argument from efficiency is consistent with Habermas's theory. For it could be explained only on the basis of some theory of truth that Habermas has rejected. For example, it could be explained on the basis of contemplative realism in the fashion of Putnam – that is, that the *de facto* success of science is explained by its realistic reference, but this is not open to Habermas. Or it could be explained on the basis of a weaker realism which accepts an element of correspondence truth in theories, while not being committed to a realist reference for *all* theoretical statements, as has been suggested above. So to defend the need for truth-claiming theories on the grounds of technical efficiency, it seems that we would need a closer relation between correspondence truth and the truth of theories than Habermas permits, and also that we would have to call in question his sharp distinction between action and discourse in science.

(d) The most illuminating reply that can be drawn from Habermas's work, regarding the need for truth-claiming theories, takes us outside empirical science and technical interest to a consideration of the place of consensus truth in social life in general. This will raise at the same time the question of the apparent relativity of discursive truth to particular forms of social life. The point will be developed in the next section, but briefly it is this. Theoretical science is part of the human goal of reflective and intersubjective self-understanding, which embraces the hermeneutic and critical sciences as well as the empirical, and involves norms and value judgements as well as empirically constituted facts. Theories are indeed a reflection of 'contemplative interest',[17] not in the sense of old-fashioned realism, but in the sense of Durkheim's symbolic representations, which unify humanity's understanding of itself and its interaction in relation to both its natural and social environments. Such symbolic representations do seem to be a universal and necessary condition of social life, and to constitute the bridge between merely biological and social needs, between nature and culture. But there is no possibility of direct application of a theory of *biological* evolution here, and much still needs to be done to justify the idea that social evolution implies such systems of symbolic understanding.

Theory as symbolic representation

In Habermas's view the domain of hermeneutic science is constituted by the interest in practical interaction between persons and social groups. In his discussions of this domain he makes use of the concept of 'symbolic interaction' as this has been developed from Durkheim, Mead, Blumer and Goffman.[18] The concept includes a view of language as the symbolic structuring of the experienced world into which every language learner is initiated, and more generally the notion of the intersubjective 'social world' into which every individual is progressively socialised, and which he or she internalises as a set of norms and rules of conduct that are not purely natural. The system of symbolic interaction constitutes the object domain of hermeneutic science: practical discourse operates upon an unreflective habitual system of social behaviour and rules to seek justification and correctness. There is a close analogy here with the object domain of the empirical sciences upon which, according to Habermas, theoretical discourse operates to seek truth.

But the relation between symbolic interaction in general and scientific theories in particular is more complex and more intimate than that analogy would suggest, and here we can perhaps go beyond Habermas's explicit statements to develop a line of thought that is implicit in his work. It is obvious that in the cosmological myths of all societies, and also in the history of Western science, cosmologies and theories have carried with them world-views and evaluations of society and nature which have gone far beyond empirical validation, and have had ideological and social functions. This property of theories has lost its claim to cognitive status in the pervasive positivism of recent interpretations of science, but in *Legitimation Crisis* Habermas wonders whether a reunification of theoretical and communicative knowledge might not result in part from a new cognitive interpretation of such world-views:

> it has in no way been determined that the philosophical impulse to conceive of a demythologized unity of the world cannot also be retained through scientific argumentation. Science can certainly not take over the functions of world-views. But general theories (whether of social development or of nature) contradict consistent scientific thought less than its positivistic self-misunderstanding. Like the irrecoverably criticized world-views, such theoretical strategies also hold the promise of meaning: the overcoming of contingencies.[19]

The suggestion is that a view of theoretical science incorporating over-all views of the natural and social worlds might be adopted, not as correspondences with the world, but as media of human communication about nature and society, in association with ethical and practical dimensions of world-views. There is therefore a need for 'understanding' in relation to nature and society that dictates the search for the 'most unnatural idea, truth', beyond the domain of technical interest into that of interpersonal communication. This operates at the level of communication between members of the scientific community in their use of languages containing theoretical terms; between scientists and the public when they attempt to convey their 'discoveries' in popular form; and in the implicit cosmology of societies, whether this is informed by consistency with the technical interest or not. In non-scientific societies it is simply an undifferentiated part of general symbolic representation; in scientific societies the difference is that there is a demand for coherence with technical interest, that is, with empirical corroboration and falsifiability. But this demand is far from being a revival of contemplative realism, for two reasons:

(a) Theoretical interpretations are always underdetermined by empirical data, and are therefore not unique for any given culture, let alone between cultures.

(b) Consistency with empirical data leaves room for the incorporation of value judgements and ideological twists within scientific theory, and in Habermas's scheme these would belong to more or less unreflective symbolic interaction rather than to technical knowledge. That there are such evaluations and ideological twists associated with natural scientific theory is amply exhibited both in styles of popularisation, for example of the ideas of the 'infinite universe' and the 'naked ape', and also in an increasing number of studies in the historical sociology of scientific ideas.[20]

It is not clear, however, that this view of the social necessity of theoretical languages can be made to fit easily into Habermas's schema. In the first place it cuts across the distinction between technical action and practical interaction – between the domains of the empirical and the hermeneutic sciences. Interpreted this way, the mythical or theoretical frameworks within which technical interest is pursued would themselves belong to pre-discursive and habitual interpersonal interaction. And yet the theoretical interpretations thus 'habitually' carried on are themselves 'discourses' about the domain of scientific objects, and are part of the process of validating the truth-claims of empirical statements. Second, at the level of theoretical discourse proper, we would have to consider the criteria of validation themselves, and this would include arguments *between* global theories and hence a great part of theoretical science as well as its philosophy. These are clearly distinct *aspects* of experimental and theoretical science, but it is difficult to regard them as sharply distinguished modes of knowledge-constitutive interest, or as clearly discriminated into 'action' and 'discourse'.[21]

The most important difficulty in reconstructing theoretical science within Habermas's framework, however, concerns the problem of relativism. The major charge against any consensus theory of truth is that it leaves truth as merely relative to a local culture. Habermas rebuts this charge by means of his theory of the ideal speech situation: roughly, that in a fully emancipated society, with symmetrical chances for all members to participate in unfettered discourse, consensus about both facts and norms is equivalent to validity. Many difficulties have been found with this view, and I shall not discuss these here. But there is one difficulty that bears particularly upon the attempt to understand theoretical truth as ideal consensus. If one accepts, along with Duhem, Kuhn and Feyerabend, that there is no ideal theoretical framework that would be uniquely 'the best' interpretation of nature even in an ideally rational society and even with 'complete' empirical evidence, then one is deprived of the notion of a supra-cultural theoretical truth. Habermas does appear to accept that there is no such ideal theory, and this is not just because historical speech situations are in fact ideologically distorted and subject to other oppressive constraints, but for the deeper reason that there is no theory that uniquely corresponds to the world. It may be just plausible to conclude that human biological and social needs are sufficiently unified to give some sense to the counterfactual idea that unconstrained consensus would define an absolute validity for *norms*, but it is not plausible to suppose that there could be any significance in a similar consensus about theoretical frameworks or paradigms. Art and culture are presumably not supposed to stand still in the unconstrained society; neither would interpretations of nature.

Why, then, in the end is Newtonian mechanics to be preferred to belief in witches? Both theories mediate an understanding of society and of nature, albeit in non-ideal societies. It is not even out of the question that certain versions of witch belief (perhaps among the Azande rather than in sixteenth-century Europe) exhibit a less 'distorted' society than that of the post-seventeenth century mechanical cosmology. The grounds of preference for Newton, if any, must have to do with technical interest and correspondence truth, not with a comparison of the states of consensus in two different societies.

Habermas might, however, develop a different interpretation of the truth of theoretical science, in which there is no claim about a convergence of theories to an ideal single limit in an ideal society but where the claim concerns *present* truth-claims.[22] The ideal consensus might be understood, not in terms of an actual sequence of future theories, but as an ideal that impinges equally upon all points of time and upon all temporary conceptual frameworks. For in terms of the debate between Popperian realism and Kuhnian paradigm-change, Habermas accepts the Kuhnian insight that actual languages and conceptual schemes change, but against Kuhn he does not accept that this results in a relativity of truth. For within the domain of empirical science, truth is a demand and a commitment *now*, which must entail abstraction from local *interests*, but cannot involve abstraction from the particularity of the local conceptual schemes in terms of which true propositions must be expressed. We may usefully compare Habermas's discussion of 'ideal history' in his review of Gadamer's *Truth and Method*.[23] Here he quotes Danto's view that historiography is a necessarily incomplete enterprise, because every historical narration incorporates judgements derived from *subsequent* events, including the 'meaning' of the narrated events in the context for which the historian writes. There cannot be any ideal 'last historian', according to Danto, because the historian's own writing of history is itself a historical event, the progress of which will itself in principle have to be written into the significance of all narrated past events, and so on. On the contrary, says Habermas, *every historian is his or her own last historian:* every historian *anticipates* the future in order to complete a story; every history includes a viewpoint on the nature and destiny of the world.

The point becomes more intelligible in the light of the scientific parallel. Every theory making truth-claims in a particular conceptual framework includes its own 'anticipations' of the total nature of the world as far as it is relevant to that theory. The commitment to anticipated consensus is the commitment to abandon falsified positions, and also to abandon conceptual schemes that do not lead to consensus. There is no last theory or theorist in the sense that science stops there, forever frozen in whatever conceptual scheme happens to be then current. But every serious theory and sincere theorist is 'the last', in the sense that *that* is where the accountability in the face of ideal consensus operates for him or her. To enter the scientific community presupposes acceptance of that accountability.

If this is the correct interpretation of Habermas's intentions, then the 'truth' of any particular theoretical framework will be in one sense culturally relative and in another sense not. *Given* a commitment to technical interest and the abandonment of empirically falsified positions, truth-judgements are relative to whatever theoretical framework emerges in the culture. But the issue between, for instance, Newton and the witches is a deeper one, for this involves a judgement about the empirical commitment itself. The superior truth-claim of Newton's theory has to appeal to a difference between a society in which the norm of empirical commitment is accepted and one in which it is not, and the judgement in favour of Newton must be justified at this level by the 'anticipation' of consensus about the normative character of the scientific attitude as such.

Objective, reconstructive and critical science
The characteristic feature of the 'objective' sciences as Habermas describes them is that they are not *reflective*. In the 'Postscript' Habermas remarks that he had previously used 'reflection' ambiguously to mean two different things:[24]

(i) There can be reflection upon the conditions of knowing as such, as in Kantian epistemology. This now becomes assimilated to programmes of *rational reconstruction,* for example analyses of rule-following in connection with social forms of life, potentially including ethics, and of conditions of competence in language-use and in logic. Unlike Kantian analyses, these presuppose intersubjectivity and abstract from the transcendental subject.

(ii) On the other hand, the Hegelian tradition developed reflection as *critique* of unconsciously produced constraints, for example Marx's critique of and emancipation from false consciousness, and Freud's disclosure of unconscious psychic distortions.

Several important distinctions between reconstructive and critical sciences follow:

(a) Reconstructive sciences have as data objective sentences and actions that are conscious creations of persons – thus their object domain is similar to that of the hermeneutic sciences. On the other hand, critical sciences have for their subject-matter 'pseudo-objects', things that are not what they seem, for example the contents of false consciousness which need unmasking, and neurotic splits of consciousness.

(b) Reconstructive sciences are general, since they concern rules of general competence that are independent of particular circumstances. Critical sciences, on the other hand, because they concern particular distortions, necessarily bear on particular individuals and groups.

(c) Reconstructive sciences explicate intuitive know-how that has been abstracted from practice – in Wittgenstein's terms they 'leave everything as it is'. They therefore, presumably, form part of discourse and share the truth-seeking functions of objective theoretical science, but without relation to technical interest. They have in this sense the status of 'pure' knowledge, which has always been the claim of logic and transcendental philosophy. Critical sciences, on the other hand, have the practical aim of changing things, whether society or the individual psyche. They are not 'neutral' since they study *deviations*: 'a critical science like psychoanalysis "must rely upon a theoretical framework which exists independently of its clinical technique, and *its* criteria of validation"'. [25] But the theoretical framework cannot be that of objectivating science, since it presupposes ordinary human knowledge of what it is to have undistorted human communication, that is, it depends on judgements of norms which cannot be given without circularity in empirical science.

So far I have attempted to explain the distinctions between the three kinds of science more or less in Habermas's own words. But their definitions lead to questions which bear also on his view of the distinction between the empirical and the human sciences. First, it is clear that the new distinction is not the same as the original empirical/hermeneutic/critical trichotomy that appeared in *KHI*. For one thing, that has been superseded by the related distinction between action and discourse. Moreover, the discussion of the *two* (not three) modes of constituting the object domains of action (namely, things and interacting persons) makes it clear that critical science does not have its own object domain, but is rather the result of reflection upon and critique of the other two. In the new account the reconstructive sciences seem to constitute an additional dimension, distinct from empirical, hermeneutic and critical sciences respectively. I shall suggest, however, that Habermas tends to overemphasise the distinctions, particularly between the empirical and reconstructive sciences. This suggestion is not made for the positivist reason that all science should be reducible to empirical science, but for the opposite reason that an empirical science can be seen to share the characteristics of the other types of science in some degree when it is described more adequately than is done in positivism.

In his discussion of the reconstructive sciences, Habermas finds that the primary question at issue is whether linguistics shares the principal characteristics of empirical science, namely its relation to the observable object domain and its capacity for theoretical *re*interpretation of that domain. He takes Chomsky's distinction between 'competence' and 'performance' to indicate that linguistics is not a science in the empirical sense. This is because competence, unlike performance, is not a behavioural concept, but is rather a 'know-how' that expresses an underlying structure of language that has to be reconstructed by eliciting speakers' intuitions. The relation between linguistic theory and data is therefore different in Habermas's view from the relation between scientific theory and data. In the latter case data may be radically reinterpreted by changing theoretical frameworks, but in the former case ordinary language is definitive – it is the structure of ordinary language that is being explicated or reconstructed, and there is no reverse feedback effect from theory upon the speaker's competence. It should be noticed that when Habermas says 'A proposal for reconstruction . . . can represent pretheoretical knowledge more or less explicitly and adequately, but it can never falsify it',[26] by contrast with the logic of empirical science, he may easily be misunderstood as holding that linguistic theory is not falsifiable *by* linguistic data. But this of course is not the case; linguistic theory is based on eliciting competence from performance and speakers' intuitions, and its categories are subject to tests by these data as with every other theoretical science. What Habermas is saying follows from the more sophisticated view of science that he described as the second defence by positivism of its essentially reductionist thesis, namely that science is *re*interpretative of ordinary experience because descriptions of experience are always theory-laden. Science changes our interpretation of, for example, the fundamental nature of matter, but his claim is that linguistics does not change our interpretation of linguistic competence in speaking, for example, English; it merely explicates what is given, though its structure is hidden within behavioural performance.

This distinction seems to me to be overdrawn, and, because it has important consequences for Habermas's views about the 'transcendental' character of the human-action framework as a whole, it is worth developing the point a little further. First, it should be noticed that when Carnap introduced his concept of 'explication' of ordinary language terms, such as (for example) 'probability', he did not deny that the disambiguation and systematic logical analysis of such terms might in turn change their use in ordinary language. It was Wittgenstein who finally broke with the Russellian programme of reconstruction of ordinary language with his dictum that 'philosophy should leave everything as it is'. But ordinary language is in any case a constantly changing phenomenon, and logical analysis may quite well be one of the agents of change. This may especially be the case where the 'ordinary language' involved is that of talk about human action. Habermas draws an analogy from the reconstruction of grammatical competence to the reconstruction of the rules and norms of social action in, for example, the philosophy of ethics. But it is surely clear that both scientific and philosophical reconstruction of concepts like human freedom and responsibility may have, indeed have had, radical effects upon the interpretations put upon 'ordinary' discourse about guilt, punishment, deviance and sickness. One has only to think of changes in attitudes towards sexual 'deviations', 'juvenile delinquency', and 'diminished responsibility' in general. 'Reconstruction' *may* feed back into its data, just as theoretical science may.

On the other hand, the reinterpretation of data by theory in science must not itself be exaggerated. It is ironic that this should now be taken by Habermas as the paradigm of *change*, where positivism saw 'the data' as the paradigm of the unchanging given. Neither view is totally adequate, for empirical science cannot be understood without some element of the given which remains resistant to changing interpretations. This is what Habermas himself recognises as pragmatic meaning, and what I called earlier the residual element of correspondence truth. Technical interest ensures a certain continuity in empirical science just as practical human interests do in the use of ordinary language, but neither is immutable.

The second difficulty about Habermas's description of reconstructive science is that it seems to presuppose that there is just one correct explication of linguistic competence, of logic, of human action, and even of theory of science and ethics. This claim is connected with the assertion that the reconstructive sciences are value-neutral and interest-free. But we have seen that even if the empirical sciences were totally interest-free (which I am shortly going to deny), this would not imply uniqueness of their theoretical frameworks. It is therefore difficult to conceive of such uniqueness in reconstructive sciences. Moreover, its possibility is not borne out by the facts – even logical theory is permeated by ideological preferences. Chomsky's version of structural linguistics has not by any means won universal acceptance, and neither has Piaget's developmental psychology; much less have the various attempts at systematising 'human-action' terminology or the theory of ethics. Even Habermas himself has suggested that Chomsky is mistaken if he thinks *universalistic* theories of linguistic competence can be ideologically neutral.[27] Reconstructive sciences, like empirical sciences, are subject to changing theoretical frameworks and, like hermeneutics and critical science, they are subject to changing ideologies.

There is a third difficulty that relates to the question of the value-neutrality of both empirical and reconstructive sciences. As I have remarked above, scientific *theories* cannot be wholly value-neutral or independent of their local ideologies. Since they are not wholly determined by empirical data, they must share to some extent the norms, presuppositions and prejudices of their own culture. *A fortiori*, this will also be true of the reconstructive sciences, which share the value commitments of critical sciences just because, unlike empirical science, they have human language and action as their subject-matter.

If the distinction between reconstructive and empirical sciences can be dissolved by these considerations, this poses serious questions for Habermas's claim that the human-action framework is not up for modification either by theoretical science or by ideological critique. He has suggested three positions that may be taken in relation to this claim:

(1) The *displacement hypothesis*, that is, the view that the human-action framework *is* reducible to current scientific theory and may be reinterpreted and modified with it. Against this position Habermas marshals anti-reductionist and particularly anti-behaviourist arguments. The applications of these arguments will, however, be limited by the objections I raised above to his radical distinctions between reconstructive and empirical science. Also, I have argued elsewhere [28] that it is doubtful whether such arguments can be conclusive in principle, though they may certainly be regarded as cogent in practice, that is, we have not, and are not likely to have in any foreseeable future, any empirically reductive theory of the totality of human action. Thus for present purposes Habermas's rejection of this kind of reductionism may be accepted.

(2) *Decisionism*. This is the name Habermas gives to the view that our current human-action framework is *chosen* more or less reflectively on the basis of values and norms held in our society, but that it is not intrinsically universal, much less *a priori*. Habermas objects to the apparent arbitrariness and relativity of this position, and attempts to rebut it by development of what he calls 'universal pragmatics' – the theory (which itself claims to be reconstructive) of the universal conditions of human communication and interaction. However, his discussion of the scientistic 'systems theories' of Luhmann and others indicates that he does not rule out the *a priori* possibility that a different human-action framework might be chosen in current social circumstances, namely the view of persons (other than the

planners) as fodder for a scientifically planned society. If Habermas's claim for his universal pragmatics is correct, it seems that such a scientistic programme would be subject to internal contradictions in some way that the 'Enlightenment' understanding of human action is not. It would of course be in conflict with the ideal speech situation. But since the justification for *this* appears to depend on assumptions about what must be presupposed in any human use of language, it cannot be appealed to without circularity to show that the scientistic programme runs into logical contradiction. To show this is to show that ideal speech is in some sense transcendental, and Habermas's attempts to show this still fall short of cogent demonstration.[29] Unless it can be shown, however, it seems that 'decisionism', with all its undesirable relativities, remains the most adequate account of the reflective human reason. Properly developed, it seems to be the account that best captures the Enlightenment ideal of relatively autonomous individual reason and individual will, without being committed to deny that natural and social structures put constraints upon that autonomy.

(3) *Transformed transcendentalism*. This is Habermas's preferred position, which is situated somewhere between *naturalism* and *a priorism*. That is to say, he seeks a theory of the human-action framework which is not transcendental in the Kantian sense, but which nevertheless is not *just* a description of contingent, though *de facto* universal, features of the evolution of the human species. But unless he can make out a stronger case for the distinctiveness of the 'pure' reconstructive sciences, this position remains unclear and the arguments for it circular.

Summary
In conclusion let me summarise the points of comment and criticism that I have made:

(1) Habermas appears to reject any element of empirical 'correspondence' in his theory of the justification of truth-claims, and to rely upon a theory of argumentation and consensus. But it remains unclear how the empirical constraint operates in the justification of truth-claims for descriptive utterance, either in science or in ordinary language, and in particular it is unclear how this constraint is related to the concept of 'consensus' truth within discourse.

(2) Habermas has argued convincingly that an instrumental interpretation of science is inconsistent with the view of theory as a redescription of the empirical world within theoretical categories, with its consequences for the theory-ladenness of empirical statements. But this argument does not exclude the possibility of instrumental interpretation of higher-level theoretical postulates that remain underdetermined by the empirical. It therefore does not follow, as Habermas contends, that truth-claims are necessarily made at all levels of a theoretical system. A question remains

about how to place the non-empirical criteria for acceptability of theories in Habermas's scheme for a universal pragmatics. In particular, is a degree of relativity of theoretical frameworks to cultural background acceptable in Habermas's theory, even when the ideal speech situation is realised? And what is the relation between such frameworks and the norms of practical action such as are incorporated in pre-scientific cosmologies?

(3) Habermas's distinction between the empirical and reconstructive sciences rests in part upon the thesis that the data of empirical sciences are always open to reinterpretation by theory, whereas the data of sciences dependent upon 'ordinary language' are not. But his account seems to exaggerate both the mutability of interpretations of empirical data, and also the immutability of ordinary language. Again, it is not clear that the theories of reconstructive sciences can be 'pure' and ideology-free any more than can empirical theories.

(4) This brings into question also Habermas's contention that the human-action framework is necessarily invariant with respect to changes of empirical science and immune to ideological critique. His transcendental arguments for this framework are not cogent enough to evade the dilemma of untenable *a priorism* on the one hand, and unacceptable *relativism* on the other.

6

Universal Pragmatics

JOHN B. THOMPSON

In recent years, the writings of Jürgen Habermas have become increasingly concerned with the development of a programme of 'universal pragmatics'.[1] Although the details of this programme remain in an unfinished form, the over-all aim is clear: to investigate the general competencies required for the successful performance of speech-acts, and thereby 'to reconstruct the universal validity basis of speech'.[2] The supposition is that such a reconstruction will in turn provide a foundation for the critique of ideology, in so far as ideology can be conceived as communication systematically distorted by the exercise of power. This attempt to establish a normative foundation for critical theory through a reconstructive analysis of everyday speech may at first appear somewhat surprising. For even though language has been a focal point of investigation for many years, it is still a topic about which there is a great deal of disagreement and dispute. Nevertheless, Habermas has proposed an original and provocative programme which demands more attention than it has sometimes received in the Anglo-American literature.[3] My hope is that the following essay will go some way towards meeting this demand. I shall begin by situating Habermas's writings on language within the context of his social theory as a whole, indicating a few of the respects in which his earlier views have been transformed by his more recent work. The second part of the essay presents an exposition of some of the central themes of universal pragmatics. In the third part, I select four of these themes and submit them to a critical examination. Finally, in the concluding part of the essay I consider some general issues and offer some constructive remarks, with the aim of indicating ways in which the obstacles encountered by Habermas's programme might be overcome.

I

The emphases and aims of universal pragmatics can be discerned throughout Habermas's earlier work. In common with other authors in the Frankfurt tradition, Habermas has always opposed the reductionist tendencies which characterise the more orthodox versions of Marxism. He expresses this opposition by insisting that a society develops not only in the dimension of technological innovation and labour but also in the dimension of communicative interaction; and however close the connection between these dimensions may be, 'there is no automatic developmental relation between labor and interaction'.[4] Communicative interaction is an autonomous sphere in which cultural traditions are historically transmitted and social relations are institutionally organised. The concern with this sphere brings Habermas into contact with hermeneutics and ordinary language philosophy. He praises these approaches for stressing the way in which language is constitutive of social and historical phenomena, but criticises their tendency to idealise this constitutive role. For language itself is dependent upon social processes which are not wholly linguistic in nature; it is, Habermas insists, '*also* a medium of domination and social force'.[5] So although the interpretation of symbolic formations may presuppose a 'deep common accord', as Gadamer maintains, one must not preclude the possibility that the latter is a consensus falsely induced by the unacknowledged exercise of power. In such cases the 'common accord' is not so much the prior condition of communication but rather the ultimate conclusion. Hence a critical theory must undertake to show both in what sense a common accord can be presupposed and operative in spite of the distorted conditions under which communication actually occurs, and in what way these distorted conditions can be explicated and criticised in the name of a consensus whose realisation is perpetually postponed.

The importance of an inquiry into the foundations of language is similarly underlined by the studies collected in *Knowledge and Human Interests*. In these studies Habermas seeks to distinguish three categories of scientific disciplines in terms of their respective knowledge-constitutive interests, which in the case of the critical social sciences is called the *interest in emancipation*. Thus in a discipline like psychoanalysis the reconstruction of developmental processes yields depth interpretations which can be corroborated if and only if patients willingly accept them as their own, thereby freeing themselves from dependence upon unrecognised constraints. Similarly, critical social science is concerned with identifying and dissolving relations of power and ideology in such a way that, in the end, 'knowledge coincides with the fulfillment of the interest in liberation through knowledge'.[6] Yet does not this alleged coincidence of knowledge and interest merely conceal the partisanship involved in the exercise of practical critique? What assurance have we that the interpretations offered by critical theory are any less ideological than the ideologies which they claim to expose? In short, how could it be established that the emancipatory interest, which Habermas places at the very heart of the critical enterprise, is anything other than pure fiction?[7] The outline of an answer to these and similar questions may be found in Habermas's 1965 Inaugural Lecture: 'The human interest in autonomy and responsibility is not mere fancy, for it can be apprehended *a priori*. What raises us out of nature is the only thing whose nature we can know: language.'[8] Habermas's subsequent work on the theory of language may be regarded as a sustained attempt to develop and defend this embryonic answer.

Despite the early anticipations of universal pragmatics, the latter programme is premissed upon two distinctions which mark a significant modification of Habermas's original views. The first of these distinctions is concerned with the concept of self-reflection, which is perhaps the central concept of *Knowledge and Human Interests*. In the 1973 'Postscript' to the latter volume, Habermas observes that this concept encompasses and conflates two elements, an element of reconstruction and an element of critique.[9] Reflection in the sense of reconstruction refers to the quasi-Kantian exercise of elucidating the conditions which render possible a form of knowledge or a mode of action. In recent years this type of reflection has been rehabilitated on a linguistic basis, assuming the form of a rational reconstruction of systems of rules which are necessarily drawn upon in everyday speech. Since these reconstructions seek merely to represent what is always and already operative, they constitute a type of knowledge which 'has always claimed a special status: that of "pure" knowledge';[10] and hence they fall outside of the epistemological scheme presented in *Knowledge and Human Interests*. Reflection in the sense of critique, on the other hand, is concerned with subjectively produced illusions that objectively constrain the social actor. Unlike the anonymous systems of rules which are the object of rational reconstruction, these illusions appertain to the particular self-formative process of an individual or group; and the critical dissolution of such illusions leads to the emancipation of the subject from previously unconscious constraints. However, the explicit distinction between reconstruction and critique does not imply that these two types of self-reflection are unrelated. On the contrary, a discipline which aspires to a critical stance cannot avoid, in Habermas's view, the exercise of rational reconstruction. For if critique 'accepts as its task the explanation of a systematically distorted communication, then it must have the mastery of the idea of undistorted communication or reasonable discourse';[11] and unfolding the idea of undistorted communication is the reconstructive task of universal pragmatics.

The second distinction underlying universal pragmatics also marks a departure from Habermas's earlier views. A central theme of *Knowledge and Human Interests* is that the logical-methodological rules for the conduct of the various sciences are linked to an interest structure which is rooted in the self-formative process of the human species, and which prejudges both the possible objects of scientific analysis and the possible meaning of the validity of scientific statements. However, in the 1973 'Postscript', Habermas concedes the criticism that this thesis is too strong:

it threatens to reduce the objectivity of the sciences to an anthropology of interests. Habermas proposes to avert this threat by introducing a distinction between action and discourse. 'Action' refers to everyday contexts of social interaction, in which information is acquired through sensory experience and exchanged through ordinary language. 'Discourse', on the other hand, designates a realm of communication which is abstracted from the contexts of everyday life. The participants of a discourse are concerned, not to perform actions or to share experiences, but rather to search for arguments and justifications; and the only motive allowed in this search is 'a co-operative readiness to arrive at an understanding'.[12] In the light of this distinction Habermas can maintain that, while the object domains of the sciences are differentially constituted by the interests which operate at the level of action, the validity-claims which these sciences raise are subject to the unitary conditions of discursive argumentation. For the objectivity attainable by science is based upon a suspension of action constraints, and this alone 'permits a discursive testing of *hypothetical* claims to validity and thus the generation of *rationally grounded* knowledge'.[13] Precisely how the validity-claims implicitly raised in action contexts can be rationally redeemed in discourse is a question which will be considered in due course.

II

Habermas introduces the programme of universal pragmatics by indicating the limitations of other approaches to language. In the dominant schools of linguistics and formal semantics, the object domain is constituted by an initial abstraction from the performative aspects of speech. Chomsky's focus on 'linguistic competence', and his tendency to treat 'performance' as an empirically limited outcome of the latter, is a case in point. Linguistic competence is conceptualised as a 'monological capability . . . founded in the species specific equipment of the solitary human organism'.[14] If this capability is to provide an adequate basis for the communicative process, then the latter in turn must be reconstructible in monological terms; and it is precisely this, Habermas contends, that cannot be done. For 'in order to participate in normal discourse, the speaker must have – in addition to his linguistic competence – basic qualifications of speech and of symbolic interaction (role-behavior) at his disposal, which we may call communicative competence'.[15] Accordingly, the analysis of language must be extended to include an investigation of the qualifications which enable a speaker, not simply to produce grammatically well-formed sentences, but to embed these sentences in successful speech-acts. Only then can the gulf be bridged between the generative competencies of speaking and acting subjects on the one hand, and the pragmatic features of concrete speech situations on the other.

The performative aspects of speech have been explored in considerable depth by the so-called 'ordinary language philosophers', such as Austin,

Searle and the later Wittgenstein. Rejecting his earlier conception of language as a formal system of representation, the later Wittgenstein turns towards a detailed examination of the ways in which expressions are actually used in everyday language-games. This is a change of emphasis with which Habermas is wholly sympathetic; but his reservation is that 'in Wittgenstein and his disciples, the logical analysis of the use of language always remained particularistic; they failed to develop it into a *theory of language games*'.[16] The elements of a more general theory can be found, Habermas suggests, in the various writings concerned with the notion of speech-act. Austin introduces this notion in order to draw attention to the fact that in uttering a sentence a person may also be performing an action and not just reporting or describing an event. Indeed even in the case of reporting and describing, as Austin subsequently points out, saying something is also doing something. Hence the way is prepared for a theory of language which would take the speech-act as its basic unit, and which would proceed to analyse and categorise its primary forms. Habermas thus regards the contributions of Austin, Searle, Strawson and others as a congenial starting-point for his programme. They are, however, only a starting-point, for they 'do not generalize radically enough and do not push through the level of accidental contexts to general and unavoidable presuppositions'.[17] Universal pragmatics therefore seeks to elucidate those performative aspects of speech which are presupposed by the ability to utter, not any particular speech-act, but speech-acts as such.

The general presuppositions of speech can be initially uncovered through an analysis of speech-acts in the 'standard form'. Such speech-acts exhibit the essential features of communicative action; and the latter, conceived dynamically as 'action oriented towards reaching an understanding' *(verständigungsorientierten Handelns)*, is regarded by Habermas as the basic type of social action.[18] The standard form can be represented by the schema 'I . . . (verb) . . . you that . . . (sentence)', or by a simple variant thereof. A speech-act which satisfies this form thus possesses a distinctive double structure. It comprises, on the one hand, an illocutionary element specified by a performative sentence in the first person present indicative with a direct object in the second person; and, on the other hand, a propositional component which contains referring and predicative expressions. The propositional component can remain invariant throughout changes in the illocutionary element, so that speech-acts in the standard form may be said to be 'propositionally differentiated out'. In Habermas's view, this internal differentiation of the standard speech-act reflects two levels upon which the speaker and hearer must move if they wish to communicate: '(a) the level of intersubjectivity, upon which the speaker/ hearer communicate *with one another;* and (b) the level of objects, *about* which they come to an understanding'.[19] The question then arises as to how the issuance of a speech-act can result in the establishment of an intersubjective relation. How is one to account for the specific *engagement* which the speaker enters into when uttering a speech-act, and which enables the hearer to rely upon the person who speaks? In the case of speech-acts which are closely connected with other social conventions, this engagement may be derivable from the validity of established norms; but what about 'institutionally unbound speech-acts', which in this respect must be regarded as the more fundamental case? In reply to such questions, Habermas submits that the relevant commitments can be accounted for only on the assumption that certain validity-claims are implicitly raised and reciprocally recognised with the utterance of every speech-act. 'In the final analysis, the speaker can illocutionarily influence the hearer and vice versa, because speech-act-typical commitments are connected with cognitively testable validity claims – that is, because the reciprocal bonds have a rational basis.'[20]

The rational basis which underlies the illocutionary force of a speech-act consists of four distinguishable validity-claims. In issuing an utterance, the speaker implicitly claims that what is said is intelligible (*verständlich*), that the propositional content is true (*wahr*), that the performative component is correct (*richtig*), and that intentions are being expressed sincerely (*wahrhaftig*). These four validity-claims, which 'competent speakers must reciprocally maintain with each of their speech-acts',[21] constitute the background consensus of normally functioning language-games. The consensus can be shaken by calling into question one or more of the claims, in which case the continuation of communicative action is dependent upon whether the relevant claim can be redeemed. The intelligibility of an utterance can be challenged by questions such as 'What does that mean?' or 'How should I understand that?' The answers to these questions are to be found in the structure of language itself; for intelligibility, in the sense of grammatical well-formedness, is a factual condition rather than a counter-factual claim of communication. The sincerity of the speaker can be impugned with questions like 'Is this person deceiving me?' or 'Is this person pretending?' These questions can only be answered by the subsequent course of interaction, for whether or not someone is expressing intentions sincerely will eventually show itself in actions. Finally, the truth of a propositional content or the correctness of a performatory component can be placed in doubt with questions such as 'Is it really as you say it is?' or 'Is it right to do what you have done?' Habermas maintains that these questions cannot be fully answered within the context of communicative action; rather, they raise 'claims of validity which can be proven only in discourse'.[22] The formal features of the discursive realm, and hence the conditions under which the claims to truth and correctness can be redeemed, are specifiable in terms of the pragmatic universals which every communicatively competent speaker must possess.

The ability to embed grammatically well-formed sentences in speech-acts presupposes, according to Habermas, that speakers have at their disposal a series of 'pragmatic' or 'dialogue-constitutive universals'. These universals are intersubjective, *a priori* linguistic elements which enable the speaker, in the course of producing a speech-act, to reproduce the general structures of the speech situation. The universals are not merely a linguistic articulation of pre-existing conditions, but rather are the very elements which establish these conditions. For 'without reference to these universals, we could not even define the recurrent components of possible speech: namely the expressions themselves, and then the interpersonal relations between speakers/hearers which are generated with the expressions, and finally the objects about which the speakers/hearers communicate with one another'.[23] Habermas proposes several categories of expressions which function as pragmatic universals.[24] First, the personal pronouns and their derivatives form a reference system between potential speakers, enabling each participant to assume the roles of 'I' and 'You' simultaneously and thereby securing the intersubjective validity of semantic rules. Second, the deictic expressions of space and time, as well as the articles and demonstrative pronouns, form a reference system of possible denotations, linking the plane of intersubjectivity upon which subjects interact with the plane of objects about which they converse. Third, the performative verbs, as well as non-performative intentional verbs and some model adverbs, form a system of possible speech-acts which enables the subject to draw certain distinctions and express certain relations 'which are fundamental for any speech situation'.[25] Habermas's contention is that the ability to enter into a conversation presupposes that subjects could deploy these various types of expression, thereby displaying the mastery of pragmatic universals which defines their communicative competence.

In developing this proposal, Habermas concentrates on the performative verbs in the third category of pragmatic universals. He seeks to show that these verbs may be divided into four basic classes; and since every speech-act in the standard form exhibits such a verb, the demonstration may be expected to provide 'a systematic account for the classification of speech acts'.[26] The first class is the 'communicatives' (to say, to ask, etc.), which are directed at the process of communication as such, and which facilitate the distinction between meaning and the fluctuating signs wherein it is expressed. The second class, the 'constatives' (to assert, to describe, etc.), are concerned with the cognitive application of sentences, enabling a subject to differentiate between a public world of being and a private world of appearance. 'Representatives' (to admit, to conceal, etc.) constitute the third class; these verbs serve to express the intentions, attitudes and feelings of the speaker, thereby making possible the distinction between the individuated self and the expressions in which it appears. The fourth class is the 'regulatives' (to order, to prohibit, etc.), which refer to norms that can be followed or broken, and which thus mark a distinction between empirical regularities and valid rules. This fourfold classification can be combined with the typology of validity-claims to yield a general model of linguistic communication. Even though all four validity-claims are implicitly raised with every speech-act, nevertheless a speaker can explicitly thematise a particular claim by employing a speech-act from one of the above classes.[27] In so doing, the subject expressly articulates one of the four regions of reality which 'must always simultaneously appear'[28] in the utterance of a successful speech-act: namely, the regions of external nature, society, internal nature and language. The general model of communication which thus emerges from Habermas's work may be summarised as in Table 6.1.

TABLE 6.1

Domains of reality	Modes of communication	Types of speech-act	Themes	Validity-claims	General functions of speech
'The' world of external nature	Cognitive: objectivating attitude	Constatives	Propositional content	Truth	Representation of facts
'Our' world of society	Interactive: conformative attitude	Regulatives	Interpersonal relation	Correctness	Establishment of legitimate social relations
'My' world of internal nature	Expressive: expressive attitude	Representatives	Speaker's intention	Sincerity	Disclosure of speaker's subjectivity
Language	—	Communicatives	—	Intelligibility	—

Source: adapted from 'What is Universal Pragmatics', pp. 58, 68.

The pragmatic universals which communicatively competent speakers have at their disposal provide the means for the construction of an ideal speech situation. The latter situation is characterised by 'pure intersubjectivity', that is, by the absence of any barrier which would obstruct the process of communication. In addition to contingent forces which impinge upon the situation from without, such barriers include the constraints which are produced by the structure of communication itself; and Habermas proceeds on the basis of the following assumption: 'the structure of communication itself produces no constraints if and only if, for all possible participants, there is a symmetrical distribution of chances to choose and to apply speech-acts'.[29] The assumption of symmetry forms the general framework of the ideal speech situation, allowing the latter to be specified further in terms of the four classes of speech-acts. Equality in the opportunity to apply communicatives means that all potential participants have the same chance to initiate and sustain discussion through questions and answers, claims and counter-claims. A symmetrical distribution of chances to apply constatives implies that all potential participants have the same opportunity to proffer interpretations and explanations, so that no preconceptions remain excluded from view. An equal opportunity to apply representatives gives all potential participants the same chance to express intentions and attitudes, creating the circumstances in which subjects become transparent to themselves and others in what they say and do. Finally, symmetry in the distribution of chances to apply regulatives entails that all potential participants have the same opportunity to order and prohibit, to obey and refuse, thereby precluding the privileges that arise from one-sided norms. The situation thus portrayed is, of course, an ideal; the conditions of empirical speech are not generally identical with those of the ideal speech situation. 'Nevertheless it belongs to the structure of possible speech', writes Habermas, 'that in the execution of speech-acts (and actions) we contrafactually proceed as if the ideal speech situation . . . were not merely fictive but real – precisely what we call a presupposition'.[30]

The claims of truth and correctness implicitly raised in communicative action can be redeemed in discourses which have the structure of an ideal speech situation. For truth and correctness, in Habermas's view, are concepts that can be analysed in terms of the discursive justification of validity-claims. A statement is true when the validity-claim of the speech-act with which it is asserted is justified; and the validity-claim is justified, according to Habermas, if and only if the statement would command the consent of anyone who could enter into a discussion with the speaker. 'The condition for the truth of statements is the potential consent of all others . . . Truth means the promise to attain a rational consensus.'[31] The circumstances under which a consensus holds as rational, and *ipso facto* as true, are precisely those of the ideal speech situation. Similarly, just as truth may be regarded as a validity-claim redeemable in an ideally structured theoretical discourse, so too correctness may be conceived as a claim which can be redeemed in a discourse of a practical nature. Hence Habermas rejects empiricist and decisionist approaches to ethics, which share the assumption that moral controversies cannot, in the last analysis, be rationally resolved. The formal properties of the discursive situation establish the conditions under which a rational consensus can be attained concerning a problematicised value or norm. Moreover, to the extent that such a consensus marks a divergence from the institutional arrangements which exist in fact, it follows that the results of practical discourse stand in a critical relation to the social world. The exercise of this critique *must* be undertaken in so far as the ideal speech situation is necessarily anticipated in every act of speech; and it *can* be undertaken in so far as every competent speaker possesses the means to construct such a situation, however distorted the actual conditions of speech may be. 'On this unavoidable fiction', submits Habermas, 'rests the humanity of relations among men who are still men.'[32]

III

The central contours of universal pragmatics have now been sketched; the extent to which they accurately reflect the linguistic terrain remains to be assessed. The programme initiated by Habermas seeks to establish, among other things, the following theses: (1) that the utterance of a speech-act implicitly raises four validity-claims; (2) that communicatively competent speakers have at their disposal a series of pragmatic universals; (3) that an ideal speech situation, which can be constructed in terms of pragmatic universals, is presupposed in everyday speech; and (4) that truth is a validity-claim that can be rationally redeemed in a discourse having the structure of an ideal speech situation. In the following sections I shall examine each of these theses in turn, reconstructing and criticising the arguments upon which they rest. I hope thereby to clarify a few of the issues which are raised by Habermas's programme, and to show that some of his contributions are, at least, in need of further defence.

The first thesis rests upon an argument which may be summarised as follows:

(i)   Every speech-act in the standard form contains an illocutionary component, represented by a performative sentence, and a propositional content which is differentiated out.

(ii)   The differentiation of the standard speech-act reflects two levels which are involved in communication: the level of intersubjectivity and the level of objects; a successful speech-act results in the establishment of a relation in which at least two subjects come to an understanding about a state of affairs.

(iii)   The establishment of such a relation can be accounted for only on the assumption that four validity-claims are implicitly raised and reciprocally recognised with the utterance of every speech-act.

The major justification for restricting the analysis to speech-acts in the 'standard form' may be found in Habermas's interpretation of Searle's principle of expressibility. According to Habermas, the principle can be reformulated as follows: 'for every interpersonal relation that a speaker wants to take up explicitly with another member of his language community, a suitable performative expression is either available or, if necessary, can be introduced through a specification of available expressions'.[33] However, even supposing that every interpersonal relation could be articulated in terms of an appropriate speech-act, it is by no means clear that the illocutionary force of the speech-act could be represented by a 'suitable performative expression'. The latter view is apparently indebted to the so-called 'performative hypothesis' of Ross, McCawley and others, a hypothesis which has been thoroughly and justly criticised in the linguistic and philosophical literature.[34] For it is not obvious what performative expression could capture the illocutionary forces involved in many indirect speech-acts, such as the distinctive *mélange* of question and request in 'Don't you think the rubbish is beginning to smell?'; [35] nor is it apparent how the performative schema 'I . . . (verb) . . . you' is to deal with more complex cases of personal pronominalisation, as may be found, for example, with reflexive verbs. Considerations such as these do not vitiate Habermas's positive programme, but they do cast some doubt upon his grounds for restricting the analysis to speech-acts in the 'standard form'.

The problematic nature of the restriction becomes increasingly evident in the third stage of the argument. There is considerable plausibility in the suggestion that when a speaker utters a speech-act, the audience is generally entitled to assume that the speaker is sincere, that he or she takes what is said to be true, and so on. There is also a clear continuity between the claims which Habermas identifies and the conditions which Searle proposes for the successful performance of a speech-act. However, it seems to me implausible and misleading to contend, as Habermas does, that all four validity-claims are necessarily raised with the utterance of *every* speech-act. In what sense does reading a poem, telling a joke, or greeting a friend presuppose the truth of what is said? Is not sincerity characteristically suspended rather than presupposed by the participants in a process of collective bargaining, or by friends engaged in the light-hearted activity of 'taking the mickey'? In what sense, precisely, does the utterance of a sentence like 'The sky is blue this morning' raise a claim to correctness which is clearly distinguishable from its intelligibility or its truth? Habermas may be right to criticise Austin for working with an undifferentiated notion of 'objective assessment'; but Habermas in turn seems mistaken to maintain that the various claims which he discerns in this notion are necessarily raised with every speech-act, albeit in an implicit and unthematic form. No doubt Habermas would deny that the above instances constitute counter-examples to his thesis, insisting instead that they must be treated as subsidiary forms of communication, as mere 'derivatives' of action orientated towards reaching an understanding. Yet such a reply would simply assume what must be shown, namely that orientation towards understanding is the basic aim of communication. So long as this assumption remains unsubstantiated, hence so far as the justification for restricting the analysis to speech-acts in the 'standard form' remains problematic, then so too the extent to which Habermas's programme qualifies as a *universal* pragmatics must be held in doubt.

A second thesis which can be elicited from Habermas's writings is that communicatively competent speakers have a series of pragmatic universals at their disposal. The argument underlying this thesis may be roughly reconstructed as follows:

(i)   The ability to enter into a conversation implies that the speaker is able (a) to relate to a world of subjects, (b) to relate to a world of objects, and (c) to draw certain fundamental distinctions.
(ii) These abilities presuppose that the speaker has mastery of (a) personal pronouns and their derivatives, (b) deictic expressions and demonstrative pronouns, and (c) performative verbs and certain intentional expressions.
(iii) The mastery of specific types of performative verbs enables the speaker to draw the distinctions which are fundamental for the speech situation; this link, together with the differential thematisation of validity-claims, provides a principle for the classification of speech-acts.

Habermas's thesis concerning pragmatic universals must be regarded as one of the more speculative aspects of his recent work. The volume of essays edited by Greenberg, to which Habermas sometimes refers in this context, is of a highly provisional and exploratory nature; and some of the inconsistencies which characterise the volume have been pointed out by subsequent authors.[36] Cases have often been made for the universality of deictic elements and personal pronouns, but there is considerably less support for the third category proposed by Habermas. Since it is the latter category which is particularly important for the construction of the ideal speech situation, it is worth investigating the relevant argument in more detail.

  Habermas contends that there are certain distinctions which are fundamental for any speech situation, and that the ability to draw these distinctions presupposes that the subject has mastery of various kinds of speech-acts. This contention raises two questions: (1) Why are precisely these distinctions fundamental to any speech situation? (2) To what extent does the ability to draw these distinctions presuppose a mastery of the various kinds of speech-acts? As regards the second question, it is not entirely clear how strongly Habermas's claim is to be construed, nor what sort of evidence he would regard as supporting or refuting his view. However, recent research on the perceptual and communicative activities of infants seems to weigh against his view, suggesting that the child may be able to make some sort of distinction between appearance and reality well before it has mastered an established system of speech-acts.[37] As regards the first question, there is a similar lack of clarity about the nature of the distinctions cited by Habermas and the grounds for treating these distinctions as fundamental. Without a more precise specification, it is difficult to judge whether the proposed distinctions are genuinely universal or merely extrapolated from the tradition of Western philosophy. Moreover, it seems possible that there may be other differentiations which are at least equally primordial, such as the differentiation, emphasised by the early Wittgenstein, between what can and what cannot be said, or the differentiation, developed by modal logic, between what is and what could be the case. Habermas appears to believe that the latter differentiation could be accommodated within his framework in terms of the intentional obfuscation of the distinctions which he regards as fundamental.[38] It may be doubted, however, whether such an account would do justice to the imaginative and creative character of language use. Language may be a medium of interrelating several worlds, but it is also, as Ricoeur insists, a medium whereby these worlds can be shattered and enlarged.[39] Habermas's proposals concerning pragmatic universals thus converge with his analysis of speech-acts in the 'standard form': poetry and humour, metaphor and multivocity, are relegated to a secondary status in the functioning and comprehension of language.

The third thesis of Habermas's programme asserts that the ideal speech situation is a necessary presupposition of communication. The argument in support of this thesis may be reconstructed in six steps:

(i)   The process of communication implies that it is possible for at least two subjects to come to an agreement about a state of affairs.
(ii) To come to an agreement implies that it is possible to distinguish between a genuine and a deceptive agreement.
(iii) A genuine agreement is an agreement induced by the force of better argument alone.
(iv) The force of better argument prevails if and only if communication is not hindered through external and internal constraints.
(v)   Communication is not hindered through internal constraints if and only if for all potential participants there is a symmetrical distribution of chances to select and employ speech-acts.
(vi) A situation in which there is a symmetrical distribution of chances to select and employ communicative, constative, representative and regulative speech-acts is an ideal speech situation.

The first step of the argument invokes the assumption of the privileged status of *verständigungsorientierten Handelns*, exploiting the ambiguity of understanding/agreement which is conveyed by the word *Verständigung*. Since it has already been suggested that this assumption is in need of further defence, no more will be said about it here. I shall pass instead to the third step of the argument, where further problems appear to arise. For although the concept of agreement may presuppose the possibility of distinguishing between genuine and illusory cases, it is difficult to see why subjects can be said genuinely to agree about something only when their agreement is induced by the force of better argument, as opposed, for example, to the feeling of compassion or the commitment to a common goal. Yet if there are, as there certainly seem to be, alternative ways in which a genuine agreement can be induced, then the momentum which allegedly leads to the presupposition of an ideal speech situation is dissipated at an early stage.

Let us suppose, none the less, that Habermas has identified a principal mode whereby genuine agreements can be distinguished from their illusory counterparts. The question then arises as to whether this mode is adequately explicated by the fourth and fifth steps of the argument. Habermas maintains that the force of better argument prevails if and only if communication is not hindered by external and internal constraints, and that internal constraints are excluded if and only if for all potential participants there is a symmetrical distribution of chances to select and employ speech-acts. What it means to speak of 'a symmetrical distribution of chances to select and employ speech-acts' is not altogether clear; and how one is to characterise the exclusion of external constraints, which seem to have been swept under the fifth step of the argument, remains uncertain. Moreover, it seems doubtful whether the elimination of internal constraints could be guaranteed by a symmetrical distribution of chances to select and employ speech-acts, however the latter stipulation may be construed. For one can imagine a debate in which all potential participants have an equal opportunity to deploy the various kinds of speech-acts; and yet in spite of this formal equality, the final decision is merely an expression of the prevailing status quo, bearing little resemblance to the quality of the arguments adduced. What Habermas's assumption of symmetry seems to neglect, and what his occasional allusions to the model of 'pure communicative action' do nothing to mitigate,[40] is that the constraints which affect social life may operate in modes other than the restriction of access to speech-acts, for example by restricting access to weapons, wealth or esteem. The neglect of these issues is closely connected to the dubious distinction between labour and interaction, and it is heavy with consequences for the attempt to use psychoanalysis as a model for critical theory. These connections and consequences cannot be pursued here;[41] but I hope that enough has been said to suggest that Habermas's argument for the presupposition of an ideal speech situation, as well as his conceptualisation of the latter, are in need of considerable attention.

The fourth thesis which I have drawn from Habermas's programme is concerned with the concept of truth. The argument underlying this thesis may be summarised in the following way:

(i)   It is statements, and not sentences or utterances, which are true or false.

(ii) Truth is a validity-claim which is connected with constative speech-acts: to say that a statement is true is to say that the assertion of the statement is justified.

(iii) The assertion of a statement is justified if and only if that statement would command a rational consensus among all who could enter into a discussion with the speaker.

(iv) A rational consensus is a consensus that is argumentatively attained under the conditions of an ideal speech situation.

The second step of the argument expresses the crucial point, which is at the same time the most problematic. For it is by no means clear that to say that a statement is true is to say that the assertion of the statement is justified. Habermas appears to treat this equation as analytic, defending it with the observation that 'truth means "warranted assertability"'.[42] If this were indeed what truth meant, then it would be meaningless to say that the assertion of a statement is justified when the statement itself is false. However, there seem to be many cases when this would not be meaningless, especially with respect to statements about events that may or may not transpire in the future. One may have very good grounds for maintaining that it will rain tomorrow, but the truth of this statement is dependent upon what happens tomorrow and not upon the grounds that one has today.[43] The third and fourth steps of the argument do not, it seems to me, alleviate this difficulty. For I have already suggested that the recourse to the conditions of ideal speech may be neither necessary nor sufficient for the attainment of a 'rational consensus'; and, as I shall now try to show, such an appeal fails to clarify an important aspect of the concept of truth.

The thesis that truth is a discursively redeemable validity-claim does not adequately elucidate what may be called the 'evidential dimension' of the concept of truth. Habermas concurs with Strawson's view that a fact is what a true statement asserts; and both of these authors justly criticise Austin and others for conceiving of facts on the model of things. However, it seems implausible to maintain, as Habermas does, that an existing state of affairs is merely the content of a proposition which has survived discursive argumentation. There are moments when Habermas relaxes this uncomfortable legislation, conceding that 'in the case of elementary empirical propositions such as "this ball is red" a close affinity exists between the objectivity of experience and the truth of a proposition as expressed in a corresponding statement'.[44] Yet Habermas does not explain why this special condition should hold for 'elementary empirical propositions' alone, nor does he clarify wherein this 'close affinity' between experience and 'corresponding statements' consists. Similar obscurities arise in the characterisation of the role of experimental data in the redemption of scientific claims to truth. Although Habermas contends that in stating a fact one is not asserting that some experience exists, he nevertheless allows that one can 'draw upon structurally analogous experiences as data in an attempt to legitimate the truth claim embodied in [a] statement'.[45] Once again, however, Habermas does not specify what kind of 'structurally analogous experiences' would be relevant here, nor how they could be 'drawn upon' to legitimate a truth-claim. He suggests that such questions could be answered by a 'non-objectivistic philosophy of science', but it is by no means clear that the answers thus provided would be wholly consistent with Habermas's current approach. For if the participants of a discourse can adduce certain kinds of experience, 'structurally analogous' though it may be, and if the discursive realm includes certain kinds of action, even though it may be 'experimental' in nature, then it is quite uncertain what remains of the distinction between contexts of action-related experience and realms of discourse, a distinction which is fundamental to the whole of Habermas's recent work. Whether the collapse of this distinction would provide a way of recovering some of the more provocative themes of Habermas's earlier writings must here be left as an open issue.

IV

In the preceding pages I have focused my critical remarks on specific themes in the programme of universal pragmatics. I have not raised any questions concerning the way in which Habermas wishes to employ universal pragmatics as a foundation for critical theory, nor have I suggested any ways in which the difficulties encountered by his programme might be overcome. In this final part of the essay I shall briefly take up these two remaining issues. The first issue may be approached in terms of the following questions: Must the exercise of critique be grounded? If so, can it be grounded through a reflection on the presuppositions of speech? In answering affirmatively to the first question, Habermas is clearly at odds with some of his predecessors in the Frankfurt tradition, as well as with many authors in other traditions of European thought. Yet if the alternative to an affirmative answer is a critique which proceeds by disclosing a discrepancy between reality and the concept which it presents of itself, but which provides no means of determining which concept is thus presented; or if the alternative is a critique which proceeds by opposing one culturally relative viewpoint to another, but which offers no way of rationally resolving these oppositions, since reason itself is regarded as merely one more viewpoint among others; or if the alternative is a critique which proceeds on the assumption that societies necessarily evolve towards ever higher stages, but which proffers no defence of this assumption and hence no cogent criteria for judging one stage to be higher than another; if indeed these are the alternatives, then it seems to me that Habermas is right to seek a foundation for critical theory.

Whether the requisite foundation can be provided through a reflection on the presuppositions of speech is much less clear. The claim that such reflection unfolds a model of idealised speech which can be used for the critique of ideology may appear somewhat vacuous, at least until one has specified precisely how it is to be so used. Habermas has not, I believe, been altogether pellucid in this respect. Sometimes he suggests that the formal symmetries of the ideal speech situation provide an adequate tool for identifying and criticising systematically distorted communication.[46] Just how this critical activity is to be carried out is not, however, explicated in any detail. Moreover, it is certainly questionable whether these formal symmetries would be sufficient to discriminate between alternative and competing views, without making some recourse to the contents of a historical tradition. As Ricoeur aptly remarks, 'man can project his emancipation and anticipate an unlimited and unconstrained communication only on the basis of the creative reinterpretation of cultural heritage'.[47] The latter objection could to some extent be met by the model which Habermas presents in *Legitimation Crisis*.[48] For the 'counterfactually projected reconstruction' of a system of norms formulated discursively would appear to provide a critical standard which is not purely formal, but which acquires its content from the conclusions attained under conditions that are formally defined. Once again, however, the model is presented at a very abstract level, and it remains to be seen whether it can be developed to avoid the obstacles that confront most formalistic approaches to practical issues.

If the criticisms which I have levelled at universal pragmatics are sound, then the spirit of Habermas's programme could be sustained only on the basis of a theory of language and action which is far more adequate than any currently available. In drawing this essay to a constructive close, I can do no more than indicate a direction of thought which seems to me promising, and which I have pursued at greater length elsewhere.[49] An idealised situation of action and speech which would be of considerable importance for a critical theory could perhaps be disclosed through a reflection on the conditions of sentential meaning. It is widely acknowledged that the meaning of a sentence can be analysed, at least partially, in terms of the conditions under which it is true; and yet the analysis cannot stop there, for the notion of the conditions under which a sentence is true must be problematicised in turn.[50] The notion of truth could be retained as a key concept in the theory of meaning only, I believe, if an account of this notion could be given which eluded the snares of a traditional correspondence theory on the one hand, and of a straightforward justificatory account on the other. Perhaps such an account could be formulated in terms of the evidence which would be adequate for the defence of the assertion that a statement is true. This account would emphasise the evidential dimension of the notion of truth, breaking down the sharp distinction between spheres of action-related experience and realms of discourse. The idea of adequacy would underline the normative character of truth; and the clarification of this character may require recourse to an idealised situation of action and speech, in which all of the modalities whereby one-sided power relations can obtain would be explicitly thematised and suspended.

The approach thus proposed might provide a way of rehabilitating some of Habermas's earlier views. For although the standards of adequacy employed in the natural sciences may have been reduced to a principle of prediction and control, there is no reason to assume, as Hesse points out, that the same principle must be adopted in the social sciences.[51] On the contrary, it could be maintained that the crucial criteria for the selection of theoretical statements in the social sciences are provided by a principle of self-reflection. The interpretations derived from an analysis of institutions and social structure may be initially disavowed by the relevant actors, who may not recognise themselves under the descriptions thereby produced. Nevertheless, the decisive condition for the acceptance of the interpretation, and hence for the truth of the theory from which it is derived, would be the ultimate appropriation of the interpretation by the subjects concerned. If the notion of 'ultimate appropriation' could be explicated by reference to the presupposed conditions of sentential meaning, then the subject could be elevated to a crucial epistemological position without capitulating to the prevailing attitudes of everyday life. Such an account would mark the reappearance of practice in the very constitution of social scientific theory, thereby recovering a central theme from the early writings of Habermas.

In conclusion, it may be helpful to summarise the major points of this essay. I began by situating universal pragmatics within the context of Habermas's social theory, and by sketching some of the provisional results which have been yielded by this programme. I then focused on four of the principal theses, reconstructing and criticising the arguments on which they rest. I suggested that Habermas's conclusions concerning validity-claims are reached by an unsubstantiated restriction to speech-acts in the 'standard form'; that his proposals concerning pragmatic universals are in need of further clarification and defence; that his argument for the presupposition of an ideal speech situation is problematic at several points; and that his analysis of truth is hard to sustain as it stands. In the final part of the essay I raised some general questions about the foundational role of universal pragmatics and offered a few constructive remarks. It is far from clear whether the difficulties which seem to vitiate Habermas's programme can be overcome; but what is clear is that the issues which it has raised, and the lines of inquiry which it has encouraged, are urgently in need of being pursued.

7

Of Gods and Demons: Habermas and Practical Reason

STEVEN LUKES

'Practical questions', according to Habermas, 'admit of truth':[1] 'just *(richtige)* norms must be capable of being grounded in a similar way to true statements'.[2] Truth, on his view, means 'warranted assertibility': this is shown when participants enter into a discourse and 'a consensus can be realized under conditions that identify it as a justified consensus'.[3] If, he writes, 'philosophical ethics and political theory are supposed to disclose the moral core of the general consciousness and to *reconstruct* it as a normative concept of the moral, then they must specify criteria and provide reasons: they must, that is, produce theoretical knowledge'.[4] Thus for Habermas judgements about moral and political questions can be rationally grounded and differences about such questions can be rationally resolved.

His position thereby contrasts with those of noncognitivists, moral sceptics, subjectivists, relativists and pluralists of various kinds, and it relies upon a conception of rationality that is sufficiently comprehensive to allow rational solution to such perennial and inherently controversial questions as: Which rules, laws, distributive arrangements, etc., are just? Is the state's claim to legitimacy valid or empty? What is the scope of legitimate authority? And so on.[5] Thus he seeks to 'vindicate the power of discursively attained, rational consensus against the Weberian pluralism of value systems, gods and demons', speaking disdainfully of the 'empiricist and/or decisionist barriers, which immunize the co-called pluralism of values against the efforts of practical reason'.[6] Habermas's rationalism has, moreover, a distinctively Hegelian dimension. He postulates the possibility of society reaching a stage of transparent self-reflection, among parties who are 'free and equal' and whose discourse has reached a stage where 'the level of justification has become reflective', in the sense that mythological, cosmological, religious and ontological modes of thought have been superseded and 'rational will-formation' can be achieved, free of dogmas and 'ultimate grounds', through ideal mutual self-understanding.[7]

Within the Marxist tradition, Habermas's position is a distinctive one. By and large, Marxists have been dismissive, even contemptuous, of morality, for reasons we shall examine below, and relatively uninterested in the problem of justifying norms and normative judgements. Among those who considered the question, Engels, Kautsky and Trotsky saw no need for such justification, though speaking of a 'really human morality which stands above class antagonisms and above any recollections of them',[8] of an unfolding 'general human morality',[9] and of the 'liberating morality of the proletariat'.[10] It was the neo-Kantian Marxists and the Austro-Marxists who explicitly raised the question of such justification, heretically distinguishing between facts and values and offering transcendental arguments purporting to justify the struggle for socialism in terms of universal values. It was, however, Lukács who developed the position that arguably accords most closely with Marx's own view on this subject: that from the privileged standpoint of the proletariat, engaged in the revolutionary transformation of the world, the subject and object of history are united, as the process of history becomes identical with the free development of consciousness and, accordingly, moral judgement becomes identical with the self-understanding of the universal class as it destroys the old world to create a new one. On this view the norms and institutions thereby created require no further justification: they are constitutive of the various ascending 'stages' of 'truly human' society. [11]

Habermas makes none of these moves, proposing instead, as an inheritor of the tradition of critical theory, to develop a mode of theorising that is grounded, in Max Horkheimer's phrase, by an interest in the future, and in particular by 'the idea of a reasonable organization of society that will meet the needs of the whole community' as a goal of human activity which is 'immanent in human work, but . . . not correctly grasped by individuals or by the common mind'.[12] However, unlike his predecessors in this tradition, Habermas makes a serious attempt to give content and grounding to the key notion of emancipation, seeing it as immanent not in work but in communication. His central idea is that

> the *design* of an ideal speech situation is necessarily implied in the structure of potential speech, since all speech, even intentional deception, is oriented toward the idea of truth. This idea can be analyzed with regard to a consensus achieved in unrestrained and universal discourse. Insofar as we master the means for the construction of the ideal speech situation, we can conceive the ideas of truth, freedom and justice, which interpenetrate each other – although of course only as ideas.[13]

His whole theory of universal pragmatics is devoted to establishing these claims and I cannot directly consider them here.[14] I shall concentrate rather on Habermas's claim to have established a vantage-point from which the social world can be critically analysed and from which one can identify ideological deception and normative power – forms of domination whose legitimacy is imposed and which rely on 'contingent and forced consensus', on 'preventing questions that radicalize the value-universalism of bourgeois society from even arising'.[15]

Let us, then, look more closely at Habermas's recent attempt to specify that critical standpoint. A social theory critical of ideology can, he writes,

> identify the normative power built into the institutional system of a society only if it starts from the *model of the suppression of generalizable interests* and compares normative structures existing at a given time with the hypothetical state of a system of norms formed, *ceteris paribus,* discursively. Such a counterfactually projected reconstruction . . . can be guided by the question (justified, in my opinion, by considerations from universal pragmatics): how would the members of a social system, at a given stage in the development of productive forces, have collectively and bindingly interpreted their needs (and which norms would they have accepted as justified) if they could and would have decided on organization of social intercourse through discursive will-formation, with adequate knowledge of the limiting conditions and functional imperatives of their society?[16]

Such ideal discourse would be solely concerned with discussing the 'bracketed validity claims' (to intelligibility, truth, rightness and sincerity) of participants' speech-acts and its sole goal would be to test them, so that

> no force except that of the better argument is exercised, and that, as a result, all motives except that of the cooperative search for truth are excluded. If under these conditions a consensus about the recommendation to accept a norm arises argumentatively, that is, on the basis of hypothetically proposed, alternative justifications, then this consensus expresses a 'rational will'. Since all those affected have, in principle, at least the chance to participate in the practical deliberation, the 'rationality' of the discursively formed will consists in the fact that the reciprocal behavioral expectations raised to normative status afford validity to a *common* interest ascertained *without deception.* The interest is common because the constraint-free consensus permits only what *all* can want; it is free of deception because even the interpretations of needs in which *each individual* must be able to recognize what he wants become the object of discursive will-formation. The discursively formed will may be called 'rational' because the formal properties of discourse and of the deliberative situation sufficiently guarantee that a consensus can arise only through appropriately interpreted, *generalizable* interests, by which I mean needs *that can be communicatively shared.* The limits of a decisionistic treatment of practical questions are overcome as soon as

argumentation is expected to test the generaliz*ability* of interests, instead of being resigned to an impenetrable pluralism of apparently ultimate value orientations (or belief-acts or attitudes).[17]

In what follows I shall examine this attempt to establish a vantage-point that purports to yield a rational basis for critical theory in order to see whether it succeeds in providing a determinate notion of emancipation (from ideology, imposed legitimacy, forced consensus, etc.) and whether it fulfils its promise of eliminating a 'decisionistic' treatment of practical questions and avoiding 'an impenetrable pluralism of apparently ultimate value orientations'.

There is, to begin with, much to be said for the practical implications of Habermas's general approach. He maintains, correctly, that any serious social analysis – and certainly a Marxist or critical theorist – must address the question: are social norms which claim legitimacy genuinely accepted by those who follow and internalise them, or do they merely stabilise relations of power? His central insight is that, in asking this (exceedingly complex) question, one must reason counterfactually and engage in a complicated thought-experiment – albeit guided by general theoretical considerations and relevant empirical evidence – in order to determine whether forms of power, manipulation, mystification, etc., are at work, shaping and deflecting the beliefs and preferences of actors in such a way as to preclude them from thinking and acting as they would otherwise autonomously do. In order to determine this, Habermas argues, we need to postulate undistorted communication among all affected by the norms in question, in which they articulate their needs and in which they both form and discover their interests and the norms that they can rationally accept as binding. Thus he writes that

> only communicative ethics guarantees the generality of admissible norms and the autonomy of acting subjects, solely through the discursive redeemability of the validity claims with which norms appear. That is, generality is guaranteed in that the only norms that may claim generality are those on which everyone affected agrees (or would agree) without constraint if they enter into (or were to enter into) a process of discursive will-formation. [18]

Habermas here reveals his firm commitment to the view (fundamentally at odds with any Leninist or Lukácsian assumption of privileged access in the imputation of interests) that people are the sole judges of their own interests, which are formed and discovered through dialogue on the part of all concerned – a political commitment to opening up public, democratic processes which Habermas has elsewhere described as 'the conversation of citizens'.[19] Contrary to the assumptions of technocrats, he has portrayed 'the depoliticization of the mass of the population and the decline of the public realm as a political institution' as 'components of a system of domination that tends to exclude practical questions from public discussion': the 'enlightenment of political will', he argues, 'can become effective only within the communication of citizens'.[20] His general approach leads him, therefore, to see democracy, not as any particular institutional form, but as a 'self-controlled learning process', in which the problem is to find 'arrangements which can ground the presumption that the basic institutions of society and the basic political institutions would meet with the unforced agreement of all those involved, if they could participate, as free and equal, in discursive will-formation'.[21]

But, aside from these admirable political implications of his approach, it remains to examine exactly *how* he proposes to establish a determinate rational basis for social criticism, an 'Archimedean point', as John Rawls might say, 'for assessing the social system' that 'is not at the mercy, so to speak, of existing wants and interests'.[22] How does Habermas propose to specify which norms and claims to legitimacy are capable of securing the rational consent of social actors – actors to a greater or lesser extent caught up in structures of 'normative power', 'illegitimate domination' that 'meets with consent', and 'contingent and forced consensus'?[23]

Habermas offers as his answer the 'model of the suppression of generalisable interests' – a hypothesis or 'counterfactually projected reconstruction' specifying of all the actors in question which of their interests are 'generalisable', how they would interpret their needs, and which norms they would accept as justified under conditions of unconstrained communication. It is true that Habermas observes that the 'social scientist can only hypothetically project this ascription of interests; indeed a direct confirmation of this hypothesis would be possible only in the form of a practical discourse among the very individuals or groups involved'. It can, he maintains, be indirectly confirmed (it would perhaps be better to say supported) through 'empirical indicators of suppressed interests'. Following Claus Offe (who likewise seeks a 'critical standard' for identifying structures that perpetuate 'suppressed, that is latent, claims and needs'), Habermas mentions specifically (1) the existence of an observed discrepancy between legal norms and actual legal practices; (2) codified rules which systematically exclude claims from the political agenda (claims which thus express suppressed interests); (3) the existence of a discrepancy between claims that are made and the level at which they are politically allowed satisfaction; and (4) comparative evidence, drawn from different political systems, which indicates, *ceteris paribus,* which possibilities are actualised when putatively repressive structures are absent or removed.[24] But before we can know whether the hypothesis of suppressed generalisable interests is either directly confirmed or indirectly well supported, we must first know what the hypothesis *is*. The prior issue is to establish whether such a hypothesis can be intelligibly advanced and what precisely it amounts to.

Two deep and connected difficulties are raised by Habermas's proposal. First, just how counterfactual is the hypothesis in question? Just how much of the real past and present are we to alter in the proposed thought-experiment? More particularly, to what extent, if at all, is the identity of the agents preserved across the transition between the actual and the imagined possible world?

There appear to be three possible answers to this last question, to each of which Habermas seems to be drawn, each of which is unsatisfactory, and none of which suits his purposes. The first is that the *actual* agents are to be imagined in conditions of undistorted communication (thus he speaks of the 'interests that would have to find expression among those involved if they [*sic*] were to enter into practical discourse').[25] The second is that *typical* or *representative* actors are to be imagined in such conditions (thus he speaks of a 'representatively simulated discourse' between groups with conflicting interests and also describes the discoursing partners as 'the members of a social system, at a given stage in the development of productive forces').[26] The third is that ideally rational, theoretically defined agents are to be imagined in such conditions (thus he speaks of the 'ideal speech situation', the participants in which must presumably be ideally constituted, having reached a level of cognitive and moral development that will enable rational consensus to be reached). The first answer suggests a counterfactual of the form 'Under (counterfactual) conditions C, the real-life actors A_1 would agree on X.' The second suggests a counterfactual of the form 'Under conditions C, typical actors A_2 (defined by, say, their membership in conflict groups or their incumbency of roles) would agree on X.' The third suggests a counterfactual of the form 'Under conditions C, ideally rational actors A_3 (defined by a theory of rationality) would agree on X.'

The problem with the first answer is that no reason is given for supposing that the actual agents would, under the conditions supposed (that is, where there is 'a symmetrical distribution of chances to select and employ speech acts and an equal opportunity to assume dialogue roles'),[27] reach the required rational consensus. Indeed, there is surely every reason to suppose that *they* would not, since *they* would continue to exhibit all kinds of traits conducive to 'distorted communication' – prejudices, limitations of vision and imagination, deference to authority, fears, vanities, self-doubts, and so on. Doubtless many of these traits will be the outcome of relations of domination and exploitation within the family and the larger society, but they will be sufficiently integral to, and internalised within, the personalities of actual people to make it implausible to suppose their eradication without those people becoming different people. Real participants in ideal communication would hold fast to their conceptions of their needs and interests and the norms they accept, to the extent that these conceptions are integral to their very identity.

The problem with the second answer is that the agents in question are constructs of a social theory which specifies relevant conflict groups or roles and their associated needs and interests, and the norms that regulate them. But, in that case, the counterfactual hypothesis will be a direct entailment of the theory and will do no more than spell out what, for the postulated conflict groups and role incumbents, are, according to the theory, negotiable or shared interests, true or self-interpreted needs and generally acceptable norms. In other words, this solution does no more than employ the counterfactual to spell out the implications of a theory accepted on other grounds, and its plausibility as a rational foundation for critical theorising is no stronger than those grounds themselves.

The problem with the third answer is a familiar one to students of Kant and Rawls. If we are asked to imagine what ideally rational agents would do under the posited conditions, the whole argument turns on the nature of those agents and the constraints set by the conditions. If these together are such that the appropriate answers are necessarily reached, then the counterfactual hypothesis emerges as vindicated but only because it has been so formulated that it must do so. Ideally rational people in an ideal speech situation cannot but reach a rational consensus.

None of these answers suits Habermas's purposes, since his aim is to identify suppressed interests, 'contingent and forced consensus' and illegitimate domination, which requires him to specify and render plausible the counterfactual hypothesis that the individuals and groups in question would, under specified alternative conditions, acknowledge *their* true interests, *their* real and unforced consensus, and the claims to legitimacy *they* genuinely accept. John Stuart Mill reasoned thus when comparing the higher and lower pleasure, deferring to the judgement of the person who had experienced both: Habermas offers a version of this argument transposed to a collective and communicative level. And Habermas is quite right to observe that Marx reasons in this way, making the crucial, further assumption that 'the consciousness of justified and, at the same time, suppressed interests' is a 'sufficient motive for conflict' to realise those interests.[28] The problem for Habermas is that none of his suggested answers to the question posed gives a plausible rendering of the counterfactual hypothesis required.

A further possible answer might be suggested: that under the imagined conditions of ideal communication, actual actors would be so transformed as to become capable of the requisite rational consensus. But this proposal encounters two severe objections. First, there is every reason to suppose that this would not be so, if socialisation processes and relations of economic and political power remain unchanged: to suppose the contrary could be described as a rationalist illusion, typical of the eighteenth century, inconceivable to a Marxist. And second, even if it were so, the greater the change from the actual agents to the ideally rational agents, capable of reaching the requisite consensus, the less relevant would be the deliberations of the latter to the purpose at hand – which is to establish how the actual participants would think and feel, were alleged structures of domination to be overthrown.

This first difficulty I have been considering can be summed up in the question: *Who* are the participants in the unconstrained discourse that is held to offer the possibility of rational consensus? The second difficulty, to which I now turn, can be summed up in the question: *What* are they supposed to agree about?

In the first place, they are to interpret their needs 'collectively and bindingly' and in such a way that 'each individual must be able to recognise what he wants' and this becomes 'the object of discursive will-formation'. This seems to amount to a strong insistence on the self-ascription of desires and needs by autonomous agents and their acceptance of responsibility for the consequences of such self-ascriptions. Moreover, Habermas stresses the public and discursive nature of such self-ascriptions.[29] Second, in the light of such public, discursively reached self-ascriptions of desires and needs, they count certain norms as 'justified' and 'legitimate' if they fulfil 'commonly accepted needs'.[30] Another way that Habermas expresses this is to say that the norms must 'express' and 'regulate' 'generalisable interests'. By 'generalisable interests' he says he means '*needs that can be communicatively shared*'. Thus rationally justified norms are those which 'express' and 'regulate' 'generalisable interests', that is needs that are publicly self-ascribed by autonomous and responsible participants in unconstrained discourse.

As yet this is a cloudy formula, and it is worth pressing on to see if clarification issues in a determinate solution. How, then, are we to recognise norms which express and regulate 'generalisable interests'? Habermas addresses this question. How, he asks, is it possible to separate by argument generalisable interests from 'those that are and remain particular'? His answer is that 'the only principle in which practical reason expresses itself' is 'the principle of universalization'.[31] He speaks of this principle as a 'bridge principle' comparable with the principle of induction:

> Induction serves as a bridge principle for justifying the logically discontinuous passage from a finite number of singular statements (data) to a universal statement (hypothesis). Universalization serves as a bridge principle for justifying the passage to a norm from descriptive indications (concerning the consequences and side effects of the application of norms for the fulfilment of commonly accepted needs).[32]

The rationally justified norms to be agreed are, then, universalised. But what does this mean? There is a good case for distinguishing three forms or stages of universalisation.[33] At the first stage, the principle of universalisation simply dictates that the rules or norms guiding and controlling human conduct make no essential reference to proper names or indexical terms: that is to say, purely numerical differences are treated as irrelevant, so that what is right (or wrong) for you or your group is right (or wrong) for me and my group, unless there are morally relevant differences between us or our situation (with no restriction as to what can count as a morally relevant difference). At the second stage, the principle dictates that the rules or norms must be subject to a further test, namely putting oneself in the other person's or group's place. This test will allow through only those norms or rules which the actors are prepared to go on applying, no matter how they might change in respect of their mental and physical qualities, resources and social status; on this test, 'differences can be fairly regarded as relevant if they look relevant from whichever side you consider them'.[34] At the third stage, a further, more stringent test is applied, namely that account is taken of rival and alternative desires, tastes, preferences, ideals and values. Now one must simultaneously take account of conflicting points of view, and seek maxims that will be acceptable from all viewpoints. This test will allow through only those norms and rules which give equal weight, in some sense, to all interests, those interests being determined by rival preferences, values and ideals.

The test at the first stage allows in all kinds of rules that are clearly partisan and unfair (e.g. all blacks should have an inferior education). Similarly the test at the second stage allows in universal rules that favour some preferences, values and ideals as against others (e.g. a puritan code of conduct). We might perhaps assume, therefore, that Habermas is thinking of the third stage of universalisation.

But the problem with the third stage of universalisation is that the test is so severe that it is not clear that any rules or norms will pass, and it is certainly very far from guaranteed that unconstrained discourse between the parties will yield action-guiding principles of this sort. There would appear to be two possible approaches to this problem. One is the highly ambitious strategy of seeking to derive, through reflection on features inherent in the human condition and general facts about society, a determinate set of principles that will pass the test. This is John Rawls's approach. The 'circumstances of justice', which are 'the normal conditions under which human cooperation is both possible and necessary', obtain wherever 'mutually disinterested persons put forward conflicting claims to the division of social advantages under conditions of moderate scarcity'. Knowing this, and accepting that 'individuals not only have different plans of life but there exists a diversity of religious and philosophical belief, and of political and social doctrines', the parties in Rawls's 'original position', operating behind a veil of ignorance (about their own natural assets, future positions and plans of life), have the task of unanimously settling on 'principles of justice that are genuinely neutral as between alternative plans of life'.[35] These principles, for Rawls, 'not only specify the terms of cooperation between persons but they define a pact of reconciliation between diverse religious and moral beliefs, and the forms of culture to which they belong':[36] they are 'principles of accommodation between different moralities',[37] intended to secure 'social cooperation among equals for mutual advantage'.[38] Two crucial and telling objections that have been made against this approach, in the Rawlsian form, are, first, that his principles are not uniquely derivable from his hypothesised choice situation, and, second, that the 'original position' and its abstract, theoretically defined inhabitants have been so artificially constructed as to yield a predetermined solution, which has therefore no independently compelling qualification for the title '*the* principles of justice'.

A less ambitious approach to applying the test at this third stage of universalisation is that of Mackie, who argues that the test is too severe: given radically divergent preferences and values and the obstinate moral disagreements arising therefrom, 'we must lower our sights a little, and look not for principles which can be wholeheartedly endorsed from every point of view, but for ones which represent an acceptable compromise between the different actual points of view'.[39] On this view of morality as compromise, there will no longer be any reason to suppose that a definitive or uniquely determinable set of rules or maxims can be arrived at through general rational argument: rather, there will be contingently different principles and rules, depending on the actual circumstances, divergences and possibilities of agreement. These must be 'invented' and 're-invented' anew in the recurrent quest for mutual accommodation.

Neither of these approaches to universalisation would seem to suit Habermas's purposes. Rawls's quest for an Archimedean point eludes him, for the reasons suggested and others,[40] while Mackie's position does not yield a uniquely rationally justified outcome, only contingent compromises. But in any case, Habermas appears to reject a basic assumption shared by both these approaches, namely that morality is a means of solving the problem posed by the conflicts generated by limited resources and limited sympathies, with a view to securing mutually beneficial co-operation. To the contrary, he explicitly distinguishes 'norms that may claim generality' from 'compromise',[41] which he describes as a case of 'normative power' involving a 'normed adjustment between particular interests' that 'takes place under conditions of a balance of power between the parties involved'. Although such compromise may be 'indirectly justifiable' through discourse, it is plainly seen as distinct from and contrasting with the case of 'interests that permit of a rational will': a compromise can be justified only where 'a balance of power among the parties involved and the non-generalizability of the negotiated interests exist'.[42]

Nor indeed is it surprising that Habermas should take this line, since the entire Marxist tradition is committed to denying that morality is a response to an inherent limitation of resources and sympathies in the human condition – a view classically expressed by Hume when he wrote that 'It is only from the selfishness and confined generosity of man, along with the scanty provision nature has made for his wants, that justice derives its origin'.[43] On the contrary, Marx and subsequent Marxists see both limitations as historically contingent and socially generated and look forward to overcoming both in a unified society of abundance.

What, then, if all this is so, does Habermas understand by the principle of universalisation as expressed in the formula 'generalisability of interests'? In truth, I find it difficult to say. A clue may lie in his attack on the Rawlsian notion of 'primary goods' as supposedly 'neutral means for attaining an indefinite multiplicity of concrete ends selected according to values'. He plausibly argues that this picture is misleading, that the Rawlsian primary goods are not compatible with all forms of life that could be chosen, but involve 'clearly circumscribed "opportunity structures"' and imply a particular underlying form of life, of private commodity production and exchange relations, and familial, occupational and civil privatism. In the light of this critique, he argues for the possibility that

> the 'pursuit of happiness' might one day mean something different – for example, not accumulating material objects of which one disposes privately, but bringing about social relations in which mutuality predominates and satisfaction does not mean the triumph of one over the repressed needs of the other.[44]

The idea seems to be that there will be an endogenous change of preferences on the part of social actors (induced by ideal discourse?) such that preferences, tastes, values, ideals, plans of life, etc., will to some large degree (to what degree?) be unified and no longer conflict. On this interpretation, the principle of universalisation would require that norms and rules pass the test that they should embody common aims, regulate shared activities and lead to common and shared satisfactions ('needs that can be communicatively shared'). But why should one suppose such a moral change to be either possible, necessary or desirable? It is true that *Legitimation Crisis* is, in part, addressed to showing such a change to be on the historical agenda in late capitalist societies and there are, of course, good arguments in favour of a more unified, less conflictual, privatised and consumerist form of life than is predominant in contemporary capitalist societies; but I cannot find in Habermas's writings any argument for the thesis that such a form of life (which is, in any case, barely even sketched, except in the most abstract possible manner) is either an appropriate interpretation of the principles of universalisation or uniquely capable of rational justification.

I turn now to the question of whether Habermas has justified his claim that his approach overcomes 'the limits of a decisionistic treatment of practical questions as soon as argumentation is expected to test the generaliz*ability* of interests'.[45] I cannot see that it does so. For the principle of universalisation, at all the three stages I have discussed, requires, at each stage, a *decision* whether or not to let one's actions and choices be guided only by maxims and norms which pass the test in question. As Mackie has remarked, 'the universalisability of moral judgements . . . does not impose any rational constraint on choices of action or defensible patterns of behaviour'.[46] At every stage it is not merely logically possible but in fact quite common for people to opt out of, or not opt into, these ways of reasoning. And this argument applies, with equal force, to Habermas's own (putative) version of the universalisation principle.

I conclude from all this that (1) these arguments do not succeed in establishing a determinate, uniquely rational basis for critical theory; (2) they do not dispense with the role of decision in moral and political thinking; and (3) they do not therefore disprove the thesis of value pluralism.

Habermas has, however, advanced a further set of considerations which are intended to provide an 'empirical' and a 'systematic' basis for the objectivity and universality of standards of rationality as he conceives them. These considerations are intended to provide further grounding for his positive claim to establish a determinate rational basis for critical theory and thereby his rejection of 'decisionism' and Weber's 'rationally irresoluble pluralism of competing value systems and beliefs'.[47] I refer to his application of Piaget's and Kohlberg's cognitive developmental psychology.

I cannot here discuss in detail Habermas's intriguing attempt to use these ideas to try to reconstruct historical materialism by incorporating within it a theory of the development of normative structures. I shall refer only to the gist of his argument, in so far as it concerns the question at issue here. His basic thought is that, since cognitive developmental psychology is 'well corroborated and . . . has reconstructed ontogenetic stages of moral consciousness', it should be possible to reconstruct these stages logically, that is, 'by concepts of a systematically ordered sequence of norm systems and behavioral controls', and at the highest stage to identify a corresponding 'universal morality, which can be traced back to fundamental norms of rational speech'.[48] With extraordinary boldness, he traces homologies between ego development on the one hand, and 'the social evolution of moral and legal representations', of 'world-views', and 'the historical constitution of collective identities' on the other.[49] Just as the ego develops from the symbiotic, through the egocentric and the sociocentric-objectivistic to the universalistic stages of development, and from preconventional through conventional to postconventional patterns of problem-solving,[50] so, Habermas argues, it should be possible to develop a 'communication theory' that would analyse 'the symbolic structures that underlie law and morality, an intersubjectively constituted world, and the identities of persons and collectivities', that would show normative structures to have their own 'internal history' which has a 'direction of development' that can be characterised by such concepts as 'universalization and individualization, decentration, autonomization, and becoming reflective'.[51] In short, the 'stages of law and morality, of ego demarcations and world-views, of individual and collective identity formations' can be seen as stages in progress towards increasing rationality, measured by 'the expansion of the domain of consensual action together with the re-establishment of undistorted communication'.[52] Such progress can be seen as a sequence of developmental stages of moral consciousness, corresponding to stages of development in interaction competence. At the final, postconventional stage, 'systems of norms lose their quasi-natural validity; they require justification from universalistic points of view'.[53]

Do these considerations help to render the 'universalistic' perspective of the highest stage, and the principles and judgements it delivers, determinate, uniquely rational and objective, and do they bypass the need for a decision to adopt it? It is notable that Kohlberg has himself argued a similar case to that of Habermas. He has claimed to 'have successfully defined the ethically optimal end-point of moral development', that 'there is a sense in which we can characterize moral differences between groups and individuals [which are themselves to be understood as differences in stage or developmental status] as being more or less adequate morally'.[54] For Kohlberg, the later stages of development are 'cognitively and ethically higher or more adequate', the final sixth stage being 'a more universalistic, moral orientation, which defines moral obligations in terms of what alternatively may be conceived as (a) the principle of justice, (b) the principle of role-taking, or (c) the principle of respect for personality', this stage being 'the most adequate exemplification of the moral'.[55] In this sense, Kohlberg argues for the 'superiority of Stage 6 judgements of duties and rights (or of justice) over other systems of judgements of duties and rights'.[56] Habermas, similarly, argues for both an empirical and a systematic 'superiority' of universal morality.[57]

But Kohlberg in fact established only that there are recurrent sequences of stages of preferred modes of moral reasoning employed by growing children in different contexts and cultures.[58] The claim that this repeated sequence is a development towards greater adequacy only makes sense if one applies specific criteria of adequacy, criteria that are themselves disputable and indeed disputed among moral thinkers, philosophical and otherwise. In Kohlberg's theory such criteria are already built into his 'scientific' theory. The claimed superiority of the later stages over the earlier and the last stage over the rest is necessitated neither by the observed data, nor by the fact that the later modes of reasoning may logically presuppose earlier modes, nor by the fact that they may imply cognitive superiority or require more elaborate conceptual thinking. There is no inherent compulsion in Kohlberg's claim that Stage 6 reasoning is ethically optimal: as Alston has observed, 'many moral philosophers who are surely at least as conceptually sophisticated as Kohlberg's Stage 6 subjects take positions in moral philosophy that reflect Stages 4 or 5'.[59] It is a claim that many can and will dispute, and it cannot be established by stipulatively defining 'moral' so that Stage 6 becomes 'the most adequate exemplification of the moral'. And the same arguments apply, *pari passu*, to Habermas's claim, *contra* Kohlberg, that there is an ultimate Stage 7 at which 'the principle of justification of norms is no longer the monologically applicable principle of generalizability but the communally followed *procedure* of redeeming normative validity claims discursively'.[60]

Indeed, these arguments can only be strengthened by considering the very disagreement between Kohlberg (and by implication Rawls[61]) on the one hand, and Habermas on the other, as to the nature of the highest stage. Kohlberg has argued that the highest stage of moral development implies the notion of justice as 'reversibility', a kind of 'ideal role-taking' which involves 'differentiating the self's perspective from the other's and co-ordinating the two so that the perspective from the other's view influences one's own perspective in a reciprocal fashion'.[62] This amounts to a moral decision procedure, which Kohlberg calls 'moral musical chairs', that is, 'going round the circle of perspectives involved in a moral dilemma to test one's claims of right or duty until only the equilibrated or reversible claims survive'.[63] (Kohlberg further claims that his decision procedure yields the same solutions as Rawls's idea of decision in the 'original position'.) By contrast, as we have seen, Habermas maintains that Kohlberg's approach is 'monological' and fails to attain 'the level of a universal ethic of speech' where self-ascriptions of interests become 'the object of practical discourse'.[64] If my interpretation of Habermas's understanding of universalisation, set out above, is correct, he assumes that such practical discourse will lead to an endogenous change of preferences and perspectives on the part of the communicators such that shared needs and 'consensual action'[65] will predominate. Yet how can one rationally resolve this difference between two such rational men? How can one conclude which is rationally and morally superior – Kohlberg's Stage 6 or Habermas's Stage 7, and the norms and judgements they respectively generate – other than by *deciding* between them? Of course, one might at this point maintain that the very distinction between 'decision' and 'rational argument' is misleading here. After all, would not any such decision be based on *reasons*: do we not decide on the basis of *rational grounds*? But neither Habermas nor Kohlberg (nor Rawls) has shown that there is a neutral or objective standpoint from which the reasons grounding alternative decisions can themselves be assessed as more or less rational.

So I conclude that this line of argument also fails to establish the critical vantage-point that Habermas seeks and that we have not yet escaped the Weberian gods and demons.

8

Labour and Interaction

ANTHONY GIDDENS

Labour and interaction: innocuous-sounding terms, but ones around which Habermas has consolidated some of the main themes in his work. It makes sense to see most of Habermas's work as concerned with what he has come to call the 'reconstruction of historical materialism' – a critical reformulation of the dominant concerns of Marx's writings, both on the level of philosophy or 'meta-theory' and on the level of the development of industrial capitalism since Marx's day. Habermas uses 'reconstruction' in a very deliberate way, as he makes clear. He is not interested, as he says, in reviving or 'restoring' traditional Marxist ideas: his preoccupation with Marx is not a scholastic or dogmatic one. As a tradition of thought which is very much alive, Marxism has no need for renewal. Rather, it is in need of a wholesale overhaul. 'Reconstruction', Habermas argues, 'signifies taking a theory apart and putting it back together again in a new form in order to attain more fully the goal it has set for itself.'[1]

The distinction between labour and interaction played a central part in Habermas's early attempts to gain a critical purchase on the shortcomings of Marx. It has not remained unmodified in his subsequent writings, and in the first two sections of this essay, I shall attempt to trace out the various contexts in which he applies the two concepts.

I

The origins of the differentiation Habermas draws between labour and interaction are to be found in his discussion of the relation between Hegel and Marx – in an analysis which is avowedly indebted to the ideas of Karl Löwith.[2] Habermas's account gives more prominence to Hegel's Jena lectures than is usually acknowledged by Hegel's interpreters, many of whom have regarded those lectures as a transitory phase in the evolution of that thinker's mature philosophy. According to Habermas, the two lecture courses Hegel gave at Jena[3] constitute a distinctive, if incomplete, perspective upon philosophy which Hegel himself came to abandon, but which for Habermas marks certain close points of connection between Hegel and Marx (even though Marx did not know of the Jena manuscripts). In the

Jena lectures Hegel treated *Geist* in the process of its formation, as a phenomenon to be explained. *Geist* is understood in terms of the communication of human beings via categories of meaning comprised in language. Language is the medium of self-consciousness and of the 'distancing' of human experience from the sensory immediacy of the here-and-now. As necessarily implying intersubjectivity, or *interaction,* language has a definite parallel to the significance of *labour* in Hegel's writings. Labour is the specifically human mode of relating to nature:

> Just as language breaks the dictates of immediate perception and orders the chaos of the manifold impressions into identifiable things, so labor breaks the dictates of immediate desires and, as it were, arrests the process of drive satisfaction.[4]

Labour and interaction are hence the two key aspects of the self-formative process of human beings in society, or of the development of human culture. In Hegel's Jena lectures, according to Habermas, labour and interaction are presented as irreducible to one another: a matter which becomes a crucial focus of Habermas's attention in his critique of Marx. Interaction is organised through consensual norms that have no logical connection to the causal processes involved in transactions with nature. This is not to say, of course, that empirically they are two separate realms of human behaviour. All labour is carried on in a social and therefore communicative context.

Even in the Jena period, Habermas accepts, Hegel interpreted labour and interaction in terms of an identity theory: *Geist* is the absolute condition of nature. In other words, Hegel's account of the self-formation of the human being was always an idealist one. While rejecting Hegel's idealism, and although not having access to the Jena lectures, Marx nevertheless was able to appropriate the notions of labour and interaction from Hegel: these appear in Marx, Habermas says, in the shape of the dialectic of the forces and relations of production.[5] The progressive development of the forces of production, therefore, manifests the human transformation of the world through labour. The self-formative process, in Marx's writings, no longer expresses the externalisation of Spirit, but is seen as rooted in the material conditions of human existence. However, the concept of labour in Marx, Habermas emphasises, remains an epistemological category: nature is only constituted for us through its mediation in human *Praxis.*[6] Marx presumes that 'nature-in-itself' exists, but this is a kind of counterpart in his thought to the Kantian 'thing-in-itself': we only directly encounter nature in our practical interchanges with it. This 'preserves', according to Habermas, 'nature's immovable facticity despite nature's historical embeddedness in the universal structure of mediation constituted by laboring subjects'.[7]

Marx's treatment of labour, in Habermas's view, is in some respects a decisive advance over that set out by Hegel. But at the same time it also represents something of a retrogressive step, because Marx does not provide an adequate epistemological support for sustaining the mutual irreducibility of labour and interaction. Marx's scheme of analysis gives a great deal of prominence to interaction, in the shape of the notion of the relations of production. The foundation of subjectivity and self-reflection in communicative frameworks of interaction is not, however, grasped epistemologically by Marx because of the dominant place accorded to the role of labour. This result stems from the very success of Marx's repudiation of Hegel's identity theory. Marx's works are thus fundamentally imbalanced, in a way which has major consequences for the later history of Marxism. In his empirical works Marx always gives strong weight to the relations of production as well as to the forces of production. Concepts which properly belong to the former, to interaction in Habermas's terms, especially domination and ideology, thus have a primary role in Marx's empirical writings. But they do not have the philosophical underpinning which labour – the material transformation of the world and of human conditions of existence – enjoys. Hence Marx's concentration upon material *Praxis* became open to a misleading emphasis: it opened the way to the collapse of interaction into labour on the level of epistemology. According to Habermas, not even Marx fully grasped the implications of this, which helped to push his work in a positivistic direction. In Habermas's words,

> Although he [Marx] established the science of man in the form of critique and not as a natural science, he continually tended to classify it with the natural sciences. He considered unnecessary an epistemological justification of social theory. This shows that the idea of the self-constitution of mankind through labor sufficed to criticize Hegel but was inadequate to render comprehensible the real significance of the materialist appropriation of Hegel. [8]

It is exactly such an epistemological justification that Habermas has sought to provide in further expanding upon the distinction between labour and interaction. The collapse of interaction into labour means that instrumentally exploitable or 'technical' knowledge – the sort of knowledge we use to attempt to control the material world – becomes regarded as characteristic of the social as well as the natural sciences. All social problems then become seen as 'technical' problems. Technical reason appears to exhaust the capabilities of human reason as a whole: the defining characteristic of positivism for Habermas. The influence of Horkheimer's and Adorno's *Dialectic of Enlightenment* on Habermas's thought is evident at this point.[9] Their 'critique of instrumental reason' converged directly with the main political thrust of Habermas's writings (in which the influence of Max Weber also looms quite large): the thesis that increased human control over nature, or over the forces of production, is not at all the same as liberation from domination. The essential difference between Habermas's position and those of the earlier Frankfurt thinkers, a difference explored particularly in the debates between Habermas and Marcuse, is that Habermas rejects the theme that scientific or technical knowledge is itself ideological in its very form. The view of Habermas, which connects his discussion of labour and interaction in Hegel and Marx with his whole conception of knowledge-constitutive interests (today abandoned by Habermas?) is that it is the *universalisation* of technical or instrumental reason, as the only form of rationality, which has to be fought against. In Marx's writings, the universalisation of technical reason is traced to the epistemological dominance of labour: but, for Habermas, the slide of Marxism towards positivism is a characteristic which Marxism shares with a great deal of modern social theory and philosophy as a whole.

II

Habermas's most systematic early attempt to elaborate the differentiation of labour from interaction appears in a critical analysis of Marcuse's views on technology.[10] Labour is equated with 'purposive-rational action' (*Zweckrationalität*), which refers, Habermas says, to 'either instrumental action or rational choice or their conjunction'. Instrumental action is action orientated to technical rules, and is founded on empirical knowledge. The technical rules involved in purposive-rational action are formulated on the basis of the predictive powers which they allow. 'Rational choice' here is a matter of deciding between strategies of action, according to the most 'efficient' way of realising goals or objectives. Interaction, on the other hand, which Habermas equates with 'communicative action', 'is governed by binding *consensual norms*, which define reciprocal expectations about behavior and which must be understood and recognized by at least two acting subjects'.[11] Communicative action is based on ordinary language communication, and depends upon the mutual understanding of social symbols. The contrast between the rules governing purposive-rational action and those governing communicative action can be pointed to by the different character of the sanctions involved in each case. Habermas here echoes a distinction made by Durkheim.[12] Non-compliance with technical rules or strategies is sanctioned by the likelihood of failure in achieving goals; non-compliance with consensual norms is sanctioned by the disapproval of, or punishment by, other members of the social community. To learn rules of purposive-rational action, in Habermas's view, is to learn skills; to learn normative rules is to 'internalise' traits of personality.

The two types of action, Habermas goes on to argue, can provide a basis for distinguishing different institutional sectors of society. There are some sectors, among which he lists the economic system and the state, where purposive-rational action is most prevalent. There are others, such as the family and kinship relations, in which 'moral rules of interaction' predominate. This classification can also be applied, Habermas believes, to illuminate over-all patterns in the development of societies. In traditional or pre-capitalist societies the scope of the sub-systems of purposive-rational action is kept confined by the pervading authority of morally binding frameworks of interaction. Capitalist society, by contrast, is one in which the expansion of sub-systems of purposive-rational action is privileged (first of all as grounded in the expanded reproduction of capital), and acts progressively to erode other institutional forms. Modern science plays a major role in this process, especially as science and technological change become more closely integrated. This leads straight through to the Habermasian themes of the 'scientisation of politics' and legitimation crisis:

> The quasi-autonomous progress of science and technology . . . appears as an independent variable on which the most important single system variable, namely economic growth, depends . . . when this semblance has taken root effectively, then propaganda can refer to the role of technology and science in order to explain and legitimate why in modern societies the process of democratic decision-making about practical problems loses its function and 'must' be replaced by plebiscitary decisions about alternative sets of leaders of administrative personnel.[13]

The passage from abstract categories of action to a more empirical concern with processes of social development is characteristic of Habermas's style of argument, and comprehensible in the light of his conception of 'epistemology as social theory'. The labour/interaction distinction remains essential to both aspects of Habermas's work in his later writings. Although at first sight the scheme of knowledge-constitutive interests advanced in *Knowledge and Human Interests* and other writings of his earlier period seems to be threefold, it is fundamentally a dichotomous one founded upon the contrast between labour and interaction. The 'interest in emancipation' lacks content, and obtains its existence from the bringing together of nomological and hermeneutic concerns in the critique of ideology. The dichotomous character of Habermas's epistemological ventures is sustained in the format of 'universal pragmatics', in his differentiation of 'theoretical-empirical' from 'practical' discourse, a differentiation that can be superimposed, as it were, upon the labour/interaction and nomological/hermeneutic distinctions. I shall not be concerned in this essay, however, with these ideas, but shall limit myself to following through Habermas's attempt to use the distinction between labour and interaction to analyse the evolution of societies.

Habermas's recent interpretation of social evolution recapitulates some of the elements of his earlier criticisms of Marx. Marx's theory, Habermas reaffirms, failed adequately to get to grips with communicative action in analysing the development of societies. Under the influence of Luhmann, Habermas is prone to employ terminology associated with systems theory. Marx, he says, located the 'learning processes' associated with social evolution in the sphere of the productive forces (i.e. in labour); but learning processes are also to be discerned in 'world-views, moral representations, and identity formations' (i.e. in interaction). We have therefore to complement the study of the development of the productive forces with that of 'normative structures'. Habermas believes that this can be done without essentially compromising the over-all determination of social change by 'economically conditioned system problems'.[14] Habermas's account of the evolution of normative frameworks of interaction is based upon the thesis (advocated also in some form by Durkheim, Piaget and Parsons among others) of a homology between personality and social development. The forms of consciousness, and the stages of their development, of the individual member of society are the same as those characteristic of society as a whole.[15]

According to Habermas, the evolution of societal learning processes can be examined in the following terms. At certain phases of their development societies meet with 'unresolved system problems' which present challenges to their continued reproduction and which cannot be handled within the existing normative order. Society must then transform itself, or its continued existence is placed in question. The nature of such a transformation, and whether it occurs at all, Habermas emphasises, are not determined by the system problems, but only by the mode in which the society responds to them, by developing new modes of normative organisation. This analysis, he claims, is still worth calling 'historical materialism'. It is materialist, because problems in the realm of production and reproduction are at the origin of the tensions which provoke system reorganisation; and it remains historical because the sources of system problems have to be sought in the contingent development of particular societies. In his account of social evolution Habermas finds archaeological justification for the integral involvement of labour and language with distinctively 'human' society. 'Labor and language', as he puts it, 'are older than man and society.' [16]

III

Having sketched in these ideas, I want to offer a brief critical appraisal of them. I am not at all happy with Habermas's formulation of the labour/interaction distinction, or with some of the uses to which he puts it, and I shall try to express some of my reservations in what follows. I hope that the reader will understand that, in so doing, I am not seeking to downplay the significance of Habermas's contributions to contemporary social theory and philosophy. I think that I have learned more from Habermas's writings than from those of any other contemporary social thinker whose work I have encountered. At the same time, I find myself in substantial disagreement with very many, perhaps most, of Habermas's major conceptions. In respect of Habermas's views upon hermeneutics, positivism and the critique of ideology, I have expressed some of my doubts elsewhere,[17] and shall not revert to these issues in the present context. Here I shall concentrate upon what seem to me to be some of the more directly 'sociological' difficulties related to the differentiation of labour and interaction.

Let me begin, however, from a more affirmative perspective. Habermas's reappraisal of the Hegel–Marx relation (more accurately put, the Kant–Hegel–Marx relation) seems to me to contain contributions of enduring significance, even if some of his interpretations of these thinkers are questionable. I do not think that the distinction between labour and interaction is itself one of those contributions, for reasons I shall come to shortly; but there is no doubt that, within the framework of Habermas's writings, the formulation of this distinction has helped him to shed light upon some very important issues. These include particularly, in my opinion, his identification of positivistic strains in Marx and the connecting of these to an analysis of the limitations of technical reason; his demonstration of the need to transcend the traditionally established division in philosophy between the 'claims to universality' of positivism and hermeneutics; and his unequivocal defence of a critical theory which insists upon the necessity of breaking with dogmatic forms of Marxism. Although some may object to the eclecticism of Habermas's work,[18] the pursuit of these themes has allowed him to bring together a diversity of erstwhile quite separate standpoints. In particular, Habermas has managed to bridge the chasm that has long separated some of the dominant Continental traditions in social theory and philosophy from those that have prevailed in the Anglo-Saxon world.

These things having been said, I do think none the less that Habermas's starting-point in the labour/interaction distinction, and his persistence with it in relatively unmodified form in his later work, have created basic inadequacies in his social theory. I shall discuss these under four headings: first, it is worth mentioning some conceptual ambiguities involved in the formulation of the distinction; second, I shall draw attention to certain problems that arise in the case of each concept taken separately; third, I shall review some implications for Habermas's analysis of institutions; and finally, I shall consider the application of the notions of labour and interaction to questions of social evolution or development. I do not claim any particular originality for the criticisms I have to offer, since Habermas's application of the concepts of labour and interaction have no doubt been scrutinised many times by previous authors.

1.   Some of the ambiguities in Habermas's use of 'labour' and 'interaction' have been pointed out by one of his leading commentators.[19] Habermas repeatedly presents the distinction as one referring to two types of action – purposive-rational action on the one hand, and communicative action on the other. One type of action is governed by technical rules, and sanctioned by the likelihood of failure to reach objectives; the other is governed by social norms, and sanctioned by convention or law. Even in his latest work, Habermas continues to write in this vein.[20] The same is the case for the sub-division he makes, within the notion of purposive-rational action, between 'strategic' and 'instrumental' action. But none of these is actually a type of action at all, as Habermas is forced to concede. They are, he says in response to this type of criticism, analytical elements of a 'complex'.[21] That is to say, they are 'idealised' features of action, like Weber's categories from which they in some part draw their inspiration. All concrete processes of labour, of course, as Habermas emphasises in his discussion of Marx, and as Marx emphasised so forcibly himself, are social – or, in Habermas's terms, involve interaction.

But this is wanting to have one's cake and eat it too. It is at best very misleading to want to use 'labour' as equivalent to an analytical element of action and at the same time continue to use it in the sense of 'social labour'; and to use 'interaction' similarly as both an analytical element and a substantive type, opposed to 'monologic' or solitary action. I think this confusion stems from an unfortunate *mélange* of ideas drawn from sources which do not really have much in common with one another. These sources are, on the one hand, the Weberian distinction between purposive-rational action and value-rational action (*Wertrationalität*: transmuted considerably by Habermas, however), and, on the other, the Marxian differentiation between the forces and relations of production. Weber's distinction was supposed to be an analytical or 'ideal-typical' one, but Marx's is not. Even within the Marxian scheme, 'labour' is not equivalent to 'forces of production', as presumably Habermas would acknowledge. But yet he continues quite frequently to slur one into the other: to assimilate 'forces of production', 'labour' and 'purposive-rational action'; and to assimilate 'relations of production', 'interaction' and 'communicative action'. These ambiguities or confusions might not matter much if there were purely terminological points at issue which could be corrected by clearer and more consistent usage. But they appear to me to lead to quite serious conceptual consequences for Habermas's work as a whole.

2.   Anyone who criticises Marx as radically as Habermas has attempted to do, even (or perhaps particularly) self-professedly in the spirit of Marxism, is bound to incur the wrath of more orthodox Marxists. Habermas's work has proved no exception. On the need for the reconstruction of historical materialism I am entirely on the side of Habermas, and have no sympathy with those who would assert dogmatically that no substantial revision of any of Marx's major concepts should be undertaken. When we consider Habermas's use of 'labour', and his criticisms of the Marxian notion of *Praxis*, the only question is whether or not these eventuate in a decisive advance over the original. I am bound to say that here I have to side with those critics who argue that they do not. Part of the reason is the very epistemological tone of Habermas's assessment of the Hegel–Marx transition. I do not share Habermas's over-all standpoint that today epistemology is only possible as social theory, and I do not think, as Habermas does, that the concept of labour remains an epistemological one in Marx – or at least, it only does so when assimilated to purposive-rational action, which in my opinion is not a justifiable equation. Habermas criticises, with some reason, the expansion of the notion of *Praxis* into a 'transcendental-logical' one, as he thinks Marcuse and Sartre have tended to do. But this sort of usage hardly exhausts the insights of the Marxian notion, if it is interpreted ontologically rather than epistemologically. Rather than attempting to make the idea of labour cover the whole gamut of associations with which it is tied in by Habermas, I think it more illuminating to distinguish labour from *Praxis*, using the former in a more restricted sense and the latter in a more inclusive one. I should regard 'labour', in other words, as 'social labour': as the socially organised productive activities whereby human beings interact creatively with material nature. Labour then remains an intrinsically social activity, among other types of activity or forms of institution. *Praxis* can be treated as the universal basis of human social life as a whole. *Praxis*, that is to say, refers to the constitution of social life as regularised practices, produced and reproduced by social actors in the contingent contexts of social life. What can be gleaned from Marx himself on these matters is fairly sketchy, but sufficient to provide clues that can be elaborated in detail.[22]

The objections that can be raised against Habermas's use of 'interaction' are at least as important as these – perhaps more important, since a goodly amount of Habermas's writing has concentrated upon interaction, as the 'neglected' side of the coin in historical materialism. The difficulties with Habermas's concept of interaction seem to me to derive from parallel sources to those concerning the notion of labour. Habermas identifies interaction with communicative action, this being governed by consensual norms. Now, his emphasis upon the hermeneutic interpretations of symbols as a methodological demand for social observation and as the medium of intersubjectivity among the members of society are quite unobjectionable – indeed, they are vital to social theory. But to treat interaction as equivalent to 'communicative action' is more than simply misleading, it is mistaken. Although Habermas insists that interaction is not reducible to labour, I would say that he himself makes a triple reduction within the notion of interaction itself: first, it is wrong to treat interaction as equivalent, or reducible, to action: second, it is wrong to treat action as equivalent, or reducible, to communicative action; and third, it is an error to suppose that communicative action can be examined solely on the level of norms. I doubt that Habermas would accept that he makes these reductions when they are thus bluntly stated. But I do not think it difficult to demonstrate that he constantly makes these elisions when he writes about interaction.

Let me develop these points somewhat. As regards the first point, perhaps the easiest way to express the matter is to say that most of Habermas's discussions of interaction do not mention *inter*action at all. To speak of interaction as a type, or even an element of action, is a misnomer. The result is that Habermas has little to say about, and proffers little in the way of concepts for analysing, the social relations that are constitutive of social systems. This may seem a banal-enough observation, but I think it is really rather significant. For it connects directly with Habermas's severing of the notion of *Praxis* into two. The production and reproduction of social life as *Praxis* involves placing as central the mechanisms whereby patterns of interaction are sustained recursively. 'Action theory', as I have tried to show elsewhere, is not the same as 'interaction theory': an adequate account of the constitution of social systems in interaction demands a conception of what I have called the 'duality of structure' in social reproduction.[23] It might be argued that, if Habermas barely touches upon these issues, this is simply an error of omission, and that the blank space could be filled in without compromising the rest of his ideas. But I think that consideration of the other two points I raised above indicates that this is not so. Action is not the same as 'communicative action', because communicative action is only one type of action. As regards this point, a lot hangs on what 'communication' is taken to mean. Again there seems some terminological ambiguity in Habermas here, in so far as he often seems to equate 'symbolic' with 'communicative'. The first does not necessarily imply, as the second normally does, some sort of intended meaning which an actor wishes to transmit to others. It might plausibly be said that all action involves symbols, but it cannot be maintained that the symbolic elements of action are equivalent to communicative intent. But Habermas quite often appears to argue as though they are, perhaps in some part because of his preoccupation with speech. In so far as he does so, he tends to move back towards the sorts of intentionalist philosophical accounts of meaning which are incompatible with other of his emphases in his discussions of hermeneutics.[24]

The third point I mentioned above can be put as follows: there is more to interaction than the norms to which it is orientated. Habermas's emphasis upon the normative components of interaction follows on plausibly enough from the identification of interaction with communicative action. But the consequence is that his social theory is surprisingly close to the 'normative functionalism' of Parsons. Both accord primacy to the norm in examining social interaction, rather than to power. It might seem somewhat surprising to make such a remark in so far as Habermas's work is presumptively directed to the critique of domination. None the less, I think it is a valid comment.[25] I should want to make the case for arguing that power is as integral a component of all social interaction as norms are.[26] Now Habermas appears to agree with this in so far as domination or power is made one of the three fundamental aspects of social organisation linked to the knowledge-constitutive interests in *Knowledge and Human Interests*. But the knowledge-constitutive interest linked to emancipation from domination is, as I have remarked, 'content-less': the critique of domination comes to turn upon freedom of communication or dialogue, rather than upon material transformations of power relations. The implications of this, I think, appear rather prominently in Habermas's formulations of the nature of critical theory, which are focused unswervingly upon the uncovering of ideology. Provocative though his formulation of an ideal speech situation is as a counterfactual model for social critique, it operates once more on the level of communication. It gives us no indication of how other problems traditionally associated with disparities of power, such as access to *scarce resources*, and *clashes of material interest,* are to be coped with in the 'good society'.

3.   The import of the critical comments I have made so far is that, in some part at least because of problems with the labour/interaction distinction, there is an 'absent core' in Habermas's writings: an adequate conceptual scheme for grasping the production and reproduction of society. This observation can be consolidated, I want to claim, if we look at those segments of his work which concern the institutional organisation of society. Here Habermas borrows in a direct fashion from Parsons's functionalism (as well as from Luhmann's systems theory, or so-called 'functional-structuralism'). Habermas has certainly not been uncritical either of Parsons or of functionalism more generally. But his disquiet with Parsons's theories, like with those of Luhmann, is mainly to do with the logical status of functionalism as an 'empirical-analytic' enquiry, rather than with the substance of those theories. The values and norms which play such a basic part in Parsons's portrayal of society cannot, Habermas argues, be accepted as 'given data' as Parsons assumes. They presuppose hermeneutic procedures of identification, and have to be opened out to the possibilities of ideology-critique.[27]

In other respects, however, Habermas seems prepared to take on board some major elements of Parsonian sociology. Among Parsons's views there are several which seem to me to be particularly questionable, and more than an echo of each of these is to be found in Habermas. The views I have in mind are Parsons's 'model of society', which accords a centrality to values and norms in social integration; the thesis that society and personality are homologous, or 'interpenetrate'; and the significance attributed to 'internalisation' in the theory of socialisation. I think major objections can be brought against all of these. The thesis of the primacy of values and norms in societal integration seems to me to be connected to a point I made previously, the tendency of Habermas to reduce interaction to communication and norms. The model of society which results – if one can judge thus far from what is clearly in Habermas's writings only a tentative approach to problems of social change – seems to embody no account of *contradiction*, and to underplay the significance of *power* and *struggle* in social development. It may be that Habermas will be able to incorporate these in his scheme in a more integral way, but he has not done so thus far. Rather, his discussion moves at the level of 'functional problems' which social systems face at certain stages of their history. 'System problems', a concept which I am not very comfortable with, are not contradictions; and Habermas has not so far given much indication of just how the identification of 'system problems' helps explain actual processes of historical change, or active social and political struggle. In lieu of a satisfactory analysis of these issues, I am more struck by the similarity of Habermas's account of social evolution to that offered by Parsons in his *Societies* [28] than I am by its closeness to Marx.

I have strong reservations about the thesis of the homology of society and personality, which has become an explicit supposition in Habermas's later writings. Although he recognises the difficulties with this conception viewed phenotypically, one cannot adopt it of course without retaining the general idea that the 'childhood of society' is like the childhood of the individual, the one a more rudimentary version of the other. But the languages of all known 'primitive societies' are as complex and sophisticated as those of the economically advanced societies, and all have rich symbolic or representational contents. The views of Lévi-Bruhl seem to me today to be less compelling than those of Lévi-Strauss. However that may be, in the present context I am more concerned to criticise the idea of society–personality homology as an analytical postulate of social theory, in which sense it is closely connected to the notion of 'internalisation'. These have been pervasive themes of Parsonian sociology, and are again related to the assumption that the value or norm is the key defining characteristic of the social (or of 'interaction'). Parsons's account of the 'internalisation' of norms supports the idea that the mechanisms providing for the integration of the individual within society and those integrating society are the same – the moral co-ordination of action through shared values. The very same values we 'internalise' in socialisation, and which form our personalities, are those which cohere the social system. The limitations of this kind of standpoint are pronounced. It further inhibits the possibility of dealing adequately with questions of power, sectional group interest and struggle. But on the level of the society–personality relation it implies a theory of social reproduction which fails to recognise the skilful and knowledgeable character of the everyday participation of actors in social practices.[29] We are led back here, I think, to the demand for a coherent conception of *Praxis*.

4. Finally, let me return to historical materialism, and to the issues posed by Marx's concepts of the forces and relations of production, the differentiation that apparently provided the main source of Habermas's labour/interaction distinction. According to Marx, the development of (class) societies can be explained in terms of the progressive elaboration of the forces of production, as they diverge from an existing set of relations of production. The controversies to which this scheme has given rise, together with the associated distinction between economic 'base' and political and ideological 'superstructure', are legion. Habermas attempts to reformulate the Marxian view on a historical level in much the same way as he did earlier in a more epistemological vein. That is to say, he asserts the independent significance of interaction, as opposed to labour, as a determining influence upon social development. I am in accord with the over-all ambition of this project, though not, for reasons I have explained, with the details of Habermas's view; because of how he conceives of 'interaction', his emphasis comes to be placed largely upon moral and cognitive orders. In his discussion of these matters Habermas admits to being influenced by the writings of 'structuralist Marxists' such as Godelier. He flirts with the idea of 'determination in the last instance',[30] and seems to want to maintain a version of the idea of social formations as exhibiting 'structures in dominance'. But I do not think that this idea is a persuasive one even at source, and in Habermas's hands it seems even more elusive. Habermas claims that, for him, 'culture remains a superstructural phenomenon', but I do not think he provides convincing demonstration of this assertion. Talk of 'economically conditioned system problems' is not only vague but suggests a view closer to Weber than that of Marx.

The problem, as I see it, is that Marx underestimated the distinctiveness of industrial capitalism, as compared with previous types of social formation. The notion of *Praxis*, in my opinion, is an essential idea which applies generically to the production and reproduction of society. But the dialectic of forces and relations of production, in anything like its classical form, is more confined in its historical scope. Only with the advent of capitalism does the accumulation process, and associated technological innovation, become the driving motor of social change. Only then does the scheme of divergence between the movement of the forces of production and the persistence of established relations of production have general application. But, of course, with the global spread of capitalism, this is nevertheless a phenomenon of world-historical significance.

9

Habermas's Theory of Social Evolution

MICHAEL SCHMID

Jürgen Habermas has developed his ideas on the foundation of a theory of evolution in various works and has repeatedly emphasised its programmatic character.[1] The theory is presented along several different lines of thought, but these, when looked at more closely, do not always form a coherent whole. The claims of a theory developed under such circumstances can only be judged in an equally limited way. In particular, the restricted scope of this essay prevents me from describing adequately the numerous connections with other theoretical and philosophical parts of Habermas's *oeuvre*. I shall also disregard the way that Habermas's evolutionary theory grew out of his debate with Niklas Luhmann's theory of society. Similarly, I should like to suspend judgement on the question of whether the illustrations of the theory are historically sound. I see my task, therefore, as twofold: first, to sketch out the content of the theory of evolution and, if possible, to systematise it; second, to examine some of the central concepts of the theory, an examination which should lead to an evaluation of it.

I

Habermas's starting-point for the development of an evolutionary theory is a reappraised historical materialism. This consists essentially in a fundamental anthropology which allows us to identify *labour* and *language* as irreducible presuppositions of any society. Only labour and language make possible the material reproduction of societies and the socialisation of their members. Given this presupposition, social evolution can be separated categorically from biological evolution; social evolution fundamentally *cannot* be treated according to the model of a biological theory of evolution. Thus the application of a criterion of biological selection (such as increased rates of reproduction) does not enable us to sketch a picture of the history of the human species; on the contrary, social evolution must be understood as the transformation and continuing reformation of social structures, and these must remain in principle identifiable as action structures.[2] Through extensive arguments Habermas has tried to substantiate the connection of reproductive labour with instrumental and/or strategic action on the one hand, and of language and communication with the competent use of normative rules on the other.[3] These distinctions are also a starting-point for his theory of evolution.

In order to sketch the theory we must present a series of definitions and explanatory theoretical links. We said above that social evolution manifests itself as a specific kind of structural change. The scope (*Wertbereich*) of the theory is therefore tied to social structures. The specific type of structures is described in different ways. Three distinct structures seem to be central.[4] (1) Structures of instrumental action: their object in the last instance is the fulfilment of the key functional problems (*Bezugsprobleme*) of material reproduction. (2) Separate from this is a power structure which derives from strategic action and which is concerned to effect the society's possible steering-performances. I regard the various kinds of differential steering requirements as a second key problem and call it, with Habermas, 'system autonomy'. (3) Finally, there is the key problem of social integration. Integration is achieved through the institutionalisation of binding normative structures. It occurs only if the relevant structures exhibit particular properties. We can list some of them: (a) normative structures must co-ordinate reciprocal behavioural expectations; (b) they must be institutionalised in comprehensive world-views and so be collectively utilisable; (c) they must therefore possess a capacity for regulating conflicts in expectations or behaviour. The different conditions underlying this capacity define the particular level of integration (*Integrationsniveau*) a society is able to attain. Habermas occasionally attempts to define this level of integration with the help of the consequences of normative structures: thus we should speak of 'integration' whenever the action-guiding norms guarantee a 'collective identity', and this in turn defines 'the individuals' membership of society (and exclusion from it)'.[5] The unquestioned nature of values and norms thereby secures social integration. Consequently, 'social integration' is also described as the 'consensual basis of normative structures'.[6] These normative structures can then be re-moulded into world-views.

Now such structures can in principle only be predicated of societies and not of a fictionally characterised species subject called 'humanity'.[7] Hence structures are always social structures. The scope of the proposed theory can thus be defined initially as pertaining to 'social structures', the characteristics and properties of which form the object domain of the theory. This definition of the theory's scope is fairly precise but in no sense conclusive, for we must remember that Habermas always tends to see social structures as consisting solely of action structures. Societies for him are 'networks of communicative actions' and structures are thus accessible only as 'structures of linguistically-produced intersubjectivity'.[8] However, if we do understand such structures expressly as action structures, we must take care to avoid thinking that social evolution is describable solely at the structural level: 'Society on its own, separated from the personality system, cannot bear the burden of evolution. The two (social system and personality system) are complementary and only when *taken together* do they produce a system capable of evolution.'[9] Reference to the personality system is thus necessary before the scope of the theory can be exhaustively defined.

In what does the *evolutionary* character of the theory consist? The answer is not provided by the above characterisation of the theory as a 'theory of structural change', since structural change is understood there only as a change in the state of fixed structural parameters. If the changes are to count as 'evolutive', they must be understood as 'cumulative processes exhibiting a certain direction'.[10] Habermas consistently uses the concept of 'developmental logic' to describe the fact that changes are *directed*. The concept plays a central role in the formulation of his theory and therefore must be rigorously defined. We can try to clarify the concept both through the formal characteristics of the process so termed and through an exposition of the methodological guidelines which its application is intended to introduce.

According to Habermas, we can speak of a developmental logic only when we can observe a factual development of specific *stages, phases,* or *steps*.[11] These different phases may be described as follows: (1) They should be discretely definable, i.e. definable as logically independent of one another. (2) The particular elements constituting phases must allow themselves to be constructed in the form of a system: they must exhibit an intrinsic structure. (3) The phases from which the completed development is formed must be capable of being ordered into an invariant sequence, so that no subsequent phase can be reached unless the previous phases of that sequence have been passed through. This means that in the next sequence the new qualitative elements must be integrated with the elements remaining from the previous phase to form a new structure (see condition 2).

Habermas deals with at least three developmental processes, each with a different object and to each of which he attributes an internal developmental logic: (1) The ontogenesis of the individual. A specific developmental logic can be documented in several spheres: in a cognitive sphere (the capacity for formal thought), a moral sphere (the capacity for moral judgement), and in a sphere of interaction (referring to an interactive competence based on normatively guided actions which are orientated to the actions of others). (2) In other places Habermas attributes a similar developmental logic to the technical development of humanity as a whole. Technical knowledge, which can be converted into instrumental action, increases by accumulation. (3) Normative structures also follow a developmental logic. In what dimension this occurs will be discussed later.

All of these internally different developmental logics share one common formal characteristic, namely that if a change does occur in response to such a logic, then it is possible to bring the various phases of this development into an *unequivocal* sequence and to order the different content of each phase according to a *criterion of higher value (Höherwertig-keit)*. This criterion is in turn *defined* in terms of at least one common property of the particular phases.

Simply knowing the developmental logic does not enable us to decide whether every possible developmental stage is in fact attained.[12] This can be done only when we know the processes that specify the conditions under which the transition to the next phase occurs. Habermas tells us nothing about the conditions for the accumulation of knowledge. In the case of the ontogenesis of the individual, processes of maturation and learning and/or a specific combination of the two can be adduced as these conditions. The development of normative structures would then depend on corresponding processes of 'collective learning'. In this context we generally find the hypothesis that learning acquired in individual experience is institutionalised in world-views and stored therein, to be used as a kind of tacit reserve in case recourse to collectively accessible experience were especially important for the resolution of system problems specific to society as a whole.[13]

However, even if this hypothesis could be expanded and substantiated, it would still not explain what is *contained* in the learning experience of these individuals. Clearly we can only find this out by defining unambiguously the phases distinguishable in the development of normative structures. When Habermas attempts this he relies on two arguments: (1) That it is possible to understand the stages of normative development of the structures of society as a whole as *equivalent* or somehow related to the ontogenesis of individual moral consciousness.[14] (2) That a reconstruction of the actual historical course of morality will substantiate the existence of such a developmental-logical sequence.[15]

(1) Drawing on the results of the developmental psychology of Piaget, Furth, Kohlberg and others,[16] Habermas describes the ontogenetic moral development of the individual in terms of a sequence of stages of moral consciousness:

At a preconventional stage, when actions, motives and acting subjects are still perceived on one level of reality, only the consequences of action are evaluated in cases of action conflict. At the conventional stage, motives can be assessed independently of concrete action consequences . . . At the postconventional stage, the systems of norms lose their naturalistic validity: they require justification from universalistic points of view.[17]

These categories for the description of individual structures of consciousness are also applied to the level of society as a whole, to characterise collective structures of moral consciousness.[18] Thus Habermas attributes to neolithic societies a conventionally structured action system with conventional models for the solution of moral conflicts, and he observes in such societies preconventional legal procedures for regulating conflicts. Early civilised cultures (*Frühe Hochkulturen*) still exhibit a conventionally structured action system but also have at their disposal world-views containing post-conventional proposals for problem-solving; yet the legal system still remains undeveloped. In modern societies the action system has at last acquired postconventional features, the world-views propagate a universalism, and the law is based on a separation of private morality and legality.

(2) In Habermas's view this sequence can be *reconstructed* through th historical development of law and morality.[19] By this he means a method (or perhaps an art) for uncovering the effective deep structures or basic rules according to which actions of any type – and particularly actions guided by norms – are performed. When we do this we also discover the developmental logic internal to the rules, that is, the logic for the way normative structures unfold. In this way we provide what the above definition required: namely, the sequential ordering of such norm structures.

Habermas sometimes gives the impression that this art of rational reconstruction is limited solely to rule systems. However, what is decisive is not the *content* of the reconstructed sequence, but rather the fact that, as structures develop, they are *capable of being represented* as if this development were aiming at the optimal fulfilment of a specific criterion. Habermas therefore suggests that it should be possible to portray 'the history of technique against the background of the ontogenetically analysed stages of cognitive development',[20] in such a way that normative rules are not implicated. It is thus important, above all, that the general argument which suggests that developments are describable as if they corresponded to a criterion of higher value should be reasonably applied and so acquire plausibility. We shall see in the next section how successful this ambition is.

Let us summarise our presentation so far of Habermas's theory of evolution: (1) we have emphasised the question of the scope of such a theory and shown what the theory's specifically *evolutive* character consists in; (2) we then clarified the concept of developmental logic; and (3) we sketched briefly the method for the rational reconstruction of advances made in accordance with this logic. This is our starting-point for a presentation of the evolutionary theory itself. Other conceptual explanations are given in the relevant context.

At the beginning we mentioned that Habermas tends to locate his theory of social evolution in the context of a reappraised historical materialism. Marx's attempt to discover the developmental laws of capitalism and to identify the specific dominant structure of the capitalist mode of production is therefore interpreted by Habermas as part of a possible evolutionary theory of society – but only as 'a part'. Marx constructed the connections between relations and forces of production in developmental-logical terms as successive stages of modes of production, but he placed too much emphasis on economic structures in the sense of purely instrumental action structures. Habermas regards the restriction of a theory of evolution to structures and rules of instrumental action as unjustified and indeed superfluous, though he does not contest Marx's analysis of the development of different modes of production either in content or in principle. As Habermas's theory of action distinguishes non-instrumental action structures, he can easily extend the scope of an evolutionary theory to include *these* structures of communicative and moral action. Furthermore, 'the development of these normative structures [is] the pacemaker of social evolution'.[21] To show exactly how this is to be understood is the task of the evolutionary theory itself.

Let us try to systematise the theory. It comprises, so far as I can tell, the following assumptions: (1) It is possible to reconstruct and to substantiate a developmental logic for the normative structures of societies.[22] (2) The developmental models or developmental stages thereby identified represent 'rules for possible problem solutions'.[23] (3) In order to clarify how these developmental stages come into existence, we need an empirical theory as to how individual learning processes reach the collectively accessible stock of knowledge. Habermas suggests that we view this as a process of institutionalisation which shows how 'individually acquired learning capacities and information' are latent in world-views before they are socially implemented, i.e. before they can be converted into *learning processes of society*. We should therefore look for the actual learning mechanisms only at the individual psychological level: 'Societies "learn" only in a metaphorical sense.'[24] (4) We therefore need a conception of the mechanism for the 'evolutionary learning' of societies which is independent of and insulated from the conditions of individual learning. To begin with, we find only a description of the fact that 'the learning capacities acquired by the individual members of society or marginal groups enter the interpretation systems of a society through exemplary learning processes'.[25] We can presume that social movements serve as vehicles for translating individual experience into world-views. But the theoretically central mechanism of 'evolutionary learning' has still not been fully explicated. We must make several more assumptions before we can finally clarify it.

(a) The learning capacities and information present in world-views define the specific *learning level* of a society.[26]

(b) This learning level sets the factual limits of a society's reaction potential when system problems occur.[27] Habermas always calls this reaction potential the 'steering capacity' of a society, and it must be understood as existing in empirical relation to power structures.[28] Unfortunately, the concept of 'system problems' is neither systematically nor clearly introduced. It generally signifies 'disturbances in the reproduction process of a society which is normatively fixed in its identity'.[29] The concept is thus clearly *not* restricted to economic steering problems. I should like to presume that system problems are generally to be understood in relation to the set of key problems *(Bezugsprobleme)* we have already identified, that is, they relate to the development of productive forces, of system autonomy and of *social integration.*

(c) The above assumption may clarify what the frequently mentioned concept of the organisation principle means and in what relation it stands to the concept of learning level. Here is one of the definitions given by Habermas:

> By organisation principles I understand those innovations made possible through learning steps which can be reconstructed in a developmental history and which institutionalise a new societal level of learning. A society's organisation principle circumscribes ranges of possibility; it determines, in particular, those structures within which changes of the institutional system are possible; it determines to what extent the available productive capacities can be socially utilised and/or whether the development of new productive forces can be stimulated; it thereby also determines how far it is possible to increase complexity and steering performance . . . A society's organisation principle may be characterised by the institutional core which determines the particular dominant form of social integration.[30]

The concept of the organisation principle is obviously intended to deal with several things. One of its functions is to link the forms of social integration with the level of learning manifested in particular world-views. Let us recall that integration is to be taken as one of the possible consequences of the normative structures which should secure collective identity. At the same time, integration is also one of the basic focal problems *(zentrale Bezugsprobleme)* of societies. It thus follows that the steering problems which particularly tend to produce crises are those which are no longer soluble within the *given* integrational forms and which consequently *compel* a society to change to a different form of organisation principle. It is obvious how improbable such an occurrence is. Both organisation principles and world-views together function to limit the conditions under which 'the transformation of the institutional and interpretative system is possible'.[31] This mutually supportive effect (which I should like to attribute to one and the same micro-process) functions, in the factual sequence of events, as a great restriction on the occurrence of 'evolutionary thrusts'. Apart from this role, the concept of the organisation principle is intended to help us characterise various types of *social formation*. Differences in the 'institutionalised cores of social integration' allow us to classify societies into different social formations.[32] It is important that this classification is made according to the reconstruction of the sequence of differential learning capacities. Hence forms of social integration are not only different from one another, but must also be classified according to the criterion of higher value incorporated in the level of learning. Societies can therefore be rated and classified according to the extent to which they exemplify the higher forms of social integration and higher problem-solving capacities.

(d) Such 'problem-solving capacities' represent natural dispositions of the corresponding learning level. These dispositions must be activated before they can be detected. Habermas suggests that they are activated by specific system problems or 'evolutionary challenges'.[33]

If we accept points (a) – (d), then we can present the mechanism of the 'evolutionary learning' of societies in the form of a two-stage argument. System problems, which can occur as contingent historical events, are tackled by a society's steering organs. The latter refer to the latent problem-solving capacities stored in world-views. So far as possible, system problems are solved *within* the established learning level which, under-stood as an organisation principle, at the same time defines the forms of social integration. Habermas willingly concedes to the Parsons–Luhmann system theory that this can be explained by a process of differentiation.

However, in the case of system problems which endanger integration because they can no longer be solved within the level of learning established by a specific organisation principle, Habermas finds that their version of system theory is incapable of explaining why societies *persist*. For him, in contrast, society can preserve its normatively secured identity in the face of evolutionary challenges by abandoning its learning level and thereby also its institutional form of integration, that is, its organisation principle. With recourse to the problem-solving capacities latent in its world-views, the society then reintegrates at a new (and in terms of developmental logic) higher stage. Habermas writes thus:

> We can also speak of an evolutionary learning process in societies insofar as they solve system problems which present evolutionary challenges. The latter are problems which overload the steering capacities contained in a given social formation. Societies can learn in an evolutionary sense by using the cognitive potential stored in world-views for the reorganisation of action systems . . . Introduction of a new organisation principle means the establishment of a new level of social integration.[34]

Only when a new, emergent organisation principle is present can 'given productive forces be implemented, new ones be generated, or social complexity be increased'.[35] To this extent, the evolutionary change of normative structures and thus of the forms of social integration is the *precondition* for further development of the relations of production: 'With its evolutionary accomplishments, a social system also acquires the conditions which make new learning processes possible.'[36] This means that once they have been incorporated into a developmental-logical process, the learning levels attained by a society become the basis for new ways of institutionalising fresh cognitive and moral content in the relevant action structures.

When we look at the theory of evolution more closely, therefore, we see that it tries to solve two quite different problems. In one case, its explanatory power applies only at a specific level of learning and hence addresses the question: 'How does a system behave within the logic of the structures attained at any given stage?'[37] Alternatively, the theory seeks to explain how a particular level of development is reached, hence how specific 'structures of collective consciousness' develop.[38] But the latter explanation has to be given quite independently of the first question, which means that it requires a different theory altogether: 'Social evolution must therefore in principle be understood as a two-staged problem-solving behaviour of macrosystems.'[39] On the one hand, we have to see the problem-solving behaviour of societies in relation to the developmental level they have attained (as incorporated in the organisation principle); we must also see the discernible steering-performances in the context of contingent steering-problems. On the other hand, if it cannot successfully explain the change in organisation principle, the evolutionary theory is itself imperfect! Such an explanation is possible, in Habermas's view, only if we can show which evolutionary learning processes are capable of generating a new organisation principle. He suggests therefore that we 'explain the evolutionary changes of social systems by referring simultaneously to developmental logics (structures of consciousness) and to historical processes (events)'.[40] An explanation of the genesis of these collective structures of consciousness (both normative and cognitive types) is thus possible only within the framework of a theory of evolutionary learning in societies.

This seems to me an adequate presentation of Habermas's theory of evolution. We now know both its scope and its object domain: namely, the mechanism of evolutionary learning in societies. We can now undertake a critical evaluation of the theory.

II

Habermas generally judges the merits of his theory of evolution by comparing it with functionalist systems theory. I shall not be investigating the rights and wrongs of this. Instead I should prefer to draw attention to certain *internal* difficulties of his theory. I shall try to present both my interpretation of it and my objections to it through a consideration of two central concepts, the organisation principle and the developmental logic.

The concept of the organisation principle

As we know, this concept carries a double load. On the one hand, it is linked by definition with the concept of developmental logic. This aspect does not concern us here. On the other hand, the organisation principle also serves to characterise specific social formations. As long as one of the explanatory problems of an evolutionary theory consists in the question of how the central structures which secure social identity manage to change, I shall assume that no such theory, regardless of which version, would be acceptable unless it has provided an unequivocal specification of the types of social formation. However, one of the dangers which may arise in this context (and which, I think, Habermas does not entirely avoid) is this: organisation principles are categorically defined only as 'abstract rules',[41] the essential characteristic of which is that they delimit the ranges of variation for structural changes. This definition is clearly insufficient for *differentiating* various types of social formations. Habermas, who, in trying to resolve this problem, argues almost exclusively within the framework of previous research, tries consistently to put these 'abstract rules' into an empirical relation with established social structures which allow for the requisite differentiation. Although the resultant classifications of social formations are not identical in all his texts, they may, with a little effort, be converted into one another. What is more important, however, is the *content* of such interpretations. Habermas locates the organisation principle of a social formation which he usually calls 'pre-civilised culture' or 'early civilised culture' in kinship structures, specifically in the institution of the family. In traditional or civilised societies the prevailing form of state domination provides the vehicle for the relevant organisation principle. By contrast, the organisation principle of modern or liberal-capitalist formations is expressed in the relations of economic classes. I shall not argue against the content of his interpretation. It can be judged only on the basis of empirical research, that is, by testing the derivations of the theory which is made concrete in this way. There is, however, a particular problem which commonly arises in this context. We should not assume that a certain social formation can be comprehensively described in terms of an organisation principle alone. There may be quite different structures empirically related to the core structure defining a social formation; and we may legitimately wish to *explain* these different structures by reference to the organisation principle. But the empirical test of such an explanation will be quite redundant if we have already semantically incorporated these different structures into the very formulation of the principle itself. So if we wish to explain the emergence of a class structure in societies integrated by political domination, we cannot at the same time *define* the organisation principle as 'political class domination' *and* in explicating *this* concept suggest that relations of production immediately possess a political form in a social formation such as that under consideration.[42] This kind of thinking clearly produces only analytical statements.

Even if we could avoid, through suitable empirical interpretations, the definitional conflation of the vehicular structures with the structures whose emergence we wish to explain, there remains a further difficulty. The theory of evolution is not, on the basis of its abstract semantics, in a position to determine what *types* of structures are to be *expected* within a given social formation, other than the core structures defined by the organisation principle. We cannot take the instances in Habermas's texts where the theory is applied as a test of the theory, but only as illustrations of it. Habermas himself would surely agree with this view.[43] My argument here should therefore be taken less as an attack on his theory than as a clarification of an important point. Evolutionary theories which are formulated at the level of abstraction of Habermas's theory – and I should like to suggest that such theories can only be formulated at this level[44] – *necessarily require an empirical interpretation* before they can be tested. It should be clear that what we criticise thereby is not the theory itself but the *interpretations* of it. This is especially so in view of the fact that the mere selection of contexts for the theory, and perhaps even our perception of those contexts, always tends to occur in the light of the most favourable possible application of the theoretical ideas. I emphasise once more that I consider this point to be noteworthy and important.[45] For it shows clearly that Habermas's theory of evolution is formulated at a semantic level which corresponds to that of classical foundation theories (e.g. utility theory in national economics or in the 'new political economy', or the rationality principle in action theory). My argument therefore ought to protect theoretical sociology from its latest misapprehension, whereby every partial interpretation or fragment of an evolutionary theory is hailed as an independent paradigm.[46] In addition, Habermas's theory has the advantage of being formulated in *non-individualistic* terms, thus promising an early end to the barren reductionism debate.[47] The reason that I still find Habermas's theory questionable lies in its application of developmental-logical arguments.

The concept of developmental logic
We discussed in detail how developmental logic should enable us to recognise a sequence of steps which can be ordered according to a criterion of higher value. Habermas sees this point alone as sufficient justification for using the concept of 'evolution'. His theory is always flexible enough to

allow for some leeway in the transition from the ontogenetic sequences of empirical developmental psychology to the developmental logic of world-views or the stages of collective consciousness. His description of the relation between the two processes as an 'homology' or a 'copy' points to a factual connection but provides no clear interpretation of it.[48] A restriction follows only from his proposed theory of the 'evolutionary learning of societies', in so far as it informs us that different organisation principles incorporate different stages of action competence and different levels of moral reflection. In fact, I can find no detailed argument for what the connection between ontogenesis and the developmental logic of world-views should look like. But if, taking Habermas's terms as literally as possible, we do assert that there is an empirical connection between the conditions of evolutionary learning and an ontogenetic developmental logic, then we come upon what seems to me to be an obscure empirical problem: can we connect the fact that different problem-solving capacities are institutionalised in structures of collective consciousness according to the organisation principle and the learning level (which is what the ascription of a developmental logic to learning levels amounts to) with the fact that the people of earlier social formations did not pass through all the stages of their possible ontogenetic development? In other words, was the process by which the action competencies of people of earlier epochs came to maturity restricted (perhaps by disruptions of their learning capacities) to preconventional or conventional stages of development? If this is the case, what kind of empirical grounds could we produce for this, independently of the fact that the relevant world-views had *no* universal or postconventional features? It seems to me much more sensible to avoid this thin ice and to separate strictly the processes of learning and maturation which guide the ontogenesis of the individual from those processes which underlie the development of world-views. We could then explain the fact that specific learning performances are assimilated into world-views by pointing out that they provide precisely the problem-solutions which guide the steering-performances of the society concerned, and moreover that the pre-adaptive expansion of such world-views is *not* rewarded when social organisation is so layered that the proposals of individual groups cannot in principle be carried through.[49] Why this is the case would then have to be capable of being explained by *application of the evolutionary theory to the processes of the collective stabilisation of knowledge*.[50] This application of the theory would have to take account of the factual structures which determine the institutionalised expansions of the stock of knowledge and also of the relevant intra- and extra-social environments of the societies under examination. The moral conservatism of traditional societies would then be the factual consequence of this complex of conditions, and we would not fall back on the highly dubious assumption that the people of earlier societies were *incapable* of reflecting upon their norms.[51] The stability of their environment would have removed the *need* for them to do this. That should suffice as an explanation.

The above is naturally only a tentative explanation and perhaps even less than that, but it does have one advantage which the postulation of developmental-logical sequences seems to me generally to obscure. It forces us to ask whether this postulation can be related to *factual evidence*, and whether the assertion that such developmental sequences actually occur has an *empirical* referent. I think I interpret Habermas's works correctly when I say that this is not his view at all. In his opinion, evolution is not a macro-process which accomplishes itself in a species subject. The epistemic character of the rational reconstructions also attests to a non-empirical interpretation of the developmental logic. These reconstructions are not empirical theories but *retrospective interpretations* which treat a factual process of development *as if* it were the optimal fulfilment of a specific criterion. Any 'as if' philosophy is obliged to define the limits of its proposed powers of explanation in the face of the all too 'freely creative moment'[52] of such fictions. Otherwise, in the context of an empirically understood theory of social evolution, the question remains as to exactly how much of the burden of explanation is in fact carried by the reconstruction of the developmental logic. I think it possible to prove not only that the postulation of a developmental logic leads to questionable assumptions about the relation between ontogenesis and the development of world-views, but also that such a logic has no explanatory powers whatsoever and in fact only burdens an evolutionary theory with irrelevant logical problems. I should like therefore to prescribe a radical cure for Habermas's theory by suggesting that *it be freed of all developmental-logical elements*. The following paragraphs are intended to show as concisely as possible that a theory of social evolution can be purified in this way without diminishing its explanatory power.

A treatment of knowledge in terms of an empirical theory of evolution which dispenses with a developmental logic seems at first to suffer from several drawbacks. Within the terms of its own assumptions, such a theory can now no longer reduce innovations to a developmental logic of world-views; not even the innovations in moral and technical knowledge (which correspond to Habermas's developmental thrusts and so to a partial definition of his organisation principle) can be so reduced. World-views are now *contingent*, in the same way as the occurrence of steering-problems in Habermas's theory. In other words, innovations in knowledge now belong to the environment of systems capable of evolution. We may now fear that a non-arbitrary definition of the organisation principle has become impossible. I think this fear is groundless, for even *with* the assumption of a developmental logic of world-views such a definition *cannot* be given. A developmental logic does not say that innovations will occur and in which form, but only that they *can be inferred* through *retrospective reconstruction.*[53] This claim is entirely irrelevant in the present context of our discussion. An evolutionary theory which regards innovations in knowledge as external factors is thus no more inadequate than one which assumes a developmental logic.

The point can be clarified by looking at a biologically interpreted theory of evolution. Darwinian theory dealt only with the selection process which describes the selection of morphological properties in strict relation to environmental changes. With cytology still in its infancy, the theory was unable to identify the mechanism which actually brings about such morphological changes. This was impossible until the invention of theories of genetic mutation and the associated molecular-biological processes. But even these theories do not explain *why* genetic mutations occur; they presuppose the occurrence of such mutations and predict only *where* they will occur and with what consequences. [54] It is thus no argument against a sociological application of evolutionary theory to say that societies do not change through biological mutation. No one disagrees with this and the point poses no problems. What is significant is that, as in the case of a biologically interpreted theory of evolution, it is in fact possible to identify a process whose mechanism produces innovations; and in the case of the sociologically applied theory, this means a mechanism which produces knowledge-content, irrespective of *what* content. The important point is that content is produced and that we are able to make theoretically plausible conjectures as to where such knowledge-innovations will occur and what consequences, if they are produced, they will have. The consequences which are particularly important for our theoretical interests are those which pertain to current integration and steering-problems. We can still remain within the framework which Habermas has designed: vehicles for innovation are personality systems which possess the property of being able to learn, perhaps even of having to learn. Such a 'theory of compulsory learning' would be of the greatest interest in this context, but even *it* would not be able to account for the content, that is, to explain *what* will be learned. This situation will in no way be changed by a developmental-logical expansion of evolutionary theory. A developmental logic of world-views does not explain how moral and cognitive innovations arise; it describes their occurrence, *if* they occur.[55] The reference to world-views and their content can thus be understood in terms of the logic of explanation as simply a specification of boundary conditions. Such a reference is, in the context of an evolutionary theory, of no theoretical relevance whatsoever.

If we bear in mind the above, we avoid the temptation to represent the development of knowledge as a *process of optimisation.*[56] If we do not resist the temptation, we make a twofold error.

(1) We burden an *empirical* theory of evolution quite unnecessarily with

normative/descriptive ambiguities in its terminology. It is quite misleading to interpret as 'progress' the fact that specific properties of knowledge permit *more* problems to be solved, without explaining *which theoretical problem* (expressible in terms of an empirical theory of evolution) would be solved by adding the dead weight of such a value-judgement to the concept of evolution. In fact – and here I suggest that my contention has apodictic value – no new theoretical problems are solved by this addition. We would receive *no new* empirical information about the factual process of evolution if, for example, we were to identify as 'progressive' or 'more advanced' the 'integrational forms of political domination in the state' in contrast to those of tribal societies,[57] and were to think we meant thereby something apart from the simple fact that the organisation principle of civilised cultures enables them to solve steering-problems which would have caused tribal societies (lacking the means for stabilising new steering-performances) to collapse. The integration processes of each social formation are simply *different*. It is true that politically integrated societies are able to integrate *more* people through collective models of integration. In this *cognitive* sense their problem-solving capacity is indeed greater. But is it the case that we could maintain this *only if* we knew that kinship forms of integration were the original ones, that these were a necessary precondition for the development of political domination, and *only if* we simultaneously supposed that this sequence of factual events was, in Habermas's sense, a developmental-logical one? I very much doubt it. That this was in fact so, that societies with quickly growing populations did not disintegrate as an empirical consequence of the formation of the state, was doubtless of no small importance for the happiness of many people. Who would disagree or morally disapprove of this? But a developmental logic, with its built-in assumption of optimisation, cannot account for the fact that all this did occur and had to occur in just this way. Our approval is of no relevance to the factual development itself.

Within the framework of an empirical theory of evolution, there are only two points which can be grasped theoretically: that a connection exists between stocks of knowledge and the steering-capacities factually delimited by the conditions of an organisation principle; and that consequently a society's degree of adaptation to its environment is measured by the type of steering-capacities factually available to it. Which stocks of knowledge can then in fact be used and referred to depends on the empirically identifiable key problems in the society, on the conditions of institutionalisation of the stocks of knowledge and on the particular social and non-social environment in which, if the relevant level of integration is to be stabilised, the action structures important for the stocks of knowledge have to be developed and maintained.

This enables us to see how, *without* innovations (which a developmental logic cannot guarantee anyway), persistent crises can set in; or alternatively how, in drastically changed environmental conditions, recourse to previous levels of integration for the important action structures can prove to be a *better* form of integration. I cannot see what further theoretically relevant information we would gain if, by accepting a developmental logic which is irrelevant to the purpose of explanation, we were allowed to call such changes in the direction of a historically prior level of integration 'regressive'.

My argument against the confusion of explanatory and evaluative viewpoints does not claim to be original.[58] It merely circumscribes the fact that Habermas by no means wishes his evolutionary theory to be understood as *exclusively* cognitive-empirical. This is not the place to examine whether a 'critical theory of society' must necessarily conceal its evaluative standpoint in its empirical investigations. But we should understand how this has come about.

The undeniable impression given by Habermas's ideas of being weighed down by value-judgements results, in my opinion, from the following argumentative strategy. First, he defines 'evolution' as a 'directed process'; but he can then give no clear theoretical grounds for the *necessity* of this definition, apart from the empirically uncashable *(uneinlösbar)* developmental logic of world-views. At the same time, a developmental logic can specify the *necessary* conditions for the further development of steering-performances only if a new organisation principle is *already present*. Since Habermas also fails to measure the performance level of an organisation principle for social integration in terms of the society's relation to an environment of societies similarly burdened with steering-problems, but instead simply refers to the assumed developmental logic of world-views, he is unable to escape the evaluative character of his judgements about different forms of social integration. The reference to a logic of world-views would only be a valid argument if it referred to an actual process and, on his own admission, this is not the case. The idea of higher value and progressiveness is thus already implicit in a developmental logic, or, as I would suggest, *built into it*. It is thus not surprising that Habermas should find other theoreticians, who do not share his belief in the factual existence of a developmental logic, lacking in a theory of evolution.[59] Such a consequence is clearly the result of Habermas's strategy of definition rather than the result of the inability of theories without a developmental logic to explain evolutionary change. In contradistinction to Habermas, the latter theories conceptualise evolutionary change as a form of structural adaptation and not on the basis of a developmental logic.

(2) This leads us to the second error involved in the idea of optimisation. Clarification of this error explains why Habermas identifies 'higher problem-solving capacities' as 'progress' and why the failure to attain them is called 'regression'.

Hypotheses of optimisation are relevant only where the augmented expression of a value can be observed in a factual dimension. I concede to Habermas that the 'augmentation of problem-solving capacities' can be understood in this sense. But this insight can be used meaningfully only as long as we know *which problems* will be better or worse solved. What is to count as a 'higher' problem-solving capacity can clearly be measured only in terms of the current steering-problems of a society; and more importantly, the latter are *specifiable* only in relation to a society's environment. Consequently, the judgement of the 'higher value' of problem-solving capacities must be sharply distinguished from their *contents*, that is, from the set of factual problems that *can* be solved at a certain time.[60] What *can be done* at a certain reconstructed level should not be identified with a possible evolutionary advantage of this ability. For we can surely posit (not merely reconstruct) environments in which postconventional norms of action would prove to be extremely harmful; similarly, societies are capable of producing pre-adaptive overloads which could seriously endanger social integration. The development of modern sciences seems to me to point quite definitely in this direction. I consider it therefore a *theoretical* error to assume that the cognitive and moral contents of world-views are relevant *as such* to adaptation. In my view, this assumption is very clearly due to the specific evaluative positions which are taken with regard to the specific content of stocks of knowledge or morality. We can surely agree about the relative justification of our positions; but I cannot derive them from the postulates of an *empirical* theory of evolution.

In sum, the assumption that optimised and accumulated knowledge can be sequentially ordered is plausible as an empirical assertion about the development of an object domain *only if* we can show that this state is the result of an empirically locatable process of selection. To show this we would have to presuppose two things: (1) that accumulation and selection in fact coincide or, in other words, that accumulations possess a selective value – an evolutionary theory can maintain this only under restricted conditions; (2) that both processes (selection and accumulation) can be co-ordinated within the same empirical subject.

Reference to a given and completed sequence of development is of little help, since it already includes the proof that previous development has satisfied its criterion of selection. Furthermore, *every* completed development is capable of being reconstructed in developmental-logical terms. We can always find a specific number of conditions without whose realisation the next steps would not have taken place. There are countless instances where, within a factual sequence of development, we will naturally discover *ex post facto* that innovations influenced the development. This will of course also prove to be the case even without our knowing the empirical subject of the supposed accumulation, as long as we can – in whatever sense – speak of growth or advancement, and this is always possible if we *already know* the relevant innovations. I do not find this procedure theoretically fruitful.

My objections against Habermas's assertions of optimisation are thus directed not against the basic theory underlying such an explanation, which should be used if a development can be characterised as both cumulative and selective, but against the supposed factuality of the explanandum. The investigations of, for example, Kuhn, Feyerabend and Toulmin into the history of science seem to me to have shown that we cannot speak of an accumulation of natural scientific knowledge towards a standard which is constitutive, optimisable and outside of time.[61] Karl Popper's theory of science makes this assumption and maintains that theories develop along the lines of a criterion of approximation towards truth.[62] His theory *in fact* forms the only basis for a reconstruction of the history of science; and of course, for this history, the development of the sciences can then be reconstructed according to a criterion of optimisation.[63] The fact that such a criterion of approximation towards truth is incapable of a consistent logical definition is, in view of this *petitio principii*, not the only index of the defectiveness of this view.[64]

If, therefore, reconstructed developmental logics *appear* to us as cumulative sequences, this is *only the result of the reconstruction itself*. That is, since developmental logics are always applied to facts *already present*, their appearing so is not the result of the factual course of things but rather of our forgetfulness, of the simple inaccessibility of the relevant facts or of our evaluative convictions. I do not possess the specialised knowledge necessary to exclude the possibility that accumulation and selection may coincide in the development of world-views. However, given a knowledge of at least some of the conditions under which traditional societies reproduce, it seems feasible to me to derive, from an evolutionary theory freed of developmental-logical elements, the following point: it seems unlikely that ontogenetically possible stages of development which clearly exist, the human organism being the vehicle of such an empirically observable sequence, are really transformed into world-views of a similar sequential order, while at the same time *there is no empirically visible carrier system for these world-views.*[65]

As a consequence of these arguments, I do not see that the development of world-views provides any grounds for the presupposition of a developmental logic. I understand neither its theoretical meaning nor its empirical sense. Nevertheless, I regard the parts of Habermas's thought which are independent of the developmental-logical arguments as perfectly plausible. A sociologically interpreted theory of evolution can be formulated only in terms of the changes in forms of structural integration and hence only as a structuralist theory. Any other version is reductive and therefore misleading. But the reconstruction of developmental logics, and particularly of completed processes of development, is theoretically arbitrary. I do not consider this to be a feature suitable for incorporation into an evolutionary theory designed to offer empirically plausible sociological interpretations.

Why does Habermas hold so rigidly to the idea of a developmental logic?

This is a problem in so far as we presume him to be aware of the counter-arguments sketched above. The answer is hidden at the end of one of his longer essays, [66] but it is clear and unequivocal. Habermas would like his evolutionary theory to be applied in discourses, where competing projections of identity are at issue. This is not the place to discuss Habermas's view of the conditions of rational discourse. But if we are to understand his position, we must note what he considers to be its essential function: 'rational discourse' should, under specific conditions, enable those participating in it to come to a consensual agreement for the rational solution of their problems. 'Rationality' is defined by (among other things) the degree of generalisability of the proposed solutions. If it were possible to prove the existence of 'invariant structures' in moral and cognitive development, this would increase the chances for a rational critique of, for instance, moralities which do not fulfil the possibilities given at a specific level of learning. The chances of a reflective self-emancipation of humanity could then draw support from the factual process of history, and the postulated partiality for reason would provide hope for an unequivocal identification of moral regressions. [67]

My critique of the developmental logic allows us no such hope. Is this merely the residual expression of a positivistically bifurcated reason? My only defence is to extend another hope: that liberation from unjustifiable constraints could be achieved without falling back on theoretical fictions, relying instead on the application of theories that identify the conditions underlying these constraints – theories which Habermas rightly calls 'emancipatory'. [68] But liberation has to come from a *commitment* to justice *(das Richtige)* . The responsibility for this commitment cannot be sought in historical processes reconstructed through developmental logic, for it lies only in ourselves.

Translated by Nicholas Saul

10

Crisis Tendencies, Legitimation and the State

DAVID HELD

Habermas's writings on advanced capitalist societies represent an important contribution to social theory. In conjunction with his colleagues he has helped to direct our understanding of the organisational principles of society away from old dogmas – dogmas asserting, for instance, that the state is merely 'a system of coercion to support the dominant class' or that it is 'a coalition balancing all legitimate interests'. Since the advantages of Habermas's work over less sophisticated approaches have been succinctly emphasised elsewhere, I shall focus this essay, first, on a brief account of his work and, second, on a number of problems which, I think, weaken its utility and scope. [1]

In *Strukturwandel der Öffentlichkeit* (1962) and *Toward a Rational Society* (a selection of essays written in the latter half of the 1960s but not published in English until 1970), Habermas documents the growth of large-scale economic and commercial organisations, the increasing interdependence of science, technology and industry, the increasing interdependence of state and society, and the extension of instrumental reason (a concern with the adequacy of means to pre-given goals) to ever more areas of life. These developments, he argues, have created a new constellation of economics and politics: 'politics is no longer *only* a phenomenon of the superstructure'.[2] The expansion of the state – symptomatic of the crisis tendencies of capitalist society – leads to an ever greater involvement of administrators and technicians in social and economic affairs.[3] It also leads, in conjunction with the fusion of science, technology and industry, to the emergence of a new form of ideology: ideology is no longer simply based on notions of just exchange but also on a technocratic justification of the social order. A perspective emerges in which political decisions *seem*, as Habermas puts it, 'to be determined by the logic of scientific-technical progress'.[4] Practical issues, underpinned by particular historical class interests, are defined as technical problems: politics becomes the sphere for the technical elimination of dysfunctions and the avoidance of risks that threaten 'the system'.

In his more recent works, *Legitimation Crisis* (1973) and *Communication and the Evolution of Society* (1979), Habermas seeks to analyse in greater detail changes in contemporary society. He does so in the context of the development of a theory of social evolution. Part of this project involves the identification of (a) the 'possibility spaces', i.e. the potential avenues of development, which a society's 'core structures' create; and (b) the crisis tendencies to which such structures are vulnerable. Although Habermas is concerned to investigate pre-civilisation (primitive communities) and traditional societies, his main focus hitherto has been on modern capitalism. He explores, in particular, the way 'advanced' (or, as he sometimes calls it, 'late' or 'organised') capitalism is susceptible to 'legitimation crisis' – the withdrawal from the existing order of the support or loyalty of the mass of the population as their motivational commitment to its normative basis is broken. It is his contention that the seeds of a new evolutionary development – the overcoming of capitalism's underlying class contradiction – can be uncovered in this and other related crisis tendencies.[5]

Habermas first provides an analysis of liberal capitalism which follows Marx closely.[6] He explicates the organisational principle of this type of society – the principle which circumscribes the 'possibility spaces' of the system – as the *relationship of wage labour and capital.* The fundamental contradiction of capitalism is formulated as that between social production and private appropriation, i.e. social production for the enhancement of particular interests. But, as Habermas stresses, a number of questions have to be posed about the contemporary significance of Marx's views. Have events in the last hundred years altered the mode in which the fundamental contradiction of capitalism affects society's dynamic? Has the logic of crisis changed from the path of crisis growth, unstable accumulation, to something fundamentally different? If so, are there consequences for patterns of social struggle? These questions informed Habermas's early writings. However, the way he addresses them from *Legitimation Crisis* onwards represents a marked elaboration of his earlier views.

The model of advanced capitalism Habermas uses follows many well-known recent studies.[7] He begins by delineating three basic sub-systems, the economic, the political-administrative and the socio-cultural. The economic sub-system is itself understood in terms of three sectors: a public sector and two distinct types of private sector. The public sector, i.e. industries such as armaments, is orientated towards state production and consumption. Within the private sector a distinction is made between a sector which is still orientated towards market competition and an oligopolistic sector which is much freer of market constraints. Advanced capitalism, it is claimed, is characterised by capital concentration and the spread of oligopolistic structures.

Habermas contends that crises specific to the current development of capitalism can arise at different points. These he lists as follows:

Point of origin (sub-systems)	System crisis	Identity crisis
Economic	Economic crisis	—
Political	Rationality crisis	Legitimation crisis
Socio-cultural	—	Motivation crisis

His argument is that late-capitalist societies are endangered from at least one of four possible crisis tendencies. It is a consequence of the fundamental contradiction of capitalist society (social production versus private appropriation) that, other factors being equal, there is either: an economic crisis because the 'requisite quantity' of consumable values is not produced; or a rationality crisis because the 'requisite quantity' of rational decisions is not forthcoming; or a legitimation crisis because the 'requisite quantity' of 'generalised motivations' is not generated; or a motivational crisis because the 'requisite quantity' of 'action-motivating meaning' is not created. The expression 'the requisite quantity' refers to the extent and quality of the respective sub-system's products: 'value, administrative decision, legitimation and meaning'.[8]

The reconstruction of developmental tendencies in capitalism is pursued in each of these dimensions of possible crisis. For each sphere, theorems concerning the nature of crisis are discussed, theories which purport to explain crisis are evaluated, and possible strategies of crisis avoidance are considered. 'Each individual crisis argument, if it proves correct, is a sufficient explanation of a possible case of crisis.' But in the explanation of actual cases of crises, Habermas stresses, 'several arguments can supplement one another'.[9]

At the moment, in Habermas's opinion, there is no way of cogently deciding questions about the chances of the transformation of advanced capitalism. He does not exclude the possibility that economic crises can be permanently averted; if such is the case, however, contradictory steering imperatives, which assert themselves in the pressure of capital utilisation, produce a series of other crisis tendencies. That is not to say economic crises will be avoided, but that there is, as Habermas puts it, no 'logically necessary' reason why the system cannot mitigate the crisis effects as they manifest themselves in one sub-system. The consequences of controlling crises in one sub-system are achieved only at the expense of *displacing and transforming* the contradictions into another. What is presented is a typology of crisis tendencies, a logic of their development and, ultimately, a postulation that the system's identity can only be preserved at the cost of individual autonomy, i.e. with the coming of a totally administered world in which dissent is successfully repressed and crises are defused. Since Habermas regards legitimation and motivation crises as the distinctive or central types of crisis facing advanced capitalist societies, I should like to give a brief *résumé* of them.

Increased state activity in economic and other social realms is one of the major characteristics of contemporary capitalism. In the interests of avoiding economic crisis, government and the state shoulder an increasing share of the costs of production. But the state's decisions are not based merely on economic considerations. While on the one hand, the state has the task of sustaining the accumulation process, on the other it must maintain a certain level of 'mass loyalty'. In order for the system to function, there must be a general compliance with the laws, rules, etc. Although this compliance can be secured to a limited extent by coercion, societies claiming to operate according to the principles of bourgeois democracy depend more on the existence of a widespread belief that the system adheres to the principles of equality, justice and freedom. Thus the capitalist state must act to support the accumulation process and at the same time act, if it is to protect its image as fair and just, to conceal what it is doing. If mass loyalty is threatened, a tendency towards a legitimation crisis is established.

As the administrative system expands in late capitalism into areas traditionally assigned to the private sphere, there is a progressive demystification of the nature-like process of social fate. The state's very intervention in the economy, education, etc., draws attention to issues of choice, planning and control. The 'hand of the state' is more visible and intelligible than 'the invisible hand' of liberal capitalism. More and more areas of life are seen by the general population as politicised, i.e. as falling within its (via the government's) potential control. This development, in turn, stimulates ever greater demands on the state, for example for participation and consultation over decisions. If the administrative system cannot fulfil these demands within the potentially legitimisable alternatives available to it, while at the same time avoiding economic crisis, that is, 'if governmental crisis management fails . . . the penalty . . . is withdrawal of legitimation'.[10] The underlying cause of the legitimation crisis is, Habermas states rather bluntly, the contradiction between class interests: 'in the final analysis . . . *class structure* is the source of the legitimation deficit'.[11] The state must secure the loyalty of one class while systematically acting to the advantage of another. As the state's activity expands and its role in controlling social reality becomes more transparent, there is a greater danger that this asymmetrical relation will be exposed. Such exposure would only increase the demands on the system. The state can ignore these demands only at the peril of further demonstrating its non-democratic nature.

So far the argument establishes only that the advanced capitalist state might experience legitimation problems. Is there any reason to expect that it will be confronted by a legitimation crisis? It can be maintained that since the Second World War, Western capitalism has been able to buy its way out of its legitimation difficulties (through fiscal policy, the provision of services, etc.). While demand upon the state may outstrip its ability to deliver the goods, thus creating a crisis, it is not necessary that this occurs. In order to complete his argument, therefore, and to show – as he seeks to – that 'social identity' crises are the central form of crises confronting advanced capitalism, Habermas must demonstrate that needs and expectations are being produced (on the part of at least a section of the population) which will 'tax the state's legitimizing mechanisms beyond their capacity'.

Habermas's position, in essence, is that the general development of late capitalism, and in particular the increasing incursion of the state into formerly private realms, has significantly altered the patterns of motivation formation. The continuation of this tendency will lead, he contends, to a dislocation of existing demands and commitments. Habermas analyses these issues, not under the heading 'legitimation crisis' (a point I shall come back to later), but under the heading 'motivation crisis'. 'I speak of a motivation crisis when the socio-cultural system changes in such a way that its output becomes dysfunctional for the state and for the system of social labor.'[12] This crisis will result in demands that the state cannot meet.

The discussion of the motivation crisis is complex. The two major patterns of motivation generated by the socio-cultural system in late capitalist societies are, according to Habermas, civil and familial-vocational privatism. Civil privatism engenders in the individual an interest in the output of the political system (steering and maintenance performances) but at a level demanding little participation. Familial-vocational privatism promotes a family-orientated behavioural pattern centred on leisure and consumption on the one hand, and a career interest orientated towards status competition on the other. Both patterns are necessary for the maintenance of the system under its present institutions. Habermas argues that these motivational bases are being systematically eroded in such a way that crisis tendencies can be discerned. This argument involves two theses: (1) that the traditions which produce these motivations are being eroded; and (2) that the logic of development of normative structures prevents a functionally equivalent replacement of eroded structures.

The motivational patterns of late capitalism are produced, Habermas suggests, by a mixture of traditional pre-capitalist elements (e.g. the old civic ethic, religious tradition) and bourgeois elements (e.g. possessive individualism and utilitarianism). Given this overlay of traditions, thesis (1) can itself be analysed into two parts: (a) that the pre-bourgeois components of motivational patterns are being eroded; and (b) that the core aspects of bourgeois ideology are likewise being undermined by social developments. Habermas acknowledges that these theses can only be offered tentatively.[13]

The process of erosion of traditional (pre-bourgeois) world-views is argued to be an effect of the general process of rationalisation. This process results in, among other things, a loss of an interpretation of the totality of life and the increasing subjectivising and relativising of morality. With regard to thesis (1b), that the core elements of bourgeois ideology are being undermined, Habermas examines three phenomena: achievement ideology, possessive individualism, and the orientation towards exchange value.[14] The idea of endless competitiveness and achievement-seeking is being destroyed gradually as people lose faith in the market's capacity to distribute scarce values fairly – as the state's very intervention brings issues of distribution to the fore and, for example, the increasing level of education arouses aspirations that cannot be co-ordinated with occupational opportunity. Possessive individualism, the belief that collective goals can only be realised by private individuals acting in competitive isolation, is being undermined as the development of the state, with its contradictory functions, is (ever more) forced into socialising the costs and goals of urban life. Additionally, the orientation to exchange value is weakening as larger segments of the population – for instance, welfare clients, students, the criminal and sick, the unemployable – no longer reproduce their lives through labour for exchange value (wages), thus 'weakening the socialization effects of the market'.

The second thesis -- that the logic of development of normative structures prevents a functionally equivalent replacement of eroded traditions – also has two parts. They are (a) that the remaining residues of tradition in bourgeois ideology cannot generate elements to replace those of destroyed privatism, but (b) that the remaining structures of bourgeois ideology are still relevant for motivation formation. With regard to (a), Habermas looks at three elements of the contemporary dominant cultural formation: scientism, post-auratic or post-representational art, and universalistic morality. He contends that in each of these areas the logic of development is such that the normative structures no longer promote the reproduction of privatism and that they could only do so again at the cost of a regression in social development, i.e. increased authoritarianism which suppresses conflict. In each of these areas the changing normative structures embody marked concerns with universality and critique. It is these developing concerns which undermine privatism and which are potentially threatening to the inequalities of the economic and political system.

But the undermining of privatism does not necessitate that there will be a motivation crisis. If the motivations being generated by the emerging structures are dysfunctional for the economic and political systems, one way of avoiding a crisis would be to 'uncouple' (an obscure notion in Habermas's writings) the socio-cultural system from the political-economic system so that the latter (apparently) would no longer be dependent on the former.[15] To complete his argument Habermas must make plausible the contention that the uncoupling process has not occurred and that the remaining structures are still relevant for some type of motivation formation, i.e. thesis (2b). His claim is that evidence from studies of adolescent socialisation patterns (from Kenniston and others) and such phenomena as the students' and women's movements indicate that a new level of consciousness involving a universalistic (communicative) ethic is emerging as a functional element in motivation formation. On this basis he argues that individuals will increasingly be produced whose motivational norms will be such as to demand a rational justification of social realities. If such a justification cannot be provided by the system's legitimising mechanisms on the one hand, or bought off via distribution of value on the other, a motivation crisis is the likely outcome – the system will not find sufficient motivation for its maintenance.

Habermas's conclusion, then, is that, given its logic of crisis tendencies, organised capitalism cannot maintain its present form. If Habermas's argument is correct, then capitalism will either evolve into a kind of 'Brave New World' or it will have to overcome its underlying class contradiction. To do the latter would mean the adoption of a new principle of organisation. Such a principle would involve a universalistic morality embedded in a system of participatory democracy, i.e. an opportunity for discursive will-formation. What exact institutional form the new social formation might take Habermas does not say; nor does he say, in any detail, how the new social formation might evolve.

In the remainder of this essay, I should like to indicate a number of areas in which Habermas's formulations lead to difficulties. The areas of concern I want to single out particularly are: the relation between legitimation and motivation crises; the analysis of components of culture and social order; the boundary conditions of crisis tendencies; and questions relating to political transformation and the role of critical theory. My critical remarks have, it should be stressed, a tentative status, for Habermas's thought in each of these areas is still in the process of development.

Legitimation and motivation crises

The novelty of Habermas's conception of crisis theory lies both in his emphasis on different types of crisis tendencies and on his formulation of the idea of crisis displacement. I do not wish to question that these notions constitute a significant contribution to the understanding of social crises: the disclosure of the relation between economic, political and socio-cultural phenomena is a vital step in overcoming the limitations of economistic theories of crisis, and of theories that place a disproportionate emphasis on the role of ideas in social change. Nevertheless, I do not think that Habermas's focus on legitimation and motivation crises is satisfactory.

In the first instance, difficulties arise because the distinction between legitimation and motivation crises is, at best, obscure. Habermas's formulation of these crisis tendencies oscillates between seeing them as distinct and conceiving of them as a single set of events. The latter position is consistent with the absence of a clear differentiation between the scarce resources to which the two types of crisis are, respectively, linked – 'generalised motivations' and 'action-motivating meaning'. As he elaborates them, legitimation and motivation crises are thoroughly enmeshed: a legitimation crisis is a crisis of 'generalised motivations', a crisis which depends on the undermining of traditional 'action-motivating meaning'; a motivation crisis is a crisis that issues in the collapse of mass loyalty. I believe the source of this ambiguity lies in an inadequate conception of the way societies cohere – that is, in a problematic emphasis on the centrality of shared norms and values in social integration and on the importance of 'internalisation' in the genesis of individual identity and social order.

For Habermas, social integration refers to 'the system of institutions in which speaking and acting subjects are socially related'. Social systems are conceived here as '*life-worlds* that are symbolically structured'. From this perspective one can 'thematize the normative structures (values and institutions) of a society'.[16] Events and states can be analysed from 'the point of view of their dependency on functions of social integration (in Parsons's vocabulary, integration and pattern maintenance)'.[17] A society's capacity for reproduction is directly connected, Habermas contends, to successful social integration. Disturbances of a society endanger its existence only if social integration is threatened; that is, 'when the *consensual foundations* of normative structures are so much impaired that the society becomes *anomic*'.[18] Although Habermas acknowledges the difference between dominant cultural value systems and meaning structures generated by individuals in their everyday lives when he criticises Parsons for not distinguishing 'institutional values' and 'motivational forces', he himself fails to utilise these distinctions adequately in his substantive analysis of capitalism.[19]

It is crucial to preserve at all levels of social theory the distinction between dominant normative prescriptions – those involved in procuring legitimation – and the 'frames of meaning' and motives of people in society. Any theory that blurs the boundaries between these, as does Habermas's crisis theory, needs to be regarded with scepticism.[20] For, as I argue below, social integration, when tied to the generation of a shared sense of 'the worthiness of a political order to be recognised' (legitimacy), is not a necessary condition for every relatively stable society.[21] Clearly, some groups have to be normatively integrated into the governing political culture to ensure a society's reproduction. But what matters most is not the moral approval of the majority of a society's members – although this will sometimes be forthcoming, for instance during wars – but the approval of the dominant groups. Among the latter, it is the politically powerful and mobilised, including the state's personnel, that are particularly important for the continued existence of a social system.[22] Habermas does acknowledge this on some occasions, but he does not pursue its many implications.[23] His failure to do so can be explained, I think, by his use of 'unreconstructed' systems concepts and assumptions.[24] Many ideas and assumptions from systems theory – in combination with concepts from action theory, structuralism and genetic structuralism – are intermingled in his work in a manner which is often unsatisfactory and difficult to disentangle.[25] These notions do not provide a suitable framework for the analysis of social cohesion and legitimation: for theories concerned with social stability must be developed without ties to the 'internalised value–norm–moral consensus theorem' and its residues.[26] What is required here is a more adequate theory of the production and reproduction of action.

Components of culture and social order
The notion of legitimation crisis presupposes that the motivation of the mass of the population was at one time constituted to a significant extent by the normative structures established by powerful groups.[27] But Habermas, in my view, overestimates the degree to which one may consider the individual as having been integrated into society, as well as the degree to which bourgeois ideology has been eroded and the extent to which contemporary society is threatened by a 'legitimation/motivation' crisis.

If one examines the substantial number of studies debating the nature of the social cohesion of capitalist societies, one thing emerges with clarity: patterns of consciousness, especially class consciousness, vary across and within specific cultures and countries.[28] To the extent that generalisations can be made, they must take account of 'the lack of consensus' about norms, values and beliefs (excepting perhaps a general adherence to nationalism).[29] Moreover, they must recognise that a 'dual consciousness' is often expressed in communities and work-places.[30] This implies a quite radical interpretation of many everyday events – often linking dissatisfactions with divisions between the 'rich and poor', the 'rulers and ruled' – and a relatively 'conservative' (defined below), privatistic interest in dominant political parties and processes. Many institutions and processes are perceived and hypostatised as 'natural', 'the way things have been and always will be'; but the language used to express and account for immediate needs and their frustration often reveals a marked penetration of ideology or dominant interpretative systems.

Although there is evidence of dissensus and various levels of class-consciousness, it is clear, none the less, that this rarely constitutes revolutionary consciousness. There is a fairly widespread 'conservatism' about conventional political processes; that is, seeming compliance to dominant ideas, a high interest in the system's output combined with low interest in political input (participation), and no coherent conception of an alternative to the existing order. The question is: What does this 'conservatism' mean? What does it entail? Does it reflect normative integration, depoliticisation, a combination of these, or something different again?

While Habermas argues that the legitimacy of the political order of capitalist society is related to 'the social-integrative preservation of a normatively determined social identity', I would argue that stability is related to the 'decentring' or fragmentation of culture, the atomisation of people's experiences of the social world. Fragmentation acts as a barrier to a coherent conception of the social totality – the structure of social practices and possibilities. The political order is acknowledged not because it is regarded as 'worthy' but because of the adoption of an instrumental attitude towards it; compliance most often comprises pragmatic acquiescence to the status quo. In certain places in his writings Habermas appears to recognise the importance of these points, but he does not accommodate them adequately.[31] By presupposing that the cultural system once generated a large stock of unquestioned values and norms – values which are now regarded as threatened by increased state intervention – his analysis detracts from a systematic appraisal of the process of 'atomisation' and of 'pragmatic' adaptation. I should like to discuss briefly the importance of the latter phenomena by indicating the significance of precisely those things that are least considered by Habermas – they include the social and technical division of labour (social and occupational hierarchies, the splits between unskilled and skilled and physical and mental labour), the organisation of work relations (relations between trade unions, management and state), and the 'culture industry' (the creation of a system of pseudo-gratifications).

Working-class consciousness, along with the consciousness of other social classes and groups, is impregnated by the work process. Analyses by Marcuse, as early as 1941, and more recently by Braverman, point to the significance of understanding the way in which the rationalisation and standardisation of production fragments tasks.[32] As tasks become increasingly mechanised, there are fewer and fewer chances for mental and reflective labour. Work experiences are increasingly differentiated. Knowledge of the total work process is hard to come by and rarely available, particularly for those on the shop floor. The majority of occupations (despite the possibility of a greater exchange of functions) tend to become atomised, isolated units, which *seem* to require for their cohesion 'co-ordination and management from above'. With the development of the capitalist division of labour, knowledge and control of the whole work process are ever more absent from daily work situations. Centralised control mechanisms and private and public bureaucracies then appear as agencies which are necessary for, and guarantee,'a rational course and order'.[33] With the fragmentation of tasks and knowledge, the identity of social classes is threatened. The social relations which condition these processes are reified: they become ever harder to grasp.

A number of factors have, furthermore, conjoined to reduce the receptivity of many people to critical thinking. Aronowitz has pointed to the way the debilitating impact of the technical division of labour is compounded not only by social divisions based on ethnicity, race and sex, but also by 'the credential routes to higher occupations, the seniority system as a basis for promotion, the classification of jobs grounded in arbitrary distinctions which have no basis in job content or skill level'.[34] Social and occupational hierarchies threaten attempts to create solidarity. Moreover, organised opposition is all too often ineffective because the representatives of these forces – although they have not lost the 'title of opposition' – are vulnerable to incorporation. This has been the fate of the trade-union movement in many countries. Its organisations have been transformed into mass organisations with highly bureaucratised leadership structures, concentrating on 'economistic' issues and acting as barriers to the expression of rank-and-file protest about, among other things, lack of control of the work process.[35] Although the exact effects of these processes constitute an empirical question, there are strong reasons to believe that they further remove from the mass of people a chance to understand and affect the institutions that impinge upon their lives.

Factors such as differentiated wage structures, permanent inflation, crisis in government finances and uneven economic development – factors which disperse the effects of economic crisis, as Habermas points out, on to 'quasi-groups', consumers, the elderly, the sick, schoolchildren – are all part of a complex series which combine to make the fronts of class opposition repeatedly fragmented, less comprehensible.[36] The 'culture industry', furthermore, reinforces this state of affairs. The Frankfurt School's analysis indicates the potency of the system of pseudo-gratifications – diversions and distractions – which the culture industry generates. As Adorno showed in study after study, while the culture industry offers a temporary escape from the responsibilities and drudgery of everyday life, it reinforces the structure of the world people seek to avoid: it strengthens the belief that misfortunes and deprivations are due to natural causes or chance, thus promoting a sense of fatalism and dependence.[37]

The analysis above is, of course, incomplete and, in many ways, partial and one-sided. The point, however, is to stress the significance of a complex of institutions and developments which seemingly fragment society and people's comprehension of it. Reference to these processes explains, I believe, the research findings which indicate that many people do not have a very coherent set of beliefs, norms and values, as well as the 'conservative' component of dual consciousness. The structural conditions of work and of many other activities atomises individuals' experience and 'draws off', and/or fails to allow access to, knowledge of the work process as a whole and of the organisational principles of society. This constitutes a crucial barrier to knowledge of dominant trends in the social totality on the one hand, and to potential solidarity on the other. The 'conservative' aspects of dual consciousness comprise in many cases a mixture of pragmatic acquiescence to existing institutions and false consciousness. Pragmatic acquiescence is involved because all men and women, who seek the maintenance of their own lives, have to act 'rationally'; that is, they have to act 'according to the standards which insure the functioning of the apparatus'.[38] Few alternatives to the status quo are perceived, and it is recognised that participation in the status quo is necessary for comfort and security. False consciousness is involved (as Habermas recognises) because the asymmetrical distribution of power ('transformative capacity') in contemporary society is mobilised (albeit often unintentionally) to prevent working people from properly understanding the reality they experience. Frames of meaning often utilised to articulate needs and account for everyday life frequently diverge from the interpretative schemes employed to make sense of traditional political institutions.[39]

Modern capitalist society's stability is linked, I believe, to this state of affairs – to what has been aptly referred to as the 'lack of consensus' in the crucial intersection of concrete daily experiences and the often confused values and interpretative schemes articulated in relation to dominant institutions.[40] Stability is dependent on the atomisation or 'decentring' of knowledge of work and politics. I suspect that modern society has never been legitimated by the mass of the population. This does not mean, of course, that the political and economic order is permanently vulnerable to disintegration or revolution. The reasons for this should be apparent; the order does not depend for its reproduction on strongly shared normative ideals.

It is because of considerations such as these that I do not find convincing Habermas's view that civil and familial privatism are dependent for their efficacy on pre-capitalist traditions. A preoccupation with one's own 'lot in life', with the fulfilment of one's own needs, is both a product of, and an adaptive mechanism to, contemporary society. The social and technical division of labour, in a society orientated towards the maximisation of profit, is, it seems, a sufficient condition for atomisation, isolation and privatism. It is for these reasons also that I do not find convincing Habermas's belief that the forces undermining achievement ideology, the orientation to exchange, etc., have further delegitimising effects. A more plausible position is that, in the context of an atomised society, changes of this kind enhance an already widespread scepticism about the virtue of existing political institutions, a cynicism and a pragmatic/instrumental orientation. Furthermore, at the empirical level there is no ready evidence to support Habermas's contention of the potentially imminent realisation of a communicative ethics – the highest stage of the human being's 'inner cognitive logic'. Contemporary changes in normative structures have, at best, a very ambiguous relationship to discursive will-formation, universality and critique.[41] On the available evidence (and in light of there being no substantial evidence in his own work), there does not seem to be a sufficient basis to locate the emergence of a principle of organisation of a 'post-modern' society.

But to disagree with Habermas's conception of the vulnerability of contemporary Western society is not to deny, of course, that the system is faced with severe challenges – challenges to the basis on which rights and obligations are structured. The question to ask, however, is not under what conditions will there be a legitimation crisis (although, it must be added, this question remains relevant to the state's personnel and to dominant groups generally), but under what conditions can the 'cognitive penetration' of the order be radically extended? Or, to put the question in the terminology used hitherto, under what conditions can pragmatic, dual, fragmented consciousness be overcome and a grasp of the social totality (the organisational principles determining the allocation of 'value' and 'meaning' and alternatives to them) be rendered possible? Answers to this question depend less, I believe, on factors affecting social identity and more on economic and political crisis tendencies in capitalism. The issues discussed below are only some of those that require analysis; they are *not* intended as a direct response to the question just raised.

The boundary conditions of system crises

System crises (economic and rationality) can, on Habermas's account, be potentially contained (although it does not follow that they will be). Containment occurs, however, only at the cost of increasing legitimation pressures on the state: the state is the interface at which the tensions of both system integration and social integration meet. Habermas's argument rests, of course, on the claim that organised capitalism can control its potential system crises. Can this claim be supported?

Most of Habermas's remarks on system crises centre upon considerations of the nation-state; that is, the focus is on the changing relation between the state and economy within an ideal-typical capitalist country. His discussion of past and present economic tendencies pays little, if any, attention to developments of international capitalism. He raises important considerations in connection with the law of value; but the referent and context is usually that of the nation-state. It is crucially important to explore the development of capitalism in one country in the context of international political economy. The capitalist world was created in dependence on an international market and is ever more dependent on international trade. Before one can conclude that economic crises can be contained (on either a national or an international level), the relationship between economic crises in the nation-state and crisis tendencies in the international market must be better analysed and explained. These issues deserve a much more substantial treatment than Habermas gives them. Without an analysis of them, Habermas's conception of the logic of crisis development can be questioned, for the political-economic constraints on capitalist development appear much less open to control and manipulation than Habermas suggests.

In his recent work on the development of the modern state, Poggi has emphasised the significance of 'the highly contingent, inherently dangerous' nature of the international system of nation-states.[42] Wallerstein's analysis of the 'European world economy' indicates the importance of comprehending economic interconnections between nation-states which are beyond the control of any one such state.[43] Disproportionate economic development and uneven development generally within and between advanced industrial societies and Third World countries have serious implications for any conception of the logic or dynamic of crisis – implications which should centre attention on the primacy of struggles over who is on the centre and periphery, who controls what resources, and over a host of other basic differences in material interests.

Furthermore, although Habermas recognises the significance of analysing different types of state activity, the nature of crisis management, and the organisational logic (rationality) of the administrative apparatus, he does not, as far as I know, stress the need for a differentiated analysis of state forms, party structures and the relation of government and party structures to socio-economic structure. This also has consequences for an analysis of crisis tendencies; for it is precisely these things, analysed in the context of international conditions and pressures, that have been shown to be crucial determinants in key cases of political and 'social-revolutionary' crisis. [44] No analytic account of crisis tendencies can claim completeness without examining these phenomena.

Political transformation and critical theory

One of the most distinctive features of the Marxist tradition – a tradition with which Habermas closely identifies – is a concern to draw from an examination of 'what exists' an account of 'what exists in possibility'. Inquiry into historical conditions and processes is linked to a desire to reveal political potentialities. In the third and final part of *Legitimation Crisis*, Habermas focuses directly on the problem of analysing potentiality. He argues that a critique of ideology, concerned both with the existing pattern of distorted communication and with how things could be otherwise, must take as its starting-point the 'model of the suppression of generalizable interests'.[45] The model permits a comparison of the normative structures of a society with those which hypothetically would be the case if norms were arrived at, *ceteris paribus,* discursively.[46] Linked to a number of assumptions about the conditions under which conflict breaks out, the model establishes the basis for what Habermas calls 'the advocacy role' of critical theory.

The advocacy role consists in 'ascertaining generalizable, though nevertheless suppressed, interests in a representatively simulated discourse between groups that are differentiated . . . from one another by an articulated, or at least virtual, opposition of interests'.[47] Using such indicators of potential conflict as discrepancies between claims and demands, and politically permitted levels of satisfaction, one can, Habermas maintains, indicate the nature of ideological repression and the level of generalisable interests possible at a given historical point. In the final analysis 'the theory serves to enlighten its addressees about the position which they occupy in an antagonistic social system and about the interests of which they could become conscious as objectively their own'.[48]

The following questions – frequently put to those in the tradition of critical theory – are pertinent: To whom is critical theory addressed? How, in any concrete situation, can critical theory be applied? Who is to be the instigator or promoter of enlightenment? It is clear that a discussion of these issues is important if Habermas is to argue successfully that the organisation of enlightenment at the social level can be fashioned after critical theory. Yet, as these issues are only discussed in Habermas's writings at a most abstract level, it is difficult to draw any specific political conclusions from his advocacy model and crisis argument. Within the terms of reference of his work on modern capitalist societies we remain very much in the dark as to political processes and events. The practical implications of his theory are left undeveloped.

Habermas might reply to this charge by saying that at the present time it is extremely difficult to draw any definite political conclusions from the state of contemporary advanced capitalist countries. He might say, moreover, that while aspects of his analysis undermine the traditional faith of orthodox Marxists, other aspects suggest the importance of social struggles over gender, race, ecology and bureaucracy, as well as over the nature and quantity of state goods and services and over economistic issues. With both of these points I would agree. However, in the context of what seems to be widespread scepticism (or cynicism) about politics – understood as traditional party politics – and the success of 'cold war' attitudes (and, of course, Stalinism itself) in discrediting socialist ideals, this does not seem enough. There is a need, greater than ever I believe, to establish the credibility of socialism, to develop concrete proposals for alternative ways of organising society and to show how these can be connected to wants and demands that crystallise in people's experience of dominant social relations.[49] In a fascinating interview for *Rinascita*, the weekly journal of the Italian Communist Party, Habermas himself appears to express sympathy for this enterprise.[50] But it is hard to see how his own investigations of advanced capitalism connect in a direct way with this project.

11

Critical Sociology and Authoritarian State Socialism

ANDREW ARATO

Jürgen Habermas has demonstrated the possibility in the West of a process of democratisation that shows the limits of technocratic rationalisation of polity and economy. Moreover, he has done this (however tentatively) while presenting advanced capitalism as a framework of political and cultural instabilities, potentially crisis- and conflict-laden. It is thus that he has reconstructed Marxism as a critical sociology. However, he has not *systematically* addressed the problem of the relationship of a Marxist critical sociology to those societies that use a version of Marxism as their 'ideology' of legitimation. While it is not necessarily his task or that of his co-workers to produce a theory of the so-called socialist societies, it is nevertheless fair to ask if those approaches and concepts of his that have universal aspiration contribute to such a *critical* theory. For today most inherited Marxist theory, from Engels and Plekhanov to Lenin and Trotsky (and even Lukács, Gramsci and Sartre), is either powerless in the face of the Soviet Union and Eastern Europe, or worse even contributes to their legitimation. In this essay I shall attempt to investigate the possible uses of Starnberg critical sociology for the study of these societies.

To begin with, I shall show (Part I) that the problem of state-socialist society is not completely absent from Habermas's critical theory. Indeed, it will be possible to derive (Part II) the principle of organisation of state-socialist society from some clues in his works and those of his colleague, Claus Offe. Next, using concepts from the Starnberg theory of capitalist development, I shall argue (Part III) that the inherent crisis tendencies of state-socialist societies can be 'managed' in the long run only if, on the level of system integration, there is a transition from a high level of penetration of the social spheres by the political institutional core (positive subordination) to a lower level of penetration (negative subordination). I shall try to show (Part IV) that negative subordination is possible only if, within the political sphere, a relative 'uncoupling' or 'disjunctivity' of political and administrative functions can be achieved; but that this disjunctivity can be protected against tendencies threatening the organisational principle of the system only if, on the level of social integration, certain conditions of legitimation are met. Finally, using the Soviet case, I shall claim (Part V) that the eclectic ideological mixture promoted in the administered public sphere can perform its function of legitimating the existing system only through some combination of economic success and activation of meanings rooted in the cultural life-world. The activation of meanings has hitherto proceeded in two directions: under the influence of legal development and under the revival of traditions and traditionalism. While the development of legality might threaten the stabilisation of the existing organisational principle even on the basis of negative subordination, the process of 'retraditionalisation' points in a conservative direction: the reinforcement of a relatively high degree of positive subordination. It will be outside the methodological limits of this essay to determine whether a combination of these two tendencies can indefinitely support some version of a 'dual state' in the different state-socialist countries.

I

Habermas never *completely* neglected the study of European social formations of the Soviet type. First of all they form, negatively, part of the background against which he has always sought to situate himself. His conception of Marxism (his critique of all objectivism and reductionism, and of the fetishism of technical development) and his concept of *Praxis* as *public* enlightenment and discourse (which led him to a critique of the Leninist-Lukácsian theory of organisation) have blocked the way towards two of the major factors necessary for the Soviet-type synthesis: the core ideological and institutional structures. I do believe that this consequence was intended. Furthermore, from the very beginning his reconstruction of Marxism has sought to make possible a thoroughly autonomous treatment of what was formerly relegated to the superstructure (politics and culture), with the unintended consequence that the two other major factors necessary for the genesis and reproduction of Soviet society (the heritage of the bureaucratic state and of cultural traditionalism) could now become accessible to analysis. This means *in principle* a break with those elements of classical Marxist theory which confront the Soviet Union with the bad alternative of unintended apology and theoretical impotence. What I shall try to show is that this openness in principle can be maintained within the framework of Habermas's late social theory, in particular within the context of his crisis theory of advanced societies.

As far as I can tell, the problem of the analysis and evaluation of Soviet and East European societies appears four times in Habermas's work. I should like to indicate these briefly in chronological order.

(1) In the important essay 'Between Philosophy and Science: Marxism as Critique' (1960) the Russian revolution and the establishment of the Soviet system are characterised as perhaps the most important of four fun-

damental 'facts against Marx'[1] that cannot be interpreted within the 'old theory'. Since this is Habermas's most extensive statement on the subject, I should like to present all of its points.

According to Habermas:

(a) The October revolution, having no immediate *socialist* aims, was initiated by a weak proletariat with peasant support, and was directed by 'Leninistically schooled professional revolutionaries'.

(b) The latter established 'a rule of functionaries and party cadres'.

(c) On the basis of this rule, Stalin initiated a 'socialist revolution bureaucratically from above, by the collectivisation of agriculture'.

(d) The system was finally stabilised after the Second World War as a world power.

(e) Nevertheless, in the face of post-war capitalist reform the system is at the very most a model for shortening the process of industrialisation in developing countries.

(f) This is because its successes in raising the productive forces at a fast rate are outweighed by the periodic regression 'from the constitutional rights attained under capitalism to the legal terror of Party dictatorship'. Thus the Soviet Union is 'far removed from the realization of a truly emancipated society'.

(g) However, the development of the productive forces affect the social structure and the apparatus of domination, and a convergence with capitalism on 'the middle ground of a controlled mass democracy within the welfare state is not to be excluded'. Nevertheless, the Soviet system may possess the means of subverting the danger of all significant social change.

(h) Finally, a Marxist analysis of Soviet Marxism of the stature of, for example, Neumann's *Behemoth* has not yet been undertaken.[2] Marcuse's *Soviet Marxism*, the most extensive work of the Frankfurt School in this area, is not apparently considered as an acceptable alternative.

(2) As is well known, in the 1960s and early 1970s Habermas thoroughly criticised and reconstructed the 'old theory'. What is the place of the Soviet Union in the 'new theory' that emerged? The next mention of the problem is a brief but important one. In an extended critique of the technocratic systems theory of Niklas Luhmann,[3] Habermas maintains that a social technology which has no room for practical questions can play an important functional role in bureaucratic socialist societies, as well as capitalist societies, in the form of the 'justification of the systematic limitation of practically consequential communication'. Such an 'ideological' role would be especially important because, in *both* forms of industrial society, genuinely ideological forms of legitimation become weaker and weaker as a result of growing system complexity, leading to an increasing legitimation deficit. Here Habermas indicates some steps towards a dynamic social theory, one that he himself only attempts to work out for advanced

capitalism. No convergence theory is indicated, but the analysis points to a common possible future of all modern societies: technocracy, though not necessarily a single form of it, since the ideological sphere alone is understood as technocratic.

(3) The next mention of the problem is in *Legitimation Crisis*. It is worth quoting the whole passage:

> I think it meaningful to distinguish four social formations: primitive (*vorhochkulturelle*), traditional, capitalist, post-capitalist. Except for primitive societies, we are dealing with class societies. (I designate state-socialist societies – in view of their political-elitist disposition of the means of production – as 'post-capitalist class societies'.) . . . The interest behind the examination of crisis tendencies in late- and post-capitalist class societies is in exploring the possibilities of a 'post-modern' society – that is, a historically new principle of organization.[4]

Here a few remarks are in order. *Vis-à-vis* the Soviet Union and Eastern Europe, Habermas seems to choose two strategies (or at least terminologies) simultaneously. On the one hand, he seems to depict them as transitional societies. The description *post*-capitalist but not yet post-modern fits in well with the quasi-orthodox idea (supported by Marcuse in *Soviet Marxism*) that some supposed achievements like central planning, state or 'public' ownership, and socialist ideological goals put the societies of the Soviet type on the road to socialism/communism, in spite of regressive phenomena (bureaucracy, terror, 'bourgeois survivals', or whatever). On the other hand, and this is more important, Habermas seems to present late capitalism and 'post-capitalism' as merely two modern forms of class society whose internal dynamics (crisis tendencies) must be analysed if we are to evaluate the chances not of their convergence in either direction but of a 'post-modern', truly emancipated society. This interpretation is supported by the essay 'On Social Identity', where the party, along with the nation-state, are rejected as bases of a new and rational social identity for the modern world.[5] We should note here again that Habermas does not go on in *Legitimation Crisis*, even on the most abstract level, to derive either the principle of organisation or the evolutionary crisis tendencies of 'post-capitalist' societies.

(4) In two essays on the theory of social evolution, 'Toward a Reconstruction of Historical Materialism' (1975) and 'Historical Materialism and the Development of Normative Structures' (1976), the problem of the historical place of societies of the Soviet type returns and is posed in terms of a simple theoretical alternative.[6] 'Bureaucratic socialism' (the so-called 'socialist transitional societies') represents either a higher stage of social evolution than 'developed capitalism', or the two are variants of the same stage of development. Here Habermas no longer considers (as he did in

1960) the convergence theory seriously. Nevertheless, it is the second alternative he inclines towards, because this would, according to him, demonstrate that the (late?) capitalist relation of state to economy is not the only possible version of *modern* society; and hence other possible alternatives *within modernity* would be conceivable, in particular a far more democratic one.

While the two societies undoubtedly share an enormous number of common characteristics as industrial-urbanised societies and welfare-warfare states, the theoretical grounds for treating them as two expressions of the same stage of development are doubtful. I am thinking of their specifically different institutional systems, and even more of their entirely 'non-simultaneous' levels of legal development. As far as Habermas is concerned, we would be able to regard bureaucratic or state socialism and advanced capitalism in terms of a single evolutionary stage *only* if they could be understood as different expressions of *the same* principle of social organisation. Following Adorno and returning to the technocracy argument, he tentatively proposes 'the autonomization of instrumental reason' as a possible basis for such a principle. Klaus Eder dispenses with all doubt and asserts that the two formations are indeed two different contemporary expressions of the same developmental stage, one that he calls 'society', i.e. a social order 'that achieves system integration through norms'.[7] It seems to me that either of these proposals (aside from their empirical dubiousness) might mean a premature leap to a level of abstraction where the critical social theory of both social formations would become difficult to develop. Without dismissing the potential importance of evolutionary theory for the study of state-socialist societies, it seems to me that an immanent reconstruction (however ideal-typical) of the principle of organisation of this social formation – the task of this study – has methodological primacy.

II

A theory of state-socialist social structure that starts out with the concepts elaborated by Habermas and Claus Offe might have several advantages over its most likely theoretical rivals. Unlike all versions of classical Marxism, Habermas and Offe do not assume the primacy of the economic (or any other sphere) in defining social formations and their logic. They have also come to reject all versions of the convergence theory, which amounts to something close to a bourgeois version of historical materialism. Unlike orthodox functionalist and systems-theoretical approaches, they neither treat social integration as merely the normative element of system integration nor do they have a methodological bias for conditions of self-adjustment, equilibrium and stability. In particular, Habermas's concept of *organisational principle* attempts to map out the limits within which a system remains self-identical, while Offe's concept of *the crisis of crisis management* seeks to show the 'limits of staying within those limits'. Finally, unlike those who first utilised the social and system integration distinction,[8] Habermas does not dogmatically affirm the absolute primacy of system integration, nor do he and Offe restrict the notions of system and social crisis to conflicts involving global subjects, i.e. classes; they do not, in other words, rush into a dogmatic stratification theory that could occlude all further independent analysis.[9]

It is in the pages devoted to the theory of social evolution that Habermas determines the concept of organisational principle in the most sophisticated manner. He defines the concept in *Legitimation Crisis* as the 'capacity of society to learn without losing its identity'.[10] An organisational principle limits three learning mechanisms in three social spheres: those of productive forces, of identity-securing interpretative systems and of institutional steering capacities. From the point of view of a general theory of action, these spheres can be reduced to two levels: *social integration*, defined as 'the system of institutions in which speaking and acting subjects are socially related', and *system integration*, 'the specific steering performances of a self-regulated system'. In his later essays we receive an importantly if slightly altered version of the concept that is even more adequate for our purposes: 'Organizational principles of society can be characterized, *in a first approximation*, through the institutional core that determines the dominant form of social integration.'[11] That is, social integration, 'securing the unity of the life-world through values and norms', is regarded as the primary task of the institutions defining a principle of organisation.

We are ready to consider the principle of organisation of state-socialist societies. Within the domain of critical sociology, Habermas and Offe present us with two alternatives.

(1) According to Habermas, state socialism is political-elitist class rule over a politically constituted but industrial system of social labour.[12] This definition focuses on the fundamental relation of class domination and implies a juridical relationship different from that of capitalism: the absence of 'free' labour. If one proceeded from this perspective, one would have to elaborate the symbolic structures of self-identification that provide in this 'socialised' society for the anonymisation of 'class' relations.[13]

(2) Following Dahl and Lindblom as well as Etzioni, Offe gives us a three-term typology that allows us to locate 'state socialism', as well as late capitalism, among industrial societies, a typology that corresponds to the three domains of learning proposed by Habermas. Given the possibility of the functional primacy of three social spheres, exchange (economy), coercive relationships (bureaucracy) and political choice (normative structures), Offe defines capitalism as the primacy of exchange economy over bureaucracy and the normative sphere;[14] presumably he would not object if one defined state socialism as the primacy of an administratively or

bureaucratically conceived political domain over both the economy and the normative-cultural sphere.

I prefer the version derived from Offe for several reasons. First of all, it is more abstract: it does not define social structure in such a way that one immediately tends to identify structural categories with those of social stratification.[15] As we shall see, it is especially useful to consider stratification in the Soviet-type societies as derivative from the specific institutional mode of domination. Second, Offe's form of the organisational principle clearly locates the three Habermasian spheres of learning under the more conventional names of economy, polity and culture. Although Offe's three-part model certainly suffers, as Habermas noticed, from an under-emphasis on social integration, which potentially leads to a screening out of the independent dynamics of the cultural sphere, it none the less indicates the institutional core responsible for social integration. The system itself identifies this core as the party, and Offe's concept of bureaucracy as the sphere of coercive relationships points to the same institution. Nevertheless, we must modify these terms if we are to avoid identifying the functional moment of arbitrary and coercive political authority with either bureaucracy, as in the endless Trotskyist and neo-Trotskyist discussions, or even with the formally separate party institution proper (as distinct from the state, secret police, etc.). Following a distinction of Ernst Fraenkel,[16] which partially coincides with Offe's categories, the political element in question should be defined as that of the 'prerogative state' (*Massnahmenstaat*), as distinct from the normative state; that is, it is the aspect of the party-state that exercises an arbitrary mode of political action unchecked by any legal limits and guarantees. The party indeed symbolises and justifies the prerogative function (hence it must be retained as a formally independent institution); but it alone does not exercise this function. Therefore, it is more accurate to speak of the 'party-state' as the structure in which the prerogative state is embedded. Accordingly, the organisational principle of state socialism is best defined as that mode of social identity that understands and legitimises itself as *the domination of the prerogative state over society*. The way in which the organisational principle of state socialism is realised in the three social spheres of the economy, the administrative-normative state and culture is indicated in Table 11.1, along with key principles of legitimation, stratification and the corresponding theories that have focused on one of the key domains in question.[17]

I cannot discuss here all the elements of this table. I would certainly maintain that it represents a plausible outline of Soviet and East European societies (except Yugoslavia) from the 1930s until the early 1960s, and perhaps including our time as well. In the 1930s, within the state-controlled sector of social life, the penetration and subsumption of economic, political and cultural moments was already accomplished, but it was only in the cataclysmic formative period of the 1920s (in Eastern

TABLE 11.1

	Economy	State	Culture
Principle of political penetration (system integration)	Industrial-redistributive command economy	Dual state of party and state bureaucracies, fused at the top ('party-state')	Dictatorship over socialisation and publicity
Key principles of legitimacy (social integration)	Rational redistribution of social optimum Welfare state	Substantive and formal justice Harmonisation of interests of nation, class or people	Social solidarity Collectivistic ethics Empirical interest subordinated to 'real' interests Social *vs* individual, positive *vs* negative freedom
Principle of stratification	(1) Redistributor – redistributed (2) Skills and educational levels of qualification	Heirarchical politocratic orders	Mass society Social atomisation Classlessness
Corresponding theories	Managerial and technocratic theories Intellectuals as a new class Historical materialist and convergence theories	Mono-organisational society Bureaucracy as new class Theories of traditional (Russian) political culture	Totalitarianism theory One-dimensionality Dictatorship over needs

Europe in the late 1940s and early 1950s) that the same logic was violently extended to society as a whole. On the other hand, it is undeniable that gradually after the death of Stalin a process of partial yet significant depoliticisation was initiated in some of the key social spheres. Since these have everywhere reached one sort of limit or another, we are justified to ask: at what point, if any, can these threaten the principle of organisation, in other words the social identity of the system?

III

Using Offe's concepts, I should like to argue that the perhaps ultimately insoluble task of all directed social change in the Soviet Union and Eastern Europe is the replacement of positive subordination (of the cultural and economic spheres to the political) by a negative subordination that nevertheless preserves the original organisational principle, i.e. the domination of the political over culture and economy.

Offe defines *positive subordination* (for him of culture and politics to the economy, for us of culture and economics to politics) as both the positive contributions and the adjustment of the contents of sub-systems to the dominant system, whereas *negative subordination* involves that partial growth of the sub-systems to independence while retaining the functional primacy of the dominant system.[18] Habermas indicates the same differentiation in his conception of liberal capitalism, where a single institutional network (the market) takes on both steering and symbolic functions, with these reverting (in part) to different sub-systems under late capitalism. Using both of their concepts, the Stalinist system can be understood as one of positive subordination that thoroughly politicises the social spheres on the basis of the ability of a single institutional network (the party-state) both to control the redistributive-command economy and to mobilise immense reserves (*vis-à-vis* some strata at least) of revolutionary-charismatic and traditional legitimacy. An entirely new stage of the system would be one based on *negative subordination*, i.e. the partial depoliticisation of economy and culture and the distribution of steering and symbolic functions among different social spheres. This new stage would be that of the *same* system because it would preserve the functional primacy of a prerogative political sphere that has irrevocably given up its goal of the total penetration of all aspects of life.

Given the socially and politically dangerous overloading of the state sphere under Stalinism with tasks of steering and symbolic self-representation, the problems of administrative and economic rationality greatly endangered the system's 'social identity'. The first but necessarily temporary response was general terror. When the party was no longer willing or able to use large-scale terror as part of its 'social cement', the task of the system became, in abstract terms, to protect its principle of organisation from the dangerous linking of deeply embedded steering problems to an increasingly difficult legitimation problem, a protection attempted by the transition to some form of negative subordination of the social spheres to politics. The 'motor' of this transition must be clarified before we can examine the possible patterns of negative subordination or 'crisis management'. Offe and Habermas have repeatedly and convincingly shown that neither voluntaristic nor systems-theoretical conceptions stressing self-regulation and equilibration can adequately account for such a 'motor'; neither an agency nor a self-regulating system can account for *both* crisis management and 'the crisis of crisis management'. Aside from the problem whether such a thing is possible in principle, even Soviet theorists admit that self-regulation is absent from their social and economic system.[19] There is, furthermore, no way of ever showing that the process of self-regulation of a system of mutually dependent parts would protect an organisational principle based on centralisation. Such protection must be and is under all state socialism a directed process. *But it is not consciously directed by a social agency,* whether the latter be a 'class', an 'order' or even the party elite itself.[20] The protection of the system's identity has an active centre, namely an institution which is not the instrument of any social agency. While it may appear trivial to assert that this institution is the hierarchically organised party-state, it is less trivial to conceive of this institution as *a selection mechanism* having functional primacy in the system as a whole. From Castoriadis and Lefort to Konrad, Szelenyi and Rakovski, the historically novel unification of the partial bureaucracies of state, economy and culture by a party has been the touchstone of 'neo' and 'post' Marxist analyses of the Soviet Union and Eastern Europe. It is, however, extremely important to stress (as have all of the interpreters just mentioned) that this unification is a successful one only in the system's ideology, that the societies in question are also the terrain of real and latent conflicts of interest.[21] Hence the concept of *selectivity*, developed by Offe, is more useful than that of unification. The party-state institution has a threefold screening function, in a sense analogous to the functions which Offe assigns to the capitalist state: to protect the existing political structure as a whole against individual bureaucracies; to eliminate the possibility of outside interests penetrating the structure of decision in any form other than their 'representation' by bureaucratic sectors; and finally to produce the ideological justifications that disguise the party-state's 'unifying' activity – to 'screen' its own screening activity even from itself.[22]

Selectivity under state socialism means that the possible 'events' that will result in administrative-political action will be drastically narrowed down. This process will be in part arbitrary but in part according to criteria determined by the party-state's factual power to penetrate and repress, its specific value and rule systems, and even more by its desire to protect its monopoly of the selectivity function against all quasi-institutions, groups, strata and elites, not to mention the underlying population itself. This protection, as well as the legitimation of the party-state summit as the ultimate instance of decision, is primarily the function of state ideologies that express in variously scientistic, *ouvrierist* and nationalist terms the one idea that the general and unified social interest is *represented* by this summit or even the 'summit of the summit'. In this representation, selectivity is veiled by entirely imaginary ideas of unity. The selectivity functions of the party-state must be disguised, veiled and legitimised unless repression and terror are to replace all other procedures of deliberate action or inaction.

The Soviet system at its most repressive required immense reservoirs of meaning, stemming from its revolutionary heritage, its ability to activate the springs of nationalism, its revival of law, etc., that were subsequently reduced and even compromised by their use. The changing memories of different generations, to whom the symbolic events of past solidarity have no personal meaning, blocked the road to that kind of loyalty without which terror itself is impossible. With the road back to Stalinism foreclosed, full *positive subordination* of society to politics became very difficult to achieve. The party-state institution of selectivity had to initiate some moves towards *negative subordination*, even if the attempted execution of negative subordination raises the question of the limits within which this very institution of selectivity – and with it the organisational principle of the system – could survive at all.

The reduction in legitimation reserves could have been compensated for initially by the increase of system rationality. Within the limits of the system, however, this increase was short-lived. The recent economic difficulties of East European state-socialist societies are now common knowledge.[23] Drastically declining rates of growth, continued and cyclical shortages, lagging productivity and technical efficiency serve as background to a period of reform which had begun in the early 1960s and which is still not exhausted in our time, at least in some countries. The system contradiction behind the economic difficulties has been interpreted variously, but I should like to single out one essential aspect. If one interprets the command-plan system as the key to the Soviet-type redistributive economies, it seems to me that perhaps the 'fundamental contradiction' must be seen as that of the plan with itself, as the self-contradiction of planning rationality. More specifically, a totally centralised command system in an increasingly complex society seems to be able to achieve economic and social development only at a cost of increasing crises of information.[24] The more it attempts to bring under its control social and economic dysfunctions due to a bizarre combination of absence yet superabundance of information, the less its ability to discover the actual needs of the population *and* to process the increasing, *uncriticised* volume of information from its extended subsidiary organs.

The problem is not only that of information/communication. Since the planning agency is ultimately dependent on the party-state hierarchy whose key function is the 'unification' and 'harmonisation' of latent and explicit social interests, the plan is unavoidably affected by various priorities adopted for the resolution of conflicts. Economic rationality is a relevant consideration, but so too are other political and social priorities. A plan that tries to integrate all of these considerations cannot be rational (according to any one criterion of rationality), or even consistent with previous or future plans that may express somewhat different constellations of interests and priorities. Furthermore, the resistance to authoritarian planning by enterprises and working operatives penetrates the plans through the distortion of information and the deliberate misinterpretation of directives. The more the plan seeks to encompass these dysfunctions, the more authoritarian and irrational it becomes.

IV

Rationality crises have a character which is entirely different from cyclical economic crises. As Habermas has shown: (1) rationality crises disorganise social life on a continuum with an uncertain threshold of tolerance; (2) bargaining and reciprocal adaptation can contain many of the disruptive consequences, some of which can be anticipated and avoided, others of which can be retroactively corrected by shifting the results towards the weakest possible strata, regions or institutions; (3) the agents of planning can be shielded from political dissent through a closed system of technical expertise supported by a full-fledged technocratic ideology.

While the state-socialist systems have already benefited from the first two of the 'advantages' of rationality crises, the third involves an internal 'disjunctivity' (Offe) between the state as planner and the party as representative of the collective interest that no Soviet-type society has been able to achieve.[25] Yet the dynamic of the whole reform period, associated above all with 'market socialism' and the proposals of Lieber-mann, Brus, Šik, Kornai and other economists seemed to point in this direction. What the reformers and their partisans in the West did not consider systematically were the limits presented to their efforts by the organisational principle of the system, limits that were indeed incorporated in their own works in the form of a gap between market socialist ideology – with all the usual economistic assumptions about the necessarily and generally democratising consequences of a market economy – and an actual programme of rather cautious decentralisation that in no way challenged the existing institutional core of society on which *all* structures of existing privilege and authority depend.[26] To be more precise, there are two types of reform ideology in state-socialist systems, one that banks on the full scientisation of the existing institutional network of planning, control and information, the other that ties any possible rationalisation of the whole to decentralisation, i.e. to some form of negative subordination. The first alternative has little importance beyond reinforcing the integration of the party itself, putting its original hyper-rationalist dreams of a totally controlled, transparent society on supposedly scientific foundations.[27] It is the second type of reform programme that expresses, however ideologically, a permanent option for the system, which must somehow rationalise its social and economic procedures and integrate an increasingly complex society without recourse to the terroristic methods of the past. Let us state a basic thesis of this essay: for the leading strata and institutions of the system which are seeking their own security, not only a return to Stalinism but also the two extremes of no reform at all and a reform involving the full decentralisation and democratisation of all social spheres are impossible and undesirable. Given the organisational principle of the society *and* minimum requirements of administrative rationality, there are two dangerous extremes for the system: too much reform and too little. Some outer limits of reform must therefore be provided by the necessity of shielding the institutional core of the prerogative state. Hence we may regard the actual reform programmes, whatever the ideologies and even intentions of individual reformers, as means of *crisis avoidance* for a system whose presuppositions cannot be threatened.

The Starnberg conception of the 'crisis of crisis management', or of 'second-order' crisis phenomena, here reveals its methodological value. In relation to capitalism Offe has repeatedly stressed that (a) there is a maximum and a minimum threshold of state intervention in the contemporary capitalist economy, and that (b) the possible extension of these thresholds depends on the degree of social integration, i.e. on the availability of necessary symbolic resources of legitimation. The adoption of this scheme for increasingly developed forms of state socialism is justified because here, too, the problem is definable as moving from positive to negative subordination – even if in the case of capitalism negative subordination means increasing state intervention in the economy, and in the case of socialism decreasing state intervention. For state socialism the *maximum* permissible level of state intervention would be primarily defined by the depth of existing steering-problems, by the political problems of the existing forms of adaptation to rationality crises and, finally, by the ideological resources that would allow a regime to weather through economic stagnation. The *minimum* permissible level of intervention would be defined, above all, by the maintenance of the integrity of the core institutional complex that specifies the identity of the system, and only secondarily by the economic dysfunctions produced by the decentralisation of controls.[28] In fact, I believe that the economically dysfunctional effects of reform have been greatly exaggerated by its opponents, who fail to distinguish between dysfunctions due to reform and those due to the incomplete nature of the reform (e.g. the resistance of workers to a new wage structure when they do not acquire independent organs of interest representation).

We may be in a position to evaluate the problems of crisis management or of second-order crisis phenomena if we turn to the problem of managing the links between economy and party-state on the one hand, and party-state and culture on the other. It has been persuasively argued that economic reform, in the manner of a significant degree of decentralisation, must involve a partial emancipation of the economic from the political hierarchy. The emancipation can be effective only if institutionalised through legal guarantees of horizontal links between economic units and of some freedom for economic interest groups. The advocates of this argument expect those achievements to 'spill over' from the economic sphere to the spheres of political administration and culture, in a sense 'reconstituting' *civil society*.[29]

The constitution or reconstitution of civil society is manifestly incompatible with the organisational principle of the state-socialist societies. Thus the problem of the successful management of the crisis of economic-administrative rationality is the problem of the successful avoidance of the spill-over of administratively executed depoliticisation. The argument for the plausibility of spill-over depends on four assumptions. The first is the unavoidability in the long run of further attempts at economic decentralisation. The second is the necessity of institutionalising the effects of decentralisation in terms of legal reform that, among other things, eliminates arbitrary political interference in the activities of economic agents. The third is that legal reform cannot be restricted to the economic sphere, because a law that purports to protect individuals cannot merely protect them as economic subjects. The fourth assumption is that the withdrawal of the party from the economy and the legalisation of the rights of economic subjects will permit the formation of interest groups. The existence of a plurality of interest groups in the economy requires a transformation of political institutions, establishing a pluralistic process of decision-making on the state level. Moreover, since these groups are not merely economic but also *social*, so too their economic rights cannot be protected unless their *human* rights are as well. The end-result of the series of assumptions is that the depoliticisation of the economy leads to the formation or re-emergence of civil society.

However attractive the projected outcome of such a spill-over may be, it seems clear that it *can be avoided*. It is possible for the political-administrative system to execute a withdrawal from the economic sphere, and even to institutionalise this in terms of legal reform, without depoliticising the socio-cultural sphere and without genuinely pluralising the political sphere itself. The possibility exists of restructuring the 'dual state', within which the prerogative state must remain predominant over the normative state. Its restructuring would combine the features of a *Rechtsstaat* in relation to a reformed economy with the elements of the political prerogative state whose limits of intervention in culture, everyday life and the non-economic dimensions of administration would be defined only by itself. In other words, in order to establish a high degree of depoliticisation of the economy without 'spill-over', the party-state structure must execute the kind of 'uncoupling' (Habermas) or 'disjunctivity' (Offe) of administrative and political institutions, or rather of those institutions that would protect the link between the prerogative state and the socio-cultural sphere from the demands of legality, rationality and publicity.

Under what conditions can the necessary internal disjunctivity of the party-state yield a stable combination of an administrative *Rechtsstaat* with its face towards a depoliticised economy and a political party-state controlling the sphere of social interests and forms of cultural discourse, self-expression and learning? As we shall see below, the very possibility of disjunctivity depends on the autonomous resources of the cultural sphere. With the prerogative state withdrawing from the economy, not only the pressure of legitimation on the party-state but also the sources of the legitimation of the party as a formally separate institution would be drastically reduced. The party's claim of being the agent of both substantive justice and *total* social welfare originally rested on its supposed *global* knowledge of all society, and its supposed representation of the *general* (national, popular or working-class) interest. With the partial abandonment of the commanding heights of the central plan (that would now be left to the relevant state ministries) and the tacit admission of selective sectoral lobbies into the party-state itself, these foundations would be decisively weakened; and the weakening of the legitimacy of the party endangers the legitimacy of the prerogative state. The outcome of this process would certainly depend on what new or old sources of legitimation could be tapped by the reconstructed institutional system. If the bulk of available cultural traditions point in the direction of the democratisation of politics and liberalisation of culture, the new institutionalisation of the party-state based on disjunctivity must be an extremely precarious one. In other words, 'spill-over' is not to be interpreted literally; it is possible only when it is met half-way by the autonomous logic of the socio-cultural sphere based on differential historical sources.

Thus the logic of the cultural sphere determines whether the most plausible strategy of crisis management is: (1) the reinforcement of positive subordination (i.e. a level of state intervention resembling the Stalinist epoch); or (2) the depoliticisation of the economy in the context of the uncoupling of administrative and political systems; or (3) an oscillation between the two. Whether a process of uncoupling or disjunctivity, if it does occur, will or will not release dysfunctional demands in the socio-cultural sphere depends on the logic of cultural traditions. Hence neither the strategies of crisis management nor their outcome can be evaluated without considering the dynamics of the socio-cultural sphere.

V

To speak of the *independent* dynamics of the socio-cultural sphere is one of Habermas's key contributions to the development of critical social theory. He initially defined this sphere as 'the cultural traditions (cultural value systems) as well as institutions that give these traditions normative power through processes of socialization and professionalization'.[30] Of course, the socio-cultural sphere is the key terrain of social integration. In this essay I shall focus on the Soviet Union, not only because it is the key political system within the constellation of states and because it is the only complex on which some of the necessary preparatory work has been done, but also because it is one of the only systems in Eastern Europe where one does not have to effect the impossible separation between integration through military occupation, through political-social compromise with the occupying power, and through indigenous mechanisms of social integration.

I have argued that any degree of disjunctivity between political (prerogative state) and administrative (legal and normative state) institutions would relieve the combined party-state from some of its burdens of legitimation, but that the same development would also tendentially endanger the already precarious legitimacy of the party, which symbolises the powers of the prerogative state based on substantive justice. Without disjunctivity in the sense that I described it, there can be no economic reform that does not risk great political dangers; and without economic reform the slowly expanding system of socio-economic rewards (consumption) can most definitely not be secured. It is Habermas's thesis that 'value' (economic) and 'meaning' are mutually substitutable within certain limits. Hence what we must discover is the capacity of the socio-cultural system to produce meaningful motivations in the context of either continued social conservatism (which endangers socio-economic rewards and indirectly the legitimacy of the party-state based on welfare and rationality) or progressive liberalisation (which endangers the party and therefore the social identity of the system). Ideally we would have to determine not only the available functional *and* dysfunctional motivations in the present, but the relationship of political ideology and motivation in the context of three developments: (1) the irreversible consequences (if any) of urbanisation and industrialisation for the traditional component in motivations; (2) the consequences for motivation of the reform/conservatism cycle itself; (3) the consequences of drastic expansion of the ideological-administrative apparatus into culture, along with the administered development of the official ideology itself.

Only four major ideological complexes are officially and semi-officially promoted in the unfree administered public sphere of state-socialist societies. One of these, Marxism-Leninism, is the symbolic system that justifies the formally separate existence of the monolithic party (defined above as the institution by which the prerogative state, the actual institutional core of the whole, identifies and justifies itself). Nevertheless, because this ideology is today entirely empty and ritualistic, it can perform its symbolic functions only by containing in ever-shifting combinations the other three, genuine ideologies: an ideology based on memories of the Leninist New Economic Policy (NEP), a nationalist-traditionalist ideology, and the already-mentioned authoritarian-technocratic ideology.

The basic continuity (in spite of a transformation of function) of

Marxism-Leninism as the hegemonic complex is a matter of record. Nevertheless, the classical dogmas of Marxist-Leninist orthodoxy, especially those concerning the transition to communism, are held increasingly cynically.[31] Thus Marxism-Leninism cannot be the *sole* means for the ideological legitimation of society: as a ritualised dogmatic quasi-religion, it is too impoverished; as a rational ideology, it is constantly endangered by the reality to which it is increasingly irrelevant. But it is still an indispensable component of the identity of the institutional core, and its dominating role in philosophy and political theory guarantees the exclusion of serious public discussion about society.[32] Thus, within the limits of the system, it can only be supplemented, not replaced.

The ideology of the NEP, based on a legally established mixed economy and the famous Leninist *smychka* between peasant and worker, was never formally renounced, even when the economy was fully politicised and the peasantry defeated and crushed. At two junctures, various ideological aspects of the NEP were revived even more dramatically: in 1936 when the 'normative state' based on law was reconstructed (largely on the precedent of late tsarist and NEP law), and in the 1960s during the period of economic reform.[33] The idea of a reformist 'return' to Lenin implies the Lenin of the NEP and not that of *War Communism* or *State and Revolution*, a Lenin that strategically combined the monolithic party with an authoritarian state and a mixed economy. We know furthermore that the NEP, conceived as a mixture of a benevolently authoritarian-welfare politics, reasonable rates of economic development and de-collectivised agriculture, retained an astonishing level of normative validity for the generation of the Second World War.[34] The Soviet system as we know it cannot survive without maintaining this ideological complex, and yet the NEP also cannot be allowed to become the ideological centre of the whole. A consistent version of the NEP would be open to all of the dangers of 'spill-over', especially in a society far more developed than that of the 1920s. To maintain some minimum resemblance between the ideology of the NEP and contemporary reality, the regime must (a) gradually improve the standard of living *both* in terms of public welfare and private consumption, and (b) slowly improve an atmosphere of public security and even legality. It is almost certain today that the first of these conditions cannot be satisfied without further steps (and serious ones) in the direction of reform. It is my belief, however, that NEP ideology is not *in itself* hostile to the self-identity of the system. The economists, planners, jurists and intellectuals who promoted it sought indeed to preserve this self-identity in a rationally reconstructed society. Rational reconstruction carries the risks that we have attempted to describe above, and after the experience of 1968 these risks appeared intolerable, though it is not at all certain that the same reforms would everywhere have the same consequence as in Czechoslovakia. As a result, the partisans of the NEP have remained ultimately weak and in the 1970s were exposed to conservative counter-attack. Such conservative counter-attacks are possible only because (and so long as) the remaining two ideological complexes retain some mobilising power among ruling strata, as well as some power to secure a significant degree of popular loyalty to the established state – or at least to secure its best replacement: apathetic, privatistic, depoliticised adaptation.

The authoritarian-technocratic ideology of extending the results of the 'scientific technological revolution' in the direction of more sophisticated socio-economic planning and control seeks to mobilise key sections of the technical intellectuals, some originally reformist and others more conserva-tive. This ideology, representing 'reform' without any substantive economic and legal concessions, could affect the population at large only by some extremely improbable level of expanding economic growth rates and above all public and private consumption. Most economists in Eastern Europe and even the Soviet Union seem to believe, however, that technocratic-authoritarian 'reform' would have the opposite consequence: namely, a continuation of the rationality crisis. So the only purpose of the ideology in question is to keep the technical and political sectors of the 'ruling elite' united – or, better still, to represent their common desire to avoid all strategies that would threaten the institutional core of the system (in particular, the selectivity which secures their relative powers and pri-vileges). In this context the experience of 1968 once again represents the ideological watershed in the Soviet Union and most East European countries.

Finally, the most important terrain of ideological legitimation is a nationalist-traditionalist complex that has also penetrated Marxist-Leninist and NEP ideologies. It hardly needs to be recalled that Marxism was 'Russified' in the process of becoming Soviet Marxism;[35] and it is perhaps even more important that the legal development of both the NEP and the post-1936 period represented a development of a complex within which Russian legal traditions (significantly different from those of the West) were a key component.[36] Indeed, whatever popular power these ideologies have in our day is shared by their rational and traditional components, which have now become inseparable. It may be completely futile to try to decide whether, as Berdyaev believed, Marxism was Russified or, as Solzhenitsyn now maintains, Russia was Marxianised. We are dealing in fact with an entirely original statist ethos that combines features of one side of Marxism (statism as against democratic socialism), one side of Russia (caesaropapist autocracy and authoritarian bureaucracy as against popular anti-statism), the Leninist self-definition of anti-capitalist intellectuals, as well as a work ethic derived from capitalism itself. So far as the Russian traditions are concerned, even its discarded populist and anti-statist components are preserved by the ruling party itself. As a result, one may speak of a nationalist-traditionalist ideological complex sustained by the combination of two sets of traditional elements: on the one hand, the heritage of 'autocracy, nationality and orthodoxy' that survives as the compulsory service state,[37] as the celebration of the imperial heritage, as an aggressive military-political ethnocentrism, as the ritualisation of ortho-dox dogma and as the cult of the autocratic personality; and on the other hand, the anti-authoritarian heritage that focuses on communitarian anti-capitalism, the ethics of collective solidarity, ideas of substantive justice and welfare, as well as the celebration of the Russian people, who supposedly possess all these qualities.[38] In the Soviet period the two sides were inseparable. Populism was the mask of autocracy, and especially during the period of the 'heroic socialist construction' and the 'Great Patriotic War' – that is, in moments of real or supposed external and internal danger – both worked sufficiently powerfully for the population as a whole. Yet autocracy could not do without the populist mask and was therefore forced to preserve and even to develop it. In moments of external danger this was done rather easily. It is only with the emergence of the Soviet Union as a great industrial and imperial power that the two moments became genuinely separable. Without genuine external threat, without the obvious necessity of enforced self-sacrifice, populism could again rediscover its anti-statist spirit; and with the autocratic centre promoting social atomisation and a puritanical work ethic,[39] the mytholo-gies of the Russian people and of the benevolent autocracy have become to some extent unstuck. Today, the opposition between the Solzhenitsyns and the ideologists of official Soviet nationality is potentially more radical than the clash between 'tsar and people' in the nineteenth century.[40] The imagined solution is, however, still the same: the synthesis of the poles in a virulent militaristic, ethnocentric, anti-semitic, Great Russian nationalism. In a very real sense the possible success of this strategy represents the ultimate alternative to what we described as the realisation of negative subordination between state and society. What then are the chances of this synthesis?

The sustenance of the eclectic ideological mix of Marxism-Leninism, NEP reformism, authoritarian technocracy and traditionalist-nationalism, and even more the displacement of the weight of the whole in the direction of virulent nationalism, depends on the cultural elements internalised through the family and education. For the bulk of the population we presume that explicit ideologies of legitimation did not play the sole or even the crucial role of social integration during the cataclysmic process of the 1930s: 'a mixture of traditional ties, fatalistic willingness to follow, lack of perspective, and naked repression (above all)'[41] have been far more important ways of ensuring the subordination of the collectivised peasantry and the newly created proletariat than 'the convincing force' of statist ideologies. None the less, for social integration to be successful there must be a complementarity between the ideologies that mobilise leading economic, political and cultural strata and the forms of motivation, loyalty, subordination and adaptation that emerge from the cultural life-world of the population. This complementarity cannot be maintained if four Habermasian theses are correct. The first asserts the impossibility of the administrative creation of meaning; the second proclaims the erosion of all dogmatically held traditions in the modern world; the third alleges the impossibility of constructing a rational social identity in the modern world around the nation-state or party elite; and the fourth acknowledges the survival of only post-auratic art, scientism and universalistic morality (embedded in legal institutions and structures) as forms of social integration that are able to withstand the critical rejection of petrified traditions.[42]

I accept the first of these theses on the basis of epistemological assumptions drawn from both Habermas and Gadamer which cannot be presented here. What I should like to argue, however, is that the second thesis is partially false, and that this deprives the third and fourth theses of some of their main force. In other words, we are obliged to consider the continued possibility of pre-rational or irrational identity formation around the nation-state; and that even if scientism, modern art and morality indicate the terrain where genuinely contemporary forms of cultural creativity must be located, in modern Russia at least this terrain hardly exhausts the symbolic systems relevant to social integration.

If we take the 1930s as our starting-point, two already-mentioned contradictory developmental tendencies can be registered in the sphere of social integration. There was first of all an obvious process of 'archaisation', the Stalinist 'resurrection of the historic Tsarist pattern of building a powerful military-national state by revolutionary means [from above] involving the extension of direct coercive controls over the population and the growth of state power in the process'. But there was also a great need, from the mid-1930s onwards in the context of a shattered fabric of traditional society and the craving of both officials and people for security, 'to regularise, to consolidate, to reinsure, to ensure a ruly and predictable working of the responsible institutions, some kind of constitutionality'.[43] It is easy to agree with Lewin that it is the clash of these two tendencies that produced the second phase of the terror, namely Stalin's violent attempt to prevent the consolidation of the power of those normal bureaucratic agencies that showed their influence in the explosion of constitutionalism and legality in a sphere previously dominated by revolutionary, substantive justice. What must also be stressed, however, is that the duality of law and terror was not abolished by the post-Stalin consolidation of law, but rather was replaced by the duality of law and politics that penetrated the structure of both law (in the form of vague, unspecific definitions of political offences) and politics. Even if the legal reforms of 1936 and especially 1953 and after were determined by needs of stability, security and rationality, even if from 1936 onwards the Soviet bureaucracy rediscovered the power of legal legitimacy, nevertheless the continuation of the 'dual state' required resources of legitimacy other than legality. In other words, the fundamental trend of legal reform would have destroyed the dual state unless the extra-legal political element could draw on a combination of charismatic-revolutionary and traditional symbolic resources. Given the terroristic trappings of charismatic autocracy, there was, after 1953, a decisive shift in the direction of tradition and even more of 'traditionalism' or traditional legitimacy. The possibility of this shift grounds the dominant, prerogative element of the dual state, and with it the organisational principle of the Soviet system.

We should not underestimate the significance of the return to law that was obviously pushed by rising *modern* social strata (bureaucrats, technical intellectuals, etc.). Today, moreover, the defence and extension of legality is the 'project' of an enormously important pressure group of modern jurists, the size and influence of which is almost entirely new in Russia.[44] Nevertheless, the re-emergence of law *was* from the outset paralleled by the revival of traditions all along the line. From the regime's side, the tsarist slogan of 'nationality, orthodoxy, autocracy' well expresses what was sought and what was in fact revived. But what was revived on the side of the population undergoing enormous sacrifices?

For the Stalinist period we are not without some empirical material. Whatever its weaknesses, the results of the 'Harvard project on the Soviet social system'[45] show that renewed traditionalism remains an important part of the social psychology of the Soviet 'citizen'. The model of the ideal society, held by the great majority of the displaced persons interviewed by the researchers, was indeed a slightly rationalised welfare-statist version of traditional Russian autocracy. The respondents had little interest in formal law, political participation, and even civil rights, with the exception of the right of privacy and family against political and administrative interference. They were also deeply imbued with the traditional attitude of the superiority of collectivistic Russia over the individualistic West. Though they revealed much dissatisfaction with the regime, their alternative loyalties based on familial *and* occupational privatism led in most cases to passive acceptance of the regime.[46] Most surprisingly, the values of those interviewed concerning family education with respect to general socialisation and occupational goals turned out to be deeply and even increasingly 'traditionalistic', in Weber's sense of the term. Inkeles and Bauer are of course right when they maintain that the regime has been successful in suppressing some of the traditional components of education, since they mean the particular traditions (strong patriarchy, orthodox religion, etc.) of the Tsarist period. These, however, do not exhaust the meaning of 'traditionalism', which I construe as the uncritical elevation of the reproduction of an existing mode of life to normative validity. What the data of the Harvard project show is that the motivation structure of their sample did not unambiguously shift from 'traditional' to 'modern' orientations, but that there was instead a noticeable rise in *traditionalistic* motivations of adjustment to a pre-given situation, as well as traditional personalistic motives (turning activity increasingly inward) in the context of a significant and remarkable fall in the level of motivations based on modern norms of achievement.[47]

As many interpreters have indicated, the effect of the regime on the traditions it fostered has always been highly selective; the only traditions which have been allowed official expression are those which reinforced the regime's political and economic goals. What the regime did not promote, at least originally, was the emergence of a traditionalistic, family-based ethic that stressed the protection of fundamental human ties through passive acceptance, adaptation and socio-political fatalism, even after the traditional religious values of the past have been discarded. This attitude is, however, greatly reinforced by the still existing extremes of political and economic centralisation and the total administration of the public sphere, which together exclude *intimate* solidarities on all except the family level. Of course, in the context of economic growth and legal security, this form of traditionalism would also be compatible with a vocational achievement ethic linked to civic privatism.[48] But in the past all traces of legal security were missing, whereas in the present and foreseeable future it is likely that economic growth will remain a problem. Hence in the Soviet Union we may count on the reinforcement of the traditionalistic features of privatism.

Can we also assume that the traditionalism of everyday life in Russia is open to the ritualistic aspects of Marxism-Leninism and to the semi-official traditional-nationalistic ideology? With respect to the first of these, the answer is probably negative, since here we are dealing with an ideology whose connection to actual communities – the substance of all traditionalism – is very remote. The official institutions of Soviet society are merely illusory communities. It may be otherwise with respect to the traditional-nationalistic ideology. In moments of military, political and social crisis related to the outside world (China, the West, Eastern Europe), the regime can probably once again activate the nationalistic and patriotic resources of legitimation that were so important in overcoming the apathy, cynicism and anomie of the population during the Second World War. But without identifiable enemies, it is at least questionable whether the atomised, privatised, family-orientated majority of the population can be indefinitely shielded from the social criticism of schools of dissidents by a massive propaganda campaign defending the existing 'Soviet way of life'.[49] While Great Russian nationalism may justify a community of interests against outside and inside 'enemies', the same ideology also represents a potential danger to the stability of the system. For Great Russian nationalism reinforces the self-consciousness and resistance of other nationalities that will soon represent over half the population of the Soviet Union.[50]

Although the actual ideological-political setting is full of dangers and ambiguities, on Habermasian grounds one would have to adopt a generally hopeful attitude. It is his belief that, in the modern world, institutions cannot be consolidated on the basis of regressive forms of legitimation. The development of law in the Soviet Union seems to bear out the point. Today the existence of a significant civil-rights movement in Russia is possible because of the large-scale replacement in civil and criminal law of traditional, substantive considerations by formally guaranteed rules and procedures. No matter how conservative jurists are personally, their work prepares the ground for a *rechtsstaatliche* transformation in the future, one that would have to be fought and suffered for by courageous individuals whatever their immediate political ideology, since legal protection of speech and assembly is desperately needed by all dissident tendencies. But to return to our own hypothesis: even the creation of some kind of modified socialist *Rechtsstaat* may still, under certain conditions, be compatible with the system's authoritarian identity principle and organisational core. To believe that legal development must necessarily overshoot this mark requires Habermas's confidence in the erosion of irrational, traditionalist structures of consciousness and the moral development of the human species. It requires, furthermore, a single logic of legal development in history, one that may be disputable in light of the continued viability of the 'dual state' in state-socialist countries, as well as the persistence and reappearance of traditionalistic structures of consciousness. In the spirit of a slightly modified version of Habermas's theory of moral development,[51] I would claim that so long as the universal moral-legal achievements of the West are preserved, the penetration of these into other contemporary settings is at least possible. But this penetration necessarily depends on what Weber called historical *Wahlverwandt-schaften*, that is, on the prior development of particular national cultural constellations and on the institutional mechanisms of the preservation or elimination of those traditions which favour or inhibit the emergence of civil society. These two aspects can be evaluated only in a framework of analysis which is both abstract-systematic *and* historical-comparative, one that would necessarily assess the possible futures of societies with the *same* state-socialist organisational principle according to their deep-seated historical *differences* and according to the developmental tendencies which are necessarily common to them all.

12

A Reply to my Critics

JÜRGEN HABERMAS

Initial reactions

That so many competent and distinguished colleagues have dealt so
seriously with publications which, as I know only too well, are at best
stimulating but by no means present finished thoughts is a source of both
embarrassment and pleasure. For all the ambivalence, satisfaction is, to be
sure, predominant. There has never been any need to complain about lack
of attention among the scholarly and political public; however, this
resonance often enough brings me to the painful awareness that I have
apparently been unable to present my theoretical approach in a comprehensible manner or, perhaps, to awaken the hermeneutic willingness
requisite for its reception. This situation has recently changed. Especially
in Anglo-Saxon countries, and also in Scandinavia and Holland, for
instance, I am encountering a critique that over-indulges me with careful
argumentation, that unsettles me with interesting objections, and that
involves me in very instructive discussions. The contributions to the
present volume are an impressive case in point. I suspect that this
well-informed interest could not have developed if Thomas McCarthy had
not subjected my work to a penetrating analysis which, for all its criticism,
represents a co-operative effort to advance the argument. I could not have
wished for a fairer and more productive partner in dialogue.

The contributions to this volume are so complex that – even without the
friendly invitation of the editors to incorporate into my response objections
published elsewhere – I run the danger of not seeing the forest for the
trees. In order to make the task somewhat more manageable, and to spare
the reader accordingly, I shall not deal with all the objections that have
been raised but only with those that strike me as the most important.
Naturally I am hopeful that my selection of themes will not turn out too
one-sided, my assessment of the objections too egocentric. To this end I
have provisionally grouped the objections – in so far as I do not for my part
treat them critically – under the following points of view. There are
objections that I accept and that force me to reflect on their consequences.
Other objections appear to me to raise serious difficulties but are for the
time being so opaque as regards their premises that I leave them to one

side. I have not been able to get clear about the intentions behind a few objections; they require, at least in so far as I am concerned, a reconstruction that I cannot carry out in this context. Finally, there are objections to themes and assumptions that I myself have treated only in a programmatic way and regard as being in need of clarification, without yet having found the time to work my way into them with sufficient intensity; this is true of the important complex of developmental logic which, without wanting to avoid a response, I shall have to leave to one side on this occasion.[1] The problems I shall deal with are ordered in such a way that the first four are of a more general nature, while the last two have a somewhat more special character. The pieces by Heller, Bubner, McCarthy, Ottmann and Lukes give me the opportunity (in sections I to IV) to clarify my own intentions, whereas my responses to Giddens, Thompson, Hesse, Held and Arato stick more closely to their texts (sections V and VI).

I.   The Marxian heritage

Agnes Heller discusses the status and claim of a critical social theory linked to Marx. We meet in the effort to carry on the Marxian tradition under considerably changed historical conditions. Heller's friendly critique touches me all the more, since I know from what perspective, from what context of life-history, *she* is speaking when she points out that I, as a Marxist theoretician, have never had organisational ties to the labour movement. If that were meant as a reproach, the response would be easy. But Heller connects with this observation the question of how, under the conditions of an academic way of life, which beyond teaching and research does not permit much more than political journalistic activity, a theory can be developed that upholds the Marxian claim to an internal relation with practice. She knows very well that a theory of society capable of holding its own can today be developed and tested only within the scientific system. She also knows that Communist Party ties today rather impede theoretical work, or at best let it be. And yet there remains the suspicion that a Marxist theory will lose the sting of its practical intent if the intellectual alienates himself or herself from the experiences and imperatives – one could say, from the sensuousness – of a social movement, even if for reasons that can scarcely be dismissed historically. Is there not then lacking, Agnes Heller asks me (and herself?), a moment of that seriousness without which all moral – and even intellectual – responsibilities slide off into abstractions?

There is a level on which I would not want to dispute this. But Heller follows the trail of this abstraction on another level; and there I cannot see the structural dissimilarities between Marxian theory on the one side, and the theoretical approach of an academic Marxism on the other.

Faced with the historical perspective suggested by an autonomous systems-functionalism of the sort proposed by Niklas Luhmann, I once employed the paradoxical formula of 'the partiality for reason'. In doing so, I wanted to recall the practical content of a critical theory aimed at revealing – and thereby indicting – the suppression of generalisable interests. The formula was in no way intended in the sense of a 'universalisation of the addressee', as if the place still occupied by the proletariat in the work of the young Lukács was to be reserved for the transcendental subject, for humanity or reason. As a matter of fact, 'reason' is neither a class nor a 'target group'; it has no body, cannot suffer, and also arouses no passion. Marx wanted to capture the embodiments of unreason. In the same sense, we are also concerned today with the analysis of power constellations that suppress an intention intrinsic to the rationality of purposive action and linguistic understanding – the claim to reason announced in the teleological and intersubjective structures of social reproduction themselves – and that allow it to take effect only in a distorted manner. Again and again this claim is silenced; and yet in fantasies and deeds it develops a stubbornly transcending power, because it is renewed with each act of unconstrained understanding, with each moment of living together in solidarity, of successful individuation, and of saving emancipation.

We should not allow ourselves to be persuaded by empiricism, of whatever hue, that the predicate 'rational' can only be applied to a subjective faculty and interpreted instrumentally in the sense of successful adaptation or self-assertion. Just as little is it the case that social formations can be observed and theoretically grasped only from the outside, like stars, by renouncing the pre-theoretical knowledge of everyday practice which ties the social scientist, literally from birth on, to the internal structure of the object.

Even Marx set out his theory in such a way that he could perceive and take up the trial of reason in the deformations of class society. Had he not found in proletarian forms of life the distortion of a communicative form of life as such, had he not seen in them an abuse of a universal interest reaching beyond the particular, his analysis would have been robbed of the force of *justified* critique. His critique would have forfeited the power of an appeal to reason; it would have been reduced to a lament or to sheer agitation. Like Marx's, my theoretical approach is guided by the intention of recovering a potential for reason encapsulated in the very forms of social reproduction. Looked at philosophically, this potential is to be reclaimed without ontological backing, without recourse to Aristotle – that is, without falling back behind Kant.

What today separates us from Marx are evident historical truths, for example that in the developed capitalist societies there is no identifiable class, no clearly circumscribed social group which could be singled out as the representative of a general interest that has been violated. This insight already separated the older generation of Frankfurt theorists, who had both fascism and Stalinism before their eyes, from their great predecessor Georg Lukács.[2] I am not certain whether this point is really at issue between Agnes Heller and myself. The following points do seem to me to be controversial: (1) if not the loss of the historical addressee, at least the meaning of this fact for a critical theory of society; further (2) my neglect of the externalisation model of social labour, of the 'romantic' features in Marx's early work generally; and finally (3) the price that I have to pay for an allegedly abstract rationalism.

(1) The destruction of the historico-philosophical certainty that the industrial working class and the European labour movement were targets for possible, theoretically induced processes of enlightenment and bearers of a politically pursued, revolutionary transformation is not, in my view, entirely a disadvantage. Today the place of very general theoretical assertions, to which organisational efforts were supposed to be directly linked, must be taken by an empirical analysis that is sensitive to contemporary history and is social-scientifically well informed – an analysis that differentiates its object not only according to stage of development, mode of production, class structure and political order, but according to national traditions, regions, subcultures and according to contingent historical constellations. At the same time, a shift of theoretical perspective which critical theory had already executed in the 1930s is now making itself felt. Theoretical attention is directed not so much to the conflict-engendering mechanisms of the economic system as to the defence mechanisms following in the wake of crisis, to the ways in which the state deals with conflicts, and to cultural integration. In consequence of this displacement of conflicts, warded off at the institutional level, to the periphery, to the geographical, social and psychological margins, the groups in which conflict potentials accumulate need not be identical with the bearers of politically enlightened and organised action.

Even if the historical addressee were not beyond the reach of the theory, the relation of the theory to a practice that might possibly be guided by it would have to be defined differently than it was in the classical doctrine. Both *revolutionary self-confidence* and *theoretical self-certainty* are gone, and not only because in the meantime bureaucratic socialism has turned out to be a worse variant of what was to be fought against.

Systems theory has sharpened our eye for the consequences of a – comparatively speaking – extremely heightened social complexity. Ideas of a total revision of existing social relations must today be measured against these risks. In highly complex societies structural alterations affect many elements at the same time and in unforseen ways. Consequently the status quo has, not entirely without reason, settled into everyday intuition as an argument.[3] I am not referring to the ideological use of this argument which misleads us into adopting an absurd rule for distributing the burden of proof, and basically exempts the status quo from the need for justificaton.[4]

Still, the argument contains a kernel of truth that must make the *juste milieu* appear more and more worth preserving, even in the eyes of those who have not given up the expectation of a long-term revolutionary transformation. One who uses the word 'revolutionary' in more than a metaphorical sense has to acknowledge that with the incalculability of interventions into deep-seated structures of highly complex societies, the risk of catastrophic alternatives ensuing also grows. To be sure, defeatism would be the wrong consequence to draw from this. The conservative rule for distributing the burden of proof obscures the dilemma: anxiously striving to avoid at all costs catastrophes that are provoked, it not only fails to protect us from catastrophe that makes its way in a quasi-natural fashion – fascistic catastrophe – but delivers us up to it.

The new ambivalences in the relation of theory to practice are fostered not only by a revolutionary uncertainty on the side of practice, but also by a fallibilistic consciousness on the side of theory. With its entrance into the academy, Marxism too had to establish itself as a theoretical approach within the reference system of organised science.[5] For a critical theory of society this has the following two consequences, among others. On the one hand, under the pincer-like pressure of theoretical generalisation and specialisation, it has to scale down philosophical questions into problems that can be dealt with scientifically; on the other hand, it has to give up the philosophical concept of science *(Wissenschaft),* which Hegel was the last to defend successfully, and acknowledge the fundamentally hypothetical character of its assertions.[6] This revision increases the distance between theory and practice; however, it frees the latter from illusory certainties and shifts decisions and responsibilities unambiguously to the side of those who have to bear the risk of the consequences of their action.

(2) Agnes Heller renews an objection that has been raised from different sides against my separation of the concepts of labour and interaction.[7] Stated briefly, this reservation is directed against the reduction of 'labour' to 'instrumental action'; the idea of labour, of productive activity, of practice – so the argument goes – is thereby robbed of its deeper dimension: the 'anthropological significance' of labour is lost. Above all, what is lost is the normative content of creativity and self-realisation; and without the rationality inherent in the externalisation, objectification and appropriation of essential human powers, the concept of alienated labour must also lose its sting. This objection brings Heller to the impressive formulation that in social reproduction there lies a claim to undistorted purposive activity no less than to undamaged communication.

I am not unaware of the weight of the tradition to which a humanistic Marxism that began in the name of the philosophy of practice *(Praxis)* can appeal. Impulses emanating from the Heideggerian Marxism of the early Marcuse and from the Husserlian Marxism of the early Sartre were picked up by Karel Kosik and Enno Paci, became fruitful in the Yugoslavian

Praxis group and in the Budapest School, and had a broad international influence, as can be seen, for instance, in the circle around the American journal *Telos*. The philosophers of practice have the intention of making visible once again the emancipatory content of Marxian theory, which has been distorted beyond recognition in Soviet Marxism, and of doing so by way of rehabilitating the anthropological concept of non-alienated labour.

It is no accident that Heller speaks in this connection of the 'romantic' features of Marx's early writings. In the introductory chapter of his book on Hegel, Charles Taylor traces this motif back through Romanticism to Humboldt and Schiller, to *Sturm und Drang,* above all to Herder. What the philosophers of practice are calling for is the legacy of a vision kindled in German classicism, the ideal of an individuality creatively realising itself. Taylor examines the model of human expressivity, of the expression of inner stirrings, in general of the objectivism of essential powers, which underlies this ideal. He emphasises two moments: first, the idealistic activistic reinterpretation of the Aristotelian concept of form – individuals can unfold their essence only through their own productive activity;[8] second, the mediation of Aristotelian and aesthetic concepts of form through the theory of reflection – the works in which subjectivity is externalised are the symbolic expression of both a creative process and a process of self-formation.[9] A result of this expressivist model of the self and self-activity is the prototypical status of aesthetic, genial productivity, which makes it possible to unite the autonomy of self-realisation with the spontaneity of self-development, and to remove from the objectivation of essential powers the moment of coercion, of doing violence to external nature or to one's own internal nature.

In the classical period these ideas became influential as ideals of cultivation *(Bildung)*; but this released motifs, especially in the circle of the *Tübinger Stiftler,* that entered into post-Kantian philosophy. Whether the expressivist model of the self-creative process of self-formation not only enriched Hegel's concept of spirit but, as Taylor believes, determined it, we can leave to one side. At any rate, however, it stimulated Hegel only to explain the structure of spirit in 'logical' terms and to ground it in *Realphilosophie.* Marx did not have at his disposal a comparable apparatus for grounding.

When Marx borrowed from Romanticism (through Hegel) the expressivist ideal of self-formation, transferred aesthetic productivity to the practical working life of the species, conceived social labour as the collective self-realisation of the producers, and, against this background, represented the activity of the modern wage-labourer at once as alienated and as the modern emancipatory force, he found himself faced with a series of difficulties. These difficulties cannot be overcome by anthropologically elucidating a concept of *Praxis* which relies on the wealth of its horizon of meaning within the history of ideas. Here I can only enumerate the difficulties without going into them in detail.

To begin with, we need an analytic clarification of the question as to whether the economic concept of labour can really be expanded into the concept of a simultaneously creative and self-formative productivity. The romantically transfigured concept called upon by Marx is hardly adequate to this task. Even supposing that this could be done, there remains the question as to whether this paradigmatic mode of activity is as universal as purposive activity and communication. If not, we could not show that the normative content of the expanded concept of production is built into the very structures of social reproduction as a claim to reason. Finally, we would have to prove that there is a dialectic of alienated labour and critical-revolutionary activity, for they are supposed to represent merely two different moments of the same circular process of externalisation, objectification and appropriation of essential human powers. Axel Honneth has elaborated this difficulty well:

> Marx did not point the way out of the basic conceptual difficulties into which his use of the concept of labour for the theory of revolution obviously brought him. The constraints of his revaluation of work within a theory of emancipation were so strong that he attempted, at all stages of development of his theory, to attribute the social-revolutionary learning process which was supposed to lead beyond capitalism to the internal relation of social labour; and he did so without developing for this reduction a model of argumentation that was convincing from the standpoint of action theory.[10]

Furthermore, Honneth traces without illusions a development of industrial labour, which, under the pressure of the imperative to rationalise, has become further and further removed from the model of the craftsman's activity. Correspondingly, the concept of labour has been purged of all normative content in industrial sociology and has been discharged from the role of an emancipatory driving-force in social philosophy. If we add to this the trends towards shortening working time and towards a corresponding devaluation of the relevance of labour within the life-world, then it becomes evident that the historical development of industrial labour is cutting the ground from under the philosophy of *Praxis*. But if the production-aesthetic revaluation of industrial labour becomes irrelevant, the whole problematic shrinks to the sober, social-political size of a 'humanisation of the working world'.[11]

Agnes Heller seems to assume, as does Anthony Giddens, that dropping the philosophically dramatised concept of labour, which identifies labour with practice in the sense of creative self-realisation, means losing the possibility of preserving the critical meaning of alienated and abstract labour. But Marx himself immediately abandoned the anthropological model of labour as externalisation, which still furnished the standard for the critique of alienated labour in the 'Paris Manuscripts', and shifted the burden of normative grounding to the labour theory of value. Later the analysis of commodity fetishism was supposed to explain the effects of reification. These effects came to pass as a result of the market taking over the function of co-ordinating action in spheres of production which had been normatively regulated in pre-capitalist societies, that is, regulated within the forms of traditional morality. In my theory of communicative action, to which I can do no more than refer here, I attempt to provide an equivalent for these reflections. I explain the alienation phenomena specific to modern societies by the fact that spheres of the communicatively structured life-world have increasingly been subjected to imperatives of adaptation to autonomous sub-systems, which have been differentiated out through media such as money and power, and which represent fragments of norm-free sociality. That the life-world remains dependent on forms of social integration, and cannot be transferred over to mechanisms for system integration without reification effects, calls for an explanation in terms of communication theory.

(3) From the controversy concerning the soundness of the philosophical concept of labour, there results finally the question as to whether the structures of purposive rationality and of linguistic understanding contain the potential for reason that can no longer be convincingly reconstructed in terms of the expressivist model of self-realisation. I shall come back to this question, which is discussed in other contributions as well. To begin with, Heller brings into play only a kind of existential mistrust against the formalism of a theory which views processes of emancipation from the perspective of establishing communicative rationality. Against this formalism she advances elements of an almost Weberian world-view: the (in the final analysis) decisionistic basis of value orientations; the fact that socio-cultural forms of life appear in the plural; and, finally, the indissolubly tragic substance of history. In my view neither the polytheism of beliefs nor the dialectic of progress – elements which I am not at all tempted to deny – can be correctly interpreted unless one resists the decisionism suggested by Nietzsche and played out by Weber in neo-Kantian terms, and by Sartre in existentialist terms.

Heller wants to stylise communicative rationality into a *particular* value, for or against which we can take sides. Her thesis can also be interpreted in a somewhat less pronounced sense as follows: if we 'decide' at all in an emphatic sense, that is, if we want to take hold of our lives in freedom and to lead them consciously, we cannot avoid taking the side of establishing communicative rationality. On the other hand, so the argument goes, a formal-pragmatic or transcendental-pragmatic grounding of the rationality-claims always involved in processes of consensus formation misleads us into losing sight of the moment of existential decision which is, in the final analysis, ungrounded. As opposed to this, my thesis is comparatively conventional. Whenever speaking and acting subjects want to arrive purely by way of argument at a decision concerning contested validity-claims of norms or statements, they cannot avoid having recourse, intuitively, to foundations that can be explained with the help of the concept of communicative rationality. Participants in discourse do not have to come first to an agreement about this foundation; indeed, a decision for the rationality inherent in linguistic understanding is not even possible. In communicative rationality we are always already orientated to those validity-claims, on the intersubjective recognition of which possible consensus depends.

In opposition to this Heller points to the abstract alternative of giving up the attitude orientated to reaching understanding in favour of a strategic orientation to success, or of 'not choosing at all but simply following drives, emotions or habits'. The possibility of choosing in this way remains abstract since it is given only from the perspective of the individual actor; from the perspective of the life-world to which the actor belongs, the modes of action are not simply at one's disposal. The symbolic structures of a life-world are reproduced in forms of cultural tradition, social integration and socialisation; and one can show that these processes *can* take place *only* through the medium of action orientated to reaching understanding. Thus for individuals who cannot acquire and maintain their identities otherwise than through carrying on traditions, belonging to social groups, participating in socialising interactions, the choice between communicative and strategic action is open only in an abstract sense. Opting for a long-run withdrawal from contexts of action orientated to reaching understanding, and thus from communicatively structured spheres of life, means retreating into the monadic isolation of strategic action; in the long run this is self-destructive. That communicative rationality, precisely as suppressed, is already embodied in the existing forms of interaction and does not first have to be postulated as something that ought to be is shown by the causality of fate which Hegel and Marx, each in his own way, illustrated in connection with phenomena of ruptured morality – the reactions of those who are put to flight or roused to resistance by fateful conflicts, who are driven to sickness, to suicide, crime, or to rebellion and revolutionary struggle.

Communicative reason operates in history as an avenging force. A theory that identifies this reason by way of structural characteristics and conceptualises it as procedural rationality – instead of mystifying it as fate – is protected against the danger of dogmatically overstating its claims precisely through being formalised. Such a theory has at its disposal standards for the critique of social relations that betray the promise to embody general interests which is given with the morality of legitimate orders and valid norms. But it cannot judge the value of competing forms of life. To be sure, the concept of communicative rationality does contain a utopian perspective; in the structures of undamaged intersubjectivity can be found a necessary condition for individuals reaching an understanding among themselves without coercion, as well as for the identity of an individual coming to an understanding with himself or herself without force. However, this perspective comprises *only* formal determinations of the communicative infrastructure of *possible* forms of life and life-histories; it does not extend to the concrete shape of an exemplary life-form or a paradigmatic life-history. Actual forms of life and actual life-histories are embedded in unique traditions. Agnes Heller is right to insist that communication free of domination can count as a necessary condition for the 'good life' but can by no means replace the historical articulation of a felicitous form of life.

For this reason it is not consistent to burden social theory in general with the task of constructing a 'system of needs', that is, the totality of a form of life. Because Heller does not approach the theory of society at a sufficiently formal level, she finds it necessary to infer a *theoretical* pluralism from the fact that forms of life appear only in the plural. Only the formalism which she believes she must criticise could keep her from first overstating the claim of theory in the sense of the philosophical tradition's emphatic concept of truth, from expecting theory to furnish utopian life projects, in order then to dispel the dangers of dogmatism, which only thus arise, by means of an ungrounded relativism.

Something similar can be said of the criticism of my proposal to grasp the historical materialist concept of progress in evolutionary terms. I have attempted to explain the stage of productive forces and the maturity of productive relations by way of learning processes in the dimensions of objectivating thought and moral practical insight, and to measure them against levels of learning characterised in terms of cognitive structures and not in terms of content. If my conjecture is correct that these structures can be hierarchically ordered (in a sense requiring further clarification), then 'progress' or evolutionary innovation relates to capacities for cognitive-instrumental mastery of natural processes and for consensual resolution of morally relevant conflicts of action. As this concept of progress does not at all touch the sensitive zones of the good life – which are, in my view, beyond the grasp of theory – the theory of social evolution permits no conclusions about orders of happiness. If the balance of happiness (which is difficult to weigh) shifts at all, it certainly does not do so in dependence on rationalisation of the life-world. Perhaps it is possible to salvage from the tragic concept of progress that Benjamin developed in his theses on the philosophy of history one aspect for a more modest and more sober historical materialism. With the implementation of new problem-solving capacities, there also arise new categories of need and denial; there is a change in the structure of burdens, which, if our intuitions do not deceive us, makes suffering both more sublime and more intense. Only the horror remains always the same, for the horrible is not to be outdone.

II.   Critique versus theory – or critical theory?

It was in 1969, in his essay 'Was ist kritische Theorie?',[12] that Rüdiger Bubner first urged the differentiation in the concept of self-reflection that he calls for in his contribution to this volume. It was, among other things, Bubner's arguments that induced me to distinguish more clearly in the meantime between self-reflection in the sense of critique and self-reflection in the sense of universalistically orientated rational reconstruction. In my 1973 'Postscript to *Knowledge and Human Interests*' I drew the following contrast:

> on the one hand it ['reflection'] denotes reflection upon the conditions of potential abilities of a knowing, speaking and acting subject as such; on the other hand it denotes reflection upon unconsciously produced constraints to which a determinate subject (or a determinate group of subjects, or a determinate species subject) succumbs in its process of self-formation. In Kant and his successors, the first form of reflection took the form of a *search for the transcendental ground* of possible theoretical knowledge (and moral conduct). What does it mean for a theory, or for theoretical knowledge as such, to ground itself transcendentally? It means that the theory becomes familiar with the range of inevitable subjective conditions which both make the theory possible *and* place limits on it . . . In his *Phenomenology* Hegel combined the self-critical delimitation of consciousness, effected by a transcendental analysis of the conditional nature of something we know naively and intuitively, with reflection in *another* sense of the term, which denotes the critical dissolution of subjectively constituted pseudo-objectivity. In other words, he embraced a concept of reflection which contains the idea of an *analytical emancipation from objective illusions.* Later Freud removed this self-critical notion of reflection from its epistemological context by relating it to the reflective experience of an empirical subject who, under the compulsive sway of restricted patterns of perception and behavior, deludes himself about his own being. By understanding these illusions the subject emancipates himself from himself.[13]

In contrast to Henning Ottmann, who refers to this revision, Bubner insists on reproaching me for continuing to confuse 'critique' in Kant's sense with 'critique' in the sense of the Young Hegelians, and indeed especially in the context of language theory. He sees here traces of a confusion that he thinks he finds already in Marx, Lukács and the older generation of the Frankfurt School. I should like to respond to this reproach by first criticising in turn Bubner's unclear imputations of an ambiguous use of language, and then taking up his special objections.

The confusion between the Kantian and the Young Hegelian senses of 'critique' cannot be found in Marx, as he abstains from any philosophical investigation aimed at a critique of the faculty of reason. Of course, Marx does attach to his 'critique' of contemporary political economy a double-edged meaning: he arrives at the theory of the 'laws of motion' of capitalism by way of dealing with other economic theories, and he thereby at the same time *unmasks the ideological content* of bourgeois economics. Marx wants to do both at once, to refute competing approaches as theories and to convict them of being ideologies. To be sure, this critique of ideology remains without practical consequence unless it is transposed through agitation and enlightenment into the political consciousness of the masses, who, in perceiving their own interests, resolve to take up the struggle. Ideology critique by itself can at most shake the legitimacy of the orders against which such a transformative practice would have to be directed. The critique of false consciousness is not identical with the overthrow of institutions that are supported by this consciousness – even if Marx does bring together these two moments in his concept of 'critical-practical activity'. This in turn receives its specifically Young Hegelian meaning only through the link Marx forges between the overcoming *(Aufhebung)* of capitalist relations of power and the idea of *overcoming philosophy,* that is, of *realising* a potential of reason that had been both expressed and retarded by philosophy.

I shall not go into this but shall return to Bubner's question as to how Marx manages to lay out his analysis of the law-like regularities of the capitalist economic system in such a way that a scientific explanation can at the same time be read as the denunciation of a self-deception, that is, as a critique of bourgeois ideology. This question can be answered only through a study of the peculiar status of his value theory and of the burden of proof it was meant to carry for the theory as a whole. On the one hand, Marx introduces his theory of value in order to be able to *translate politico-economic statements* concerning anonymous functional interconnections of the economic cycle – which unconsciously penetrate and steer the action orientations of participants – *into sociological-historical statements* concerning the action contexts of which actors are intuitively aware. On the other hand, Marx implants in the theory of value, however inconspicuously, the *normative core* of rational natural law, that is, the idea that things would go well in bourgeois society only so long as the equivalents exchanged represented not merely what was alleged to be equivalent, but what was in fact – according to the standard of the labour power expended – equivalent. Thus an analysis of exchange processes carried out in terms of value theory made possible at the same time a critical judgement regarding the illusionary reflection of these processes in the consciousness of the participating actors.

When, under the altered historical circumstances of the 1930s, the interests of the Frankfurt School shifted from a political economy meant to explain crises to a theory of culture meant to explain why in developed capitalist societies the crisis of the economy and of the state did *not* lead to the expected disintegration, the theory of value – which had become problematic for other reasons as well – had to lose its privileged position. Ironically it was philosophy, in which bourgeois ideals were preserved, that once again – after the attempt to overcome it had failed – took on central importance. In the form which it assumed in the *Zeitschrift für Sozialforschung,* critical theory renewed the affirmative moment in its relation to the philosophy of the bourgeois epoch. The theory of society had to take from the latter the concept of reason, without which it lost its normative basis. 'Reason', wrote Marcuse in an essay expanding on Horkheimer's programmatic delimitation of critical theory in relation to traditional theory, 'is the fundamental category of philosophical thought, the only one by means of which it has bound itself to human destiny.'[14] And he goes on:

> Reason, mind, morality, knowledge, and happiness are not only categories of bourgeois philosophy, but concerns of mankind. As such, they must be preserved, if not derived anew. When critical theory examines the philosophical doctrines in which it was still possible to speak of man, it deals first with the camouflage and misinterpretation that characterized the discussion of man in the bourgeois period.[15]

To be sure, the ideology-critical confrontation with the tradition could aim at 'the truth content of philosophical concepts and problems'[16] and achieve an *appropriation of its systematic content* only because critique was *guided by theoretical assumptions.* At that time critical theory was still based on the Marxist philosophy of history, that is, on the conviction that the forces of production were objectively developing an explosive force. Only on that presupposition could critique limit itself to 'bringing to consciousness potentialities that have emerged within the maturing historical situation itself'.[17] And only then can Marcuse affirm:

> For the theory, these are exclusively potentialities of the concrete social situation. They become relevant only as economic and political questions and as such bear on human relations in the productive process, the distribution of the product of social labor, and men's active participation in the economic and political administration of the whole.[18]

Without a *theory* of history, there could be no immanent *critique* that set out from the forms of objective spirit and distinguished between 'what men and things could be and what they actually are'. Critique would be delivered over, in a historicist manner, to the standards of any given epoch. Bubner confuses this position with that adopted in the *Dialectic of*

Enlightenment. At that time, in 1941, Horkheimer and Adorno – and soon Marcuse as well – had lost their historico-philosophical faith in the rational potential of bourgeois culture which was to be set free in social movements under the pressure of developed forces of production. With that, the principal 'lever' of the theory was also lost. Since that time the development of productive forces and critical thinking have appeared in the perspective of a cloudy mixture with, and assimilation to, their opposite: instrumental reason, having become total, embodies itself in totalitarian society. With this the classical form of critical theory fell apart.

Marcuse and Adorno drew opposite conclusions from this critique of instrumental reason, with which the critique of ideology had in fact rendered itself independent of its theoretical context. Whereas Marcuse shifted the historically eclipsed claim to reason back below the threshold of culture by way of a theory of instincts – in order to obtain an equivalent for reason in the archaic grounds of a rebellious subjectivity[19] – Adorno consistently renounced any attempt to gain back normative foundations. He gave himself over to the negativism of a thinking that saw in the solitary experience of a self-denying philosophy, going round in its own aporias, the only possibility of at least pointing to the contents of reason – however powerless – disguised in esoteric art.

Thus neither Marx nor critical theory fell prey to the error that Bubner chalks up to them. Of course, *today* we have good reasons that might keep us from blindly following Marx in his value-theoretic reflections, or the older Frankfurt School in its philosophy of history, or Adorno and Marcuse in their desperate attempts to find a way out of the dead end of totalised critique. My own efforts can be understood in connection with the undertaking that critical theory broke off at the start of the 1940s.[20] My intention is to renew a critical social theory that secures its normative foundations by taking in the experience of thought gained along the way from Kant through Hegel to Marx, and from Marx through Peirce and Dilthey to Max Weber and George Herbert Mead, and by working them up into *a theory of rationality.* This is a matter of explicating a concept of reason that falls prey neither to historicism nor to the sociology of knowledge, and that does not stand abstractly over against history and the complex of social life. Only with this attempt can the Kantian meaning of 'critique' – which the Austro-Marxists, expecially Max Adler, invoked *in an unmediated way* against the Kautskyianism of the Second International – attain a position of honour within the Hegelian-Marxist tradition. I first connected self-reflection in the Kantian and Freudian senses in *Knowledge and Human Interests,* and explained myself on that point in the above-mentioned 'Postscript' of 1973.

Bubner does not mention the difficulty for the construction of *Knowledge and Human Interests* that results from this explanation. Thomas McCarthy formulates it very clearly in his book:

In trying to do justice to the theoretical character of theory (rational reconstructions as 'pure' knowledge) and the practical character of practice (critique as bound to the system of action and experience), Habermas seems to have reintroduced the gap between theory and practice, between reason and emancipation that *Knowledge and Human Interests* tried to close. More specifically, if it is only reflection in the sense of critique that pursues a direct interest in liberation from the self-deception embedded in systematically distorted communication; and if the identification of reason (in its purest form) with reflection makes sense only if reflection is understood as the reconstruction of the universal presuppositions of speech and action, then it seems to follow that the interest in emancipation is not proper to reason as such but only to a particular employment of reason: critical self-reflection. 'Transcendental' reflection appears to be an exception to the 'interest-ladenness' of cognition; it pursues neither the technical, the practical, nor the emancipatory interests. It is, in this sense, 'interest-free' – and we are back to something like the traditional notion of disinterested reason. Or, at most, it pursues an interest in the completion of transcendental reflection itself – and we are back to something like a 'pure' interest in explicating the implicit presuppositions of reason. In either case the radical claims of the theory of cognitive interests would have to be considerably trimmed.[21]

For the time being I shall have to accept this objection; I want to come back to the problem only after I can judge more precisely the (altered?) position of a theory of cognitive interests in the light of the theory of communicative action. My view today is that the attempt to ground critical social theory by way of the *theory of knowledge,* while it did not lead astray, was indeed a roundabout way. Bubner's objections are also aimed at the second, direct way leading into social theory, through the *theory of language.*

I shall try to render Bubner's objections sufficiently precise to enable me to divide up the problem-complex and deal with it step by step.

(1) *Language as a 'fact of reason'.* It strikes me as not entirely fair to nail me to one rather strongly formulated sentence from my inaugural lecture at Frankfurt University in 1965,[22] which was delivered as a series of theses, even though I have since attempted in a number of essays to develop the idea that was there introduced only in a programmatic way. I share Wittgenstein's view that language and understanding are equally original, mutually elucidating concepts. If, in a certain analogy to Kant's critique of reason, we seek to answer the question concerning how a use of language orientated to reaching understanding is possible, we come across an intuitive knowledge possessed by subjects capable of speech and action, a

knowledge which the growing child has to learn in order to be able to use it in communicative action as an adult. The rational reconstruction of this pre-theoretical knowledge can be carried on from a universalistic perspective, whether the investigations are directed to hypothetically assumed universal competencies of a grammatical or of a pragmatic sort.

Proposals for reconstruction are hypotheses that stand open to the testing and revision usual for rational reconstructions. To this extent I do not share the Kantian *a priorism*. The intuitive, non-reconstructed knowledge has no *theoretical* certainty, even for the communicative actors themselves – my original formulation does suggest this reading – but rather that kind of everyday certainty that is characteristic of background knowledge in the life-world, and even more so of the background knowledge that is constitutive of this world.

If it is the case that using language with an orientation towards achieving understanding requires of participants in communication an orientation to validity-claims that are in principle criticisable, and if it makes sense to reconstruct the philosophic concept of reason in the light of the role that these validity-claims play in processes of reaching understanding in everyday life or in argumentative discourse, then the telos of understanding inherent in language can, in analogy to the Kantian usage, be called a 'fact of reason'. Naturally a comparison of this sort stands in need of further differentiations.

(2) *Speech, actions, knowledge.* Bubner would like to see the relation to reason, which he allows for in connection with knowledge, detached from speech and action, and thus also from society (understood as life-world). I do not think it makes sense to speak at all of the rationality of knowledge; we should rather reserve the predicate 'rational' for the *use* of knowledge in linguistic utterances and in actions. *Communication* and *purposive activity* stand in internal relation to grounds or reasons, because subjects capable of speech and action employ knowledge in speaking and acting, and connect with their utterances, at least implicitly, claims to validity (or to success). I use the term *communicative action* for that form of social interaction in which the plans of action of different actors are co-ordinated through an exchange of communicative acts, that is, through a use of language (or of corresponding extra-verbal expressions) orientated towards reaching understanding. To the extent that communication serves mutual understanding (and not merely mutual influencing), it can take on the role in interaction of a mechanism for co-ordinating action, and thus make possible communicative action. Viewed from the perspective of the participants, it then serves to establish interpersonal relations; from the perspective of social science, it is the medium through which the life-world shared by the participants in communication is reproduced. To be sure, social systems are not wholly comprised of such life-world contexts reproduced through communicative action; only to the degree that they are

does the rational internal structure of the mechanism of reaching under-standing also affect society.

This concept in no way signifies an attempt to cede primacy to practical reason. The validity-claims interwoven into everyday practice – claims to propositional truth, normative rightness, and subjective truthfulness or authenticity – are equally primordial aspects; it is only in the modern period that they have been isolated from one another to the extent that cultural traditions can be dealt with under any given one of these aspects, and traditional problems can be sorted out in terms of questions having to do with truth, justice, or taste. Only at the cost of Occidental rationalism itself could we rescind the differentiation of reason into those rationality complexes to which Kant's three critiques of reason refer. Nothing is further from my intention than to make myself an advocate of such a regression, to conjure up the substantial unity of reason.

(3) *Ideal and reality*. Nothing makes me more nervous than the imputation – repeated in a number of different versions and in the most peculiar contexts – that because the theory of communicative action focuses attention on the social facticity of recognised validity-claims, it proposes, or at least suggests, a rationalistic utopian society. I do not regard the fully transparent society as an ideal, nor do I wish to suggest *any* other ideal – Marx was not the only one frightened by vestiges of utopian socialism. [23] Five brief reminders should suffice on this point.

(a) The ideal speech situation has its place in the theory of truth. Using this model I tried (very crudely) to clarify the formal-pragmatic presup-positions of argumentative speech. Discourses are islands in the sea of practice, that is, improbable forms of communication; the everyday appeal to validity-claims implicitly points, however, to their possibility. Only to this extent are idealisations *also* built into everyday practice. But I do wish to hold fast to the strict distinction between communicative action in the naive attitude and reflectively achieved understanding in regard to hypothetical validity-claims – in spite of the reservations of Herbert Schnädelbach.[24]

(b) The counterfactual element occupies a central place in everyday action. This is true, however, with the following qualifications:

(i) Pure modes of using language are the exception; normally the orienta-tions to truth, rightness and truthfulness claims are combined in a syndrome that is broken up only temporarily under the pressure of problems that arise.

(ii) Negotiated descriptions of situations, and agreements based on the intersubjective recognition of criticisable validity-claims, are diffuse, fleeting, occasional and fragile.

(iii) Naturally, communicative acts take on explicitly linguistic forms only in exceptional cases; nevertheless, the semantic content of indirect expressions, presuppositions, non-linguistic expressions, gestures, etc., is of a linguistic nature.

(iv) Not all interactions fall into the category of action orientated to reaching understanding; the proportion of strategic interactions, in which participants are orientated to consequences and success and not to the building of consensus, increases with the degree of formalisation of an action system on the one hand, and with the degree of de-institutionalisation on the other; often actions of the two types are mixed together, and in complicated ways.

(c) Formal-pragmatic analysis starts with idealised cases of the communicative action that is typical of everyday life *in modern societies.* The rationalisation of the life-world that depends on this form of achieving understanding has arisen from a process of differentiation that reaches back into archaic times; in the course of it, profane and sacred forms of practice, actions orientated to understanding and those orientated to success, communicative actions and discourses, have first been separated. In modern societies 'non-contemporaneous' forms of achieving understanding interfere with one another.

(d) The rational properties of speech that can be thrown into relief by the model of individual, context-free speech-acts are also relativised by the fact that the presuppositions of action orientated to reaching understanding are often only *supposedly* fulfilled. False consensus may be based on error or on deception, but also on the circumstances that participants in interaction deceive themselves about the strategic attitudes they have in fact adopted. The pseudo-consensus that depends on inconspicuous (for the participants) violations of necessary conditions for processes of consensus formation is characteristic of systematically distorted communication.

(e) Finally, the picture is complicated by the necessity, in differentiating forms of achieving understanding, for carefully separating questions of structure and developmental logic from questions of causality and developmental dynamics. Contrary to Bubner's surmise, I am far from wanting to renew the dialectic self-movement of the concept in language-theoretic terms. The rationalisation of life-world structures and the corresponding alteration in the forms of the intersubjectivity of possible understanding, which I *describe* in structural terms, can be *explained* only in connection with the evolutionary dynamics of the social system. To this extent the analysis of the rational potential of using language with an orientation to achieving understanding does not relieve the theory of society from the burden of that dialectic of labour and interaction that the Hegel of the Jena period presented in his own way.

(4) *The central importance of communicative action.* My previous remarks have relativised the position of the model of action orientated to reaching understanding. But then this raises the question as to why just this model – which deviates in many ways from everyday communicative practice – should provide the key to the analysis of actions and life-worlds:

'Not all forms of linguistic communication are in themselves potential realisations of the social model of mutual recognition.' It is precisely in this respect that Bubner sees the decisive difference from the Kantian analysis of universal and necessary – and in this sense transcendental – conditions of experience and judgements of experience. McCarthy's second objection in his contribution to this volume is aimed at the same point. To be sure, he does go on there to describe my line of defence. Before addressing myself to this, I should like to introduce a few clarificatory distinctions.

Communication and purposive activity are two equally fundamental elements of social interactions. These interactions fall into two classes, depending on the mechanism for co-ordinating action: communicative action and strategic action. In the one case co-ordination takes place by way of building consensus, in the other case by way of complementing interest situations. In the former case communication in language *has to* serve as the medium for co-ordinating action; in the latter it *can* do so. To the extent that strategic interactions are linguistically mediated, language serves as a *means of influencing*. With reference to sanctions, ego brings alter to decisions from which ego expects consequences favourable to the attainment of its own ends. In doing so, ego does not – as it does in communicative action – first have to get involved in the consensus-forming function of language. If, on the other hand, ego and alter *harmonise* their plans of action with one another, that is, if they pursue their individual ends only under the condition of a communicatively produced consensus regarding the given situation, they have to make use of language in a manner orientated to reaching understanding. The central importance which the basic concepts of communicative action have for social theory can now be made plausible in several steps.

First, it would have to be shown in detailed analyses that all non-strategic interactions are derivates of action orientated to reaching under-standing. Then it would have to be demonstrated through conceptual analysis that the rational potential of language can be put into effect only in communicative action, because linguistic communication is, so to speak, by nature aimed at building consensus and not at influencing. And finally, we would have to show, conceptually as well as empirically, that the symbolic structures of the life-world can be reproduced only through the medium of action orientated to understanding. (Arguments of this kind are sketched above in my response to Agnes Heller.)

(5) *The sophistic danger.* Bubner is not alone in raising the objection that my attempt to establish internal relations among reason, language and society falls into the errors that Plato criticised so clearly in connection with his sophistic opponents. The objection that the discourse theory of truth breaks down the barriers between grounded conviction and rhetorical illusion (Ilting) is, in the neo-conservative polemics which have become so routine, sharpened into the reproach that the communication theory of

society delivers up the tradition-dependent, historically rooted world of everyday life to the utopias, and thereby to the lust for power of intellectuals obsessed with enlightenment (Maurer). This strategy rests on the taken-for-granted premiss that the Platonic way of reading the history of philosophy needs no further grounding. Moreover, it suggests that recourse to substantial reason, to a metaphysical world-view, is not only possible but unproblematic. Maurer, who vehemently inflates the sophism reproach ('discourse as the alibi of gangsters'), leaves no doubt on that point:

> Philosophy arose in confrontation with sophistry. It is a complex of theoretical and practical philosophy, such that practical norms follow from theoretical insight. The Sophists referred the question of norms back to the practice in which norms were allegedly posited ('Man is the measure of all things'); philosophy criticised this solution because it was at bottom no solution. For the question, which is in the first instance theoretical: what do we want to do, or what are we supposed to do? would never arise if it were not a problem for practice, leading beyond it and bursting its taken-for-granted and autonomous character. Thus philosophy considered the question of norms to be resolvable only if there are pre-given, theoretically knowable norms, already developing *teleologically* in reality, and if technical positing is an extension of such development.[25]

I shall let this rest with an indication of where the burden of proof lies. One who uses 'sophist' as an insult, so as to spare oneself arguing, must first explain the sense in which the procedural rationality developed in the modern age and spelled out by modern philosophy can be so ominous; one must show, second, that in science or philosophy there can today still be found truths whose validity is based in the final analysis on something other than agreement brought about through argumentation. Post-empiricist philosophy of science has provided good reasons for holding that the unsettled ground of rationally motivated agreement among participants in argumentation is our only foundation – in questions of physics no less than in those of morality.

III.   Reason and nature – reconciliation at the cost of re-enchantment?

Against the background of the rather diffuse polemic that I enjoy in the Federal Republic, it seems advisable to clarify the basic intention which keeps me, like the older generation of Frankfurt theorists, a good distance from metaphysical or epistemological attempts to provide ultimate foundations. I am, however, convinced that we can connect up with Kant's transcendental mode of posing questions without having to take over his method and his basic assumptions. Joel Whitebook has characterised this intention well:

Habermas seems concerned to avoid two equally unacceptable alternatives. He does not want to assert that the validity of fundamental norms
can be demonstrated with the rigor sought by 'traditional theory'. Yet
he is equally opposed to the sceptical contention that these concepts are
arbitrary, in the sense of either being the mere products of convention
or of biological adaptation in any simple sense. While the validity of
these principles may not be demonstrable in a completely compelling
fashion, there are nevertheless 'good reasons' for their acceptance.[26]

Whatever differences may otherwise exist, this is the strategy I pursued
both in *Knowledge and Human Interests* and in my later work on
communication theory. I have tried to take up the universalistic line of
questioning of transcendental philosophy, while at the same time detrans-
cendentalising the mode of procedure and the conception of what is to be
shown:

> It is somewhat ironic that Habermas, who is often accused of hyper-
> rationalism by the hermeneuticists, requires so large an element of
> judgement at the very base of his scheme. The way in which one 'comes
> to terms' with the transcendental standpoint ultimately bears a closer
> resemblance to aesthetic taste or Aristotelian *phronesis* than to empha-
> tic philosophic proof. While Habermas' transcendental scheme is meant
> to serve a theoretical function of grounding our knowledge which is
> analogous to traditional *Ursprungsphilosophie,* the scheme itself is not
> grounded in as emphatic a fashion as one generally finds in *first
> philosophy.*[27]

The renunciation of ultimate foundations, be they of a traditional or of a
critical sort, exacts a price that from time to time brings upon me the
reproach of eclecticism. I am referring to the necessity of linking up with
various reconstructive approaches and corresponding lines of empirical
research, with the aim of ascertaining whether the results of the specialised
sciences fit together within the overlapping theoretical perspectives that
interest me. I do not accept a hierarchy of sciences in the sense of the
priority of *a prioristic* knowledge or formal science; this I learned from
C. F. von Weizsäcker.[28] The coherence theory of truth is certainly too weak
to explain the concept of propositional truth; but it comes into its own at
another level, the metatheoretical, where we put together the individual
pieces of theory like a puzzle. On this point William E. Connolly
understands me correctly (even if 'speculation' is perhaps not the right
expression):

> The mode of speculative theory Habermas practices generates a form of
> discipline unavailable to more insulated inquiries. In a speculative

theory, claims articulated in one domain can be checked for their consistency, or, more permissively, consonance, with assumptions accepted in others. Judgements reached with confidence in one area can be brought to bear on issues posed in more problematic or mysterious areas of a theory. And, since every specialized theory necessarily draws upon uninvestigated assumptions in a variety of allied fields, one could argue that speculative theory, when it is done well, provides more clarity and discipline than theory of the more restrained sort. The more encompassing the theory, the greater the variety of coherence tests each of the component parts must pass.[29]

If we let this stand for the moment as the description of a *basic philosophical intention,* this intention can be correlated just as closely with an implicitly associated *self-understanding of modernity.* To the extent that philosophy takes on the tasks of a theory of rationality, it will have to explain Occidental rationalism's decentred understanding of the world which developed in modern Europe with the differentiation of the 'value spheres' of science, morality and art, and with the ideals of bourgeois society and of the democratic constitutional state. This way of looking at things has been articulated from Kant to Weber. It is not at all incompatible with the counter-reckoning of modernity drawn up from Marx to Lukács and Horkheimer; for this critique of the capitalist model of modernisation can – if it is not to fall back behind Kant – be orientated to the idea of an uncompleted *project,* diverted from its goal, garbled in its intentions, often unrecognisable, a project of modernity at variance with itself, which has even been transformed into its opposite. Of course, the weight has shifted within the Marxist tradition as well. With his gift for stylisation, Whitebook assigns me a middle position in this spectrum:

> Because he introduces the categorical distinction between instrumental and practical reason, Habermas can determine the proper amount of discontinuity, as it were, between capitalism and a free society. Against Marx, who tends to see socialism as continuous with capitalism on the technical level insofar as he sees a socialist society as the nearly automatic outcome of the development of the forces of production, Habermas insists on the need for practical enlightenment and formation of a new conception of the good life. And against the early Frankfurt School, Habermas appreciates the sedimented norms of bourgeois society so that the gap between capitalism and socialism does not have to be so radical as to be impossible. *Habermas, in short, asserts the enlightenment heritage of practical reason against its legacy of technical reason in order to achieve the fulfillment of the former.*[30]

If one keeps in mind this connection between my basic philosophical intention and an understanding of modernity derived from – or 'bound to'? – the Enlightenment, then it is quite understandable that the themes which have dominated the 1970s – the destabilising intervention into ecological systems and natural milieux, the destruction of traditional forms of life, the threat to the communicative internal structures of life-worlds, the depletion of non-regenerable natural and cultural resources, the negative side-effects of capitalist growth, monetarisation, legalisation, bureaucratisation, and so on – could be transposed into just as many motives for doubting such a theoretical orientation. Thomas McCarthy draws these reservations together in the question of how we can put our fragmented world *back together* again. Against the Kantian move of analytic differentiation, he invokes the Hegelian promise of a 'non-regressive reconciliation' of speaking and acting subjects with external nature, society and internal nature. If reason is divided into the instrumental and the communicative, that which holds the two moments together shrinks to the procedural concept of argumentative grounding. There are above all two misgivings that arise in regard to this formalistic construction. First, it seems to preclude as irrational a non-objectivistic relation to nature; second, it seems to allow for no mediation between the universal structures of knowing, speaking and acting on the one hand, and historically developed traditions on the other. Against this, I should like to show that my conception is less rigid in respect to mediations between reason and nature than McCarthy, Ottmann and others suppose.

Henning Ottmann develops the thesis that my specifications of instrumental and communicative rationality are drawn too narrowly to permit an adequate distinction between external nature as a means for us and nature as an end-in-itself. The human race is, to be sure, thought of as a product of natural evolution, of *natura naturans* in Schelling's terms; but the analysis of the faculty of reason – so the objection runs – is laid out in such a way that the knowing and acting subject could never encounter a nature-in-itself from this perspective, something that could set limits to his or her interest in disposing over an objectified nature. In Ottmann's essay two aspects are conflated which I should like to treat separately in what follows: the ethical and the epistemological. On the one hand, he introduces the ecological problematic, which gives emphatic voice to nature's demand to be treated as an end-in-itself. If the 'colonial war' of society against nature today turns back on the aggressor, we need an ethic that has recourse to a teleology holding sway in the orders of nature itself, in the sense of a renewed cosmological ethic reaching behind the conditions of unimpaired interpersonal relations.[31] On the other hand, Ottmann develops this critique from an epistemological standpoint. He doubts that the relation of nature-in-itself to those two moments released from it – the *subjective nature* of humans and the *nature objectivated* in knowledge and action – can at all be thought in transcendental-pragmatic terms. I shall discuss these two complicated problems, at least to the point at which it becomes clear from the kinds of problems involved that the aporetic consequences do not so much put in question the approach from which they arise as perform the function of throwing light on the limits of human reason.

(1) McCarthy has worked out in a very penetrating way the paradoxes of the *epistemological* concept of a nature-in-itself.[32] If one construes the logic of investigation in the objectivating sciences along the lines of a pragmatism with a transcendental turn, that is, in the way that Karl-Otto Apel interprets the work of C. S. Peirce,[33] and if one looks back from this standpoint to the theory of knowledge implicit in Marx, then the concept of a nature-in-itself forces itself upon us, the concept of a nature from which the subjective nature of knowing and acting subjects proceeds – or is thought of as proceeding – equally primordially with the objective nature they find before them. McCarthy shows how this concept unavoidably falls into the aporetic double-role of an epistemological *limit concept* and a *basic concept* supporting evolutionary materialism.

The concept of a 'nature-in-itself' that I introduced in *Knowledge and Human Interests* is an ironic refrain on the Kantian thing-in-itself, in so far as it is meant to preserve in the nature constituted 'for us' the realistic connotations of a contingently existing reality independent of us. The resistance that reality opposed to false interpretations forces us to *construe* nature as something existing in itself, though it is scientifically accessible to us only as objectivated. The concept plays a similar role in regard to subjective nature viewed epistemologically: the necessary subjective conditions of possible experience. These are, to be sure, accessible only in the transcendental orientation, that is, by way of rationally reconstructing pre-theoretical knowledge; but pragmatism has to reject the assumption of a transcendental consciousness, without origins as it were. The connection between the way in which nature is objectivated and the structures of feedback-monitored action – a connection disclosed by transcendental pragmatics – makes it necessary to construe subjective nature as something arising under contingent conditions, something *proceeding from* 'nature-in-itself'.

In both cases 'nature-in-itself' is a postulate motivated by epistemological reflections; and this postulate cannot be linked in an unmediated way to the results of empirical research, since this research obeys for its part the logic of investigation of the objectivating sciences. Nevertheless, that postulate establishes a perspective from which a reconstruction of natural history can be undertaken as a prehistory of the socio-cultural form of life. The older ethnology coming from Üxhüll and Portmann – and already given a neo-Darwinian turn by Konrad Lorenz – can, with the analyses of the 'worlds' specific to species, serve as an example of the idea of a privative access to *natura naturans* that is guided by a pre-understanding of the life-world specific to humans, an idea developed in the Romantic philosophy of nature, especially in Schelling's doctrine of potency. (On the other hand, the biology employing a systems-theoretic approach, which many ecologists celebrate as a new science, should not be loaded with ontological notions of an objective teleology set in nature itself.)

Let us assume for the moment that such attempts to find a theoretical access to 'nature-in-itself' are not condemned from the start to absurdity. Then a transcendental-pragmatic theory of knowledge encounters a series of difficulties, which McCarthy enumerates:

(i) Because the statements about domains of objectivated nature that are obtained in the framework of the nomological sciences cannot be transformed into statements which, though about the same object domain, are obtained from a categorically different, internal perspective, we find ourselves confronted with a striking hiatus: the loose ends of an objectivating natural science and of an interpretative approach to nature cannot be tied together.

(ii) A non-objectivistic account of the natural prehistory of the socio-cultural life-world would shift the boundary for interpretative science lower on the scale of nature; and the boundaries drawn between humankind and (the rest of) nature by the theory of cognitive interests would have to become blurred. It is unclear how far we can penetrate into nature from an interpretative, internal perspective – as far as it shows signs of subjectivity and intersubjectivity? as far as we identify matter as living nature? Or can, as the mystics among the natural philosophers believed, even the minerals open their eyes in the end?

(iii) Finally, it is important to note that the approaches to an interpretative account of natural history – phenomenological, morphological, anthropological-evolutionary – have not overcome the stage of natural *philosophy*; that they have not been able to develop into alternatives *within* science.[34] Since the transition to modern science in the seventeenth century, they have belonged rather to the apocryphal traditions; and it is not very likely that the internal history of natural science which began at that time had external origins, that it was only institutional decisions which ended the debates with alternative forms of knowing nature.[35]

Do we have to understand such difficulties as the result of a questionable, too rigidly set out, theoretical programme, as McCarthy thinks? Or do they not simply speak for the view that while we can indeed adopt a performative attitude to external nature, enter into communicative relations with it, have aesthetic experience and feelings analogous to morality with respect to it, there is for *this* domain of reality only one *theoretically*

SCHEMA 1   *Formal-pragmatic relations*

Basic attitudes	Domains of reality		
	(1) External nature	(2) Society	(3) Internal nature
(1) Objectivating	Cognitive-instrumental relation	Cognitive-strategic relation	Objectivistic relation to self
(2) Norm-conformative	Moral-aesthetic relation to non-objectivated environment	Obligatory relation	Censorious relation to self
(3) Expressive		Self-presentation	Sensuous-spontaneous relation to self

fruitful attitude, namely the objectivating attitude of the natural-scientific, experimenting observer?

I should like to support this view with the following reflections. The structures of a (in Piaget's sense) decentred understanding of the world that are determinative for the modern period may be characterised by the fact that the acting and knowing subject can adopt *different* basic attitudes towards the same world. We can obtain nine fundamental relations by combining basic attitudes and formal world concepts, as Schema 1 illustrates.

I cannot systematically examine these formal-pragmatic relations here; I shall confine myself to intuitive references to characteristic forms of expression which might serve as illustrations. The cognitive-instrumental relation (1.1) can be illustrated by assertions, instrumental actions, observations and the like; the cognitive-strategic (1.2) by social actions of the purposive-rational type; the obligatory (2.2) by normatively regulated actions; self-presentation (3.2) by social actions of the dramaturgical, Goffmanian type. An objectivistic relation to oneself (1.3) can be expressed in theories (e.g. empiricist psychology or utilitarian ethics), but also in reified, pseudo-communicative relations; a censorious relation to oneself (2.3) can be illustrated both by such superego phenomena as guilt feelings and by defence reactions; a sensuous-spontaneous relation to oneself (3.3) can be found in affective expressions, libidinous stirrings, creative accomplishments, and the like. For illustrating an aesthetic relation to a situation, that is, to a non-objectivated environment (3.1), we can point trivially to works of art, to phenomena of style in general, but also to just those interpretative sciences that seek access to nature-in-itself. The phenomena that are exemplary for a moral-practical, a 'fraternal', relation to nature are most unclear, if one does not want to have recourse here as well to mystically inspired philosophies of nature, or to taboos (e.g.

vegetarian restrictions), to anthropomorphising treatment of house pets, and the like.

Even this provisional attempt at characterisation shows that, of the pragmatic relations between actors and their outer or inner environments which became formally possible through 'disenchantment', only a few were selected and articulated as standardised forms of expression. This differential in exploiting formal possibilities can have external or internal grounds. It could reflect a culture-specific and society-specific exploitation of the rationality potential offered by modern structures of consciousness, that is, a selective pattern of societal rationalisation. My conjecture, however, is that *only a few of these formal-pragmatic relations are suitable for the accumulation of knowledge.* But then it does not make sense to demand of a reason separated into its movements a reconciliation *at the level* of the scientific system, or *at the level* of the cultural tradition generally. We cannot expect to be able to use the experiential potential gathered in non-objectivating dealings with external nature for purposes of knowledge and to make them theoretically fruitful. Precisely from the perspective of the theory of knowledge, which has to orientate itself to *successful* examples of theory formation, the internal obstacles become visible which modern science places in the way of all attempts *to re-establish the unity of reason in the theoretical dimension.* Such attempts would have to lead back to metaphysics, and thus behind the levels of learning reached in the modern age into a re-enchanted world.

(2) A similar point can be made in regard to the relation of reason and nature from the *ethical standpoint* as well. Just as the transcendental-pragmatic theory of knowledge considers that the logic of the objectivating sciences binds the knowing subject to an attitude, from the perspective of which nature as an ultimate purpose drops out, so too ethical universalism (likewise situated in the Kantian tradition) supposes that the norm-conformative attitude of morally acting subjects *restricts* their view to interpersonal relations – here, too, nature-in-itself cannot become a theme. Ottmann agrees with Whitebook that the communications-theoretic grounding of a discourse ethic makes the defect of anthropocentrism particularly clear. 'As opposed to all forms of naturalistic ethics [i.e. cosmological–natural-law moral theories] anthropocentrism holds that man is the only locus of value and the only being that commands respect in the universe.'[36] This description suggests the objection that formalistic ethics have to ignore our experiences of non-objectivated dealings with nature which have unmistakably moral qualities. The impulse to provide assistance to wounded and debased creatures, to have solidarity with them, the compassion for their torments, abhorrence of the naked instrumentalisation of nature for purposes that are ours but not its, in short the intuitions which ethics of compassion place with undeniable right in the foreground, cannot be anthropocentrically blended out.

Compassion and solidarity do, however, appear in a discourse ethic that is consistently thought through to the end, at least as limit concepts. Such an ethic certainly isolates those questions that are posed from the standpoint of justifying actions and discursively redeeming norms of action; it stylises questions of the good life, and of the good life together, into *questions of justice,* in order to render practical questions accessible to cognitive processing by way of this abstraction. But the guiding idea, that a norm is valid only if it would meet with the approval of those involved under conditions of discursive will-formation, points to dimensions of an 'unlimited community in communication' (Apel) that lead to aporias. One of the embarrassments was discussed by Horkheimer and Benjamin in the 1930s.[37] If one understands ethics not only as an explication of the question concerning the grounding of normative statements, but as a theory that includes questions concerning the historical realisation of moral-practical rationality, there arises a problem which Christian Lenhardt, under the influence of Walter Benjamin, has formulated as follows. Let us assume that it is only by virtue of the suffering and sacrifice of past generations that subsequent generations can enjoy an institutionalised freedom, can enjoy, if not exactly a just order, then procedures that minimise injustice – could they call a world that had such a basis a 'just' world?[38]

Peukert cites a passage from a letter of Horkheimer to Benjamin of 16 March 1936:

> The thought that the prayers of the persecuted in direst need, that those of the innocents who must die without clarification of their situation, that the final hopes for a superhuman authority, are to no avail, and that the night in which no human light shines is also devoid of any divine light, is monstrous. Without God, eternal truth has just as little a foothold as infinite love – indeed they become unthinkable concepts. But is atrocity ever a cogent argument against the assertion or denial of a state of affairs? Does logic contain a law to the effect that a judgement is false when its consequence would be despair?[39]

Against the background of a discourse ethic, we might construe Horkheimer's reflection as follows. If one does not constrict the universality of the unlimited community in communication to one's contemporaries, but counterfactually includes past generations in the circle of those without whose potential agreement the claim to justice could not be vindicated, this may be sufficient for the *logic* of practical discourse. But the posthumously obtained approval of the victims remains abstract, because it lacks the force of reconciliation – it cannot later drown out the protest expressed in their lifetimes. There remains a stain on the idea of a justice that is bought with the irrevocable injustice perpetrated on earlier generations. This stain cannot be washed away; it can at most be forgotten. But this forgetting would have to leave behind traces of the repressed. The contradiction that is inherent in the idea of complete justice, owing to its in principle irredeemable universalism, cannot be dissolved. Benjamin's reflection has its place here. Those born later can compensate for the contradiction contained in the idea itself only by supplementing the abstract thought of universality with the anamnetic power of a remembering that goes beyond the concepts of morality itself. This remembering is actualised in compassionate solidarity with the despair of the tormented who have suffered what cannot be made good again. In this respect 'compassion', compassion for the violation of moral or bodily integrity, is a limit concept of the discourse ethic, just as nature-in-itself is a limit concept of the transcendental-pragmatic theory of knowledge.

Anamnetic solidarity follows as a postulate from the universalistic approach of the discourse ethic; but the relation established through compassion itself lies beyond moral-practical insights. It would become accessible to moral consideration only if this ethic were extended beyond the domain of interpersonal relations to our relationship with creatures that cannot fulfil the conditions of responsible action. With these living creatures – who are indeed *affected* by the normatively regulated, morally relevant behaviour of humans, but who could not, even counterfactually, step out of the position of those affected and take up the role of *participants* in practical discourses – nature-in-itself would come into view in a certain way, and not only the nature instrumentalised by us.

As Ottmann shows, such an extension of the ethical perspective is suggested by the ecological problematic. The latter makes clear that with the heightening of our technical power of disposing over nature, there also comes increased responsibility for the natural processes set in motion by our interventions. However, this problematic can be dealt with satisfactorily within the anthropocentric framework of a discourse ethic. Joel Whitebook makes this point with arguments that I shall not repeat here. He comes to the conclusion 'that the proper norms for regulating the relation between society and nature would somehow follow from the communicatively conceived idea of the human good life without reference to nature as an end-in-itself '.[40] He adds to this an observation worthy of note:

> Even if it could be shown *theoretically* that it is not necessary to move from the standpoint of anthropocentrism to formulate solutions for the environmental crisis, a question would still remain at the level of *social psychology*. For it is difficult to imagine how the conflict between society and nature is going to be resolved without a major transformation in our social consciousness of the natural world, e.g. a renewed reverence for life.[41]

What Whitebook refers to as a 'socio-psychological' necessity is the transition to a morality that includes the compassionate relation of humans to nature as a cosmically expanded solidarity with everything that is capable of suffering and that in this vulnerability calls for reverence. From this can be derived, for example, precepts for a vegetarian way of life, presumptions against experimenting with animals, among other things. The ethics of animal protection and vegetarianism – to stick with these two examples – extends the circle of one's 'neighbours' even beyond the potential participants in a (already counterfactually constructed) communication community to all *affected* living creatures with whose suffering we can empathise. All those creatures rescued by Noah's Ark *should* enjoy the protection of subjects with whom we interact on the level of equals.

Our intuitions tell us that attempts to open up a *moral access* to nature-in-itself are by no means absurd; but we should not permit ourselves to be cajoled by these intuitions into ignoring the difficulties that we encounter here, just as with the analogous attempts to gain *theoretical access* to nature-in-itself:

(i) Between a discourse ethic and a naturalistic ethic there is a yawning gap, because the in principle egalitarian relation of reciprocity built into communicative action – a relation from which the meaning of normative validity-claims and the ideas of freedom and equality derive – cannot be carried over into the relation between humans and nature in any strict sense. In neo-Aristotelian attempts to restore natural law, the rather paternalistic relation of caring-for (*Fürsorge*) is given a prominent place; and this is not just an accident. 'Caring-for' is a category that can lay claim to ethical status *only* in relation to those who can be released into autonomy and responsibility.

(ii) An ethic that gets rid of its 'anthropocentrism' extends the circle of addressees lower in the scale of nature; but again, the limits of empathy into alien life remain blurry. And is it not the case that the precepts of sympathetic solidarity soon come to a halt – namely already with plant life – if they are not to come into conflict with the firmer imperatives of the self-preservation of the human race?

(iii) Finally there is the basic philosophical question of how a naturalistic ethic could be adequately grounded today without recourse to the substantial reason of religious or metaphysical world-views, how it could be grounded at the level of learning attained in the modern understanding of the world.

I do not mean to construe these difficulties as the consequences of a questionable theoretical programme, but again as a sign that, while in our dealings with external nature we can indeed have feelings analogous to moral feelings, the *norm-conformative attitude* to this domain of external nature does not yield any problems susceptible of being worked up cognitively, that is, problems that could be stylised to questions of justice

SCHEMA 2   *Complexes of rationality*

Basic attitudes	Worlds			
	1	2	3	1
3	Art			
1	Cognitive-instrumental rationality			
	Science *Technology*	*Social technologies*		
2	Moral-practical rationality			
		Law	*Morality*	
3			Aesthetic-practical rationality	
			Erotics	*Art*

from the standpoint of normative validity. On the other hand, the discussion from Kant to Adorno concerning natural and artistic beauty could provide grounds for the thesis that the *expressive attitude* to external nature opens up a domain of experience that can be exploited for *artistic production.*

Evidently the differentiation of cultural spheres of value is due to special *family relationships between basic formal-pragmatic attitudes* (that are to be rendered methodically useful) *and corresponding domains of reality.* These affinities make possible the development of rationality complexes that can be united at the level of cultural tradition only at the cost of de-differentiation; and that means a re-enchantment of the world. If the affinities represented in Schema 2 actually hold – and are not merely the expression of a particular culture – the moralisation of our dealings with external nature cannot, any more than can a non-objectivating knowledge of nature, be carried out *at the same level* that Kant attained in his moralisation of social relations and Newton attained in his objectivating knowledge of nature.

The objectivating attitude to external nature and society circumscribes a complex of cognitive-instrumental rationality, within which the production of knowledge can take the form of scientific and technical progress (including social technologies). The fact that area (1.3) remains empty represents my assumption that nothing can be learned about internal nature *qua* subjectivity in an objectivating attitude. The norm-conformative attitude to society and internal nature circumscribes a complex of moral-practical rationality, within which the production of knowledge can take the form of systematically working out legal and moral representations. That the area (2.1) remains empty indicates my scepticism regarding the possibility of rationalising fraternal intercourse with a non-objectivated nature, for instance in the form of interpretative sciences of nature. Finally, the expressive attitude towards internal and external nature circumscribes a complex of aesthetic-practical rationality, within which the production of knowledge can take the form of an authentic interpretation of needs, that is, an interpretation which has to be renewed in each changed set of historical circumstances. That the area (3.2) remains empty is meant to indicate that expressively determined forms of inter-action (e.g. counter-cultural forms of life) do not of themselves form any structures susceptible of rationalisation; they are rather parasitical, in-asmuch as they remain dependent on innovations in other value spheres. If these rationality complexes derived in formal-pragmatic terms from basic attitudes and world-concepts point to precisely those three cultural value spheres that were differentiated in modern Europe, this does not amount to an objection against the systematic claim of the schema. On Weber's view, modern structures of consciousness emerged from a universal-historical process of disenchantment.

The unity of reason that McCarthy, Ottmann and others invoke is not to be had at the level of the cultural spheres of value. On the other hand, in the communicative practice of everyday life, in which cognitive explana-tions, moral expectations, expressions and evaluations interpenetrate, this unity is in a certain way *always already* established. That need for reconciliation which Hegel registered against Kant springs from one-sided rationalisation of this everyday practice – as we can learn in turn from Marx's critique of Hegel. This need first arises in modern societies, where, under the pressure of the burdens resulting from capitalist modernisation, the life-world and communicative interaction are denied that uncon-strained interplay of the cognitive with the moral-practical and the aesthetic-expressive on which they are by their very structures dependent.

IV.   Reason and history – the critique of ethical formalism

The critique of the dubious blessings of the abstract universalism of a theory of rationality connected with the Kantian problematic also raises questions concerning the relation of reason and history. Let us assume for the moment that in everyday communicative action those aspects of rationality that are separated out in science, morality and art, and dealt with in isolation, are still intimately interlaced. Then there are two contrasting spheres standing in need of mediation: on the one hand the culture of experts, on the other the everyday communicative practice nourished by traditions, embedded in cultural forms of life, intertwined in individual life-histories – in short, the life-world. In the syndromes of the life-world background, and in the tradition-dependent hermeneutics of everyday communication, utterances of different types refer to one another; by contrast, in the expert culture the transfer of validity between statements with descriptive, normative, expressive and evaluative content is brought to a halt initially, so that problems can be worked out under some *one* aspect of rationality. The achievement of cultural modernity consists in detaching the formal structures of reason from the semantic contents of traditional world-interpretations, that is, in letting reason come apart into its different moments. The reverse side of this *rendering autonomous* of science, morality and art is, however, a *splitting off* from the streams of tradition that nourish the processes of reaching understanding in everyday life. Reason becomes *abstract* and therewith arises the problem of how cognitive potentials accumulated by way of independent logics *(eigensinnig)* can be freed from their esoteric forms and supplied to a life-world whose traditional substance is increasingly depreciated. How can those abstractions, which are at the root of the modern understanding of the world and of a reason come apart into its moments, be 'transcended', without our having to pay the price of de-differentiation involved in an impotently simulated, regressive enchantment of the world? This is McCarthy's question. It is a question that arises particularly for a practical reason in the shape of a formalistic ethic that consistently works out the independent logic *(Eigensinn)* of normative questions, that works out the idea of justice. For ethics is concerned with problems that have their actual place only in everyday practice.

With respect to the general question concerning the historical embedding of practical reason, we can distinguish two positions. One insists on the context-boundedness of the faculty of moral judgement and contests the view that a universalistic ethic is at all possible. The other asserts that the independent logic of moral-practical rationality can be developed only by way of ethical universalism; but it also recognises that the abstract universality of such an ethic, unavoidable as it is, poses a problem of mediation. This second position does not, anymore than the first, require us to sacrifice the pluralism of historically concrete life-forms and life-histories to the abstractions of a perfectly just order. Ethical universalism does indeed have a utopian content, but it does not *sketch out* a utopia.

I do not wish to return here to my own discussion of Gadamer's hermeneutic position. This debate was recently subjected to a first-rate analysis by Jack Mendelson. He comes to the following conclusion:

On the issues of epistemology versus ontology, the relation of reason to authority, and the need to mediate *verstehen* through an explanatory understanding guided by theory, Habermas' arguments seem valid. But the controversy with Gadamer has some implications for Habermas' approach which did not emerge explicitly in their confrontation. In particular the question of the relation of critical theory to tradition needs to be raised in a somewhat different manner.[42]

Thus even a well-disposed critic finds lacking the mediation that a discourse ethic developed in communications-theoretic terms would have to establish between itself and its addressees – between, on the one side, its abstract insights, *radically ignoring all content* and concentrating only on the sense of normative grounding, and on the other side, the historical reality, the *already operative* ideas of justice, the orientations of *already present* social movements, the *existing* forms of freedom. Mendelson is right to point out

> that the historical potential of the ideal speech situation for becoming the actual organizing principle of a society can only come to fruition in a society which comes close to articulating it on the level of more historically specific and conscious traditions, for instance, in the Western democracies of the twentieth century. While in a sense the ideal of rational consensus may be immanent in language *per se* and not simply in an actual culture, it becomes politically relevant as an ideal to be consciously striven for only in societies which have begun to approach it on the level of their own cultural traditions . . . From this point of view, communication theory and the immanent interrogation of historically specific traditions are not alternatives but complementary steps in a single process.[43]

In an unpublished manuscript Seyla Benhabib sharpens this point. She declares a normative theory that does not ascertain its own historical conditions of origin and of application, that does not enter into the historical context of the everyday language-games of its addressees, to be worthless. Practical reason ought not to be set out only in abstract universality; it has to be 'situated'. Benhabib is concerned with a question that turns up again in Steven Lukes's contribution to this volume. In order that human beings of flesh and blood can satisfy the idealised conditions of practical discourse, there is required a process of self-formation from which the theory may not grandly abstract:

> Universal pragmatics proceeds at a level of abstraction from the standpoint of which each and every individual is a being capable of consensus and discourse. Whether or not this is a necessary 'transcendental illusion' of every ordinary communication context, universal pragmatics reconstructs a system of rules which will be *recognized* to be binding by acting and speaking agents only of a certain sort. These have attained, or can attain, a level of moral and practical *Bildung* which corresponds to the level of abstraction of universal pragmatics. The commitment to consider all individuals as potential participants in discourse presupposes a universalistic commitment to the potential equality, autonomy, and rationality of individuals. This commitment is

rendered cogent either by a completed, or by a yet-to-be completed *Bildungsprozess*.[44]

Neither the willingness nor the ability to consider moral questions from the hypothetical and disinterested perspective of a participant in practical discourse falls from heaven; they result from *interests* that are formed only under certain social conditions, as well as from *learning processes* and *experiences* that are open to social groups only in certain situations. The same holds for the new interpretations that allow our needs and interests to appear in another light and thereby open new opportunities for consensus. However these innovations arise, it is not through discourse that they gain the power to convince and are spread abroad; this happens only in *social movements*.

I do not want to contest these statements. To the degree that they are directed against the blind spot of transcendentally orientated theories, they have a justified critical point; but they ought not to be given a false value in argumentation. Drawing on similar observations, Benhabib and Lukes argue for opposite positions. Whereas Lukes is fundamentally sceptical about the cognitive claim of moral judgements, Benhabib is asserting the right of historically situated morality *(Sittlichkeit)* against an abstractly universal morality *(Moral)*. I regard both positions as false – the historico-philosophical no less than the sceptical.

One can learn from the course of critical theory why the foundation of the critique of ideology in a philosophy of history developed cracks. Assumptions about a dialectical relation between productive forces and productive relations are pseudo-normative statements about an objective teleology of history. For the critical theory of the 1930s this counted as the motor force behind the realisation of a reason set forth in bourgeois ideals. This mixing of descriptive and normative contents was present in the basic concepts of historical materialism. It is possible to avoid this confusion without surrendering the leading intention behind the theory, if we ascertain the rational content of anthropologically deep-seated structures in a transcendentally orientated analysis which is initially unhistorical. It is not so important whether one approaches this goal through the theory of knowledge or through the theory of language. But this way of proceeding has an important consequence. From the cognitive structures of knowing, acting and understanding that can be found in the intuitive knowledge of competent members of modern societies, there is no way back to a theory of history which does not *a fortiori* carefully separate problems concerning the logic of development from those concerning the dynamics of development. Through this move I have myself attempted to free historical materialism from its historico-philosophical ballast.[45]

As this procedure requires a clear analytic cut between social evolution and history, critique can no longer draw upon the guiding thread of philosophy of history. It must be orientated to the possibility of learning processes opened up by a level of learning already achieved historically. The critique of ideology can no longer set out directly from concrete ideals intrinsic to forms of life, but only from formal properties of rationality structures. These are of course expressed in concrete forms of life, in particular cultural traditions, institutions, patterns of justification, identity formations, and so on; but they vary in accord with *universal* points of view. A developmental-logical delimitation of the ranges of variation does not, however, prejudge questions concerning the dynamics of historical processes. This double abstraction – of social evolution from the historical concretion of forms of life, and of the development of cognitive structures from the historical dynamic of events – removes that confusion in basic concepts to which philosophy of history owes its existence. But, as we shall see, it also requires that we give up critically judging and normatively classifying totalities, world-views, epochs, forms of life and cultures, complexes of life as a whole.

First I should like to take up the three main objections of Steven Lukes, who draws sceptical conclusions from his doubts regarding the abstract universality of a discourse ethic.

(1) To begin with, Lukes turns the aforementioned problem concerning the relation between discourse and the real context of action into a question of foundations. The conditions set forth for participating in practical discourse are, he argues, idealised to such a degree that we cannot imagine how actors who are tied to their social contexts even into the innermost regions of their persons could possibly be equal to the role of participants in discourse. And if one does try to imagine it, the actors lose their flesh and blood, take on unearthly forms. But this would prejudge the question of how discursive agreement can be attained in practical questions.

Unfortunately Lukes develops this objection in connection with the model of suppressed generalisable interests. However, in this model the basic assumptions of the discourse ethic are in no way explained; they are *presupposed* as correct. The discourse ethic is here merely *applied*, and not even for the purpose of clarifying practical questions but for the theoretical purpose of making it possible, in empirically ascribing interests, to distinguish between general and particular interests. Lukes wants to criticise the discourse ethic itself and not one of its applications. For this reason I shall transpose his objections into the perspective of the first person, that is, of one who is frontally attacking a normative theory.

The discourse ethic refers to those presuppositions of communication that each of us must intuitively make when we want to participate seriously in argumentation. My position is that those who understand themselves as taking part in argumentation *mutually suppose*, on the basis of the pre-theoretical knowledge of their communicative competence, that the

actual speech situation fulfils certain, in fact quite demanding, precondi-
tions. I shall leave aside the question of whether these presuppositions of
communication can be adequately reconstructed in the form of the 'ideal
speech situation' that I proposed. I shall also put aside the question of the
extent to which the requirements that we have to set as participants in
discourse are actually realised. We are forced, only as it were in a
transcendental sense, to suppose that these requirements are, under the
given empirical limitations, *sufficiently* realised; for so long as we do not
consider external and internal constraints to be sufficiently neutralised to
exclude in our eyes the danger of a pseudo-consensus based on deception
or self-deception, we cannot *suppose* that we are taking part in argumentation.

In view of this thesis, the two cases that Lukes discusses cannot be
sharply separated.[46] From the perspective of the participants, both are true
simultaneously: naturally those taking part identify themselves as 'real-life
actors'; but at the same time they 'have to' suppose that they can for the
time being sufficiently satisfy the formal conditions of the ideal speech
situation. This is by no means a question of fictively transforming their real
characters into intelligible ones. On the contrary, if the actors do not bring
with them, and into their discourse, *their* individual life-histories, *their*
identities, *their* needs and wants, *their* traditions, memberships, and so
forth, practical discourse would at once be robbed of all content. The two
cases of the 'real-life' and the 'rational' actors, the roles of participants in
real communication communities and in that community presupposed as
ideal, can be sharply separated only from the perspective of the third
person, say of a social scientist, who applies the model of suppressed
generalisable interests. Such an observer has to watch for empirical
indicators upon which he or she can base hypothetical extrapolations.
From the observed behaviour he or she extrapolates to the kind of
positions for which the observed actors would have had good grounds in
their action contexts, if (counterfactually) they had been given the
opportunity to take part in a corresponding argumentation among those
affected. But even here the *hypothetically undertaken* transition from 'real
life' to discourse amounts only to a methodological setting aside of 'false
consciousness' and not to a neutralisation of life-forms and life-histories.[47]

(2) Lukes's second criticism is directed to the idea of generalising
interests, whereby interests appear under descriptions that must themselves be able to stand up under discursive examination. I find it awkward
here that Lukes does not take up the basic assumptions of the discourse
ethic as they have been discussed, for example, by Thomas McCarthy[48] or
Robert Alexy.[49] The following paragraph summarises the comprehensive
theoretical programme:

Communication that is oriented toward reaching understanding inevitably involves the reciprocal raising and recognition of validity-claims. Claims to truth and rightness, if radically challenged, can be redeemed only through argumentative discourse leading to rationally motivated consensus. Universal-pragmatic analysis of the conditions of discourse and rational consensus show these to rest on the supposition of an 'ideal speech situation' characterized by an effective equality of chances to assume dialogue roles. This unavoidable (but usually counterfactual) imputation is an 'illusion' constitutive of the very meaning of rational argumentation . . . Thus the universal-pragmatic conditions of possibility of rationally justifying norms of action or evaluation have themselves a normative character. The search for the fundamental principles of morals properly begins with a reflective turn, for these principles are built into the very structures of practical discourse.[50]

I do not claim to have carried out this programme; but the outline suffices to locate the position of the universalisation thesis. On the basis of a formal-pragmatic analysis of action orientated to reaching understanding, the first thing to be clarified is what it means for actors to orientate themselves to validity-claims (action theory). Then there is the problem of what it means to redeem validity-claims discursively; this problem calls for an investigation of the communicative presuppositions of argumentative speech (discourse theory of truth) and an analysis of the general procedural rules of argumentation (logic of discourse). It is in the framework of a logic of *practical* discourse – that is, of argumentation keyed to dealing with questions of practice (in contrast to questions of truth) – that we encounter basic questions of ethics, not only questions concerning the *meaning* of normative statements but questions concerning the possibility of *grounding* them. The works of Karl-Otto Apel are important in this connection. They are concerned above all with two problems: with the mode of grounding that relies on rational reconstruction of universal and unavoidable presuppositions of knowledge, action and understanding in language; and with the normative content of the formal structure of rational speech.[51] His central thesis is that the fundamental principle of universalisation can be 'derived', in the sense of 'transcendental-pragmatic' grounding, from general presuppositions of communication.

All this is by no means uncontroversial.[52] But only in this way could I explain the *status* that the principle of universalisation assumes in the discourse ethic. The *meaning* of this principle was already explained by George Herbert Mead in his interesting interpretation of Kantian moral philosophy.[53] The idea of 'universal discourse' turns up again in Kohlberg – who was introduced to Mead by his teacher, Charles W. Morris – under the name of 'ideal role-taking'. These expressions signify a procedure that is both open to hypothetical anticipation and susceptible of being actually carried out, a procedure that is meant to secure the impartiality of moral judgement. The exchange of arguments – unlimited in principle and unconstrained – among all those involved functions as a touchstone of whether a norm can be counted on to meet with grounded approval, that is, whether its claim to validity rightfully stands. A norm of action has validity only if all those possibly affected by it (and by the side-effects of its application) would, as participants in a practical discourse, arrive at a (rationally motivated) agreement that the norm should come into (or remain in) force, that is, that it should obtain (retain) social validity. The basic principle of universalisation[54] is *not* exhausted by requirements such as the following:

(a) that the universal *form* of normative sentences should exclude their referring to, or being addressed to, specific groups and individuals;
(b) that norms should be publicly defensible (Gewirth) and generally teachable (Baier);
(c) that the judging individual should be able to accept with reason the consequences and the side-effects that result when *everyone* follows a contested norm (Singer); or
(d) that the judging individual should test whether everyone who found himself or herself in the same situation could accept such a norm (Hare).

The point of discourse-ethical universalisation consists rather in this, that only through the communicative structure of a moral argumentation involving *all* those affected is the *exchange of roles* of each with every other forced upon us. Only an actually carried out discourse offers any guarantee of the possibility of objecting to any norm that does not fulfil the following condition: that the consequences and side-effects for the satisfaction of the interests of *every* individual, which are expected to result from a *general* observance of the norm, can be accepted with good reason by *all*.

McCarthy sums up a corresponding discourse-ethical interpretation of the categorical imperative in the following sentence: 'The emphasis shifts from what each can will without contradiction to be a universal law, to what all can will in agreement to be a universal norm.'[55] If I am not mistaken, this version of the universalisation principle takes into account Lukes's second and third interpretations. If that is so, I do not understand why he regards this requirement as too strong. He seems to assume that there is a zero-sum relationship between the individual differentiation of needs and the generalisability of collective interests. But there are enough counter-examples – from traffic rules to basic institutional norms – to make it intuitively clear that increasing scope for individual options does not decrease the chances for agreement concerning presumptively common interests. The discourse-ethical way of reading the universalisation principle does not rest – not even implicitly – on assumptions about the quantitative relation between general and particular interests. Particular interests are those that prove on the basis of discursive testing not to be susceptible of generalisation and thus to require compromise. A unified society of abundance would be a necessary condition for the functioning of the universalisation principle only if we had to suppose that the alternative needs (wishes, inclinations, values, and so forth), which normative regulation is supposed to take into account, exclude *a priori* consensual regulation at a higher level of abstraction. I am not sure whether this is what Steven Lukes has in mind.

(3) Lukes's third objection is directed against a use of Kohlberg's theory of the development of moral consciousness that is, he maintains, guilty of a naturalistic fallacy. In fact, this theory is based on an interesting kind of division of labour between philosophy and psychology, that is, between rational reconstruction of everyday moral intuitions on the one hand, and empirical investigation of moral development on the other. This division of labour stands in need of further clarification. And for this one has to take a close look at the constructivist concept of learning. According to that concept, every growing child who passes from one (cognitive or socio-moral) stage of thought to the next can be brought by maeutic means to explain why his or her way of judging things is now able to solve given problems better than at the previous stage. In the case of moral judgements this is the line of natural insights that the moral philosopher takes up. For both the psychologist's subject and the moral philosopher adopt the same *performative attitude,* that of one making moral judgements, and, at the reflective level, the *perspective of one taking part* in practical discourses. In both cases their moral judgements – whether they express the moral intuitions of the layperson or they assume the theoretical form of a reconstruction of the layperson's knowledge – are subject to the standards of *normative rightness.* This is different from the attitude of the psychologist and from the validity-claim that he or she connects with an empirical theory. The psychologist, too, identifies the learning processes of the growing child in light of the criterion that the individual being tested can, at a higher stage, criticise his or her own previous judgements. But in contrast to the person being tested and to his or her reflecting alter ego, the moral philosopher, the psychologist explains such learning processes from the third-person *perspective of an observer* such that empirical assumptions are orientated exclusively to the claim to *propositional truth.*

This important distinction is veiled by some of Kohlberg's own formulations: 'The scientific theory as to why people factually *do* move upward from stage to stage, and why they factually *do* prefer a higher stage to a lower, is broadly the same as a moral theory as to why people *should* prefer a higher stage to a lower.'[56] But in other passages Kohlberg unmistakably emphasises the *complementary* relation between the normative theory that the psychologist has to borrow from moral philosophy, and the empirical theory for which he or she uses the former as input. The psychologist has to *presuppose* the validity of the normative theory which he or she draws on in describing the formal properties of postconventional judgements. To be sure, if this theory does not stand up in the context of developmental-psychological assumptions, the shadow of doubt falls indirectly upon it as well:

> While moral criteria of adequacy of moral judgement help define a standard of psychological adequacy or advance, the study of psychological advance feeds back and clarifies these criteria. Our psychological theory as to why individuals move from one stage to the next is grounded on a moral-philosophical theory which specifies that the later stage is morally better or more adequate than the earlier stage. Our psychological theory claims that individuals prefer the highest stage of reasoning they comprehend, a claim supported by research. This claim of our psychological theory derives from a philosophical claim that a later stage is 'objectively' preferable or more adequate by certain *moral* criteria. This philosophic claim, however, would for us be thrown into question if the facts of moral advance were inconsistent with its psychological implications.[57]

The success of the empirical theory, which can be true or false, also functions as a kind of coherence test for the rightness – for the normative validity – of the philosophically executed reconstruction of the intuitions expressed in everyday moral judgements. 'Science, then, can test whether a philosopher's conception of morality phenomenologically fits the psychological facts. Science cannot go on to justify that conception of morality as what morality ought to be.'[58]

Even if one avoids naturalistic fallacies, there remains the uncomfortable question of whether, through the interplay of normative ethics and empirical science, there does not after all creep in an element which must prejudge in an unfortunate way the philosophical discussion between rival approaches in moral theory. To the degree that one regards the evidence for an empirical theory of moral development, say Kohlberg's, as sufficient, one also has to make a choice among competing ethics, and indeed a choice in favour of that theory which has 'stood up' in the specified way. But then empirical arguments are employed in the same indirect way in a debate, concerning which philosophy has held, and rightly so in my view, that it has to be settled with *another kind* of argument.

However, this problem exists only so long as psychological theory asserts that there are also different stages of postconventional morality. It is only then that there can arise discussions like that about the demarcation of a fifth from a sixth stage, or about the introduction of a seventh. There are always implicitly also discussions about who is right, utilitarians or contractualists, Kant, Rawls or Apel; and one cannot escape the feeling that these discussions are being conducted in the wrong place. This consequence drops out if we follow an interesting line of argument advanced by McCarthy.

Anyone who responds to moral-practical questions in a hypothetical attitude and in the light of principles stands, as it were, on the same level as the moral psychologist and the moral philosopher. He or she is not merely using a special competence in a naive way, but is incipiently already involved in reconstructing. The manner in which a question is resolved postconventionally already betrays an implicit theory regarding what it means to ground a normative proposition. But then competing views of this kind can just as little be placed in a hierarchy from a developmental-logical standpoint as can the corresponding 'higher' forms of moral philosophy. McCarthy's thesis is all the more plausible to me as it agrees with the empirical evidence. In the Starnberg Institute we have always had difficulty differentiating among postconventional stages, both in the development of law and in ontogenesis. Even Kohlberg can, according to the most recent rescoring of his material, no longer apprehend test subjects for this sixth stage.

(4) Even if we accept McCarthy's argument, the voice of cognitive developmental psychology does not of course become entirely silent in the debates among moral philosophers. For the position of ethical scepticism that Steven Lukes represents is untenable if theories of moral development of the Piagetian type are not false *in their very conception*. Within Kohlbergian theory, the category of judgements scored as '4½' still presents difficulties, in respect both to classification of data and to theoretical explanation. The regression hypothesis, which has to do in any case only with aspects of developmental dynamics, can explain the *time of first appearance* of this sceptical, partly nihilistic, partly relativistic consciousness; but it cannot explain the *possibility of its stabilisation*. I should like to offer the following line of interpretation for this.

The development from conventional to postconventional consciousness can be viewed from two perspectives. With the ability to think hypothetically about moral-practical questions, the youth fulfils the necessary and sufficient conditions for *breaking away from the conventional mode of thought;* but this step does not yet prejudge the choice between two alternative paths of development, which can be globally characterised as follows. There are different ways in which the youth can use his or her newly won distance from a world of conventions that lose the naive force of social validity by being hypothetically ordered within a horizon of possibilities and thus reflectively depreciated. On the one hand, the youth will attempt to preserve from the lost world of *de facto* valid norms the *sense of validity* of norms and ought-sentences at the new level of reflection. In this case the youth has to restructure the basic concepts of the moral without surrendering the ethical perspective. He or she has to relativise the social validity of actually existing norms in the light of a normative validity that satisfies standards of rational grounding. Holding fast in this way to the reconstructed sense of normative validity is a necessary condition for the *transition to the postconventional mode of thought.* On the other hand, the youth can be freed from the conventional mode of thought without passing over to the postconventional. In this case he or she understands the collapse of the world of conventions as an insight into a false cognitive claim with which norms and ought-sentences were connected until then. Then basic moral concepts require in retrospect an explanation in their cognitively devalued, conventional form. The youth has to work through the dissonance that persists: the dissonance between the moral intuitions by which his or her unreflective everyday consciousness and action continue to be determined, and the (supposed) insight into the illusory character of this conventional consciousness – which, despite its devaluation in reflection, is by no means put out of operation in everyday life. In place of a postconventionally renewed *ethical consciousness,* there appears a *meta-ethical explanation* of moral illusions. This explanation can overcome those dissonances all the more easily, the more it is possible to reconcile the theoretical scepticism with the intuitions that continue to be operative in practice. In this respect, for example, Max Weber's ethical scepticism, which also leaves theoretically untouched the existential character of value attachments, accomplishes more than the ethical naturalism that explains away moral intuitions as emotional attitudes. From the perspective of Kohlbergian theory, these meta-ethical versions have to submit to classification from developmental-logical standpoints, and to subordination to cognitivist ethics.

(5) These latter ethics – whether in contract-theoretical or Kantian form, whether they integrate utilitarian points of view more or less strongly – certainly do retain something of that abstract universality which has called forth the critique of the hermeneuticists. If one takes McCarthy's argument seriously, one is no longer able to order cognitivist ethics from a developmental-logical standpoint; one has to return them to the debate of the philosophers and thus to the historical context of this debate as well. This context, however, is shaped by a modernity in which, with moral and legal theory, a value sphere specialised in questions of justice has been differentiated and rendered independent in respect to complex everyday practice. It is through this that the problem of mediation arose with which we began this discussion.

In a work on 'Reason, Emancipation and Utopia',[59] Albrecht Wellmer criticises the short-circuiting that occurs when one ignores the mediations between the ethic of discourse and the practice of life and thinks one can directly take from this ethic the standards for something like an ideal form of life. In a passage open to criticism, I have myself used a short-circuited formulation of this kind, which I should like hereby to retract: 'no historical society coincides with the *form of life* that we anticipate in the *concept* of the ideal speech situation'.[60] With the discourse ethic as a guiding thread, we can indeed develop the formal idea of a society in which all potentially important decision-making processes are linked to institutionalised forms of discursive will-formation. This idea arose under specific historical conditions, together with the idea of bourgeois democracy. But it would be a short-circuit of the type Wellmer criticises to think 'that we have thereby also formulated the ideal of a form of life which has become perfectly rational – there can be no *such* ideal'.[61]

Wellmer makes it clear that standards of procedural rationality hold only for dealing with questions that are sorted out according to some one universal aspect, for example that of justice or normative rightness; and that the corresponding learning processes can be understood in light of these standards as an approximation (at best asymptotic) to ideal limit values. But we cannot undertake to appraise forms of life centred on communicative action simply by applying the standards of procedural rationality. These forms of life comprise not only institutions that come under the aspect of justice, but 'language-games', historical configurations of habitual practices, group memberships, cultural patterns of interpretation, forms of socialisation, competencies, attitudes, and so forth. It would make no sense to want to judge these syndromes as a whole, the totality of a form of life, from the standpoint of individual aspects of rationality. If we do not wish to renounce altogether standards for judging a form of life to be more or less misguided, distorted, unfortunate or alienated, if it is really necessary, the model of sickness and health presents itself. We privately judge life-forms and life-histories according to standards of normalcy that do not allow for approximation to ideal limit values. Perhaps we should speak instead of a balance among moments incomplete in themselves, an equilibrated interplay of the cognitive with the moral and the aesthetic-expressive. However, the attempt to specify an equivalent for what was once meant by the idea of the good life ought not to mislead us into *inferring* an idea of the good life from the formal concept of reason with which the decentred understanding of the world in the modern age has left us.

> For this reason we can specify only certain *formal conditions* of a rational life – such as *a universalistic moral consciousness, a universalistic law, a collective identity that has become reflective,* and so forth. But insofar as we are dealing with the possibility of a rational life in the substantial sense, with the possibility of a rational identity, there is no ideal limit value describable in terms of formal structures. There exists rather only the success or failure of the efforts to achieve a form of life in which the unconstrained identity of individuals, along with uncon-

strained reciprocity among individuals, becomes an experiencable reality.[62]

In speaking of a 'rational life in the substantial sense', Wellmer does not mean to suggest a return to the conceptual apparatus of substantially rational world-views.[63] But if one has to renounce this, there remains only the critique of the distortions inflicted on forms of life in capitalistically modernised societies in two ways: through devaluation of their traditional substance; and through subordination to imperatives of a one-sided rationality limited to the cognitive-instrumental.

V. On the theories of action, communication and science
The objections by Giddens, Thompson, Hesse, Held and Arato have a more strongly analytic character; they are directed less against the architectonics of the whole theory and thus do not force me to expound my own approach to the same extent as the contributions discussed to this point. My responses can stay closer to the relevant texts.

Action theory
I shall begin with Anthony Giddens's theses on the theory of action.[64] They involve essentially four objections.

(1) I shall start with the three critical remarks on my concept of interaction.

(a) Evidently I expressed myself so unclearly in earlier works that Giddens basically misunderstands my concepts of action. As Schema 3 shows, I am far from equating action with interaction.[65] The distinction between orientation to success and orientation to reaching understanding is decisive for the construction of my typology of action. In the model of purposive-rational action the actor is orientated to the realisation of an end; the success of his or her actions is measured by the extent to which he or she succeeds, through intervening in the world (or through forgoing such intervention), in bringing the intended state of affairs into existence. Actions orientated to success are termed *instrumental* when they are understood as following technical rules and can be appraised from the standpoint of the efficiency of goal-orientated intervention in the physical

SCHEMA 3   *Types of action*

Action	Actor	
	Orientated to success	Orientated to reaching understanding
Non-social	Instrumental action	—
Social	Strategic action	Communicative action

world. Actions orientated to success are termed *strategic* only if they are understood as following rules of rational choice and can be appraised from the standpoint of the efficiency of influencing the decisions of rational opponents. Instrumental actions (as well as the corresponding tasks) can be *combined* with social actions as elements of roles; strategic actions are themselves a class of interactions. I speak of *communicative actions* when social interactions are co-ordinated not through the egocentric calculations of success of every individual but through co-operative achievements of understanding among participants. In communicative action participants are not orientated primarily to their own success but to the realisation of an agreement which is the condition under which all participants in the interaction may pursue their own plans.

Communicatively achieved agreement is based on the intersubjective recognition of criticisable validity-claims – however merely implicit this may be. Agreement cannot be imposed by one side. An objectively forced agreement, or even one merely suggested, can count subjectively as an agreement only so long as the contingency of its accomplishment is not perceived. On occasion I have expanded this typology with two variants. In latently strategic interaction, at least one of the participants is deceiving the other(s) regarding the non-fulfilment of the conditions of communicative action which he or she apparently accepted; this is the case of *manipulation*. In the case of *systematically distorted communication*, at least one of the participants is deceiving *himself or herself* regarding the fact that he or she is actually behaving strategically, while he or she has only apparently adopted an attitude orientated to reaching understanding. From this there results the classification shown in Schema 4.[66]

S<small>CHEMA</small> 4

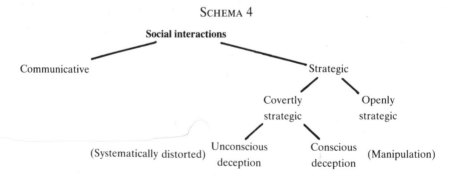

(b) I do not identify either action, social action or communicative action with speech-acts. Only the last distinction requires commentary, since I have not always differentiated adequately between speech and communicative action.[67] Patterns of social action can develop only where some mechanism guarantees that participants' plans of action are co-ordinated with one another in a sufficiently conflict-free way, and that ego's offers are accepted by alter. The mechanism for co-ordinating action either provides for an *objective* harmony of action plans – as in the case of the market, which exploits the complementarity of existing interest situations – or it opens up the possibility that the *subjects themselves* undertake to harmonise their plans, as is the case with language as a medium of reaching understanding. Thus in communicative action the interpretative accomplishments of the actors and the corresponding communicative acts have the status of a mechanism for co-ordinating action which is shunted into the creation of consensus. The goal-directed actions that the actors perform in carrying out their linguistically co-ordinated plans exhibit, as do all actions, the structure of purposive activity.

There is little difficulty in delimiting speech from action when the action sequence to be analysed in terms of these concepts is sufficiently complex. It is more difficult in the case of an elementary speech-act which represents a communicative action but does not stand in a context such that it can be *understood* as an act of reaching understanding that co-ordinates *other* actions. A command (together with the corresponding yes/no position taken by the addressee) can be understood as a communicative act (language) only if one understands it in the sequence of ego's antecedent plans of action and alter's subsequent actions, as an action-co-ordinating element within an interaction. As soon, however, as one considers the command in isolation, the same occurrence can be described either as an act of reaching understanding or as a communicative action that requires reaching understanding. The two aspects are analytically separable. Only under the description of communicative action does the structure of purposive activity stand out in this occurrence; we then suppose that ego is pursuing some goal with its command. When we describe the occurrence of a communicative act, an observer can always still impute to the actor the pursuit of an end; but ego is not itself communicating in the attitude of one acting purposively. In the act of reaching understanding, the actor is not interested first of all in having his or her command *carried out*, but rather in alter accepting the validity-claim that ego connects with its utterance. Reaching understanding is a peculiar 'goal': it cannot be pursued through communication in the same way as a goal can through teleological action. Because participants in communication want to arrive at an understanding about something in a world, the sought-for consensus cannot, from their point of view, itself be a state in the world which the actors set as their goal.

(c) Contrary to Giddens's view, the concept of communicative action goes decidedly beyond the normativistic model of action. According to this concept, interaction is regulated not through a normative consensus that is fixed in an *a priori* way, but through the participants' own fallible accomplishments of reaching understanding. Normatively directed action *à la* Parsons represents (alongside of expressive self-presentation and constative speech action) one of three pure cases of the complex type: action orientated to reaching understanding. In this latter model, actors, with their intersubjectively shared life-world behind them as a resource for processes of reaching understanding, simultaneously stand over against three worlds: not only the social world of legitimately regulated interpersonal relations, but also the objective world of existing states of affairs, and each's own subjective world of experiences to which he or she has a privileged access.

This point touches on the further problem of an alleged confusion of *analytic aspects of action* with *types of action*. The above-mentioned *pure cases* (or ideal types) of action orientated to reaching understanding are of course the results of an idealising abstraction. The pure cases of constative speech actions, normatively regulated action and self-presentation each emerge from one of the three analytic viewpoints from which any communicative action must be simultaneously open to analysis. What is isolated by the concept of the mode of employing language – by the concepts of the cognitive, interactive and expressive uses of language – that is, concentration on a given one of the three validity-claims, can, in the case of individual communicative actions embedded in their contexts, only be separated analytically. In the same way, certain elements of action orientated to reaching understanding can even be analysed from the viewpoint of the strategic use of symbolic expressions. The more diffuse an action situation is, the more it requires situating within conversation itself, all the more do the participants in interaction, who cannot always fall back on the costly means of meta-communication, have to rely on means of indirectly achieving understanding. Thus they can 'give' their counterparts 'something to understand', 'induce' them to form an idea or make a decision. Even in these cases, however, the means of communication used in a strategic way have to serve the goal of coming to an understanding; otherwise we would not be dealing merely with strategic *aspects* of an interaction sequence aimed as a whole at reaching understanding, but with another type of action.

Thus strategic and communicative actions are introduced as two genuine types of interaction. I am in fact supposing that the actors themselves, in every phase of interaction, can know – however vaguely and intuitively – whether they are adopting a strategic-objectivating attitude towards the other participants or are orientated to consensus. Through deception and self-deception arise the mixed forms mentioned above; and it is often difficult for an observer to make a correct ascription. But subjectively the two basic attitudes that discriminate between action orientated to success and action orientated to understanding can by no means be understood only as different analytic aspects of the same behaviour. This is not even true in the standard case of the rhetorician who wants to convince the audience through means of persuasion. The rhetorician knows, at least in retrospect, when and how he or she wanted to manipulate the public. The

Janus face of rhetoric, which is mirrored in the ambiguous meaning of the word 'persuasion', arises from the perspective of the addressees, not from that of the speaker.

It is of course possible to construe strategic action as a *limit case* of communicative action by theoretically varying the (relevant) features. The model of strategic action remains if, starting from the case of communicative action, one thinks away step by step all the presuppositions of the use of language orientated to achieving understanding, if one abstracts, that is, from the consideration that the participants have regard for normative contexts, that they mean what they say, that they put forward the truth of propositions before others as a validity-claim. (For the egocentric calculation of success it suffices if each privately attributes or denies truth-value to his or her views or to those of others.) This *limit case* of communicative action ought not to be confused with the *pure cases* of communicative action.[68]

After these preliminary clarifications I can deal with the remaining objections briefly.

(2) Giddens thinks that I assimilate productive forces to purposive-rational action, productive relations to communicative action. But in fact the two pairs of concepts lie at different levels. I too never entertained any doubts about that. None the less, there exists between productive forces and the type of purposive-rational action an analytically explicable connection, inasmuch as the knowledge implemented in forces of production, embodied in technologies, organisations and competencies, is meant to improve the productivity of labour, in general to improve the purposive-rational application of means in gaining control over nature and over co-operating human beings.[69] The relations of production, as institutions that regulate legitimate access to the means of production, refer by contrast to another type of action. They make up the core component of a political, legal and social order that provides contexts for action orientated to reaching understanding.

However, productive forces and relations lie at a different conceptual level than the action concepts referring to simple interactions. The former concepts refer to components of a society as a whole – be they potentials a society can use for processes of production, that is, for its exchange with external nature, or basic institutions which, with the distribution of the means of production and social power, establish the interest structure of society, that is, a differential pattern of possibilities for the socially recognisable satisfaction of needs.

(3) The separation of the analytically different levels of action and system of action (or society) is especially important for Giddens's distinction between *labour* and *Praxis*. By 'labour' Marx understood as a rule 'socially organised labour' (and not merely the conjunction of individual instrumental actions). If one wants now to analyse this complex concept

from the standpoint of the theory of action, it is advisable to distinguish the *institutionalisation* of behavioural patterns from the *organisation* of co-operation within the division of labour on the one hand, and from the task elements on the other. In social labour we are dealing essentially with a combination of communicative and instrumental action.

Giddens wants to distinguish from this a concept of practice that is supposed to be related to the constitution of action complexes and to their reproduction. I do not think that this choice of conceptual strategy is a fortunate one, because the basic epistemological concept of 'constitution', which refers to the formation of object domains, causes confusion in social theory. It suggests that speaking and acting subjects 'produce' their social life-context in a way similar to that in which they make products of instrumental action. I prefer to introduce the concept of the *life-world* as a complementary concept to communicative action; and I understand communicative action as the same *medium* through which the symbolic structures of the life-world are *reproduced.* At the same time, instrumental actions, that is, interventions in the objective world, present themselves as the medium through which the material substratum of the life-world is reproduced, that is, through which the life-world develops processes of exchange with external nature. From the perspective of an outside observer who objectivates the life-world, these 'material exchange processes' can be analysed as functional interconnections and as self-regulating systems. From the viewpoint of this conceptual strategy, it is advisable, first, to separate clearly concepts of action from those of society, second, to distinguish between society as a symbolically structured life-world (a concept developed from the perspective of action theory) and society as a system (a concept obtained by the way of methodical objectification of the life-world), in order, third, to develop from this a *two-level concept of society* and corresponding concepts of social reproduction. The latter cannot be reduced, as Giddens proposes, to *Praxis*. The overextension of action concepts in a theory of constitution remains stuck in metaphors; the basic concept of the philosophy of *Praxis* gives us at best an anthropomorphistic concept of society.

(4) Finally, Giddens charges that in the framework of my theory 'power' can only have the sense of an ideological distortion of communicative relations.[70] He is renewing against me the objections that conflict theorists like Coser, Lockwood and Dahrendorf raised against Talcott Parsons at the end of the 1950s.[71] In this debate I am in fact on Parsons's side, as I believe that his theory is complex enough to take into account all those phenomena for which his opponents wanted to work out a more special approach. On the other hand, I in no way wish to adopt certain idealistic premises of Parsonian social theory, and I insist on the methodological primacy of action theory in relation to systems theory. I cannot go into that here.[72]

The concept of force *(Gewalt)* already has a central place in the action theory sketched above: to the degree that interactions cannot be co-ordinated through achieving understanding, the only alternative that remains is force exercised by one against others (in a more or less refined, more or less latent manner). The typological distinction between communicative and strategic action says nothing else than this. The concept of power *(Macht)*, however, I should like to reserve for the level of action *complexes* (or of society). I am inclined, on the one hand, to agree with Hannah Arendt in regarding communicatively shared convictions as a source of legitimate power, and the communicative practice of everyday life in the life-world as a generator of power that is acknowledged without coercion *(Zwang)*.[73] On the other hand, both the Weberian concept of domination *(Herrschaft)*, in the sense of institutionalised mixtures of power and force, and the Parsonian concept of power, as a sub-system-forming medium (to be sure, only for problems of employing authorisations to power in modern societies), are useful.[74]

I am attempting to arrive at a suitable approach to the critical analysis of class structures through integrating these three concepts. With the communicative concept of power, we can make the institutionalisation of relations of force comprehensible as a transformation of force into a power outfitted with the appearance of legitimacy.[75]

If one introduces *force* as an alternative to the action-co-ordinating mechanism of reaching understanding, and *power* as a product of action orientated to reaching understanding, one gains the advantage of being able to grasp the forms of indirectly exercising force that predominate today. I mean that pathogenic force that inconspicuously enters the pores of everyday communicative practice, and can develop its latent influence there to the extent that the life-world is delivered over to imperatives of independent sub-systems and reified along paths of one-sided rationalisation.

Universal pragmatics
The theory of communicative action is based on an analysis of the use of language orientated to reaching understanding. With the concept of communicative action, the action-co-ordinating, binding effect of the offers made in speech-acts moves to the centre. Through these offers, participants in communication establish interpersonal relations through intersubjective recognition of criticisable validity-claims.[76] What is peculiar about this mechanism of reaching understanding is that ego can, in a certain sense, rationally motivate alter to accept its offer; that is, ego can motivate alter by its readiness to cover the claim it has raised through providing grounds or reasons. What stands behind the reciprocally raised validity-claims in communicative action are potential reasons as a (kind of) security reserve, rather than sanctions or gratifications, force or money, with which one can influence the choice situation of another in strategic

action. What counts in a given case as a reason or ground also depends of course on the background cultural knowledge that the participants in communication share as members of a particular life-world. The analyses of speech-acts that I have previously published focus on a question that arises from the perspective of action theory: How can we explain the rationally motivating power of offers made in speech-acts? This focus does not come through very clearly in John B. Thompson's contribution to this volume. I shall comment upon the four themes dealt with by Thompson, and in the same order.

(1) As the actor relates with an utterance simultaneously to something in the objective world, to something in the social world, and to something in his or her own subjective world, Thompson's first thesis has to be supplemented with respect to this third world-relation (and the linguistic representations of the speaker's intentions implied in part by the semantic content of performative expressions). And now to the individual objections.

The methodological decision to *begin* my analysis with speech-acts in standard form is independent of special assumptions about the representation of illocutionary components in the grammatical deep-structure. I am assuming only that the standard form explicitly calls attention to just those features that are *essential* for the rational binding effect of using symbolic expressions with an orientation to reaching understanding. It is all the same whether these expressions take the shape of elliptically contracted, indirect or propositionally non-differentiated speech-acts – as is usual in the context-dependent practice of everyday life – or whether they take the shape of extraverbal, for instance bodily, expressive gestures. To be sure, only those expressions that can be *expanded* into explicit speech-acts come into consideration. If one understands the principle of expressibility in this sense, symbolic forms like dance, music, painting, etc., drop out of consideration.[77]

For purposes of my analysis, this selectivity is harmless, since such expressions do not as a rule take over functions of co-ordinating action. Of course there are expressions – such as, for example, sacred actions – that resist being expanded and yet are important for functions of co-ordination. The binding force of these diffuse expressions can be explained in the light of a systematic history of the differentiation of the validity basis of speech, that is, in developmental-logical terms. The reference-point for such a reconstruction of forms of reaching understanding remains, however, the use of language differentiated according to validity-claims, which is characteristic of modern everyday worlds.

A brief remark on the remaining counter-examples. I do not understand bargaining as a case of communicative action; a silent greeting is as a rule the non-linguistic equivalent of an illocutionarily abbreviated speech-act, the meaning of which can be expanded with reference to the underlying norm of action; indirect speech-acts can likewise be expanded – if necessary through modifying available expressions or introducing new ones. As I have suggested elsewhere, jokes, fictional representations, irony, games, and so on, rest on intentionally using categorial confusions which, in the wake of the differentiation of validity-claims and corresponding modes (being/illusion, is/ought, essence/appearance), are seen through as category mistakes.[78]

With his example of a context-free reporting expression, 'The sky is blue this morning', Thompson indeed touches upon a difficulty of orthodox speech-act analysis that has in the meantime caused me to expand my basic formal-pragmatic assumptions. The methodological limitation to the standard form goes a step too far in neutralising context. The model of the speech-act has to take into account not only such familiar elements as utterance, action situation, speaker, hearer and the yes/no positions he or she takes, but also the background of the life-world shared by speaker and hearer, and thus the culturally transmitted, prereflexively certain, intuitively available, background knowledge from which participants in communication draw their interpretations.[79] In coming to an understanding about something by way of their speech-acts, participants in communication not only take up a frontal relation to three worlds: in doing so, they have at their backs a context-forming life-world that serves as a resource for processes of achieving understanding.

(2) Thompson inquires about the grounds for such basic formal-pragmatic distinctions as those among three *validity-claims* (truth, rightness, truthfulness) that speakers raise with their utterances, three *worlds* (objective, social, subjective) to which speakers relate in their utterances, three *basic attitudes* (objectivating, norm-conformative, expressive) which they thereby adopt and among which they can establish continuous transitions in a performative attitude, and three *classes of speech-acts* (constative, regulative, representative) that indicate three *pure modes of language-use* (cognitive, interactive, expressive). I could ground these and similar distinctions only by *carrying through* the formal-pragmatic analysis that I have *begun* in my published works. One can contest such reconstructive efforts by adducing counter-examples, such that the claims for their adequacy, universality, and so on, are invalidated.

Thompson would have to show in this way that, for example, the logical arguments for assuming exactly three validity-claims are false. If one examines the ways in which the validity of a standard utterance as a whole can be contested, one finds, in my view, precisely three aspects under which a hearer can, if need be, say no. He or she can say no to the truth of the statement asserted (or of the existential presuppositions of a mentioned propositional content), to the rightness of the utterance in relation to a normative context (or to the rightness of an underlying norm of action itself), and finally to the truthfulness or sincerity of the intention expressed by the speaker. One arrives at the same result through formal-pragmatic investigation of elementary sentences with descriptive, normative and expressive contents, and through the pragmatic logic of the corresponding (types of) argumentation specific to questions of truth, justice and self-deception.[80] Furthermore, the decentred understanding of the world, the development of which can be found both in ontogenesis and in the changing structures of world-views, also speaks for the universality of the distinction among exactly three worlds.

The two distinctions that Thompson puts forward as additional candidates hit upon what are probably universal features of the human mind; but they do not refer to formal properties of speech-acts. The hypothetical attitude towards experiences and commands, which first enables us to distinguish between *possible* and *existing* states of affairs and between *obtaining* (i.e. socially recognised) and *valid* norms, marks a general stage in the cognitive development of the individual. The distinction, equally universal in my opinion, between what can and what cannot be said is related – as the transcendental theory of language in Wittgenstein's *Tractatus* also shows – to differences between the implicit background knowledge of the life-world and linguistically explicit knowledge. The one is immediately certain but prereflective – we are not cognisant *of* this knowledge. The other is connected with criticisable validity-claims and is thus fallible – we have or express this knowledge in the consciousness that it might turn out to be invalid.

For the rest, I readily admit that the formal-pragmatic analyses I have carried out so far neglect the dimension of time and thus do not take account of phenomena having to do with linguistic creativity, with creative ways of dealing with language.[81]

(3) Thompson's third objection relates to what the ideal speech situation accomplishes. I am not claiming that a valid consensus can *come about* only under conditions of the ideal speech situation. The communicative practice of everyday life is immersed in a sea of cultural taken-for-grantedness, that is, of consensual certainties. To this life-world background of actual processes of reaching understanding, there also belong normative convictions and empathetic identifications with the feelings of others. As soon, however, as an element of this naively known, prereflexively present background is transformed into the semantic content of an utterance, the certainties come under the conditions of criticisable knowledge; from then on disagreement concerning them *can* arise. Only when this disagreement is stubborn enough to provoke a discursive treatment of the matter at issue do we have a case concerning which I am claiming that a *grounded* agreement cannot be reached unless the participants in discourse *suppose* that they are convincing each other only by force of better arguments. Should one party make use of privileged access to weapons, wealth or standing, in order to *wring* agreement from another party through the

prospect of sanctions or rewards, no one involved will be in doubt that the presuppositions of argumentation are no longer satisfied.

(4) The fourth objection is directed against the discourse theory of truth. The 1972 essay in which I developed my thesis has found a lively resonance. A number of objections have so impressed me that I am planning an extensive response. I cannot here anticipate that response in a few words. If one wants to explain the binding effect of speech-acts in interactions, the rational motivation of yes/no responses to validity-claims receives a central place. In this latter connection, an opponent's yes or no to a proponent's assertion has an exemplary significance, for argumentative dispute about the truth of statements has always drawn the interest of philosophers.

What the opponent contests is the claim that the proponent raises for his or her statement, namely, that the conditions for the validity of 'p' are satisfied. This truth-*claim* advanced for 'p' is certainly not identical with the truth or validity of 'p'. 'P' is true if the truth conditions for 'p' are satisfied; but to raise the corresponding validity-claim is to offer to defend in argument against opponents the assertion that the truth-conditions for 'p' are satisfied. The one cannot be equated with the other. The point of the discourse theory of truth is that it attempts to show why the question of what it means for the truth-conditions of 'p' to be satisfied can only be *answered* by explaining what it means to redeem or to ground with arguments the claim that the truth-conditions for 'p' are satisfied. *In this way the apparently clear distinction between explicating the meaning of truth and specifying the criteria for ascertaining truth is relativised.* Explaining the procedural meaning of discursively redeeming truth-claims is identical neither with the one nor with the other. Thus discourse – whose general communicative presuppositions have been elucidated – is not a sufficiently operationalised procedure, adherence to which could be checked like the application of a criterion. The *criteria* of truth lie at a different level than the *idea* of redeeming validity-claims which is expounded in terms of the theory of discourse. Criteria change with standards of rationality and are subject in their turn to the dictate of argumentative justification. What can count in a given instance as a good reason is something that depends on standards about which it must be possible to argue. The only thing exempted from this argument is that prior knowledge which is shared by all competent speakers, which is of course merely intuitive and thus in need of reconstruction, and to which we have recourse when we are supposed to explain what it means to enter into argumentation.

If we get clear about this basic idea, the explanation of the validity of predictions in terms of the theory of truth does not at all present an insoluble problem. The truth-conditions of a statement about the future cannot be fully satisfied at the time when it is asserted. For predictions one can prospectively raise only the claim that they will *come true*. Only the retrospective claim that they have come true is equivalent to the truth-claim raised for a corresponding statement without a temporal index.

On the other hand, I regard as justified the admonition that I have hitherto not taken the 'evidential dimension' of the concept of truth adequately into account. This objection is taken up by Mary Hesse as well.

On the theories of truth and science
During the past decade I have been only cursorily occupied with questions in the theory of science and have lost the feeling for the relevant discussions. Otherwise I would have responded to Hesse's impressive 1972 article,[82] as well as to others.[83]

In the light of the debate set off by Kuhn and Feyerabend, I see that I did in fact place too much confidence in the empiricist theory of science in *Knowledge and Human Interests*. But in her earlier attempt to overcome the rigid dualism between natural and human sciences – I do not know if this is still her position – Hesse overshot the mark in *one* respect. She did not take seriously enough the central idea of Dilthey and Rickert. The natural sciences also have to deal with hermeneutic problems on the theoretical, but especially on the meta-theoretical level; however, they do not have first to gain access to their object domain through hermeneutic means. The difference between the observer's access to a physically measurable object domain from the third-person perspective, on the one hand, and access to a symbolically prestructured object domain in the performative attitude of a participant in communication, on the other hand, has consequences not only for research *technique*; they reach deeply into the *logic* of investigation in the objectivating and the meaning-understanding sciences.[84] However, this is not our theme. I should like instead to take up the critique advanced by Mary Hesse in this volume; in doing so I shall stick to the order of her own sections.

(1) Like Thompson, Hesse criticises me for not making clear the connection between the objectivity of experience (interpreted in the sense of transcendental pragmatism) and the truth of propositions (conceived in terms of the theory of discourse). The discourse theory of truth is said to be strong where Tarski's correspondence theory is weak,[85] namely in regard to explaining the intersubjective sense of truth. But its weakness, according to Hesse, lies where she sees the strength of the correspondence theory, namely in regard to the question of how the truth of elementary observation sentences is rooted in experiences that we have in our feedback-monitored dealings with corresponding objects. I see the question, the relevance of which I do not dispute, as a problem for a theory of *knowledge* which elucidates in transcendental-pragmatic terms the life-world basis of possible experiences. I do not see it as a problem for the theory of *truth*; for owing to the peculiar problem-free character of what is taken for granted in the life-world in the domain for which Hesse brings the

correspondence theory into consideration, questions of truth cannot even be posed. To be sure, as soon as such prereflexive experiences are expressed, for example as formulated in such basic statements as 'This ball is red', they lose the status of being beyond question which is enjoyed by knowledge that remains in the background. Transposed into the semantic content of communicative utterances, experiences are transformed into judgements and connected with a validity-claim. And yet something of the life-world's problem-free character still remains attached primarily to elementary observation sentences so long as they are embedded in everyday language-games. The question of their truth is posed when we can no longer assure ourselves of their validity through simple ostensive procedures, when circumstances arise which render problematic *in a persistent way* validity-claims previously concealed behind habituation. At that moment we are already moving in the sphere of argumentative speech, where in principle only reasons count.

For this reason the type of sentence to which the correspondence theory is orientated is not suitable as a model through which the meaning of truth can be made clear; in my view it is, as Hesse rightly remarks, a limit case. The discourse theory of truth does not start with basic sentences; it chooses as paradigmatic cases statements that call for grounding even at first sight: hypothetically general and modal statements, counterfactual and negative statements, to which the human mind owes its progress. This does not, to be sure, exempt the discourse theory of truth from the obligation urged by Hesse, to explain how empirical limitations operate in the process of justifying truth-claims connected with descriptive statements. What is above all of interest here is the role of the experimental action which transforms experiences into data. Experimental action does not lie on the same level as the instrumental action of naive or scientised practice. In its function of producing data, which is always gathered with a view to testing hypothetical validity-claims, experimental action is related to discourse from the start.[86] This is a vague expression; I readily admit that the 'evidential dimension' of the concept of truth is badly in need of further clarification.

(2) I am completely in agreement with the five points that Hesse puts forward to characterise my position on the question of the constitution of an object domain interpreted in the light of constantly changing theory-languages. Prior to all theory, there is constituted in the behavioural system of instrumental action a basis in the life-world for possibilities of reaching understanding; this basis explains why we can *refer to the same phenomena* through the lenses of *different theories*, even if these phenomena, when transformed into data, have to be described in connection with those very theories.

Hesse raises here the interesting question of why, if we explain the basis of experience in pragmatistic terms, we should not also understand the entire theoretical progress of objectivating science as a non-discursive continuation of animal learning behaviour. Why should not the technical cognitive interest that guides us already in the constitution of the object domain evoke the contemplative illusion of truth in Nietzsche's sense: truth as a life-saving fiction? Hesse wants to give an instrumentalist interpretation to theory-formation itself, to the 'higher-level theoretical postulates' that always remain empirically underdetermined. Then the discursive elucidation of truth-claims could not be uncoupled from the technical cognitive interest in such a way as I propose. One would have to assume rather that the highly unnatural idea of truth is itself an instrument that makes the expansion of our technical mastery over an objectivated nature all the more efficient.

I have difficulties with such a view, and not only because of the familiar objections – formulated among others by Popper – against instrumentalist concepts of truth, but above all because I cannot bring such a view into accord with the *counterfactual formulations* – already clearly stressed by Peirce – of a pragmatism with a transcendental turn.

However that may be, Hesse picks up another thread at this point. She herself points out that an instrumentalist concept of truth is incompatible with the role that validity-claims (such as propositional truth) play in communicative action, in general, in establishing and maintaining the intersubjectivity of a life-world inhabited in common. This can be taken into account only by a concept that does not explain the truth of propositions exclusively from the standpoint of the object relation.

(3) To be sure, Hesse gives this argument a peculiar twist. She speaks of the 'social necessity' of the functions of world-views for which modern science has to offer an equivalent after the decline of religious and metaphysical world-views. Hesse appears to assume that scientific theories, if only they are 'strong' enough, can *simultaneously* provide technically useful knowledge and satisfy collective needs for meaning. A consensus concept of truth then might provide the measure of fulfilment of this second function.

I am unhappy with this proposal for the following reasons. If, with Max Weber, we regard cultural modernity as characterised by the independent differentiation of three special spheres of value (science, morality and art), science cannot take over the function of meaning-creation for the communicative practice of everyday life, unless it be in an interplay of all three expert cultures which, by way of being mediated with contexts of the life-world, have to bring the moments of reason separated at the level of culture into contact with one another again on the level of everyday practices. But no world-views would thereby be restored; rather, new forms of practice would arise. The unity of reason has become unattainable at the level of cultural interpretative systems ever since the latter were detached in the modern period from the validity syndrome of everyday communication and split up under abstract individual aspects of validity.

In this connection Hesse proposes an interpretation of the universality of validity-claims that I find exceptionally attractive. We cannot simultaneously *assert* a proposition or *defend* a theory and nevertheless anticipate that its validity-claims will be refuted in the future. Only in the performative attitude can we put forward assertions, and this attitude compels us (with the gentle but irresistible force of transcendental necessity) to advance a claim that bursts all local and temporal limits, *transcends* all cultural and historical bounds. On the other hand, we advocate this claim, which could meet with recognition in the forum of an unlimited community in communication, *here and now*. Thus the 'final consensus' that we anticipate for a particular statement or a special set of statements does not signify that we have to represent to ourselves the limit value of a cumulative progress of knowledge in the form of an 'actual sequence of future theories'. 'Final consensus' expresses only an idea that is implicitly posited with the concept of truth, an idea that determines the assertoric meaning of assertions, each *in its place and at its time*. This idea can be actualised only as a perspective bound to particular situations, though it *requires* that we neutralise all merely situation-bound, perspectivistic limitations.

It is somewhat different with the concept of reality as the correlate of all statements whose claims would be upheld in the last days by the judgement of the unlimited community in communication. Peirce's language-theoretic concept of reality is connected with the idea of a convergence point towards which the lines of all theoretical descriptions run in the end. But this idea, too, is always here and now, and indeed is in force only at the moment in which we *raise* a validity-claim with the conviction that it can be discursively redeemed. This may explain why it would be senseless for us to reckon with future theories as we do with the appearance of events. The truth of tomorrow is an empty concept. It escapes prediction not because of contingent limitations but for categorial reasons. Anyone who seriously puts forward a theoretical proposition unavoidably finds oneself in the role of the 'last' theoretician.

It seems to be doubtful, however, that these features of the discourse-theoretic understanding of truth support that version of historicism that Hesse wants, if I am not mistaken, to advocate – in agreement with deconstructionists like Richard Rorty[87] – in order to render the endangered humanity of the historical world compatible with the dehumanised reality of the objectivating sciences, which have been robbed of all human meaning.

(4) If I understand her correctly, Hesse's critique of my distinction between nomological and reconstructive sciences is directed against assertions that I did not put forward in the sense in question. The essentialism which, in my view, attaches to reconstructions of pretheoretical knowledge

of competently knowing, speaking and acting subjects is not meant to deny that we are dealing here with fallible hypotheses, just as in the objectivating sciences. However, in the attempt to transform implicit abilities into explicit knowledge, the *terminus a quo* is connected with the *terminus ad quem* internally and thus in a *different* way than an existing state of affairs is connected with its theoretical description when the latter is based on a nomological theory.

VI.   On the analysis of modern societies

David Held has recently published a book on the Frankfurt School[88] which complements the standard study by Martin Jay.[89] Despite the predominantly descriptive and systematising character of his presentation, Held develops in the parts of the book dealing with my work a profusion of critical perspectives which would require a treatment of their own.[90] On another front, Andrew Arato belongs to a remarkable circle of younger American social scientists and philosophers who are gathered around Paul Piccone's journal *Telos,* some of whom were in contact with Albrecht Wellmer when he was teaching at the New School for Social Research in New York. In recent years so many productive impulses have come out of this circle that I am unable to react to them here.[91] I shall restrict myself to brief replies to the two essays contained in this volume.

Legitimation problems and the 'motivation crisis'

The argumentation sketch that I laid out in *Legitimation Crisis* was meant to further understanding in regard to questions of crisis theory that can be dealt with empirically. It was the framework for a series of empirical studies carried out at the Starnberg Institute in the mid-1970s.[92] In the course of our investigations the complexity of the research programme, among other things, proved to be an obstacle. But David Held's objections relate in essence to the analytical consistency of the lines of inquiry, not to the attempts to deal with them empirically.

There were in fact obscure points in the conceptual demarcation between a legitimation crisis and a motivation crisis, as I could not clearly connect the paradigms of 'life-world' and 'system'. I am dealing with this theme in the soon-to-appear *Theorie des kommunikativen Handelns.*[93] If, as a first step, we conceptualise society as the life-world and see this as centred on communicative action, then three components of the life-world, culture, society and personality, can be correlated with the components of action orientated to reaching understanding. As Schema 5 shows, the maintenance of the symbolic structures of the life-world can be analysed in these dimensions.

The individual reproduction processes can be evaluated according to standards of the rationality of knowledge, the solidarity of members, and the responsibility of the adult personality. Of course, the measures vary

SCHEMA 5 *Contributions of reproduction processes to maintaining the structural components of the life-world*

Reproduction processes	Structural Components		
	Culture	Society	Personality
Cultural reproduction	Interpretative schemata susceptible to consensus ('valid knowledge')	Legitimations	Behavioural patterns influential in self-formation, educational goals
Social integration	Obligations	Legitimately ordered interpersonal relations	Social memberships
Socialisation	Interpretative accomplishments	Motivation for norm-conformative actions	Capability for interaction ('personal identity')

within these domains according to the degree of structural differentiation in the life-world. The extent of the needs for consensual knowledge, legitimate orders and personal autonomy is dependent on this. Disturbances in reproduction manifest themselves in the respective domains of culture, society and person as a loss of meaning, anomie or mental illness (psychopathologies). In each case there are corresponding withdrawal phenomena in the other domains (see Schema 6).

I am supposing, furthermore, that in modern societies two sub-systems have been differentiated out through the media of money and power, namely the capitalist economic system and a rationalised (in Weber's sense) state administration. Each forms a complementary environment for the other, and each is involved in exchange with its environment through its medium, so that the Parsonian 'interchange paradigm' can find application in this domain of interaction between state and economy. With the transition to the capitalist mode of production and the modern system of states, the material substratum of the life-world can be analysed from the standpoint of an action system that is stabilised through functional interconnections and has become independent in relation to the life-world. What I then (in 1973) treated under the catchwords 'economic crisis' and 'rationality crisis' has its place here; they can be traced back to deficits in the production of economic values and in the state's organisational achievements.

SCHEMA 6 *Crisis phenomena connected with disturbances in reproduction*

Disturbances in the domain of	Structural Components			
	Culture	Society	Person	Evaluative dimension
Cultural reproduction	Loss of meaning	Withdrawal of legitimation	Crisis in orientation and education	Rationality of knowledge
Social integration	Insecurity of collective identity	Anomie	Alienation	Solidarity of members
Socialisation	Breakdown of tradition	Withdrawal of motivation	Psychopathologies	Accountability of the person

Naturally the economic and the administrative systems of action have to be anchored in the life-world by way of institutionalisation of the money and power media. This means that the symbolically structured life-world is connected with the functional imperatives of the economy and administration through private households and the legal system; it is thereby subject to the limitations of material production within the framework of existing productive relations. On the other hand, the economy and the polity, especially the occupational system and the administrative system of domination, are dependent on accomplishments of the symbolic reproduction of the life-world, namely on individual skills and motivations, as well as on mass loyalty.

If, in the interaction between life-world and system, disturbances develop which, depending on one's point of view, can be represented as *disequilibriums* or as *pathologies*, it is necessary to make a clear distinction that still escaped me in *Legitimation Crisis*: a distinction between the deficits that inflexible structures of the life-world can give rise to in maintaining the economic and political systems on the one hand, and manifestations of deficiences in the reproduction of the life-world itself on the other. Empirically the two are connected in a feedback process; but it makes sense to separate analytically the *withdrawal of motivation* affecting the occupational system and the *withdrawal of legitimation* affecting the system of domination, on the one side, from the *colonialisation of the life-world* that is manifested primarily in phenomena of loss of meaning, anomie and personality disorders, on the other side. In 1973 I used the misleading catchphrase 'motivation crisis' for deformations of the life-world which make themselves felt in modern societies as the destruction of traditional forms of life, as attacks on the communicative infrastructure of life-worlds, as the rigidity of a one-sidedly rationalised everyday practice, and which come to expression in the consequences of impoverished cultural traditions and disturbed socialisation processes. Now I would rather conceive of motivation crisis as a parallel case to legitimation crisis; and I would want to distinguish from both of these the pathological manifestations of a colonialised life-world.

I am grateful to David Held for making me clarify these points. If this proposal is acceptable, however, his other reservations are taken care of. For it is then a matter of definition that life-worlds can be integrated only through communicative action (and through norms and values). It remains of course an empirical question as *to what extent* the need for integration in modern societies, which exceeds the social-integrative capacity of extensively rationalised life-worlds, can be covered by achievements of system integration. It is the mistake of a systems theory *à la* Luhmann that it analytically prejudges *this* question by no longer distinguishing at all in the dimension of societal integration between social integration that takes effect in connection with action orientations and systematic integration that is related to action consequences.

I think that my approach is sufficiently flexible to take into account all the phenomena that Held rightly points to. When imperatives of social and system integration are in conflict with one another, the competition can be relieved in heavily stratified societies as follows: the political system's need for legitimation is covered by the high cultures, while popular cultures provide for passive acceptance of a repression that appears to allow of no alternatives. In more levelled societies, segmentation of the labour market and fragmentation of consciousness, for example, can fulfil a similar function. In both cases the need for normatively secured or communicatively achieved agreement is decreased and the scope of tolerance for merely instrumental attitudes, indifference or cynicism is expanded.

The evolutionary status of bureaucratic socialism

Arato correctly notes that the analysis of bureaucratic socialism is a blind spot in the Frankfurt tradition of research. He puts to productive use a few remarks on this theme that he finds in Offe's and my own work. My reactions to his stimulation will have to be rather provisional and non-binding; I am not really well versed in the relevant studies – and for this there is hardly a plausible excuse.

Arato hesitates to conceive capitalist and state-socialist societies as two variants of the same developmental level because they exhibit different organisational principles, in particular a non-simultaneity of legal development. He differentiates the two systems in light of the functional primacy asserted in the one case by the exchange economy over state and culture, and in the other case by the administrative action system over economy and culture. These arrangements limit the learning and problem-solving capacities of society differently in each case. In the post-Stalinist, not yet liberalised societies of 'real socialism', learning capacities are further constricted by the fact that economy and culture are 'positively subordinated' to the state, whereas in capitalist societies the economy asserts its primacy over the other two systems by way of 'negative subordination'. Arato's question, then, is whether there is at all a possibility in post-Stalinist societies for a transition from the positive to the negative mode of subordination; and how, in that case, the likelihood of such a development could be assessed in connection with empirical indicators.

Perhaps the phenomena that Arato has in view can be made somewhat clearer by separating the *initial conditions* of modernisation from the two *paths of development* along which modernisation takes place, depending on whether it is induced by endogenously produced problems of *economic* processes of accumulation or by the *state's* efforts at rationalisation. The initial conditions of societal modernisation include an extensively rationalised life-world, in which money or power can be anchored as media, that is, can be institutionalised through positive law. If this condition is fulfilled, an economic and an administrative system can be differentiated out; these systems are complementarily related to one another and carry out the exchange with their environments through such media. Only at this level of differentiation can modern societies arise, first capitalist and, in demarcation from these, bureaucratic socialist societies. The path of capitalist modernisation is opened under the condition that the economic system can develop an independent dynamic and can take the lead with endogenously produced problems. This is the case when the economy, with the institutionalisation of wage labour and the establishment of the state based on taxation, achieves a relative autonomy in relation to private households and public administration. The path of modernisation has to take a different course when the administrative system of action, on the basis of state-controlled means of production and institutionalised one-party rule, gains a similar autonomy in relation to its environments, the economy and the political public sphere, and does so through the medium of binding decisions.

In bureaucratic socialism *crisis tendencies* arise from the planning administration, as they do in capitalism from the market economy, as soon as the administrative, or the economic, rationality of action orientations comes into contradiction with itself through unintended systematic effects. Arato speaks of the self-contradiction of planning rationality in a way similar to that in which Marx spoke of the self-contradiction of exchange rationality. These crisis tendencies are dealt with not only in the subsystem in which they arise, but also in the complementary system of action. Just as the capitalist economy is dependent on the organisational accomplishments of the state, the specialist planning bureaucracy is dependent on the self-steering accomplishments of the economy. Arato focuses on these problems of subordination. Developed capitalism also oscillates between a policy of the 'self-healing powers' of the market and state interventionism. But the structural dilemma is more clearly marked on the other side, where Arato observes a hopeless oscillation between increased central planning and decentralisation, between economic policies orientated more heavily either to production or to consumption.

As Arato also takes the cultural system into consideration, he comes across the pathological deformations of the life-world that result from the interaction of the state and economy, on the one side, with the communicative practice of everyday life, on the other. Marx tied the subsumption of living labour under dead labour (i.e. labour that had congealed into capital) to symptoms of *reification*. One can understand this also as an effect of overstressing the money medium through which economic imperatives intrude deeply into the communicatively structured life-world of employees and consumers. The overextension of the medium of legal-administrative power results in a similar intrusion of systemic mechanisms into the life-world. The points of incursion are not private households, but politically relevant memberships. Here, too, a sphere relying on social integration, namely the political public sphere, is transferred over to system-integrative mechanisms. But the effects are different; in place of the reification of communicative relations, we have the *shamming* of communicative relations in bureaucratically desiccated, coercively harmonised domains of pseudo-democratic will-formation. This *politicisation* is in a certain way symmetric with *reification*. The life-world is not assimilated to the system, to formally organised domains of action subject to law; rather, the systematically independent organisations of the state are fictively transposed back into the horizon of the life-world: the system is draped out as a coercively integrated life-world.

If this model, introduced here in a speculative manner, is useful, we are faced with precisely the question that Arato takes up in the last section of his essay: What resistance does the life-world itself pose to such an instrumentalisation for imperatives either of an economy set loose in its own dynamic or of a bureaucracy rendered autonomous? Can the structures of the life-world – however warped, yet none the less tenacious in their own proper logic – stop processes of reification or politicisation? Through an analysis of the three components of the cultural tradition influential today, and of those constellations that can make their way among them, Arato gives us a plausible answer to this question for the case of the Soviet Union.

Translated by Thomas McCarthy

Notes and References

Throughout the notes and references, English translations of Habermas's works are abbreviated as follows:

TP   *Theory and Practice,* trans. J. Viertel (Boston: Beacon Press, 1973; London: Heinemann, 1974).

TRS   *Toward a Rational Society: Student Protest, Science, and Politics,* trans. J. J. Shapiro (Boston: Beacon Press, 1970; London: Heinemann, 1971).

KHI   *Knowledge and Human Interests,* trans. J. J. Shapiro (Boston: Beacon Press, 1971; London: Heinemann, 1972).

LC   *Legitimation Crisis,* trans. T. McCarthy (Boston: Beacon Press, 1975; London: Heinemann, 1976).

CES   *Communication and the Evolution of Society,* trans. T. McCarthy (Boston: Beacon Press, 1979; London: Heinemann, 1979).

References to German and French texts have been retained; but wherever possible the editors have added the English equivalent in square brackets.

Editors' introduction
1. See section 2a of our Select Bibliography.
2. M. Horkheimer, 'Die gegenwärtige Lage der Sozialphilosophie und die Aufgaben eines Instituts für Sozialforschung', in *Sozialphilosophische Studien* (Frankfurt: Athenäum Fischer, 1972) p. 41.
3. Throughout the introduction, publication dates refer to the original German editions; non-italicised titles in English indicate that the volume has not been translated. For full bibliographical details, see sections 1a and 1b of our Select Bibliography.
4. 'Technology and Science as "Ideology"', in *TRS*, p. 103.
5. See H. Marcuse, 'Industrialization and Capitalism in the Work of Max Weber', in *Negations,* trans. J. J. Shapiro (Harmondsworth: Penguin, 1968) pp. 201–26.
6. *TP*, p. 41.
7. *KHI*, p. vii.
8. J. Habermas, *Zur Logik der Sozialwissenschaften* (Frankfurt: Suhrkamp, 1970) p. 287.
9. *TP*, p. 9.
10. 'What is Universal Pragmatics?', in *CES*, p. 5.
11. 'Technology and Science as "Ideology"', p. 101.
12. 'Toward a Reconstruction of Historical Materialism', in *CES*, p. 148.
13. *LC*, p. 113.

14. In this volume, p. 31
15. Ibid, p. 56.
16. Ibid, p. 72.
17. Ibid, p. 86.
18. Ibid, p. 126.
19. Ibid, p. 148.
20. Ibid, p. 159.
21. Ibid, p. 222.
22. Ibid, p. 238.
23. Ibid, pp. 243–4.
24. Ibid, p. 251.
25. Ibid, p. 273.
26. Ibid, p. 280.

1   Habermas and Marxism (Agnes Heller)

1. J. Habermas, 'Literaturbericht zur philosophischen Diskussion um Marx und den Marxismus' (1957), in *Theorie und Praxis* (Frankfurt: Suhrkamp, 1971).
2. See *LC*, pp. 125–8.
3. This has been elaborated in detail in my book on philosophy: *Die Philosophie des linken Radikalismus* (Hamburg: VSA, 1978).
4. In the concrete analysis of late capitalism, Habermas reintroduces the problem of motivation when discussing the motivational crisis of capitalism. These considerations, however, do not enter into his general theory.
5. Personal communication. Haupt planned to write a paper on this subject before he died.
6. The lack of a theory of organisation in Marx does not contradict the fact that he preferred some organisations to others and attributed different tasks to different organisations.
7. When I refer to 'human reason', I always mean the transcendental deduction of rational communication.
8. I apply the notion of 'class struggle' in Habermas's sense of struggle between groups with different or contradictory interests.
9. *TP*, p. 32 (translation modified).
10. Ibid, p. 37.
11. Robert Owen, *The Revolution in the Mind and the Practice of the Human Race* (London, 1849) pp. 87, 93 (emphasis added).
12. The German term *Sittlichkeit* encompasses all social rules which imply hidden or overt obligations; 'ethical' is only a rough translation.
13. Of course, even the most alienated work is not completely bereft of goal-rationality. However, if the (relative) final goal of the process of production is not envisaged by the individual, and if he or she cannot relate his or her activity consciously to the whole, then the goal-rationality is distorted and loses its creativity. That is why it is not enough to decide in some rational communication about the general goals of production; it would be necessary for all concerned in a productive model of self-management to discuss all the concrete goals of a production process.
14. As Habermas says, 'It is not evolutionary processes that are *irreversible* but the structural sequences that a society must run through *if* and *to the extent that* it is involved in evolution' (*CES*, p. 141).
15. Lukács made the same theoretical proposal and conceived of the indicators of progress very much as Habermas does. See his *Ontology of Social Being* (London: Merlin, 1978).

16. *CES*, p. 146.
17. Ibid, p. 147.
18. *Zur Rekonstruktion des Historischen Materialismus* (Frankfurt: Suhrkamp, 1976) p. 250 (second emphasis added) ['History and Evolution', trans. D. J. Parent, *Telos*, 39 (Spring 1979) p. 44].
19. In preparation for the volume this essay has been modified and reduced by the editors.

2   Habermas's concept of critical theory (Rüdiger Bubner)
1. Preface to the first edition of *Critique of Pure Reason*, trans. Norman Kemp Smith (London: Macmillan, 1929).
2. Cf. Karl Löwith, *From Hegel to Nietzsche* (New York: Holt, Rinehart & Winston, 1964); D. McLellan, *The Young Hegelians and Karl Marx* (London: Macmillan, 1969).
3. See the influential studies by J. Zelený, *Die Wissenschaftslogik und 'Das Kapital'* (Frankfurt: Europ. Vlgsanst., 1969); L. Althusser, *Lire le Capital* (Paris: Maspero, 1965) [*Reading Capital*, trans. B. Brewster (London: New Left Books, 1970)]; and, more recently, R. Bubner, 'Logik und Kapital', in *Dialektik und Wissenschaft* (Frankfurt: Suhrkamp, 1973); E. M. Lange, L. Nowak, W. Diederich and H. F. Fulda, 'Marx' Methodologie', *Neue Hefte für Philosophie*, 13 (1978).
4. G. Lukács, *History and Class Consciousness*, trans. R. Livingstone (London: Merlin, 1971).
5. M. Horkheimer, 'Traditionelle und Kritische Theorie', in *Kritische Theorie II* (Frankfurt: S. Fischer, 1968) p. 162 [*Critical Theory*, trans. M. J. O'Connell *et al.* (New York: Herder & Herder, 1972) p. 231].
6. *KHI*, chs 2,3.
7. T. Adorno, *Ästhetischen Theorie*, in *Gesammelte Schriften*, 7, ed. G. Adorno and R. Tiedemann (Frankfurt: Suhrkamp, 1970).
8. See the recent collection of essays, *Materialien zur ästhetischen Theorie Adornos: Konstruktion der Moderne*, ed. Lindner and Ludke (Frankfurt, 1980).
9. J. Habermas, 'Erkenntnis und Interesse' (1965) [*KHI*, pp. 301–17].
10. *KHI*, pp. 314–15.
11. Cf. ibid, ch. 9.
12. I. Kant, *Critique of Practical Reason*, trans. L. W. Beck (New York: Garland, 1949), section 7; related literature: D. Henrich, 'Der Begriff der sittlichen Einsicht und Kants Lehre vom Faktum der Vernunft', in *Festschrift Gadamer. Die Gegenwart der Griechen im neueren Denken*, ed. D. Henrich *et al.* (Tübingen: Mohr, 1960).
13. G. W. F. Hegel, *Phenomenology of Spirit*, trans. A. V. Miller (Oxford University Press, 1977) ch. 4.
14. K. Marx, 'Economic and Philosophical Manuscripts' (1844), in *Karl Marx: Early Writings*, ed. and trans. T. B. Bottomore (New York: McGraw-Hill, 1964).
15. J. Habermas, 'Arbeit und Interaktion', in *Theorie und Praxis* (Frankfurt: Suhrkamp, 1971) [*TP*, pp. 142–69].
16. M. Horkheimer and T. Adorno, *Dialectic of Enlightenment*, trans. J. Cumming (New York: Herder & Herder, 1972).
17. J. Habermas, 'Bewusstmachende oder rettende Kritik – Die Aktualität W. Benjamins' (1972), in *Kultur und Kritik* (Frankfurt: Suhrkamp, 1973) ['Consciousness Raising or Redemptive Criticism – the Contemporaneity of Walter Benjamin', trans. P. Brewster and C. H. Buchner, *New German Critique*, 17

(Spring 1979)]. In section 7 Habermas dismisses my suspicion ('Was ist kritische Theorie?', *Philosophische Rundschau*, 16 (1969)) that there is sophistry here. The dismissal, however, does not convince me.

18. See J. Habermas, 'Vorbereitende Bemerkungen zu einer Theorie der kommunikativen Kompetenz', in J. Habermas and N. Luhmann, *Theorie der Gesellschaft oder Sozialtechnologie – Was leistet die Systemforschung?* (Frankfurt: Suhrkamp, 1971) p. 121.

19. Ibid, p. 140.

20. Cf. my 'Kant, Transcendental Arguments and the Problem of Deduction', *Review of Metaphysics*, 28 (1975).

21. 'Vorbereitende Bemerkungen', p. 141. Cf. Kant, *Critique of Pure Reason*, A 293 H.

22. J. Habermas, 'Was Heisst Universalpragmatik?', in *Sprachpragmatik und Philosophie*, ed. K.–O. Apel (Frankfurt: Suhrkamp, 1976) pp. 201ff [*CES*, pp. 1–68]. Habermas here differs from his colleague Apel, who has since radicalised the allusions to transcendental philosophy into a demand for 'ultimate grounding'; cf. 'Das Problem der philosophischen Letzbegründung im Licht einer transzendentalen Sprachpragmatik', in *Sprache und Erkenntnis, Festschrift G. Frey*, ed. B. Kanitscheider (Innsbruck: Inst. für Sprachwissenschaft d. Univ. Innsbruck, 1976).

23. For example, J. Habermas, 'Wahrheitstheorien', in *Wirklichkeit und Reflexion, Festschrift W. Schulz*, ed. H. Fahrenbach (Pfullingen: Neske, 1973).

24. J. Habermas, *Legitimationsprobleme im Spätkapitalismus* (Frankfurt: Suhrkamp, 1973) especially part III [*LC*, part III].

25. I have attempted elsewhere to demonstrate what is meant by this: *Handlung, Sprache und Vernunft. Grundbegriffe praktischer Philosophie* (Frankfurt: Suhrkamp, 1976).

3   Rationality and relativism: Habermas's 'overcoming' of hermeneutics (Thomas McCarthy)

1. J. Habermas, 'A review of Gadamer's *Truth and Method*', in *Understanding and Social Inquiry*, ed. F. Dallmayr and T. McCarthy (Notre Dame University Press, 1977) pp. 335–63; H.–G. Gadamer, 'On the Scope and Function of Hermeneutical Reflection', in *Philosophical Hermeneutics* (Berkeley: University of California Press, 1976) pp. 18–43; J. Habermas, 'Der Universalitätsanspruch der Hermeneutik', in *Hermeneutik und Ideologiekritik*, ed. K.–O Apel *et al.* (Frankfurt: Suhrkamp, 1971) pp. 120–59; and H.–G. Gadamer, 'Replik', in ibid, pp.283–317. For an overview see T. McCarthy, *The Critical Theory of Jürgen Habermas* (Cambridge, Mass.: M.I.T. Press, 1978) pp. 169–93.

2. See *The Critical Theory of Jürgen Habermas*, pp. 261ff; and T. McCarthy, 'On the Changing Relation of Theory to Practice in the Work of Jürgen Habermas', in *Proceedings of the 1978 Biennial Meeting of the Philosophy of Science Association (PSA 1978)*, vol. 2, ed. P. Asquith and I. Hacking (East Lansing, Michigan, 1979).

3. H.–G. Gadamer, *Truth and Method* (New York: Seabury, 1975) pp. 263–4.

4. See Richard Rorty, *Philosophy and the Mirror of Nature* (Princeton University Press, 1979).

5. See *The Critical Theory of Jürgen Habermas*, chs 3, 4.

6. Habermas considers this formulation in his contribution to *Transzendentalphilosophische Normenbegründungen*, ed. Willi Oelmüller (Paderborn: Schöingh, 1978) p. 114.

7. J. Habermas, 'What is Universal Pragmatics?', in *CES*, p. 2.

8. Ibid, pp. 8ff, 21ff.
9. See *The Critical Theory of Jürgen Habermas*, ch. 4. Habermas uses the phrase 'something like a minimal ethics' to characterise the implicit normative presuppositions of discourse in *Transzendentalphilosophische Normenbegründungen*, p. 114.
10. 'What is Universal Pragmatics?', p. 25.
11. *Transzendentalphilosophische Normenbegründungen*, pp. 138–9.
12. S. Kanngiesser remarks that one might be 'tempted to say that according to Habermas the function of language consists in permitting the formulation of the classical philosophical problems'. See *Sprachpragmatik und Philosophie*, ed. K.–O. Apel (Frankfurt: Suhrkamp, 1976) pp. 273–393, here p. 351.
13. 'What is Universal Pragmatics?', p. 3.
14. Ibid, p. 2 and n. 2, pp. 208–10.
15. *Transzendentalphilosophische Normenbegründungen*, p. 156.
16. Ibid, p. 138.
17. Ibid, p. 224. The same point can be made in another way through an analysis of various pathologies and their origins in pathogenic structures of communication in the family. See Habermas, 'Stichworte zur Theorie der Sozialisation', in his *Kultur und Kritik* (Frankfurt: Suhrkamp, 1973) pp. 118–94; and 'Die kommunikative Organisation der inneren Natur', unpublished manuscript (1974).
18. *Transzendentalphilosophische Normenbegründungen*, p. 128.
19. Ibid, p. 146.
20. Ibid, p. 128.
21. In a manuscript on *Handlungsrationalität und gesellschaftliche Rationalisierung*, to be published by Suhrkamp in 1981; the contrasts are developed on pp. 48ff of the manuscript.
22. Ibid, pp. 253–4.
23. Ibid, pp. 257–8.
24. See especially *CES*.
25. J. Habermas, *Zur Logik der Sozialwissenschaften* (Frankfurt: Suhrkamp, 1970) pp. 121–2.
26. *TRS*, p. 91.
27. For a relevant bibliography see Patricia Teague Ashton, 'Cross-cultural Piagetian Research: an Experimental Perspective', *Harvard Educational Review*, 45 (1975) pp. 475–506; and *Piagetian Psychology: Cross-Cultural Contributions*, ed. P. R. Dasen (New York: Halsted, 1977) especially Dasen's introduction, pp. 1–25.
28. Susan Buck-Morss, 'Socio-economic Bias in Piaget's Theory and its Implications for Cross-cultural Studies', *Human Development*, 18 (1975) pp. 40–1, cited by Dasen in *Piagetian Psychology*, p. 6.
29. Dasen, *Piagetian Psychology*, p. 8.
30. See Ashton, 'Cross-cultural Piagetian Research'.
31. Dasen, *Piagetian Psychology*, p. 11.
32. Ibid, p. 7.
33. John C. Gibbs, 'Kohlberg's Stages of Moral Judgment: a Constructive Critique', *Harvard Educational Review*, 47 (1977) p. 55.
34. This is Habermas's characterisation in *CES*, p. 205.
35. *CES*, pp. 101–2.
36. Gibbs, 'Kohlberg's Stages of Moral Judgment', p. 55.
37. Thus in 'The Claim to Moral Adequacy of a Highest Stage of Moral Judgement' (*Journal of Philosophy*, 70 (1973) pp. 630–46; reprinted in *Essays in Moral Development*, vol. 2, Harvard University Center for Moral Develop-

ment, pp. 145–75; citations from the latter edition) Kohlberg writes: 'the developing human being and the moral philosopher are engaged in fundamentally the same moral task . . . The task is arriving at moral judgements in reflective equilibrium . . . between espoused general moral principles and particular judgements about situations . . . The process continues to lead to revision, sometimes of our principles, sometimes of our intuition as to what is right in a concrete situation' (p. 149). On this view, stages represent theories or principles through which concrete experiences are interpreted (assimilated), and which are revised to accommodate these experiences. They are 'equilibrium points in the successive revisions of principles and concrete experiences in relation to one another' (ibid). Thus in posing hypothetical moral dilemmas to subjects, the moral psychologist elicits both their concrete normative judgements (moral intuitions) and the justifications they offer for them (moral theories, meta-ethical and normative) (p. 172). The individual's moral theory is viewed as 'a conscious reflection upon his actual normative judgements' (ibid). And this implies a relation between moral philosopher and moral agent that is increasingly symmetrical: 'the familiar concerns of moral philosophy correspond to the "natural" concerns or modes of reflection at our highest stages' (p. 174). Moral philosophy or 'formal moral theory' emerges from this 'post-customary level of "reflective" moral discourse' in which subjects attempt to justify and systematise their concrete judgements (ibid). In fact, Kohlberg goes so far as to say that even the 'philosopher's formal moral theory is an elaboration of certain portions of his "natural" moral stage structure' (ibid). Now this view of moral philosophy as systematising modes of reflective thought that are part and parcel of higher-stage morality clearly relativises the pre-reflective-intuition/reflective-reconstruction asymmetry on which Habermas relies so heavily. While he attributes the 'same performative attitude of a participant in practical discouse' to both the moral subject and the moral philosopher, he regards the latter as the 'reflecting alter ego' of the former and emphasises the differences between 'the lay member's moral intuitions' and the 'expert's reconstruction of them' ('Interpretive Social Science *vs* Hermeneuticism', unpublished paper read at the University of California, Berkeley in 1980, p. 24). One could argue, however, that moral theory is less properly characterised as a 'philosophical reconstruction of moral intuitions' (ibid, p. 23) than as an aspect of the active reconstruction of moral judgement in the process of development.

38.   Kohlberg recognises this in a certain way: 'The isomorphism of psychological and normative theory generates the claim that a psychologically more advanced stage of moral judgement is more morally adequate by moral-philosophic criteria. The isomorphism assumption is a two-way street. While moral philosophical criteria of adequacy of moral judgement help define a standard of psychological adequacy or advance, the psychological advance feeds back and clarifies these criteria . . . Our psychological theory claims that individuals prefer the highest stage of reasoning they comprehend, a claim supported by research. This claim of our psychological theory derives from a philosophical claim that a later stage is 'objectively' preferable or more adequate by certain *moral* criteria. This philosophical claim, however, would for us be thrown into question if the facts of moral advance were inconsistent with its psychological implications' ('The Claim to Moral Adequacy', p. 148). The 'moral criteria' in question are taken largely from 'the formalist tradition in philosophic ethics from Kant to Rawls' (ibid). That is, the focus is narrowed to questions of 'duties and rights' to the exclusion of questions of 'ultimate

aims or ends' and of 'personal worth or virtue' ('From Is to Ought: How to Commit the Naturalistic Fallacy and Get Away With It in the Study of Moral Development', in *Cognitive Development and Epistemology*, ed. T. Mischel (New York: Academic Press, 1971) p. 214), and morality is regarded as having to do with 'conflicts between competing claims' (ibid, p. 192), the moral aim being 'to make decisions which anyone could agree with in resolving social conflicts' (ibid, p. 218) or, at another level, to discover a 'universal prescriptive principle' (ibid, p. 221). Moral 'theorists', whether lay members or philosophers, would of course want to debate much of this. It is not at all clear how the adequacy of this very construal of morality emerges from the 'inner logic' of moral development, how (for instance) higher stages 'include lower stages as components reintegrated at a higher level' (ibid, p. 186 – how does Kant 'include' Aristotle or Acquinas, or for that matter Zen Buddhism?), or how the higher stages capture 'the visible core of lower stages of morality' (ibid, p. 221), especially if they abstract from precisely the concern with ends, virtues, self-perfection, etc., with which these 'lower stages' are so preoccupied.

39. A case in point is Habermas's own critique of the positivist equation of knowledge with science; the complementarity of 'philosophical' and 'empirical' considerations is obvious.

40. *CES*, p. 74.

41. Ibid, p. 107. This is consistent with Habermas's earlier critique, following Hegel, of the monadological presuppositions of Kant's autonomous self; see 'Labor and Interaction: Remarks on Hegel's Jena *Philosophy of Mind'*, in *TP*, pp. 142–69. This point, as well as those which follow, is developed at length by Fred R. Dallmayr in his *Contributions to a Post-Individualist Theory of Politics* (Amherst, Mass.: University of Massachusetts Press, forthcoming).

42. *CES*, pp. 93–4. This conception of a 'seventh stage' going beyond formalist moral consciousness and reintegrating the 'field dependency' of earlier stages in a higher synthesis might provide a perspective for righting the imbalance arising from the focus on autonomy at the expense of attachment. See Carol Gilligan, 'In a Different Voice: Women's Conception of the Self and of Morality', *Harvard Educational Review*, 44 (1977) pp. 481–517; and 'Woman's Place in a Man's Life Cycle', *Harvard Educational Review*, 49 (1979) pp. 431–46.

43. *KHI*, p. 35 (translation modified).

44. Ibid, p. 26. See *The Critical Theory of Jürgen Habermas*, pp. 110–36.

45. *KHI*, p. 34.

46. Ibid, p. 41.

47. *TP*, pp. 21–2.

48. This might provide conceptual foundations for the type of 'non-regressive reconciliation with nature' envisioned in some of the projects for an 'ecological science'. For a review of the issues at stake see Joel Whitebook, 'The Problem of Nature in Habermas', *Telos*, 40 (1979) pp. 41–69.

49. *TP*, p. 40.

4   Cognitive interests and self-reflection (Henning Ottmann)

1. *KHI*, pp. 301ff.

2. There comes to mind above all Habermas's dialectical theory of the social sciences, as it already had been outlined in the 'Positivismusstriet' and in the discussion of contemporary analytic and hermeneutic philosophy of the social sciences. See Habermas's contributions to T. W. Adorno *et al., Der Positivismusstriet in der deutschen Soziologie* (Neuwied: Luchterhand, 1969) [*The*

Positivist Dispute in German Sociology, trans. G. Adey and D. Frisby (London: Heinemann, 1969)]; and J. Habermas, *Zur Logik der Sozialwissenschaften* (Frankfurt: Suhrkamp, 1970).

3. The situation is very lucidly described by A. Wellmer, 'Empirisch-analytische und kritische Sozialwissenschaft', in *Kritische Gesellschaftstheorie und Positivismus* (Frankfurt: Suhrkamp, 1969) pp. 53ff [*Critical Theory of Society,* trans. J. Cumming (New York: Seabury, 1974)].

4. Some of the differences between the teachings of orthodox Marxism and critical theory are summarised by Habermas in 'Between Philosophy and Science: Marxism as Critique', in *TP*, pp. 195ff.

5. The latter contention may be too strongly put with regard to the 'bourgeois' elements in Adorno's and Horkheimer's theories. It can, however, be justified, if one considers the radicality with which the totality of civil society and 'traditional' theory is criticised.

6. Some readers might miss an interpretation of Heidegger and Scheler, especially on the grounds that both anticipated the triad of cognitive interests: M. Heidegger, *Sein und Zeit* (Tübingen: Max Niemeyer, 1927) section 41 [*Being and Time,* trans. J. Macquarrie and E. Robinson (Oxford: Blackwell, 1978)]; see T. Kisiel, 'Habermas' Reinigung von reiner Theorie', in *Materialien zu 'Erkenntnis und Interesse',* ed. W. Dallmayr (Frankfurt: Suhrkamp, 1974) p. 310. K.-O. Apel reminds us of Scheler's 'Herrschafts-', 'Bildungs-' and 'Erlösungswissen', in *Transformation der Philosophie,* Bd I (Frankfurt: Suhrkamp, 1973) p. 31. Some of the modern authors not presented in *Knowledge and Human Interests,* like Popper or Wittgenstein, are discussed elsewhere (for instance, in *Zur Logik der Sozialwissenschaften).*

7. *KHI*, p. 314.

8. *TP*, pp. 8, 14ff.

9. Ibid, pp. 8, 14; *KHI*, p. 35.

10. *KHI*, p. 34: 'the contingency of nature as a whole'.

11. Ibid, p. 196.

12. Ibid, pp. 196–7.

13. Ibid, pp. 197–8.

14. *TP*, p. 8 (emphasis added).

15. *KHI*, p. 314.

16. Ibid, pp. 313–14.

17. Nichols has pointed out that psychoanalysis 'must rely upon a theoretical framework which exists independently of its clinical technique, and *its* criteria of validation': C. Nichols, 'Science or Reflection: Habermas on Freud', *Philosophy of the Social Sciences,* 2 (1972) p. 265.

18. Böhler tries to distinguish between transcendental 'formal and universally valid reflection' ('formal emancipatory knowledge for the sake of knowing') and the historical self-reflection which aims at a liberation of a particular subject in a concrete historical situation ('practical emancipatory knowledge for the sake of action'): D. Böhler, 'Zur Geltung des emanzipatorischen Interesses', in *Materialien zu 'Erkenntnis und Interesse',* pp. 359–60. Similarly, see K.-O. Apel, 'Wissenschaft als Emanzipation?', in the same volume, pp. 341–2.

19. *TP*, pp. 22–3.

20. J. Habermas, 'Vorbereitende Bemerkungen zu einer Theorie der kommunikativen Kompetenz', in J. Habermas and N. Luhmann, *Theorie der Gesellschaft oder Sozialtechnologie – Was leistet die Systemforschung?* (Frankfurt: Suhrkamp, 1971) pp. 101–42; J. Habermas, 'Stichworte zur Theorie der Sozialisation' and 'Notizen zum Begriff der Rollenkompetenz', in *Kultur und*

Kritik (Frankfurt: Suhrkamp, 1973) pp. 118–95, 195–232; J. Habermas, 'Moralentwicklung und Ich-Identität', in *Zur Rekonstruktion des Historischen Materialismus* (Frankfurt: Suhrkamp, 1976) pp. 63–92 [*CES*, pp. 69–94]. In the latter volume one also finds a 'reconstruction' of the theory of evolution (pp. 129ff) [*CES*, pp. 130ff].

21. J. Habermas, 'Nachwort' (1973), in *Erkenntnis und Interesse*, p. 392 ['A Postscript to *Knowledge and Human Interests*', trans. C. Lenhardt, *Philosophy of the Social Sciences*, 3 (1975) p. 171].

22. 'Vorbereitende Bemerkungen zu einer Theorie der kommunikativen Kompetenz', pp. 136ff.

23. *TP*, 25ff, 38ff.

24. '[The] vindicating superiority of those who do the enlightening over those who are to be enlightened is theoretically unavoidable, but at the same time it is fictive and requires self-correction: in a process of enlightenment there can only be participants' (*TP*, p. 40).

25. The new distinctions themselves seem to be problematic. The 'reconstructable' theories may have come too close to the classical interest-free theory. And there may be, above all, too sharp a separation between action and experience on the one hand and discourse on the other.

26. Schöpf has criticised Apel's interpretation of psychoanalysis with arguments which equally apply to Habermas's interpretation. A. Schöpf, 'Review of *Transformation der Philosophie*, Bd. I and II', *Philosophisches Jahrbuch*, 83 (1976) pp. 418–19.

27. *KHI*, pp. 256, 346.

28. Ibid, pp. 205ff.

29. J. G. Fichte, 'Grundlage der gesamten Wissenschaftslehre' (1794), in *Ausgewählte Werke in sechs Banden*, Bd I, ed. F. Medicus (Darmstadt: Wissenschaftliche Buchgesellschaft, 1962) pp. 275ff; J. G. Fichte, 'Über den Grund unseres Glaubens an eine göttliche Weltregierung' (1798), in *Ausgewählte Werke*, Bd III, p. 129.

30. 'The pressure of reality and corresponding degree of societal repression then depend on the degree of technical control over natural forces as well as on the organization of their exploitation and the distribution of the goods produced. The more the power of technical control is extended and the pressure of reality decreased, the weaker becomes the prohibition of instincts compelled by the system of self-preservation' (*KHI*, p. 275). See also *KHI*, p. 280.

31. 'Discourse is no institution at all, it is the anti-institution as such' (*Theorie der Gesellschaft oder Sozialtechnologie*, p. 201).

32. *KHI*, p. 280.

33. For example, H. Freyer, 'Über das Dominantwerden technischer Kategorien in der Lebenswelt der industriellen Gesellschaft', in *Gedanken zur Industriegesellschaft* (Mainz: von Hase und Koehler Mainz, 1970); A. Gehlen, *Die Seele im technischen Zeitalter* (Hamburg: Rowolt, 1975).

34. J. Habermas, 'The Scientization of Politics and Public Opinion', in *TRS*, pp. 62–81.

35. J. Habermas, *Strukturwandel der Öffenlichkeit* (Neuwied: Luchterhand, 1971); and 'The University in a Democracy: Democratization of the University', in *TRS*, pp. 1–13.

36. Following Arendt and Bloch, Habermas sometimes refers to the fundamental difference between the moral-political realm of freedom and the economic realm. However necessary as a precondition for freedom, the satisfaction of hunger and needs is not in itself a moral or political category. For instance, see 'Nachgeahmte Substantialität', in *Philosophische-politische Profile* (Frankfurt: Suhrkamp, 1971) p. 217.

37. 'Bewusstmachende und rettende Kritik – Die Aktualität Walter Benjamins', in *Kultur und Kritik,* p. 324, see also p. 318 ['Consciousness Raising or Redemptive Criticism – The Contemporaneity of Walter Benjamin', trans. P. Brewster and C. H. Buchner, *New German Critique,* 17 (Spring 1979) p. 46, see also p. 42].
38. *TRS,* p. 88.
39. Following Varagnac's three-stage theory, we can distinguish three cultural epochs and corresponding 'paradigms' for interpreting nature: hunter-and-scavenger-culture (realm of 'animals'), farmer-and-shepherd-culture (realm of 'plants' and 'organisms'), and industrial-technical-culture (lifeless, 'inorganic' matter). A. Varagnac, *De la prehistoire au monde moderne* (Paris: Plon, 1954).
40. Glaser rightly criticises Bloch's and Marcuse's magical utopia of technology: W. R. Glaser, *Soziales und instrumentelles Handeln* (Stuttgart: Kohlhammer, 1972) pp. 103ff.
41. In a forthcoming paper, 'Praktische Philosophie und technische Welt' *(Zeitschrift für philosophische Forschung),* I have proposed an open dialectic between 'nature' and 'freedom', in which not only freedom but also nature has to be recognised as an 'end-in-itself'. Neither freedom nor nature can encompass the respective other 'kingdom of ends'.
42. *KHI,* p. 191.
43. Ibid, p. 131.
44. Ibid, pp. 27, 35.
45. Ibid, p. 33.
46. G. W. F. Hegel, *Jenaer Realphilosophie,* ed. J. Hoffmeister (Hamburg: Felix Meiner, 1969) pp. 198ff.
47. Some of the difficulties of a materialistic transcendental 'constitution' are elucidated by T. McCarthy, *The Critical Theory of Jürgen Habermas* (Cambridge, Mass.: M.I.T. Press, 1978) pp. 110ff.
48. The structure of this *Reflexionsverhältnis* resembles the logic of the master–slave dialectic. Theunissen has lately brought to light the crypto-politic of the Hegelian *Reflexionslogik*: M. Theunissen, *Sein und Schein* (Frankfurt: Suhrkamp, 1978).
49. *KHI,* p. 276.
50. 'Nachgeahmte Substantialität', pp. 208ff.
51. J. Habermas, *Protestbewegung und Hoschschulreform* (Frankfurt: Suhrkamp, 1969) pp. 43ff (n. 6).
52. *KHI,* p. 284.
53. *Zur Logik der Sozialwissenschaften,* p. 283.
54. 'Einrücken in den Traditionszussamenhang': H.-G. Gadamer, *Wahrheit und Methode* (Tübingen: Mohr, 1972) p. 274 [*Truth and Method* (London: Sheed & Ward, 1975) p. 258].
55. We have to pass over Habermas's thesis that the extra-linguistic sources of distorted communication call for a 'meta'-hermeneutic founded in 'reconstructable' theories.
56. Hegel in his Bern period contrasted 'positivity' as a form of petrified life with 'subjectivity' and 'reason'. But already in his later years at Frankfurt, under the influence of Hölderlin, Fichte and a new interpretation of Christianity, he developed a dialectic for which 'positivity' itself belonged to 'life' and 'spirit'. See also Gadamer, *Wahrheit und Methode,* pp. 256ff [*Truth and Method,* pp. 241ff].
57. Contrary to Habermas, Marcuse's transformation of psychoanalysis at least takes as its point of departure the Freudian 'inseparability' of instinctual

sacrifice and culture: for example, *Triebstruktur und Gesellschaft* (Frankfurt: Suhrkamp, 1967) pp. 9ff.

58. A. Gehlen, *Anthropologische Forschung* (Reinbeck: Rowolt, 1975) pp. 74ff; *Die Seele im technischen Zeitalter*, pp. 57ff. The genesis, functions and categories of institutions are described in *Urmensch und Spätkultur* (Frankfurt: Akad. Vlgsges. Athenaion, 1975).

59. 'Bewusstmachende und rettende Kritik', p. 343 ['Consciousness Raising or Redemptive Criticism', pp. 58–9].

60. N. Luhmann, 'Systemtheoretische Argumentation: Eine Entgegnung auf Jürgen Habermas', in *Theorie der Gesellschaft oder Sozialtechnologie*, p. 320.

61. Schelsky has shown the difficulties with regard to the example of religion in modern times: H. Schelsky, 'Ist Dauerreflexion institutionalisierbar?', in *Auf der Suche nach Wirklichkeit* (München: Wilhelm Goldmann, 1979) pp. 268–98.

62. N. Luhmann, 'Systemtheoretische Argumentation', pp. 326ff.

63. Apel's idea of critical reflection and 'unlimited community of communication' seems to gravitate more in the direction of such a 'regulative idea'.

64. The model of social critique is characterised as follows: 'How would the members of a social system, at a given stage in the development of productive forces, have collectively and bindingly intepreted their needs (and which norms would they have accepted as justified) if they could and would have decided on an organization of social intercourse through discursive will-formation and with adequate knowledge of the limiting conditions and functional imperatives of society?' (*LC*, p. 113).

65. Spaemann describes the differences between the justification of 'legitimate power' and the interest in liberation from power and authority as such as the fundamental difference between traditional practical philosophy and critical theory. R. Spaemann, 'Die Utopie der Herrschaftsfreiheit', in *Zur Kritik der politischen Utopie* (Stuttgart: Klett-Cotta, 1977) pp. 104–27.

66. J. Rawls, *A Theory of Justice* (Oxford: Clarendon, 1972) pp. 20ff. The 'reflective equilibrium' can be interpreted as a 'coherence theory' of norm justification: N. Hoerster, 'John Rawls' Kohäreztheorie der Normbegründung', in *Über John Rawls' Theorie der Gerechtigkeit*, ed. O. Höffe (Frankfurt: Suhrkamp, 1977) pp. 57–77; K. G. Ballestrem, 'Metholdologische Probleme in Rawls' Theorie der Gerechtigkeit', in the same volume, pp. 108–31.

5 Science and objectivity (Mary Hesse)

1. *KHI*, chs 5 and 6, and appendix.

2. 'A Postscript to *Knowledge and Human Interests*', trans. C. Lenhardt, *Philosophy of the Social Sciences*, 3 (1973) pp. 157 and (especially) 179.

3. See especially 'A Postscript'; and 'What is Universal Pragmatics?', in *CES*, p. 1.

4. F. P. Ramsey, *The Foundations of Mathematics* (London: Routledge & Kegan Paul, 1931) p. 155.

5. T. McCarthy, *The Critical Theory of Jürgen Habermas* (Cambridge, Mass.: M.I.T. Press, 1978) p. 295.

6. This does not appear to be quite the same usage as that of the translator of *KHI*, where 'objectivate' means to give form to a symbolic system in order to make it into a vehicle of communicative action, as, for example, the construction of an intersubjective 'social world'. In this translation 'objectify'

is used for constitution (in the Kantian sense) of the objects of instrumental action or of natural science, which are taken to be separate from and external to the subject. (Cf. translator's note 23, *KHI*, p. 323.)

7. 'A Postscript', p. 167.
8. *TP*, pp. 20–1 (my italics).
9. 'A Postscript', p. 170.
10. Ibid, p. 174. I have attempted to do justice to both the pragmatic correspondence elements of empirical truth, and to their consensus or coherence elements, in my *The Structure of Scientific Inference* (London: Macmillan, 1974) chs 1 and 2.
11. 'A Postscript', pp. 161–2.
12. Ibid, p. 162.
13. Recent English-language critques of Habermas from the point of view of realism include G. Gutting, 'Habermas's Philosophy of Natural Science', *Proceedings of the 1978 Biennial Meeting of the Philosophy of Science Association (PSA 1978)*, vol. 2, ed. P. D. Asquith and I. Hacking (East Lansing, Michigan, 1979); and N. Stockman, 'Habermas, Marcuse, and the *Aufhebung* of Science and Technology', *Philosophy of the Social Sciences*, 8 (1978). Gutting argues for the independence of the 'theoretical attitude', and Stockman argues for realism on the grounds that acceptance of the 'technical interest' as definitive for science is itself a socially conditioned and ideologically motivated position.
14. 'A Postscript', pp. 171-2. Habermas's appeal here to the Copenhagen interpretation of quantum mechanics as an example of stable descriptive language is, however, misleading, because natural-language denotations do not entail the whole ontology of classical physics, as has become clear, for example, in discussions of alternative quantum logics.
15. Ibid, p. 180. The points 1–5 that follow here first appeared in my 'Habermas's Consensus Theory of Truth', *PSA 1978*, vol. 2.
16. 'A Postscript', pp. 180, 185.
17. The phrase comes from Gutting, 'Habermas's Philosophy of Natural Science', though he gives it the realist interpretation rejected here.
18. See especially 'Moral Development and Ego Identity', in *CES*, p. 69.
19. *LC*, p. 121.
20. I have discussed the evaluative aspects of scientific theories in 'Theory and Value in the Social Sciences', in *Action and Interpretation*, ed. C. Hookway and P. Pettit (Cambridge University Press, 1978), and in 'The Strong Thesis of Sociology of Knowledge' (forthcoming).
21. For a discussion of this point, see J. B. Thompson, *Critical Hermeneutics: A Study in the Thought of Paul Ricoeur and Jürgen Habermas* (Cambridge University Press, 1981) pp. 130ff and 196ff.
22. The rest of this section closely follows arguments that first appeared in my 'Habermas's Consensus Theory of Truth'.
23. In *Understanding and Social Inquiry*, ed. F. R. Dallmayr and T. McCarthy (Notre Dame University Press, 1977) p. 335.
24. 'A Postscript', p. 182. See also 'What is Universal Pragmatics?', pp. 8ff.
25. 'A Postscript', p. 184, quoting Christopher Nichols.
26. 'What is Universal Pragmatics?', p. 16.
27. 'Toward a Theory of Communicative Competence', *Inquiry*, 13 (1970) p. 360.
28. 'Theory and Value in the Social Sciences'.
29. See, for example, John B. Thompson, 'Universal Pragmatics', Chapter 6 in this volume.

6   Universal pragmatics (John B. Thompson)

1.   The major essays of Habermas which discuss various aspects of universal pragmatics are, in order of publication, as follows: 'Toward a Theory of Communicative Competence', in *Recent Sociology*, no. 2, ed. Hans Peter Dreitzel (New York: Macmillan, 1970) pp. 114–48; 'Vorbereitende Bemerkungen zu einer Theorie der kommunikativen Kompetenz', in Jürgen Habermas and Niklas Luhmann, *Theorie der Gesellschaft oder Sozialtechnologie – Was leistet die Systemforschung?* (Frankfurt: Suhrkamp, 1971) pp. 101–41; 'Wahrheitstheorien', in *Wirklichkeit und Reflexion: Walter Schulz zum 60. Geburtstag,* ed. Helmut Fahrenbach (Pfullingen: Neske, 1973) pp. 211–65; 'Was heisst Universalpragmatik?', in *Sprachpragmatik und Philosophie,* ed. Karl-Otto Apel (Frankfurt: Suhrkamp, 1976) pp. 174–272; 'Some Distinctions in Universal Pragmatics', *Theory and Society,* 3 (1976) pp. 155–67. A slightly revised version of 'Was heisst Universalpragmatik?' has appeared in English as 'What is Universal Pragmatics?', *CES,* pp. 1–68. It should be noted that, although I shall be concerned only with Habermas's work, he is not the only author who has sought to develop the programme of universal pragmatics. Other contributions, such as those of Karl-Otto Apel, may be found in *Sprachpragmatik und Philosophie.*
2.   'What is Universal Pragmatics?', p. 5 (translation modified).
3.   For an unsympathetic and largely uncomprehending critique, see Y. Bar-Hillel, 'On Habermas' Hermeneutic Philsosophy of Language', *Synthese,* 26 (1973) pp. 1–12. Critical discussions which are far more perceptive, and to which I am greatly indebted, may be found in Thomas McCarthy, 'A Theory of Communicative Competence', *Philosophy of the Social Sciences,* 3 (1973) pp. 135–56; Anthony Giddens, 'Habermas's Critique of Hermeneutics', in his *Studies in Social and Political Theory* (London: Hutchinson, 1977) pp. 135–64.
4.   *TP,* p. 169.
5.   J. Habermas, *Zur Logik der Sozialwissenschaften* (Frankfurt: Suhrkamp, 1970) p. 287.
6.   *TP,* p. 9.
7.   These and similar questions are confronted by Habermas in the 1971 'Introduction' to *Theory and Practice.*
8.   *KHI,* p. 314.
9.   Cf. J. Habermas, 'A Postscript to *Knowledge and Human Interests'*, trans. C. Lenhardt, *Philosophy of the Social Sciences,* 3 (1973) pp. 157–89. Many of the revisions which Habermas makes in the 'Postscript' can also be found in the 1971 'Introduction' to *Theory and Practice.*
10.   'A Postscript', p. 184.
11.   J. Habermas, 'Summation and Response', trans. M. Matesich, *Continuum,* 8 (1970) pp. 128–9.
12.   *TP,* p. 18.
13.   Ibid, p. 20.
14.   'Toward a Theory of Communicative Comptence', p. 131.
15.   Ibid, p. 138.
16.   'A Postscript', p. 160.
17.   'What is Universal Pragmatics?', p. 8.
18.   For an illustration and explication of the relations between Habermas's many categories of action, see *CES,* pp. 208–10 (see also pp. 40–1).
19.   'Vorbereitende Bemerkungen', p. 105.
20.   'What is Universal Pragmatics?', p. 63 (italics removed).

21. 'Wahrheitstheorien', p. 220.
22. *TP,* p. 18.
23. 'Vorbereitende Bemerkungen', p. 110.
24. The following categorisation is a modification and simplification of Habermas's account, which varies somewhat from one publication to the next.
25. 'Toward a Theory of Communicative Competence', p. 142.
26. Ibid, p. 148.
27. The exception is the claim of intelligibility, which must be fulfilled by every speech-act in the same way. See 'What is Universal Pragmatics?', p. 57.
28. 'What is Universal Pragmatics?', p. 66.
29. 'Vorbereitende Bemerkungen', p. 137.
30. Ibid, p. 140.
31. 'Wahrheitstheorien', p. 219.
32. 'Vorbereitende Bemerkungen', p. 120.
33. 'What is Universal Pragmatics?', p. 40.
34. The publications in which the performative hypothesis is expounded and defended include the following: J. R. Ross, 'On Declarative Sentences', in *Readings in English Transformational Grammar,* ed. R. A. Jacobs and P. S. Rosenbaum (Waltham, Mass.: Ginn, 1970) pp. 222–72; J. D. McCawley, 'The Role of Semantics in a Grammar', in *Universals of Language,* ed. Emmon Bach and R. T. Harms (New York: Holt, Rinehart & Winston, 1968) pp. 125–70; J. M. Sadock, *Toward a Linguistic Theory of Speech Acts* (New York: Academic Press, 1974). For a summary of the critical literature, see Gerald Gazdar, *Pragmatics: Implicature, Presupposition, and Logical Form* (New York: Academic Press, 1979) ch. 2. The performative hypothesis is also criticised by Searle in his review of *Toward a Linguistic Theory of Speech Acts* (see *Language,* 52 (1976) pp. 966–71). Searle dismisses the hypothesis as 'a breath-taking and prima facie implausible claim', a dismissal which places considerable strain on Habermas's interpretation of the principle of expressibility.
35. For discussions of the complexities involved in analysing indirect speech-acts, see some of the essays in *Syntax and Semantics, Volume 3: Speech Acts,* ed. Peter Cole and Jerry L. Morgen (New York: Academic Press, 1975); and *Proceedings of the Texas Conference on Performatives, Presuppositions, and Implicatures,* ed. Andy Rogers, Bob Wall and John P. Murphy (Arlington, Virginia: Center for Applied Linguistics, 1977).
36. Cf. *Universals of Language,* ed. Joseph H. Greenberg (Cambridge Mass.: M.I.T. Press, 1963). Critical discussions of this volume may be found in Hans-Heinrich Lieb, 'Universals of Language: Quadaries and Prospects', *Foundations of Language,* 12 (1975) pp. 471–511; and Hansjakob Seiler, 'Universals of Language', in *Proceedings of the Eleventh International Congress of Linguists,* volume I, ed. Luigi Heilmann (Bologna: Società editrice il Mulino, 1974) pp. 75–99.
37. A summary of some of the evidence is provided by T. G. R. Bower, 'The Visual World of Infants', *Scientific American,* 215 (December 1966) pp. 80–92. See also Michael A. K. Halliday, 'Early Language Learning: a Sociolinguistic Approach', in *Language and Man: Anthropological Issues,* ed. William G. McCormack and Stephen A. Wurm (The Hague: Mouton, 1976) pp. 97–124.
38. Cf. 'Some Distinctions in Universal Pragmatics', pp. 365–7.
39. See especially Paul Ricoeur, 'Creativity in Language', trans. D. Pellauer, *Philosophy Today,* 17 (1973) pp. 97–111.

40. Habermas emphasises that the application of the thesis of symmetry to representative and regulative speech-acts presupposes a reference to the organisation of action contexts, and hence 'the emancipation of discourse from the constraints of action is possible only in the context of pure communicative action' ('Wahrheitstheorien', pp. 255–6). This does not mitigate the problem because communicative action is defined so as to exclude considerations of interest and strategy, of power and persuasion; thus the latter are not thematised and suspended by the model of pure communicative action, but are simply ignored.

41. For a pertinent discussion, see Anthony Giddens, 'Habermas's Critique of Hermeneutics', especially p. 152.

42. 'Wahrheitstheorien', p. 240; the allusion is to Dewey. Weaker versions of Habermas's thesis are suggested by Thomas McCarthy in 'A Theory of Communicative Competence', pp. 149–50. However, if my interpretation of Habermas is correct, then such attenuations do not seem to obviate the present difficulty, which is that the truth of a statement is not settled when its assertion has been justified, irrespective of whether that justification is characterised as the 'meaning', 'condition' or 'criterion' of truth. As I shall suggest later, it may be possible to overcome this difficulty by distinguishing between the justified assertion of a statement and the justified assertion that a statement is true.

43. Similar arguments against a straightforward justificatory analysis of truth are offered by Michael Dummett, 'What is a Theory of Meaning (II)', in *Truth and Meaning: Essays in Semantics,* ed. Gareth Evans and John McDowell (Oxford: Clarendon Press, 1976) pp. 67–137; and Hilary Putnam, 'Reference and Understanding', in *Meaning and the Moral Sciences* (London: Routledge & Kegan Paul, 1978) pp. 97–119.

44. 'A Postscript', p. 170.

45. Ibid, p. 169.

46. Cf. 'Toward a Theory of Communicative Competence', pp. 144–6.

47. Paul Ricoeur, 'Hermeneutics and the Critique of Ideology', in his *Hermeneutics and the Human Sciences: Essays on Language, Action and Interpretation*, ed. John B. Thompson (Cambridge University Press, 1981) p. 97. For a similar reservation expressed in more Anglo-Saxon terms, see Steven Lukes, 'The Critical Theory Trip', *Political Studies*, 25 (1977) pp. 408–12.

48. *LC*, pp. 111–17.

49. See my *Critical Hermeneutics: A Study in the Thought of Paul Ricoeur and Jürgen Habermas* (Cambridge University Press, 1981).

50. The seminal essay for current work on truth-conditional semantics is Donald Davidson, 'Meaning and Truth', *Synthese,* 17 (1967) pp. 304–23. Some of the issues raised by this essay are pursued by the papers in *Truth and Meaning*; the contribution by Michael Dummett is particularly provocative. It may be objected that to grant truth a privileged position in the analysis of meaning is to begin from a starting-point which is even narrower than Habermas's. Perhaps this objection could be averted if, first, principles could be established which would show how utterances in different moods were related to indicative sentences, and, second, a notion of truth could be formulated which would be freed from reference to a pre-given object domain.

51. Cf. Mary Hesse, 'Theory and Value in the Social Sciences', in *Action and Interpretation: Studies in the Philosophy of the Social Sciences*, ed. Christopher Hookway and Philip Pettit (Cambridge University Press, 1978) pp. 1–16.

7 **Of gods and demons: Habermas and practical reason (Steven Lukes)**
1. *LC*, p. 111.
2. J. Habermas, 'Wahrheitstheorien', in *Wirklichkeit und Reflexion: Walter Schulz zum 60. Geburtstag*, ed. H. Fahrenbach (Pfullingen: Neske, 1973), p. 226. 'I suspect', he adds, 'that the justification of the validity claims contained in the recommendation of norms of action and of evaluation can be just as discursively tested as the justification of the validity claims implied in assertions. Of course the grounding of just *(richtigen)* commands and evaluations differs in the structure of argumentation from the grounding of true statements. The logical conditions under which a rationally motivated consensus can be attained differ as between practical and theoretical discourse' (ibid, pp. 226–7). Habermas uses the term *'richtig'* in such a way as to imply that there is a truth of the matter as to whether norms, commands or evaluations are *richtig* or not.
3. Ibid, pp. 239–40.
4. *CES*, pp. 202–3.
5. Ibid, p. 200. On this point see R. J. Bernstein, *The Restructuring of Social and Political Theory* (New York: Harcourt Brace Jovanovich, 1976).
6. *LC*, p. 107. The passage by Max Weber, to which Habermas refers, is the following: 'What man will take upon himself the attempt to "refute scientifically" the ethic of the Sermon on the Mount? For instance, the sentence, "resist no evil", or the image of turning the other cheek? And yet it is clear, in mundane perspective, that this is an ethic of undignified conduct; one has to choose between the religious dignity which this ethic confers and the dignity of manly conduct which preaches something quite different; "resist evil – lest you be co-responsible for an overpowering evil". According to our ultimate standpoint, the one is the Devil and the other the God, and the individual has to decide which is God for him and which is the Devil. And so it goes throughout all the orders of life' (*From Max Weber: Essays in Sociology*, trans. H. H. Gerth and C. Wright Mills (London: Routledge & Kegan Paul, 1949), p. 148). For a no less eloquent statement of the same viewpoint see Leszek Kolakowski's 'Ethics without a Moral Code', *Triquarterly*, 22 (1971) esp. pp. 172–4.
7. *CES*, pp. 186, 185, 184.
8. F. Engels, *Anti-Dühring* (Moscow: Foreign Languages Publishing House, 1959).
9. K. Kautsky, *Ethics and the Materialist Conception of History* (Chicago: Charles H. Kerr & Co.) p. 160.
10. L. Trotsky, *Their Morals and Ours* (New York: Pathfinder Press, 1972) p. 37.
11. For this interpretation of Lukács and Marx, see L. Kolakowski, *Main Currents of Marxism*, 3 vols (Oxford: Clarendon Press, 1978).
12. M. Horkheimer, *Critical Theory* (New York: Seabury Press, 1973) p. 213.
13. J. Habermas, 'Toward a Theory of Communicative Competence', *Inquiry*, 13 (1970) p. 372.
14. They are admirably treated in John B. Thompson's essay in this volume (ch. 6).
15. *CES*, pp. 188, 198.
16. *LC*, p. 113.
17. Ibid, pp. 107–8.
18. Ibid, p. 89.
19. *TRS*, p. 75.
20. Ibid.
21. *CES*, p. 186.

22. J. Rawls, *A Theory of Justice* (Oxford: Clarendon Press, 1972) p. 261.
23. *LC,* p. 111; *CES,* pp. 202, 188.
24. *LC,* p. 114.
25. Ibid.
26. Ibid, pp. 117, 113.
27. T. McCarthy, *The Critical Theory of Jürgen Habermas* (London: Hutchinson, 1978) p. 306.
28. *LC,* p. 114.
29. This is one of many interesting points of convergence with Rawls, who also stresses the importance of publicity: see *A Theory of Justice,* pp. 177ff.
30. 'Wahrheitstheorien', p. 245.
31. *LC,* p. 108.
32. 'Wahrheitstheorien', p. 245.
33. In what follows, I am indebted to the discussion of this question in J. L. Mackie, *Ethics: Inventing Right and Wrong* (Harmondsworth: Penguin, 1977) ch. 4.
34. Ibid, pp. 91–2.
35. *A Theory of Justice,* pp. 226–30. Rawls even claims that 'to see our place in society from the perspective of this position is to see it *sub specie aeternitatis*: it is to regard the human situation not only from all social but also from all temporal points of view' (ibid, p. 587). Ronald Dworkin, similarly, has argued that the constitutive political morality of liberalism rests on the idea that 'government must be neutral on what might be called the question of the good life', that 'political decisions must be, as far as is possible, independent of any particular conception of the good life, or of what gives value to life' ('Liberalism', in *Public and Private Morality,* ed. S. Hampshire (Cambridge University Press, 1978) p. 127).
36. *A Theory of Justice,* p. 221.
37. J. Rawls, 'Fairness to Goodness', *Philosophical Review,* 84 (1975) p. 539.
38. *A Theory of Justice,* p. 14.
39. Mackie, *Ethics,* p. 93.
40. For an argument in support of this claim, see the present author's *Essays in Social Theory* (London: Macmillan, 1977) ch. 10.
41. *LC,* p. 89.
42. Ibid, p. 112.
43. D. Hume, *A Treatise of Human Nature,* book III, part II, section II, ed. L. A. Selby-Bigge (Oxford: Clarendon Press, 1888) p. 495. For an interesting discussion of 'morality as compromise', see Arthur Kuflick, 'Morality and Compromise', in *Compromise in Ethics, Law and Politics: Nomos XXI,* ed. J. R. Pennock and J. W. Chapman, this being the *Yearbook of the American Society for Political and Legal Philosophy* (New York University Press, 1979).
44. *CES,* pp. 198–9.
45. *LC,* p. 108.
46. Mackie, *Ethics,* p. 99.
47. *LC,* p. 100.
48. J. Habermas, *Zur Rekonstruktion des Historischen Materialismus* (Frankfurt: Suhrkamp, 1976) p. 205 ['History and Evolution', trans. D. J. Parent, *Telos,* 39 (Spring 1979) p. 8]; *LC,* p. 95.
49. *CES,* pp. 99, 102, 110.
50. Kohlberg's six stages of moral consciousness are: (1) punishment-obedience orientation, involving maximisation of pleasure through obedience; (2) instrumental hedonism, involving maximisation of pleasure through exchange of equivalents; (3) 'good-boy/nice-girl' orientation, involving concrete

morality of gratifying interactions; (4) law-and-order orientation, involving concrete morality of a customary system of norms; (5) social-contractual legalism, involving civil liberties and public welfare; and (6) ethical-principles orientation, involving moral freedom.

51. *CES*, pp. 116–17.
52. Ibid, p. 120.
53. Ibid, p. 156.
54. L. Kohlberg, 'From Is to Ought: How to Commit the Naturalistic Fallacy and Get Away with It in the Study of Moral Development', in *Cognitive Development and Epistemology,* ed. T. Mischel (New York: Academic Press, 1971) pp. 153, 176.
55. Ibid, pp. 208, 218.
56. Ibid, pp. 214–15.
57. *LC*, p. 95.
58. See the critique of Kohlberg by William Alston in *Cognitive Development and Epistemology.* Also see P. R. Dasen, 'Cross-cultural Piagetian Research: a Summary', *Cross Cultural Psychology,* 3 (1972) pp. 23–40.
59. Alston, in *Cognitive Development and Epistemology,* p. 275.
60. *CES*, p. 90.
61. Rawls claims support from the ideas of Piaget and Kohlberg, in seeking to indicate 'the major steps whereby a person would acquire an understanding of an attachment to the principles of justice as he grows up in this particular form of a well-ordered society' (*A Theory of Justice,* p. 461; see sections 69–72). On the other hand, *contra* Kohlberg, Rawls is clear that the claimed superiority of his theory of justice 'is a philosophical question and cannot, I believe, be established by the psychological theory of development alone' (ibid, p. 462). Kohlberg, reciprocally, sees Rawls's theory as consonant with his own.
62. L. Kohlberg, 'Justice as Reversibility', in *Philosophy, Politics and Society,* 5th series, ed. P. Laslett and J. Fishkin (Oxford: Blackwell, 1979) p. 266.
63. Ibid, p. 262.
64. *CES*, p. 90.
65. Ibid, p. 110.

8 Labour and interaction (Anthony Giddens)

1. J. Habermas, 'Historical Materialism and the Development of Normative Structures', in *CES*, p. 95.
2. See J. Habermas, 'Remarks on Hegel's Jena *Philosophy of Mind*', in *TP,* p. 168; Karl Löwith, *From Hegel to Nietzsche,* trans. D. E. Green (New York: Anchor Press, 1967).
3. *Hegel's Philosophy of Mind,* trans. W. Wallace and A. V. Müller (Oxford: Clarendon Press, 1971), and *System der Sittlichkeit,* ed. G. Lasson (Hamburg: F. Meiner, 1967).
4. 'Remarks on Hegel's Jena *Philosophy of Mind*', in *TP,* pp. 153–4.
5. Ibid, p. 168.
6. *KHI,* pp. 28–34.
7. Ibid, p. 34.
8. Ibid, p. 45.
9. Habermas has spoken in a recent interview of the strong impression that the *Dialectic of Enlightenment* made upon him in his early intellectual career (interview with Habermas by Detlef Korster and Willem van Reijen, Max-Planck-Institut, Starnberg, 23 March 1979, p. 6).

10. 'Technology and Science as "Ideology"', in *TRS*. This essay also makes plain the significance of certain ideas of Max Weber for Marcuse and Habermas.
11. Ibid, pp. 91–2.
12. Durkheim distinguished between what he called 'utilitarian', or technical, and 'moral' sanctions. In the latter, the sanction is defined socially, in the former by objects and events in nature. Emile Durkheim, 'Determination of the Moral Fact', in *Sociology and Philosophy* (London: Cohen & West, 1953).
13. 'Technology and Science as "Ideology"', p. 105.
14. 'Historical Materialism and the Development of Normative Structures', pp. 97–8.
15. Habermas makes various qualifications to this assertion, however. See *CES*, pp. 102–3 and 110–11.
16. 'Toward a Reconstruction of Historical Materialism', in *CES*, p. 137.
17. See my 'Habermas's Critique of Hermeneutics', in *Studies in Social and Political Theory* (London: Hutchinson, 1977).
18. Cf. Göran Therborn, 'Habermas: a New Eclectic', *New Left Review*, 63 (1970).
19. Thomas McCarthy, *The Critical Theory of Jürgen Habermas* (London: Hutchinson, 1978) pp. 24–6.
20. See, for example, his portrayal of the two concepts in 'Historical Materialism and the Development of Normative Structures', pp. 117–19.
21. J. Habermas, 'A Postscript to *Knowledge and Human Interests*', trans. C. Lenhardt, *Philosophy of the Social Sciences*, 3 (1973).
22. As I have tried to do in *Central Problems in Social Theory* (London: Macmillan, 1979) pp. 53–9.
23. Ibid, *passim*.
24. Cf. my *New Rules of Sociological Method* (London: Hutchinson, 1976) pp. 68–9 and 86–91.
25. I have made the same argument previously in 'Habermas's Critique of Hermeneutics'.
26. *Central Problems in Social Theory*, pp. 88–94.
27. J. Habermas, *Zur Logik der Sozialwissenschaften* (Frankfurt: Suhrkamp, 1970) pp. 170ff.
28. Talcott Parsons, *Societies: Evolutionary and Comparative Perspectives* (Englewood Cliffs, N.J.: Prentice-Hall, 1966).
29. Cf. *Central Problems in Social Theory*, pp. 101–3 and *passim*.
30. 'Toward a Reconstruction of Historical Materialism', pp. 143–4.

9 Habermas's theory of social evolution (Michael Schmid)

1. Habermas develops his ideas in the following works: 'Theorie der Gesellschaft oder Sozialtechnologie? Eine Auseinandersetzung mit Niklas Luhmann', in J. Habermas and N. Luhmann, *Theorie der Gesellschaft oder Sozialtechnologie – Was leistet die Systemforschung?* (Frankfurt: Suhrkamp, 1971) pp. 142–290, especially pp. 270–86; *Legitimationsprobleme im Spätkapitalismus* (Frankfurt: Suhrkamp, 1973); *Zur Rekonstruktion des Historischen Materialismus* (Frankfurt: Suhrkamp, 1976). For remarks on the programmatic character of his theory, see *Legitimationsprobleme*, p. 7 [*LC*, p. xxv]; *Rekonstruktion*, pp. 9, 44 [*CES*, pp. 95, 128].
2. Cf. *Rekonstruktion*, pp. 131ff, 156 [*CES*, p. 141], 188 [*CES*, pp. 171–2].
3. Cf. J. Habermas, *Erkenntnis und Interesse* (Frankfurt: Suhrkamp, 1968); 'Vorbereitende Bemerkungen zu einer Theorie der kommunikativen Kompetenz', in *Theorie der Gesellschaft oder Sozialtechnologie*, pp. 101–41; 'Was heisst Universalpragmatik?', in *Sprachpragmatik und Philosophie*, ed. K.–O.

Apel (Frankfurt: Suhrkamp, 1976) pp. 174–272 [*CES*, pp. 1–68]; *Rekonstruktion*, pp. 12ff [*CES*, pp. 98ff], 132ff.

4.   Cf. *Rekonstruktion*, pp. 32ff, 152ff [*CES*, pp. 117ff, 138ff]; *Legitimationsprobleme*, pp. 16, 19 [*LC*, pp. 14, 16].

5.   *Rekonstruktion*, pp. 156, 25 [*CES*, pp. 141–2, 111].

6.   *Legitimationsprobleme*, p. 12 [*LC*, p. 3].

7.   *Rekonstruktion*, p. 154 [*CES*, p. 140].

8.   Ibid, pp. 12, 30 [*CES*, pp. 98, 116].

9.   Ibid, p. 133.

10. Ibid, p. 155 [*CES*, p. 141]; *Legitimationsprobleme*, p. 28 [*LC*, p. 15].

11. *Rekonstruktion*, pp. 67, 90 [*CES*, pp. 73–4, 220–1], 134.

12. Cf. ibid, pp. 14, 67ff [*CES*, pp. 100, 73ff].

13. Cf. ibid, pp. 36ff [*CES*, pp. 121ff], 134ff; 160ff, 169ff, 176 [*CES*, pp. 145ff, 154ff, 160].

14. Cf. ibid, pp. 35 [*CES*, p. 120], 134.

15. Cf. ibid, pp. 136ff, 171ff [*CES*, pp. 156ff], 232 ['History and Evolution', trans. D. J. Parent, *Telos*, 39 (Spring 1979) p. 29]. In making this assertion Habermas generally relies on the arguments of K. Eder, *Zur Entstehung staatlich organisierter Gesellschaften* (Frankfurt: Suhrkamp, 1976) and R. Döbert, *Systemtheorie und die Entwicklung religiöser Deutungssysteme* (Frankfurt: Suhrkamp, 1973). As we shall see, I view this claim with great scepticism.

16. See H. Furth, *Intelligenz und Erkennen* (Frankfurt: Suhrkamp, 1972) [*Piaget and Knowledge* (Englewood Cliffs, N.J.: Prentice-Hall, 1969)]; L. Kohlberg, *Zur kognitiven Entwicklung des Kindes* (Frankfurt: Suhrkamp, 1974); J. Piaget, *Das moralische Urteil beim Kind* (Frankfurt: Suhrkamp, 1973) [*The Moral Judgement of the Child* (Glencoe, Ill.: Free Press, 1948)].

17. *Rekonstruktion*, pp. 172–3 [*CES*, p. 156].

18. Ibid, pp. 172ff [*CES*, pp. 157ff].

19. On the method of 'reconstruction', see *Theorie der Gesellschaft oder Sozialtechnologie*, pp. 172ff; *Rekonstruktion*, pp. 215ff ['History and Evolution', pp. 16ff].

20. *Rekonstruktion*, pp. 185–6 [*CES*, pp. 168–9]. On p. 216 ['History and Evolution', p. 17], Habermas seems to view his own proposal rather more sceptically.

21. Ibid, p. 35 [*CES*, p. 120].

22. Cf. ibid.

23. Ibid, p. 36 [*CES*, p. 121].

24. Cf. ibid, pp. 36 [*CES*, p. 121], 133, where Habermas talks in the same sense of a 'domain-specific theory of learning' for the developmental-logical conversion processes between personality and societal systems.

25. Cf. ibid, pp. 169ff, 176 [*CES*, pp. 154ff, 160].

26. Cf. ibid, p. 176 [*CES*, p. 160].

27. Cf. ibid, pp. 235 ['History and Evolution', p. 32], 36ff [*CES*, pp. 121ff].ff].

28. Ibid, pp. 235 ['History and Evolution', p. 32], 40 [*CES*, p. 125].

29. Cf. ibid, p. 36 [*CES*, p. 121].

30. Ibid, pp. 168–9 [*CES*, pp. 153–4].

31. Ibid, p. 234 ['History and Evolution', p. 31].

32. Cf. ibid, pp. 169, 179 [*CES*, pp. 154, 162–3], 235 ['History and Evolution', p. 32].

33. Cf. ibid, pp. 36, 176 [*CES*, pp. 121, 160], 242ff ['History and Evolution', pp. 38ff].

34. Ibid, p. 176 [*CES*, p. 160].

35. Ibid, p. 35 [*CES*, p. 120].
36. Ibid, p. 131.
37. Ibid, p. 155 [*CES*, p. 141].
38. Ibid, p. 232 ['History and Evolution', p. 29]. In a similar manner, Habermas requires a genetic explanation for the formation of the structures of consciousness (see ibid, p. 142).
39. Ibid, p. 234 ['History and Evolution', p. 31].
40. Ibid, p. 233 ['History and Evolution', p. 30].
41. Cf. ibid, p. 169 [*CES*, p. 153].
42. Cf. *Legitimationsprobleme*, pp. 33–4 [*LC*, pp. 18–20]; *Rekonstruktion*, pp. 138–9.
43. Cf. *Rekonstruktion*, pp. 145, 173 [*CES*, pp. 131, 157–8].
44. In our article, 'System und Evolution: Metatheoretische Vorbemerkungen zu einer soziologischen Evolutionstheorie' (*Soziale Welt*, Jg. 26 (1975) pp. 386ff), B. Giesen and I have already pointed out that in its exact sense an evolutionary theory is only a partially interpreted calculus which still requires to be interpreted in terms of empirical co-ordinates.
45. This conception of theory refers, of course, to the early positivist understanding of theory, as in H. Feigl's 'The "Orthodox" View of Theories: Remarks in Defense as well as Critique', in *Analyses of Theories and Methods of Physics and Psychology*, ed. M. Radner and S. Winokur (Minneapolis: University of Minnesota Press, 1970) pp. 3–16. Apart from one or two drawbacks, this conception does have the merit of making clear why a fundamental examination of theoretical assumptions requires an altogether *different* theory, or, as Feyerabend recently said, an altogether different 'tradition'. See P.K. Feyerabend, *Wissenschaft für freie Menschen* (Frankfurt: Suhrkamp, 1978) [*Science in a Free Society* (London: New Left Books, 1978)]; also the same author's *Der wissenschaftstheoretische Realismus und die Autorität der Wissenschaften* (Braunschweig: Vieweg & Sohn, 1978). Where a fundamental examination is possible without a 'break from tradition', we are in fact dealing with a reciprocal critique by two applied versions of one and the same theory.
46. In the same way it is possible to put an end to the fragmentation of the sociological tradition into different schools and to show that Durkheim, Weber and Marx are representatives of the same paradigm. We also avoid the error of either failing to take these thinkers into consideration when defining paradigms, or of classifying them according to eccentric criteria, as is the case with G. Ritzer's *Sociology: A Multiple Paradigm Science* (Boston: Allyn & Bacon, 1975). For a contribution in this direction, see my 'Soziologische Evolutionstheorie: Ein makrosoziologishes Erklärungsmodell' (manuscript, 1979).
47. See B. Giesen and M. Schmid, 'Methodologisher Individualismus und Reduktionismus', in *Psychologie statt Soziologie?*, ed. G. Eberlein and H.-J. von Kontratowitz (Frankfurt: Campus, 1977) pp. 24–47.
48. Cf. *Rekonstruktion*, pp. 21, 36 [*CES*, pp. 106–7, 121], 136; 164 [*CES*, pp. 148–9], 248 ['History and Evolution', p. 42].
49. S. Toulmin has offered one such explanation in his *Human Understanding, vol. 1: The Collective Use and Evolution of Concepts* (Princeton University Press, 1972). Durkheim's theory of the *modus operandi* of tradition also contains apt comments on the subject; see his *Über die Teilung der sozialen Arbeit* (Frankfurt: Suhrkamp, 1978) pp. 332ff [*The Division of Labor in Society*, trans. G. Simpson (New York: Free Press, 1933)]. Habermas's theory of evolutionary learning *could* of course be understood in this way, if it abandoned its concern with developmental logic.

50. See M. Polanyi, 'The Stability of Beliefs', *British Journal for the Philosophy of Science,* 3 (1952) pp. 217ff.
51. I am no specialist in the development of world-views, but in K. Eder's *Entstehung staatlich organisierter Gesellschaften,* I am unable to find the claim that 'primitive man' was incapable of reflection. Equally, I am unable to discover in Lévi-Strauss's work an unequivocal statement to the effect that 'primitive man' possessed only a reduced capacity for thought; on the contrary, I find unconcealed admiration for the intellectual achievements of native tribes *(Naturvölker).* I may, however, be mistaken in this.
52. H. Vaihinger, *Die Philosophie des Als-Ob* (Leipzig: F. Meiner, 1924) p. 83.
53. Cf. *Rekonstruktion,* pp. 38 [*CES,* p. 123], 233, 249 ['History and Evolution', pp. 30, 43].
54. Thus the theory of biological selection treats mutations as 'instantaneous', and the Hardy-Weinberg law of population genetics even ends up by presupposing that no mutation occurs. Cf. M. Ruse, *The Philosophy of Biology* (London: Hutchinson, 1973) pp. 13, 15. Conversely, molecular genetics deals only with the chemical processes which facilitate inheritance and does not seek to explain the occurrence of mutations. See D. Hull, *Philosophy of Biological Science* (Englewood Cliffs, N.J.: Prentice-Hall, 1974) p. 23 and *passim.*
55. Cf. *Rekonstruktion,* p. 38 [*CES,* p. 123].
56. This follows logically from the concept of developmental logic and from the assumption that developmental-logical processes are accomplished as 'accumulation'. See *Legitimationsprobleme,* p. 22 [*LC,* p. 10].
57. Cf. *Rekonstruktion,* pp. 179ff [*CES,* pp. 163ff].
58. It goes back as far as Max Weber; see M. Weber, *Gesammelte Aufsätze zur Wissenschaftslehre* (Tübingen: Mohr, 1968) pp. 518ff. Substantially the same argument can be found in J. D. Y. Peel's *Herbert Spencer: The Evolution of a Sociologist* (New York: Basic Books, 1971) pp. 131ff. Peel argues against Herbert Spencer's attempt to justify the adoption of ethical standpoints through the use of an evolutionary theory. Spencer came upon the same insoluble problems we have shown to be present in Habermas's theory of evolution.
59. For a contrasting view, see N. Luhmann, 'System theoretische Argumentationen: Eine Entgegnung auf Jürgen Habermas', in *Theorie der Gesellschaft oder Sozialtechnologie,* pp. 369ff.
60. This is another reason why I do not find the evolutionary theories of Bellah and Döbert empirically convincing. See R. S. Bellah, 'Religiöse Evolution', in *Religion und gesellschaftliche Entwicklung,* ed. C. Seytarth and W. M. Sprondel (Frankfurt, 1973) pp. 267ff; and R. Döbert, *Systemtheorie und die Entwicklung religiöser Deutungssysteme* (Frankfurt: Suhrkamp, 1973). Both should be classified as theories of 'general evolution'.
61. See S. Toulmin, *Human Understanding,* vol. 1; T. S. Kuhn, *The Structure of Scientific Revolutions* (University of Chicago Press, 1962); P. K. Feyerabend, *Wissenschaft für freie Menschen,* and *Der wissenschaftstheoretische Realismus und die Autorität der Wissenschaften.*
62. See K. R. Popper, *Conjectures and Refutations: The Growth of Scientific Knowledge* (New York: Basic Books, 1965) pp. 233ff, 391ff.
63. See I. Lakatos, 'History of Science and its Rational Reconstruction', in *Boston Studies in the Philosophy of Science,* vol. 3, ed. R. C. Buck and R. S. Cohen (Dordrecht: D. Reidel, 1970) p. 118.
64. D. Miller, 'Popper's Qualitative Theory of Verisimilitude', *British Journal for the Philosophy of Science,* 25 (1974) pp. 166–77; P. Tichy, 'On Popper's

Definitions of Verisimilitude', *British Journal for the Philosophy of Science,* 25 (1974) pp. 155–60.

65. See J. H. Steward, *Theory of Cultural Change* (Urbana: University of Illinois Press, 1972); M. Sahlins, *Stone Age Economics* (Chicago: Aldine, 1972). Max Weber's explanation of the structural change in the constitution of ancient Israel is a clear indication that it is in principle possible to do without a developmental logic. The same applies to his investigation of the decline of classical culture. See Weber's *Gesammelte Aufsätze zur Religionssoziologie,* Bd 3, (Tübingen: Mohr, 1920) pp. 1ff, 87ff; and his 'Die sozialen Gründe des Untergangs der antiken Kultur', in *Soziologie – Weltgeschichtliche Analysen-Politik* (Stuttgart: Kröner, 1956) pp. 1ff. Weber's thesis on Protestantism manages without a developmental logic, as does Durkheim's theory of structural changes in segmented societies. An excellent example of sensible work in this field is D. Goetze's 'Entwicklungsgesellschaft und Kulturanthropologie: Zu einer Protheorie der Entwicklung', *Die Dritte Welt,* Jg 6 (1978) pp. 323–44.

66. Cf. *Rekonstruktion,* p. 250 ['History and Evolution', p. 44].

67. Cf. ibid, p. 180 [*CES,* pp. 163–4]; *Legitimationsprobleme,* pp. 194ff [*LC,* pp. 142ff].

68. See *Erkenntnis und Interesse,* pp. 244, 262ff [*KHI,* pp. 197–8, 214ff]; and *Technik und Wissenschaft als 'Ideologie'* (Frankfurt: Suhrkamp, 1968) p. 158. I should be happy if R. Bernstein (*The Restructuring of Social and Political Theory* (Oxford: Blackwell, 1976) p. 218) were correct when he understands Habermas to believe that there exists no direct link between the conditions of political decision and an emancipatory theory. He bases his interpretation, as I have done, on references to Habermas's own writings; see *Theorie und Praxis* (Frankfurt: Suhrkamp, 1968) p. 33 [*TP,* p. 28].

10 Crisis tendencies, legitimation and the state (David Held)

1. See Boris Frankel, 'The State of the State after Leninism', *Theory and Society,* 7 (1979) pp. 199–242.
2. *TRS,* p. 101.
3. Ibid, pp. 63–4, 106–7.
4. Ibid, p. 105.
5. See *LC,* part II.
6. Ibid, ch. 4
7. Cf., for example, James O'Connor, *The Fiscal Crisis of the State* (New York: St. Martin's Press, 1973); Andrew Schonfield, *Modern Capitalism* (London: Oxford University Press, 1965); and the work of Claus Offe on the capitalist state, e.g. 'Political Authority and Class Structure', in *Critical Sociology,* ed. P. Connerton (Harmondsworth: Penguin, 1976) pp. 388–421.
8. *LC,* p. 49.
9. Ibid, pp. 49–50.
10. Ibid, p. 69.
11. Ibid, p. 73.
12. Ibid, p. 75.
13. Ibid, pp. 81–4.
14. Ibid, pp. 84–92.
15. Ibid, pp. 90, 117ff.
16. Ibid, p. 4. By contrast, Habermas speaks of system integration 'with a view to the specific steering-performances of a self-regulated *system.* Social systems are considered here from the point of view of their capacity to maintain their boundaries and their continued existence by mastering the complexity of an

inconstant environment' (ibid, p. 4). Both perspectives, 'life-world' and 'system' are, Habermas stresses, important.

17. Ibid, pp. 4–5.

18. Ibid, p. 3 (my emphasis).

19. Cf., for example, his discussion in *Zur Logik der Sozialwissenschaften* (Frankfurt: Suhrkamp, 1970) pp. 181–2; and *LC*, pp. 75–6.

20. See Anthony Giddens, *Central Problems in Social Theory: Action, Structure and Contradiction in Social Analysis* (London: Macmillan, 1979) especially pp. 85–7, 101–3, for an elaboration of this point.

21. Habermas explicates this concept of legitimacy in 'Legitimation Problems in the Modern State', in *CES*, pp. 178–205. My argument owes a good deal to Michael Mann, 'The Ideology of Intellectuals and Other People in the Development of Capitalism', in *Stress and Contradiction in Modern Capitalism*, ed. Leon N. Lindberg *et al.* (Lexington, Mass.: D. C. Heath, 1975), and to Giddens, *Central Problems in Social Theory*, ch. 2.

22. But even a crisis of legitimacy among some of these groups, it should be stressed, can leave a social system quite stable so long as the system's coercive organisations remain effective. See Theda Skocpol, 'State and Revolution: Old Regimes and Revolutionary Crises in France, Russia, and China', *Theory and Society*, 7 (1979).

23. Cf. *LC*, p. 22.

24. Cf. Thomas McCarthy, *The Critical Theory of Jürgen Habermas* (Cambridge, Mass.: M.I.T. Press, 1978) p. 379.

25. Habermas has stressed the necessity for unifying systems-theoretic perspectives with insights from other approaches. But he has not, as yet, formulated an integrated framework for inquiry. This task appears to be the topic of his current research. But until it is published the methodological framework of his work will remain unclear. Cf. 'Toward a Reconstruction of Historical Materialism' and 'Historical Materialism and the Development of Normative Structures', in *CES*, especially pp. 125, 169; and *Zur Logik der Sozialwissenschaften*, pp. 164–84.

26. Cf. Giddens, *Central Problems in Social Theory*, p. 87.

27. Habermas argues that with the development of the liberal-capitalist social formation the economic sub-system took over certain socially integrative tasks, i.e. integration was accomplished in part through exchange relations. But although he emphasises the importance of understanding the ways in which social integration achieved through norms and values is replaced with a system integration operating through exchange (and the ideology of the exchange of equivalents), he also emphasises how the loyalty and support of the proletariat to the political order is dependent upon pre-capitalist traditions. See *LC*, pp. 20–6; and 'Legitimation Problems in the Modern State', in *CES*, p. 190.

28. See, for example, Michael Mann, *Consciousness and Action Among the Western Working Class* (London: Macmillan, 1973); and Anthony Giddens, *The Class Structure of the Advanced Societies* (London: Hutchinson, 1977).

29. Mann, 'The Ideology of Intellectuals and Other People in the Development of Capitalism', p. 276. A strong case can be made that the only groups highly committed to dominant ideologies are those that created them, i.e. the dominant classes and groups. See Nicholas Abercrombie and Bryan S. Turner, 'The Dominant Ideology Thesis', *British Journal of Sociology*, 29 (1978).

30. Cf. Michael Mann, 'The Social Cohesion of Liberal Democracy', *American Sociological Review*, 35 (1970); and Giddens, *The Class Structure of the Advanced Societies*, ch. 11.

31. See Habermas's early work, especially *Toward A Rational Society* and *Strukturwandel der Öffentlichkeit,* for important analyses of the expansion of instrumental reason into everyday life. *Toward a Rational Society* is a considerable aid to understanding the impersonal nature of domination.
32. Cf. Herbert Marcuse, 'Some Social Implications of Modern Technology', *Studies in Philosophy and Social Science,* 9 (1941); and Harry Braverman, *Labor and Monopoly Capital: the Degradation of Work in the Twentieth Century* (New York: Monthly Review Press, 1974).
33. Marcuse, 'Some Social Implications of Modern Technology', pp. 430–1.
34. Stanley Aronowitz, *False Promises: the Shaping of American Working Class Consciousness* (New York: McGraw-Hill, 1973) p. 408. Although Aronowitz focuses on factors that have affected the American working class, his analysis has more general implications.
35. Cf. Aronowitz, *False Promises,* ch. 4; and Mann, *Consciousness and Action Among the Western Working Class,* especially chs 2 and 3.
36. Cf. *LC,* pp. 38–9.
37. For a more detailed analysis of Adorno's views see my *Introduction to Critical Theory: Horkheimer to Habermas* (London: Hutchinson, 1980) ch. 3.
38. Marcuse, 'Some Social Implications of Modern Technology', p. 424.
39. The mode in which the latter are understood can be traced back, in part, to schooling, learning to labour, and to the culture industry – to socialisation processes which embody ideas and theories about life which do not coincide with many people's own accounts of the 'realities of working life'. Cf., for example, Paul Willis, *Learning to Labour: How Working Class Kids Get Working Class Jobs* (Westmead: Saxon House, 1977).
40. See Mann, 'The Social Cohesion of Liberal Democracy', pp. 436–7.
41. It might be objected that Habermas's case could be made stronger by reference to his theory of social evolution and his theory of the logic of development of normative structures. But these theories cannot, in my view, be drawn upon until they are more fully elaborated.
42. Gianfranco Poggi, *The Development of the Modern State: A Sociological Introduction* (London: Hutchinson, 1978) ch. 5.
43. Immanuel Wallerstein, *The Modern World-System* (New York: Academic Press, 1974). Habermas recognises the importance of this issue for understanding 'the *external aspect* of the new [modern] state structures', but he does not explicate their relevance for the logic of crisis tendencies.
44. See Theda Skocpal, *States and Social Revolutions: A Comparative Analysis of France, Russia and China* (Cambridge University Press, 1979). The significance of analysing state forms – focusing, in particular, on the changing relation between parliament and administrative branches – has recently been stressed in the debate over the development of corporatism. See, for example, Bob Jessop, 'Corporatism, Parliamentarism and Social Democracy', in *Patterns of Corporatist Intermediation,* ed. P. Schmitter and G. Lehmbruch (Beverly Hills: Sage, 1979).
45. See *LC,* pp. 111-17.
46. Ibid, p. 113.
47. Ibid, p. 117.
48. *TP,* p. 32 (translation modified).
49. Cf. Frankel, 'The State of the State after Leninism', pp. 232–9.
50. A translation of this interview has appeared in *New Left Review,* 115 (May–June 1979).

11 Critical sociology and authoritarian state socialism (Andrew Arato)

1. J. Habermas, *Theorie und Praxis* (Neuwied: Luchterhand, 1967) pp. 161–3 [*TP*, pp. 184–6].
2. In later editions of this essay, the partial exception in the Polish context of Modzelewski's and Kuron's 'Open Letter' is noted.
3. J. Habermas, 'Theorie der Gesellschaft oder Sozialtechnologie', in J. Habermas and N. Luhmann, *Theorie der Gesellschaft oder Sozialtechnologie – Was leistet die Systemforschung?* (Frankfurt: Suhrkamp, 1971) pp. 265–7.
4. *LC*, p. 17.
5. J. Habermas, 'On Social Identity', *Telos*, 19 (Spring 1974).
6. *CES*, pp. 152, 158.
7. K. Eder, 'Zum Problem der logischen Periodisierung von Produktionsweisen', in *Theorien des Historischen Materialismus*, ed. U. Jaeggi and H. Honneth (Frankfurt: Suhrkamp, 1977) pp. 511, 520.
8. D. Lockwood, 'Social Integration and System Integration', in *Explorations in Social Change*, ed. Zollschan and Hirsch (Boston: Houghton Mifflin, 1964); and F. Parkin, 'System Contradiction and Political Transformation', *European Journal of Sociology*, 13 (1972).
9. N. Mouzelis, 'Social and System Integration', *British Journal of Sociology*, 25 (1974).
10. *LC*, p. 4; see also pp. 7–8, 16.
11. J. Habermas, 'History and Evolution', trans. D. J. Parent, *Telos*, 39 (Spring 1979) pp. 144, 148, 156.
12. *LC*, pp. 17ff.
13. Cf. A. Arato, 'Systems of Reproduction and Histories of the State', *Telos*, 35 (Spring 1978), under the heading of 'Understanding Bureaucratic Centralism'.
14. C. Offe, 'Crisis of Crisis Management', *International Journal of Politics*, 6 (1976) p. 33.
15. C. Offe, *Strukturprobleme des kapitalistischen Staates* (Frankfurt: Suhrkamp, 1972); J. Cohen, 'System and Class: the Subversion of Emancipation', *Social Research*, 45 (Winter 1978), and 'The Problem of Class Analysis in Advanced Capitalism', New York, New School for Social Research dissertation, 1979.
16. E. Fraenkel, *The Dual State* (New York: Oxford University Press, 1941).
17. The categories used, in a slightly altered form, are drawn primarily but not exclusively from recent works by M. Rakovski, 'Marxism and Soviet Societies', *Capital and Class*, 1 (Spring 1977); M. Rakovski, *Towards an East European Marxism* (London: Allison & Busby, 1978), an incomplete translation of *Le Marxisme face aux pays de l'est* (Paris: Savelli, 1977); G. Konrad and I. Szelenyi, *The Intellectuals on the Road to Class Power* (New York: Harcourt Brace Jovanovich, 1979); F. Feher and A. Heller, 'Forms of Equality', *Telos*, 32 (Summer 1977); and F. Feher, 'The Dictatorship over Needs', *Telos*, 35 (Spring 1978). In my opinion all of these suffer slighty from a one-sided extension of the structural principle of politics, culture or economy to the whole.
18. C. Offe, 'Crisis of Crisis Management', pp. 35–6.
19. M. Lewin, *Political Undercurrents in Soviet Economic Debates* (Princeton University Press, 1974); and R. Laird, '"Developed" Socialist Society and the Dialectics of Legitimation in the Soviet Union', *Soviet Union/Union Soviétique*, 4 (1977).
20. This is true especially because there is not and cannot be (except in the ideology) an agency in Soviet society to whom the society as a whole and the

relationship of its parts to the whole is transparent. Cf. C. Castoriadis, 'The Social Regime in Russia', *Telos,* 38 (Winter 1978–9).

21. Cf. essays in *Interest Groups in Soviet Politics,* ed. H. Skilling and F. Griffiths (Princeton University Press, 1971).
22. Offe, *Strukturprobleme,* pp. 65ff.
23. Cf. Lewin, *Political Undercurrents.*
24. Ibid; and F. Parkin, 'System Contradiction and Political Transformation', *European Journal of Sociology,* 13 (1972).
25. Yugoslavia is the possible exception, and perhaps this proves that it is not a Soviet-type society.
26. Cf. Rakovski's excellent discussion in *Towards an East European Marxism.*
27. C. Lefort, *Un homme en trop. Reflexions sur 'L'Archipel du Goulag'* (Paris: Seuil, 1976); Feher, 'The Dictatorship over Needs'; but see Laird, '"Developed" Socialist Society and the Dialectics of Legitimation in the Soviet Union'.
28. I do not believe the crisis of crisis management can be sought in the demonstration (on the level of system integration) of the inevitable coincidence of permissible maximum and minimum levels of political intervention (where even the maximum would be too little from the point of view of maintaining the primacy of the political, and even the minimum too much from the point of view of economic rationality); rather, it must be sought in the analysis (on the level of social integration) of the difficulties of legitimating either or both a strategy based on undiminished levels of intervention and/or one based on reform.
29. Lewin, *Political Undercurrents,* pp. 164–5, 178, 236–8; and Konrad and Szelenyi, *The Intellectuals,* pp. 231–2.
30. *LC,* p. 149, n. 15.
31. Compare H. Marcuse, *Soviet Marxism: A Critical Analysis* (New York: Random House, 1958) with Castoriadis, 'The Social Regime in Russia', and V. Zazlavsky, 'The Problem of Legitimation in Soviet Society', in *Conflict and Control,* ed. Vidich and Glassman (Beverly Hills: Sage, 1979).
32. M. Vajda, 'Is Kadarism an Alternative?', *Telos,* 39 (Spring 1979).
33. H. Berman, *Justice in the USSR: An Interpretation of Soviet Law* (Cambridge, Mass.: Harvard University Press, 1963); R. Sharlet, 'Stalinism and Soviet Legal Culture', in *Stalinism,* ed. R. Tucker (New York: Norton, 1977); and Lewin, *Political Undercurrents.*
34. R. Bauer, A. Inkeles and C. Kluckhohn, *How the Soviet System Works* (New York: Knopf, 1956).
35. R. Dutschke, *Versuch Lenin auf die Füsse zu Stellen* (Berlin: Wagenback, 1974).
36. Berman, *Justice in the USSR.*
37. R. Tucker, 'Stalinism as Revolution from Above', in *Stalinism,* ed. Tucker.
38. F. Barghoorn, *Soviet Russian Nationalism* (New York: Oxford University Press, 1956).
39. V. Zazlavksy, 'The Problem of Legitimation in Soviet Society', and 'The Rebirth of the Stalin Cult in the USSR', *Telos,* 40 (Summer 1979).
40. M. Cherniavsky, *Tsar and People* (New Haven: Yale University Press, 1961).
41. *LC,* p. 22.
42. *LC,* pp. 70, 79, 84–9; 'On Social Identity', pp. 98–9; 'History and Evolution', pp. 115, 197.
43. M. Lewin, 'The Social Background of Stalinism', in *Stalinism,* ed. Tucker.
44. D. Barry and H. Berman, 'The Jurists', in *Interest Groups in Soviet Politics,* ed. Skilling and Griffiths.

45. Cf. Bauer, Inkeles and Kluckhohn, *How the Soviet System Works*; and R. Bauer and A. Inkeles, *The Soviet Citizen* (Cambridge, Mass.: Harvard University Press, 1959).
46. Bauer, Inkeles and Kluckhohn, *How the Soviet System Works,* pp. 138–42, 236–9, 150–4, 171–8.
47. Bauer and Inkeles, *The Soviet Citizen,* pp. 220–6, especially pp. 221ff.
48. *LC,* pp. 76–7.
49. Zazlavsky, 'The Rebirth of the Stalin Cult in the USSR'.
50. H. Carrère d'Encausse, *L'Empire éclaté* (Paris: Flammarion, 1978).
51. Cf. A. Heller, 'Habermas and Marxism', in this volume (Chapter 1).

12 A reply to my critics (Jürgen Habermas)

1. In addition to the contribution by Michael Schmid (Chapter 9), cf. also the dissertations by M. Müller, 'Das Konzept der Entwicklungslogik' (Frankfurt, 1978), and C. Fleck, 'Der prominente Überbau, Studien zur Sozialisations-theorie und Evolutionstheorie von Jürgen Habermas' (Graz, 1979).
2. Cf. H. Dubiel, *Wissenschaftsorganisation und Politische Erfahrung* (Frankfurt: Suhrkamp, 1978).
3. N. Luhmann, 'Status quo als Argument', in *Studenten in Opposition,* ed. H. Baier (Bielefeld: Bertelsmann Universitätsverlag, 1968) pp. 73ff.
4. H. Lübbe, *Fortschrittsorientierung als Problem* (Freiburg: Rombach, 1975) pp. 32ff.
5. A. Wellmer, *Critical Theory of Society* (New York: Seabury Press, 1971).
6. Cf. my discussion with Herbert Marcuse, in J. Habermas, S. Bovenschen *et al., Gespräche mit Herbert Marcuse* (Frankfurt: Suhrkamp, 1979) [*Telos,* 38 (1978–9) pp. 124–53].
7. J. Keane, 'On Tools and Language', *New German Critique,* 6 (1975) pp. 82ff; Ben Agger, 'Work and Authority in Marcuse and Habermas', *Human Studies* (1979) pp. 191ff; and above all J. Arnasson, *Zwischen Natur und Gesellschaft* (Frankfurt, 1976), ch. 3, and 'Review of Habermas' *Zur Rekonstruktion des Historischen Materialismus', Telos,* 39 (1979) pp. 201ff.
8. 'First, realizing the human form involves an inner force imposing itself on external reality, perhaps against external obstacles. Thus where Aristotelian philosophy saw the growth and development of man and the realization of human form as a tending towards order and equilibrium constantly threatened by disorder and disharmony, the expressivist view sees this development more as the manifestation of an inner power striving to realize and maintain its own shape against those the surrounding world might impose. Thus the ideal realization is one which not only conforms to the idea, but is also internally generated; indeed these two requirements are inseparable in that the proper form of man incorporates the notion of free subjectivity' (Charles Taylor, *Hegel* (Cambridge University Press, 1975) p. 15).
9. 'The second important strand in expressivism is the notion that the realization of a form clarifies or makes determinate what the form is. If we return to our guiding analogy, the way in which an action or gesture can express what is characteristic about a person, we can see that there are two aspects which can be united in this idea. Something I do or say can express my feelings or aspirations in the sense of making these clear to others or to myself. In this sense we can speak of someone's actions as expressions of his feelings or desires when they carry out what he wants, or realize his aspirations. These two aspects can be separated: I can bring my desires to verbal expression without acting, I can act and remain an enigma to myself and others; but they often do go together, and frequently we are inclined to say of ourselves or

others, that we did not really know what we wanted until we acted. Thus the fullest and most convincing expression of a subject is one where he both realizes and clarifies his aspirations' (ibid, p. 16).

10. A. Honneth, 'Arbeit und instrumentales Handeln', in *Arbeit, Handlung, Normativität*, ed. A. Honneth and U. Jaeggi (Frankfurt: Suhrkamp, 1980) p. 197.

11. The demand for autonomy in the work-place is related to another problem. Like the complementary demand for democratic control of entrepreneurial decisions, it has to do with the organisation of domination, that is, with the institutional framework of social labour, or the relations of production. Honneth takes this as his point of departure in an effort to save the foundations of a philosophy of *Praxis* after all. He tries to spin the moral-practical consciousness 'with which the subjects of labour react to the experience of a capitalistically instrumentalised working activity' out of a 'critical concept of labour'. With this concept he hopes to capture the logic of 'the violations of norms and the practices of resistance that have become routine' in some industrial sectors. Let us grant for the moment that this kind of subversion is motivated by the desire for an activity in which 'the monitoring that accompanies action and the structuring of the activity suitable to the object are left to the labouring subject'; even then, the rationality of the rights sued for, however implicitly, derives not from any 'logic of appropriation', but from the logic of practical discourse. Honneth commits a genetic fallacy: the justified desire for autonomy in the work-place may well spring from 'the experience of work that has been destroyed by the techniques of production'; but the justification of normative regulations that help this repressed interest obtain its rights follows the logic of practical discourse and not the logic of a labour practice which is supposed to be located somewhere between instrumental action and action orientated to reaching understanding. Norms for the organisation of labour are also norms of action that regulate tasks and interactions.

12. Reprinted in K.–O. Apel, C. V. Bormann *et al.*, *Hermeneutik und Ideologie-kritik* (Frankfurt: Suhrkamp, 1971) pp. 160ff.

13. 'A Postscript to *Knowledge and Human Interests*', *Philosophy of the Social Sciences*, 3 (1975) pp. 157–89, here pp. 182–3.

14. H. Marcuse, 'Philosophy and Critical Theory', in *Negations* (Boston: Beacon, 1968) p. 135.

15. Ibid, p. 147.

16. Ibid, p. 148.

17. Ibid, p. 158.

18. Ibid, pp. 142–3.

19. J. Habermas, 'Psychic Thermidor and the Rebirth of Rebellious Subjectivity', *Berkeley Journal of Sociology*, 25 (1980) pp. 1ff.

20. A. Honneth, 'Communication and Reconciliation', *Telos*, 39 (1979) pp. 45ff; J. Habermas, 'Die Frankfurter Schule in New York', *Süddeutsche Zeitung* (2–3 August 1980).

21. T. McCarthy, *The Critical Theory of Jürgen Habermas* (Cambridge, Mass.: M.I.T. Press, 1978) pp. 101–2.

22. 'The human interest in autonomy and responsibility is not mere fancy, for it can be apprehended a priori' (*KHI*, p. 314).

23. With reference to a similar objection by Gadamer, Mendelson writes: 'Does critical theory ever claim to achieve such transparency or even orient to it as a regulative or normative ideal? It is necessary, according to Habermas, to distinguish between those inevitable preunderstandings which derive simply

from one's participation in culture, and those false preconceptions which are anchored in systematically distorted forms of communication. Critical theory hopes to elicit a self-reflection in which the addressee penetrates and dissolves the latter. Its normative ideal is the complete elimination of systematic blockages to communication with oneself or others. But it certainly does not claim to bring to consciousness *all* the addressee's preconceptions – an impossible task. In this sense, Habermas agrees that we are "more being than consciousness"' (J. Mendelson, 'The Habermas–Gadamer Debate', *New German Critique*, 18 (1979) pp. 62–3.

24. H. Schnädelbach, *Reflexion und Diskurs* (Frankfurt: Suhrkamp, 1977).
25. R. K. Maurer, 'Jürgen Habermas' Aufhebung der Philosophie', *Philosophische Rundschau*, Beiheft 8 (Tübingen, 1977) p. 4.
26. J. Whitebook, 'The Problem of Nature in Habermas', *Telos*, 40 (1979) p. 48.
27. Ibid, p. 51.
28. C. F. von Wiezsäcker, *Die Einheit der Natur* (München: Hanser, 1971).
29. W. E. Connolly, 'Review of T. McCarthy, *The Critical Theory of Jürgen Habermas*', *History and Theory*, 3 (1979) pp. 397–8.
30. Whitebook, 'The Problem of Nature in Habermas', p. 68.
31. H. Jonas, *Das Prinzip Verantwortung* (Frankfurt: Insel, 1979).
32. McCarthy, *The Critical Theory of Jürgen Habermas*, pp. 113–25.
33. K.-O Apel, *Der Denkweg von Charles S. Peirce* (Frankfurt: Suhrkamp, 1975).
34. G. Böhme, W. v.d. Daele and W. Krohn, 'Alternativen in der Wissenschaft', *Zeitschrift für Soziologie*, 1 (1972) pp. 302ff.
35. G. Böhme, W. v.d. Daele and W. Krohn, *Experimentelle Philosophie* (Frankfurt: Suhrkamp, 1977).
36. Whitebook, 'The Problem of Nature in Habermas', p. 52.
37. Cf. the excellent analysis by H. Peukert in *Wissenschaftstheorie, Handlungstheorie, Fundamentale Theologie* (Düsseldorf: Patmos, 1976), pp. 273ff.
38. C. Lenhardt, 'The Proletariat and its Masses. An Essay on Anamnestic Solidarity', paper presented at the Max-Planck-Institut, Starnberg, 1975.
39. Peukert, *Wissenschaftstheorie*, p. 282.
40. Whitebook, 'The Problem of Nature in Habermas', p. 61.
41. Ibid, p. 64.
42. Mendelson, 'The Habermas–Gadamer Debate', p. 68.
43. Ibid.
44. S. Benhabib, 'Procedural and Discursive Norms of Rationality', paper presented in the Max-Planck-Institut at Starnberg, 1980, pp. 38–9.
45. *CES*.
46. I can leave to one side the subsequent case of representation of individual participants. Within the proposed model, discourse carried on through representation can be ascribed to a higher-level community in communication, formed once again discursively, whereby the way of organising will-formation (e.g. the question: imperative mandate versus independence of delegates) is dependent in turn on will-formation in the constituting communication community.
47. The application of this model certainly involves methodological difficulties in the case of pre-modern societies, generally of actors to whom we cannot ascribe a modern understanding of the world. Here we need additional assumptions concerning the rationalisation of the life-world, that is, concerning the evolution of world-views, of institutionalised levels of justification, and of forms of reaching understanding.
48. *The Critical Theory of Jürgen Habermas*, pp. 310–32.

49. Robert Alexy, *Theorie der Juristischen Argumentation* (Frankfurt: Suhrkamp, 1978).
50. McCarthy, *The Critical Theory of Jürgen Habermas,* p. 325.
51. K.–O. Apel, 'Das Apriori der Kommunikationsgemeinschaft und die Grundlagen der Ethik', in *Transformation der Philosophie,* vol. II (Frankfurt: Suhrkamp, 1973) pp. 358ff [*Towards a Transformation of Philosophy* (London: Routledge & Kegan Paul, 1980)]; K.–O. Apel, 'Sprechakttheorie und transzendentale Sprachpragmatik, zur Frage ethischer Normen', in *Sprachpragmatik und Philosophie* (Frankfurt: Suhrkamp, 1976) pp. 10ff; K.–O. Apel, 'Das Problem der Letztbegründung im Lichte einer transzendentalen Sprachpragmatik', in *Sprache und Erkenntnis,* ed. B. Kanitschneider (Innsbruck: Inst. f. Sprachwissenschaft d. Univ. Innsbruck, 1976) pp. 55ff; and W. Kuhlmann, 'Ethik der Kommunikation', in K.–O. Apel *et al., Praktische Philosophie, Ethik,* vol. 1 (Frankfurt: Suhrkamp, 1980) pp. 292ff.
52. W. Oelmüller (ed.), *Transzendentalpragmatische Normenbegründungen* (Paderborn: Schöningh, 1977), and *Normenbegründung, Normendurchsetzung* (Paderborn: Schöningh, 1978).
53. G. H. Mead, *Mind, Self and Society from the Standpoint of a Social Behaviorist* (University of Chicago Press, 1934).
54. R. Wimmer, *Universalisierung in der Ethik* (Frankfurt: Suhrkamp, 1980).
55. *The Critical Theory of Jürgen Habermas,* p. 326.
56. L. Kohlberg, 'From Is to Ought', in *Cognitive Development and Epistemology,* ed. T. Mischel (New York: Academic Press, 1971) p. 223.
57. L. Kohlberg, 'The Claim to Moral Adequacy of a Highest Stage of Moral Judgement', *Journal of Philosophy,* 70 (1973) pp. 630–46; reprinted in *Essays in Moral Development,* vol. 2 (Harvard University Center for Moral Development) pp. 145–75, here pp. 148–9.
58. Ibid.
59. A. Wellmer, 'Thesen über Vernunft, Emanzipation und Utopie', unpublished manuscript, 1979.
60. J. Habermas and N. Luhmann, *Theorie der Gesellschaft oder Sozialtechnologie – Was leistet die Systemforschüng?* (Frankfurt: Suhrkamp, 1971) pp. 140–1.
61. Wellmer, 'Thesen', p. 32.
62. Ibid, p. 53.
63. Ibid.
64. A. Giddens, 'Habermas's Critique of Hermeneutics', in *Studies in Social and Political Theory* (London: Hutchinson, 1977) pp. 165ff.
65. This schema is taken from J. Habermas, 'Aspects of the Rationality of Action', in *Rationality Today,* ed. T. Geraets (Ottawa University Press, 1979) p. 195.
66. Ibid, p. 196.
67. For example, a false impression is conveyed by the table in which I derive the analytic units for an analysis of speech-acts using idealising procedures, not from communicative acts but from social actions (in *CES,* p. 40).
68. The type distinction between communicative and strategic action should not exclude the case of legitimately regulated action in one's own interest *(Interessenhandeln),* and thus Max Weber's standard case of the pursuit of interests organised through civil law. In this case, it appears as if the actor simultaneously adopts the two alternative basic attitudes in the same action: he or she behaves with an orientation to success in relation to other participants in interaction; he or she behaves in a norm-conformative way (and thus with an orientation to achieving understanding) in relation to the

legal system that authorises the strategic behaviour. As a matter of fact, the ╳ two attitudes do not collide, since actors, standing in an actual ego–alter relation as participants in interaction, orientate themselves on the one hand to a concretely present other, whereas on the other hand, as legal persons and members of a formally organised system of action, they orientate themselves to the higher-level, abstract community of their legal cosubjects. This latter, virtual, level can be actualised as soon as the legal framework itself is made thematic; then the same actors encounter one another as legal cosubjects at the level of interaction as well – now with the attitude orientated to understanding of those who know that they have to arrive at an agreement (even if it be by way of legal proceedings, which, though they are set up again as normatively regulated strategic interaction, are basically consensual). It is in this sense that Robert Alexy conceives juridical argumentation as a 'special case of general practical discourse'. See his *Theorie der Juristischen Argumentation,* pp. 161ff.

69. For definitions of the concepts of productive forces and productive relations, see *CES,* pp. 138–9.
70. Cf. also Giddens, *Studies in Social and Political Theory,* p. 157.
71. Cf. also A. Gouldner, *Die Intelligenz als Neue Klasse* (Frankfurt: Campus, 1980) pp. 69ff [*The Future of Intellectuals and the Rise of the New Class* (New York: Seabury Press, 1979)].
72. J. Habermas, 'Talcott Parsons: Konstruktionsprobleme der Gesellschaftstheorie', in *Verhandlungen des 20. Deutschen Soziologentages* (forthcoming).
73. J. Habermas, 'Hannah Arendt's Communications Concept of Power', *Social Research,* 44 (1977) pp. 3–24.
74. J. Habermas, 'Bemerkungen zur Medientheorie von T. Parsons', in *Verhalten, Handlung und System,* ed. W. Schluchter (Frankfurt: Suhrkamp, 1980).
75. Cf. my discussion with Luhmann in *Theorie der Gesellschaft,* pp. 250–7.
76. Cf. *CES,* pp. 59–65.
77. Cf. ibid, p. 40, schema.
78. J. Habermas, 'Some Distinctions in Universal Pragmatics', *Theory and Society,* 3 (1976) pp. 155–67.
79. Cf. J. Searle, 'Literal Meaning', in *Expression and Meaning* (Cambridge University Press, 1979). I am indebted for a number of suggestions to the seminar on 'background knowledge' offered jointly by J. Searle and H. Dreyfus at the University of California, Berkeley, in the winter term of 1980.
80. Questions of taste introduce new complications having to do with the relation of evaluations to normative sentences on the one side, and to expressive sentences, on the other. The adequacy of standards of value has something in common with the rightness of norms of action; on the other hand, the authenticity of works of art, in connection with which standards of value are formed and authenticated, has more in common with the sincerity of expressions.
81. On this point, see the interesting remarks of Peukert, *Wissenschaftstheorie,* pp. 269–70.
82. M. Hesse, 'In Defence of Objectivity', *Proceedings of the British Academy,* 58 (1972).
83. For instance, the critique of W. Franzen (which misses my point) in 'Die Geisteswissenschaften und die Praxis', *Man and World,* 9 (1976) pp. 113ff.
84. This thesis has since been further developed by G. H. von Wright, *Explanation and Understanding* (London: Routledge & Kegan Paul, 1971); R. J. Bernstein, *The Restructuring of Social and Political Theory* (Oxford: Black-

well, 1976); K.-O. Apel, J. Manninen and R. Tuomela, *Neue Versuche über Erklären und Verstehen* (Frankfurt: Suhrkamp, 1978); K.-O. Apel, 'Types of Rationality Today', in *Rationality Today,* ed. Geraets; and K.-O. Apel, *Die Erklären-Verstehen-Kontroverse in Transzendentalpragmatischer Sicht* (Frankfurt: Suhrkamp, 1979).

85. In so far as the latter does not merely specify formal conditions that every substantial theory of truth has to satisfy.

86. Cf. Schnädelbach, *Reflexion und Diskurs.*

87. R. Rorty, *The Mirror of Nature* (Princeton University Press, 1980).

88. D. Held, *Introduction to Critical Theory* (London: Hutchinson, 1980).

89. M. Jay, *The Dialectical Imagination* (Boston: Little, Brown, 1973).

90. Held, *Introduction to Critical Theory,* pp. 379ff.

91. I have in mind works by Seyla Benhabib, Paul Breines, Jean Cohen, Carol Gould, Dick Howard, Jeremy Shapiro, among others.

92. R. Döbert and G. Nunner-Winkler, 'Das Problem der Normalität aus entwicklungslogischer Perspektive', in M. Cramer and P. Gottwald (eds), 'Verhaltenstherapie in der Diskussion, Vorträge a.d. 5. Kongress d. Ges. z. Förderg. d. Verhaltenstherapie', *Sonderheft d. Mitteilungen der GVT e. V., 1973,* pp. 182–92; R. Döbert and G. Nunner-Winkler, *Adoleszenzkrise und Identitätsbildung* (Frankfurt: Suhrkamp, 1975); R. Döbert and G. Nunner-Winkler, 'Adoleszenzkrise, moralisches Bewusstsein und Wertorientierungen', in H. Hurrelman (ed.), *Sozialisation und Lebenslauf* (Reinbek: Rowohlt, 1976); R. Döbert and G. Nunner-Winkler, 'Zum Zusammenhang von Adoleszenzkrisenverlauf, moralischen Bewusstsein und Wertorientierungen', in R. M. Lepsius (ed.), *Zwischenbilanz der Soziologie. Verhandlungen des 17. Deutschen Soziologentages* (Stuttgart: Enke, 1976); K. Eder, 'Komplexität, Evolution und Geschichte', in *Theorie der Gesellschaft oder Sozialtechnologie. Beiträge zur Habermas–Luhmann–Diskussion* (Frankfurt: Suhrkamp, 1973) pp. 9–42; K. Eder, *Die Entstehung staatlich organisierter Gesellschaften* (Frankfurt: Suhrkamp, 1976); R. Funke, 'Organisationsstrukturen planender Verwaltungen, dargestellt am Beispiel von Kommunalverwaltungen und Stadtplanungsämtern', *Schriftenreihe 'Städtebauliche Forschung' des Bundesministers für Raumordnung Bauwesen und Städtebau, Nr. 03.027* (Bonn-Bad, Godesberg, 1974); R. Funke, 'Planungskritik als Bürokratiekritik? Zur internen Struktur planender Verwaltungen', in R. R. Grauhan (ed.), *Lokale Politikforschung* (Frankfurt: Campus, 1975); G. Müller, U. Rödel, Ch. Sabel, F. Stille and W. Vogt, *Ökonomische Krisentendenzen im gegenwärtigen Kapitalismus* (Frankfurt: Campus, 1978); C. Offe, *Strukturprobleme des kapitalistischen Staates. Aufsätze zur politischen Soziologie* (Frankfurt: Suhrkamp, 1972); C. Offe, 'Advanced Capitalism and the Welfare State', in *Politics and Society,* vol. 2, no. 4 (1972) pp. 479–88; C. Offe, 'Krisen des Krisenmanagements – Elemente einer politischen Krisentheorie', in M. Jänicke (ed.), *Herrschaft und Krise* (Opladen: Westdeutscher Verlag, 1973) pp. 197ff; C. Offe, *Berufsbildungsreform. Eine Fallstudie über Reformpolitik* (Frankfurt: Suhrkamp, 1975); C. Offe and V. Ronge, 'Fiskalische Krise, Bauindustrie und die Grenzen staatlicher Ausgabenrationalisierung', in *Leviathan (2) 1973,* pp. 189–220; R. Rödel and V. Brandes, 'Inflation – die historische Perspektive', in *Politische Ökonomie – Geschichte und Kritik. Handbuch III: Inflation–Akkumulation–Krise* (Bonn/Frankfurt: Europäische Verlagsanstalt, 1975); V. Ronge, 'The Politicization of Administration in Advanced Capitalist Societies', in *Political Studies,* vol. XX, no. 1 (1974) pp. 89–93; V. Ronge, 'Der "polit-ökonomische Ansatz" in der Verwaltungsforschung,' in P. Grottian and A. Murswieck (eds), *Handlungsspielräume*

der Staatsadministration (Hamburg: Hoffmann & Campe, 1974); V. Ronge, 'Entpolitisierung der Forschungspolitik', in *Leviathan 1975*, pp. 307–37; V. Ronge, *Forschungspolitik als Strukturpolitik* (München: Piper, 1977); V. Ronge, 'Bankpolitik im Spätkapitalismus. Politische Selbstverwaltung des Kapitals?' in *Starnberger Studien 3* (Frankfurt: Suhrkamp, 1979); V. Ronge and G. Schmieg, *Restriktionen politischer Planung* (Frankfurt: Athenäum, 1973).

93. To be published by Suhrkamp Verlag, Frankfurt.

Select Bibliography

The following bibliography is a selection of Habermas's writings and of the secondary literature. We make no attempt to provide a comprehensive list. A complete bibliography of Habermas's work has been compiled by Görtzen and van Gelder (see section 2b below); and a full bibliography of the secondary literature is in preparation. We therefore cite only those writings of Habermas and others which are readily accessible and which, in the editors' opinion, are of most interest.

1. Works by Habermas

(a)   *Books in German (in order of publication)*
Strukturwandel der Öffentlichkeit. Untersuchungen zu einer Kategorie der bürgerlichen Gesellschaft (Neuwied: Luchterhand, 1962).
Theorie und Praxis. Sozialphilosophische Studien (Neuwied: Luchterhand, 1963). Republished with four new essays and a new introduction in 1971 (Frankfurt: Suhrkamp).
Zur Logik der Sozialwissenschaften, Beiheft 5 of *Philosophische Rundschau*, 14 (1966–7). Republished with additional essays in 1970 (Frankfurt: Suhrkamp).
Erkenntnis und Interesse (Frankfurt: Suhrkamp, 1968). Republished with postscript in 1973 (Frankfurt: Suhrkamp).
Technik und Wissenschaft als 'Ideologie' (Frankfurt: Suhrkamp, 1968).
Protestbewegung und Hochschulreform (Frankfurt: Suhrkamp, 1969).
Theorie der Gesellschaft oder Sozialtechnologie – Was leistet die Systemforschung?, with Niklas Luhmann (Frankfurt: Suhrkamp, 1971).
Philosophische-politische Profile (Frankfurt: Suhrkamp, 1971).
Legitimationsprobleme im Spätkapitalismus (Frankfurt: Suhrkamp, 1973).
Kultur und Kritik. Verstreute Aufsätze (Frankfurt: Suhrkamp, 1973).
Zur Rekonstruktion des Historischen Materialismus (Frankfurt: Suhrkamp, 1976).

(b) *Books in English (in order of publication)*
Toward a Rational Society: Student Protest, Science, and Politics, trans. J. J. Shapiro (Boston: Beacon Press, 1970; London: Heinemann, 1971). Translation of selected essays from *Tecknik und Wissenschaft als 'Ideologie'* and *Protestbewegung und Hochschulreform*.
Knowledge and Human Interests, trans. J. J. Shapiro (Boston: Beacon Press, 1971; London: Heinemann, 1972). Translation of *Erkenntnis und Interesse*.
Theory and Practice, trans. J. Viertel (Boston: Beacon Press, 1973; London:

Heinemann, 1974). Translation of selected essays from 1971 edition of *Theorie und Praxis* and one essay from *Technik und Wissenschaft als 'Ideologie'*.

Legitimation Crisis, trans. T. McCarthy (Boston: Beacon Press, 1975; London: Heinemann, 1976). Translation of *Legitimationsprobleme im Spätkapitalismus*.

Communication and the Evolution of Society, trans. T. McCarthy (Boston: Beacon Press, 1979; London: Heinemann, 1979). Translation of 'Was heisst Universal-pragmatik?' and selected essays from *Zur Rekonstruktion des Historischen Materialismus*.

(c) *Essays in German and English (in order of publication)*
This section lists some of the essays which are not included in the above volumes. If an essay originally published in German has been translated into English, then only the English version is cited. In the case of translated essays the original date of publication is given in square brackets.

'The Analytical Theory of Science and Dialectics', in T. W. Adorno *et al.*, *The Positivist Dispute in German Sociology*, trans. G. Adey and D. Frisby (London: Heinemann, 1976) pp. 131–62 [1963].

'A Positivistically Bisected Rationalism', in *The Positivist Dispute in German Sociology*, pp. 198–225 [1964].

'The Public Sphere: an Encyclopaedia Article', *New German Critique*, 3 (1974) pp. 49–55 [1964].

'Discussion of "Value-Freedom and Objectivity"', in *Understanding and Social Inquiry*, ed. F. Dallmayr and T. McCarthy (University of Notre Dame Press, 1977) pp. 66–72 [1965].

'A Review of Gadamer's *Truth and Method*', in *Understanding and Social Inquiry*, pp. 335–63 [1967, 1970].

'Toward a Theory of Communicative Competence', in *Recent Sociology*, no. 2, ed. H. P. Dreitzel (New York: Macmillan, 1970) pp. 114–48.

'Summation and Response', *Continuum*, 8 (1970) pp. 123–33.

'Why More Philosophy?', *Social Research*, 38 (1971) pp. 633–54 [1971].

'Consciousness-raising or Pure Critique: the Contemporaneity of Walter Benjamin', *New German Critique*, 17 (1979) pp. 30–59 [1972].

'Wahrheitstheorien', in *Wirklichkeit und Reflexion: Walter Schulz zum 60. Geburtstag*, ed. H. Fahrenbach (Pfüllingen: Neske, 1973) pp. 211–65.

'What does a Crisis Mean Today? Legitimation Problems in Late Capitalism', *Social Research*, 40 (1973) pp. 643–67 [1973].

'A Postscript to *Knowledge and Human Interests*', *Philosophy of the Social Sciences*, 3 (1973) pp. 157–89 [1973].

'On Social Identity', *Telos*, 19 (1974) pp. 91–103 [1974].

'The Place of Philosophy in Marxism', *Insurgent Sociologist*, 5 (1975) pp. 41–8 [1974].

'Habermas Talking: an Interview' (interviewed by Boris Frankel), *Theory and Society*, 1 (1974) pp. 37–58.

'Some Distinctions in Universal Pragmatics', *Theory and Society*, 3 (1976) pp. 155–67 [1975].

'Sprachspiel, Intention und Bedeutung: zu Motiven bei Sellars und Wittgenstein', in *Sprachanalyse und Soziologie*, ed. R. Wiggershaus (Frankfurt: Suhrkamp, 1975) pp. 319–40.

'Legitimationsprobleme der Religion' (with Sölle, Bahr and others), in H. G. Bahr *et al.*, *Religionsgespräche: Zur gesellschaftlichen Rolle der Religion* (Darmstadt: Luchterhand, 1975) pp. 9–31.

'History and Evolution', *Telos*, 39 (1979) pp. 5–44 [1976].

'Hannah Arendt's Communications Concept of Power', *Social Research*, 44 (1977) pp. 3–24 [1976].
'A Test for Popular Justice: the Accusations against the Intellectuals', *New German Critique*, 12 (1977) pp. 11–13 [1977].
'Der Ansatz von Habermas', in *Transzendentalphilosophische Normbegründung*, ed. W. Oelmüller (Paderborn: Schöningh, 1978).
'Theory and Politics: A Discussion with Herbert Marcuse, Jürgen Habermas, Heinz Lubasz and Telman Spengler', *Telos*, 38 (1978–9) pp. 124–53 [1978].
'Conservatism and Capitalist Crisis' (interview conducted by Rinascita), *New Left Review*, 115 (1979) pp. 73–84.

2. Works on Habermas
(a) *Books*
This section lists books, collections of essays and special issues of journals in which a substantial part of the volume is devoted to a discussion of Habermas's work. Priority is given to material in English.

Adorno, T. *et al.*, *The Positivist Dispute in German Sociology*, trans. G. Adey and D. Frisby (London: Heinemann, 1976).
Apel, K.-O. *et al.*, *Hermeneutik und Ideologiekritik* (Frankfurt: Suhrkamp, 1971).
Bauman, Zygmunt, *Hermeneutics and Social Science: Approaches to Understanding* (London: Hutchinson, 1978).
Bauman Zygmunt, *Towards a Critical Sociology: An Essay on Commonsense and Emancipation* (London: Routledge & Kegan Paul, 1976).
Bernstein, Richard, *The Restructuring of Social and Political Theory* (Oxford: Blackwell, 1976).
Connerton, Paul, *The Tragedy of Enlightenment: An Essay on the Frankfurt School* (Cambridge University Press, 1980).
Connerton, Paul (ed.), *Critical Sociology: Selected Readings* (Harmondsworth: Penguin, 1976).
Continuum, 8 (1970).
Cultural Hermeneutics, vol. 2, no. 4 (February 1975).
Dallmayr, W. (ed.), *Materialien zu Habermas' 'Erkenntnis und Interesse'* (Frankfurt: Suhrkamp, 1974).
Giddens, Anthony, *New Rules of Sociological Method: A Positive Critique of Interpretative Sociologies* (London: Hutchinson, 1976).
Held, David, *Introduction to Critical Theory: Horkheimer to Habermas* (London: Hutchinson, 1980).
Kortian, Garbis, *Metacritique: The Philosophical Argument of Jürgen Habermas*, trans. John Raffan (Cambridge University Press, 1980).
Leiss, William, *The Domination of Nature* (Boston: Beacon Press, 1974).
McCarthy, Thomas, *The Critical Theory of Jürgen Habermas* (Cambridge, Mass.: M.I.T. Press, 1978).
Mueller, Claus, *The Politics of Communication: A Study in the Political Sociology of Language, Socialization, and Legitimation* (New York: Oxford University Press, 1973).
Negt, Oskar, *Die Linke antwortet Jürgen Habermas* (Frankfurt: Europäishe Verlangsanstalt, 1968).
Negt, Oskar and Kluge, Alexander, *Öffentlichkeit und Erfahrung. Zur Organisationsanalyse von bürgerlicher und proletarischer Öffentlichkeit* (Frankfurt: Suhrkamp, 1972).
O'Neil, John (ed.), *On Critical Theory* (New York: Seabury Press, 1976).
Philosophy of the Social Sciences, vol. 2, no. 3 (September 1972).

Radnitzky, Gerard, *Contemporary Schools of Metascience* (Chicago: Henry Regnery, 1973).
Sennat, Julius, *Habermas and Marxism: An Appraisal* (Beverly Hills: Sage, 1979).
Shroyer, Trent, *The Critique of Domination* (New York: George Brazillier, 1973).
Theunissen, Michael, *Gesellschaft und Geschichte: Zur Kritik der kritischen Theorie* (Berlin: de Gruyter, 1969).
Thompson, John B., *Critical Hermeneutics: A Study in the Thought of Paul Ricoeur and Jürgen Habermas* (Cambridge University Press, 1981).
Tuschling, Burkhard, *Habermas – Die 'offene' und die 'abstrakte' Gesellschaft* (Berlin: Argument, 1978).
Wellmer, Albrecht, *Critical Theory of Society*, trans. J. Cumming (New York: Seabury Press, 1974).

(b) *Essays*
This section lists essays that are not contained in the volumes mentioned in section (a). Priority is given to critical material which is in English.

Bar-Hillel, Y., 'On Habermas' Hermeneutic Philosophy of Language', *Synthese*, 26 (1973) pp. 1–12.
Blanchette, Oliva, 'Language, the Primordial Labor of History: a Critique of Critical Social Theory in Habermas', *Cultural Hermeneutics*, 1 (1974) pp. 325–82.
Dallmayr, Fred R., 'Reason and Emancipation: Notes on Habermas', *Man and World*, 5 (1972) pp. 79ff.
Disco, Cornelis, 'Critical Theory as Ideology of the New Class', *Theory and Society*, 8 (1979) pp. 159–214.
Frankel, Boris, 'The State of the State after Leninism', *Theory and Society*, 7 (1979) pp. 199–242.
Giddens, Anthony, 'Habermas's Critique of Hermeneutics', in his *Studies in Social and Political Theory* (London: Hutchinson, 1977) pp. 135–64.
Görtzen, Rene and van Gelder, Frederik, 'Jürgen Habermas: The Complete Oeuvre. A Bibliography of Primary Literature, Translations and Reviews', *Human Studies*, 2 (1979). This bibliography will be reprinted in the forthcoming second edition of Thomas McCarthy, *The Critical Theory of Jürgen Habermas* (Cambridge, Mass.: M.I.T. Press, 1st edn. 1978).
Held, David and Simon, Larry, 'Habermas's Theory of Crisis in Late Capitalism', *Radical Philosophers' News Journal*, 6 (1976) pp. 1–19.
Hesse, Mary, 'Habermas's Consensus Theory of Truth', in *Proceedings of the 1978 Biennial Meeting of the Philosophy of Science Association*, vol. 2, ed. P. D. Asquith and I. Hacking (East Lansing, Michigan, 1979).
Hesse, Mary, 'In Defence of Objectivity', *Proceedings of the British Academy*, 58 (1972) pp. 275–92.
Hohendahl, Peter Uwe, 'Critical Theory, Public Sphere and Culture. Jürgen Habermas and his Critics', *New German Critique*, 16 (1979) pp. 89–118.
Honneth, Axel, 'Communication and Reconciliation', *Telos*, 39 (1979) pp. 45–61.
Howard, Dick, 'A Politics in Search of the Political', *Theory and Society*, 1 (1973) pp. 271–306.
Keane, John, 'On Tools and Language: Habermas on Work and Interaction', *New German Critique*, 6 (1975) pp. 82–100.
Leiss, William, 'The Problem of Man and Nature in the Work of the Frankfurt School', *Philosophy of the Social Sciences*, 5 (1975) pp. 163–72.
McCarthy, Thomas, 'A Theory of Communicative Competence', *Philosophy of the Social Sciences*, 3 (1973) pp. 135–56.

Mendelson, Jack, 'The Habermas–Gadamer Debate', *New German Critique,* 18 (1979) pp. 44–73.

Overend, Tronn, 'Enquiry and Ideology: Habermas's Trichotomous Conception of Science', *Philosophy of the Social Sciences,* 8 (1978) pp. 1–13.

Ricoeur, Paul, 'Hermeneutics and the Critique of Ideology', in his *Hermeneutics and the Human Sciences: Essays on Language, Action and Interpretation,* ed. and trans. John B. Thompson (Cambridge University Press, 1981) pp. 63–100.

Schmidt, Friedrich W., 'Hegel in der kritischen Theorie der "Frankfurt School"', in *Aktualität und Folgen der Philosophie Hegels,* ed. Oskar Negt (Frankfurt: Suhrkamp, 1971) pp. 21–61.

Schmidt, James, 'Offensive Critical Theory', *Telos,* 39 (1979) pp. 61–70.

Scott, John P., 'Critical Social Theory: An Introduction and Critique', *British Journal of Sociology,* 29 (1978) pp. 1–20.

Shapiro, Jeremy J., 'The Dialectic of Theory and Practice in the Age of Technological Rationality: Herbert Marcuse and Jürgen Habermas', in *The Unknown Dimension: European Marxism since Lenin,* ed. Dick Howard and Karl E. Klare (New York: Basic Books, 1972) pp. 276–303.

Shroyer, Trent, 'The Re-Politicization of the Relations of Production: An Analytic Interpretation of Jürgen Habermas's Analytic Theory of Late Capitalist Society', *New German Critique,* 5 (1975) pp. 105–28.

Stockman, Norman, 'Habermas, Marcuse and the *Aufhebung* of Science and Technology', *Philosophy of the Social Sciences,* 8 (1978) pp. 13–55.

Therborn, Göran, 'Jürgen Habermas: A New Eclectic', *New Left Review,* 67 (May–June 1971) pp. 69–83.

Whitebook, Joel, 'The Problem of Nature in Habermas', *Telos,* 40 (1979) pp. 41–69.

Winfield, Richard, 'The Dilemma of Labor', *Telos,* 24 (1975) pp. 115–28.

Woodiwiss, Tony, 'Critical Theory and the Capitalist State', *Economy and Society,* 7 (1978) pp. 175–92.

Notes on Contributors

Andrew Arato is associate professor in philosophy and social theory at the Cooper Union and visiting lecturer in sociology at the Graduate Faculty of the New School for Social Research, New York. He is the co-author of *The Young Lukács and the Origins of Western Marxism* (1979), and he is currently preparing a volume entitled *Marxism West, Europe East*. Originally from Hungary, his long-term research project is concerned with tradition and modernity in Eastern Europe.

Rüdiger Bubner, until recently professor of philosophy in Frankfurt, is now professor at the University of Tübingen. His publications include *Theorie und Praxis* (1971), *Dialektik und Wissenschaft* (1973), *Handlung, Sprache und Vernunft* (1976) and *Zur Sache der Dialektik* (1980). He has published many essays on hermeneutics and critical theory, as well as on other topics in classical and contemporary philosophy.

Anthony Giddens is fellow of King's College and lecturer in sociology at the University of Cambridge. He has written widely on problems in social theory and the philosophy of social science. Among his many books are *Capitalism and Modern Social Theory* (1971), *The Class Structure of the Advanced Societies* (1973), *New Rules of Sociological Method* (1976), *Studies in Social and Political Theory* (1977) and *Central Problems in Social Theory* (1979).

Jürgen Habermas was professor of philosophy and sociology at the University of Frankfurt until 1971. He is currently co-director of the Max Planck Institute in Starnberg and visiting professor at Frankfurt. The provisional title of his most recent book is *Theorie des kommunikativen Handelns*.

David Held is lecturer in politics at the University of York. In addition to writing several essays on critical theory and political economy, he has published *Introduction to Critical Theory: Horkheimer to Habermas* (1980). He is now working on problems concerning the relation between democracy, bureaucracy and socialism.

Agnes Heller is reader in sociology at La Trobe University. As a student and associate of Lukács, she worked in Hungary until 1973, when she and other members of the Budapest School were rendered 'politically unemployed'; she left for Australia in 1977. She has published some forty books in ten languages, the most important of these being *The Ethics of Aristotle and the Ancient Ethos* (1966), *Renaissance Man* (1967), *Everyday Life* (1970), *Theory of Needs in Marx* (1976), *On Instincts* (1977) and *A Theory of Feelings*.

Mary Hesse is fellow of Wolfson College and professor of philosophy of science at the University of Cambridge. She is also a fellow of the British Academy and was recently Stanton Lecturer in Cambridge. Her publications include *Forces and Fields* (1961), *Models and Analogies in Science* (1963), *The Structure of Scientific Inference* (1974) and *Revolutions and Reconstructions in Philosophy of Science* (1980).

Steven Lukes is fellow and tutor in politics and sociology at Balliol College, Oxford. He has taught at many universities in Britain, France, Canada and the USA. In addition to numerous essays on a wide range of topics, he has published *Emile Durkheim* (1973), *Individualism* (1973), *Power: A Radical View* (1974) and *Essays in Social Theory* (1976).

Thomas McCarthy is associate professor and chairman of the department of philosophy at Boston University. He has taught at the Universities of California and Munich and conducted research at the Max Planck Institute in Starnberg. Author of *The Critical Theory of Jürgen Habermas* (1978) and co-editor of *Understanding and Social Inquiry* (1977), he has also translated two of Habermas's major works.

Henning Ottmann teaches philosophy and political theory at the University of Munich. He is well known in Germany for his work on Hegel, having published *Das Scheitern einer Einleitung in Hegels Philosophie* (1973) and *Individuum und Gemeinschaft bei Hegel,* Bd 1 (1977); the second volume of the latter study will appear soon. He has also written articles on Gehlen, Rawls and Hegel.

Michael Schmid is lecturer in sociology at the University of Augsburg. He is the author of *Leerformeln und Ideologiekritik* (1972) and *Handlungsrationalität–Kritik einer dogmatischen Handlungswissenchaft* (1979), and co-author of *Basale Soziologie* (1976) and *Erklärung und Geschichte* (1976). He has written numerous essays on action, evolution and the methodology of social science.

John B. Thompson is research fellow at Jesus College, Cambridge. He is the author of *Critical Hermeneutics: A Study of the Thought of Paul Ricoeur and Jürgen Habermas* (1981), and he has edited and translated a collection of essays by Paul Ricoeur entitled *Hermeneutics and the Human Sciences* (1981). He is currently working on problems in the analysis of ideology.

JH -- "A Reply"

1) emphasis on "a theory of _rationality_" p. 232